西方人文社科
经典原著选读：英、汉

翁学东　编著

光明日报出版社

图书在版编目（CIP）数据

西方人文社科经典原著选读：英、汉 / 翁学东编著. --北京：光明日报出版社，2022.12
　ISBN 978-7-5194-7021-0

　Ⅰ.①西… Ⅱ.①翁… Ⅲ.①人文科学—名著—介绍—西方国家—英、汉②社会科学—名著—介绍—西方国家—英、汉 Ⅳ.①Z835

中国版本图书馆 CIP 数据核字（2022）第 249526 号

西方人文社科经典原著选读：英、汉
XIFANG RENWEN SHEKE JINGDIAN YUANZHU XUANDU YINGHAN

编　　著：翁学东	
责任编辑：梁永春	责任校对：乔宇佳
封面设计：中联华文	责任印制：曹　净

出版发行：光明日报出版社
地　　址：北京市西城区永安路 106 号，100050
电　　话：010-63169890（咨询），010-63131930（邮购）
传　　真：010-63131930
网　　址：http://book.gmw.cn
E - mail：gmrbcbs@gmw.cn
法律顾问：北京市兰台律师事务所龚柳方律师
印　　刷：三河市华东印刷有限公司
装　　订：三河市华东印刷有限公司
本书如有破损、缺页、装订错误，请与本社联系调换，电话：010-63131930

开　　本：170mm×240mm	
字　　数：433 千字	印　　张：24.5
版　　次：2023 年 3 月第 1 版	印　　次：2023 年 3 月第 1 次印刷
书　　号：ISBN 978-7-5194-7021-0	
定　　价：99.00 元	

版权所有　　翻印必究

文本选择说明（代自序）

本书是作者在开设《西方人文社科经典原著选读》研究生课程基础上逐渐形成的。在中央财经大学开设此课程的目的，是为了提高研究生的综合人文素养，拓宽人文社科研究的视野，尝试突破学科研究领域的限制，启发学科交叉研究的选题。本书内容是西方古代文本部分，主要由古希腊、罗马作者及古希伯来作者所写作品组成（由于众所周知的原因，古希伯来作者的作品被删除），所有文本均为英文译本，因而可使我们对古代地中海文明有初步的认识和理解。

本书是为了教学的需要，文本的选择遵循一定的主观性原则和可读性原则，因为经典古籍译文很多，所以也遵循易得性和方便性原则。由于不同学者所掌握资料的权威性不同，本书将来可以不断汲取专家学者的意见和建议，不断改进和提高文本的质量。由于篇幅所限，多数文本只能选取部分内容，从这个意义上说，本书希望起到"抛砖引玉"的作用，有兴趣的读者可以根据自己的需要去阅读全文。由于本书选择的是不同译者、不同时代的文本，作者对书中所有的神名、人名、地名做了统一性的注释，由于作者本人知识系统的局限，也难免会出一些差错，希望读者和专家学者批评指正，避免以讹传讹。

首先，我们选择了赫西俄德（Hesiod）的《神谱》（*Theogony*），赫西俄德是和荷马同时代的人，他的《神谱》将古希腊神话传说中天神的起源进行了梳理和总结。尤其是对奥林匹斯诸神之前第一代神和第二代神十二泰坦之间的关系进行了整合，对奥林匹斯主神宙斯及其后代也进行了总结。第二篇我们选择了古罗马诗人奥维德（Ovid）的代表作《变形记》（*the Metamorphoses*），同样是关于希腊神话的故事，奥维德补充了荷马之后关于罗马的神话传说，更重要的是他用优美的文字，将看似不相关联的故事，有机地联结起来，我们选择了忒拜城（Thebes）的建立者——卡德摩斯（Cadmus）家族的悲剧，和珀尔修斯（Perseus）的英雄事迹等内容。第三篇是荷马（Homer）史诗《伊利亚特》（*Iliad*）中的第二十四卷，《伊利亚特》是从特洛伊战争的第一英雄阿喀琉斯（Achilles）与希腊人主帅阿伽门农（Agamemnon）之间的矛盾冲突开始讲起，最后以特洛伊大王子赫克托（Hector）战死在与阿喀琉斯的对决之中，特洛伊国王普里阿姆（Priam）来到阿喀琉斯的大营，向阿喀琉斯赎回自己儿子的尸体而结束的。第四篇是荷马的另一部史诗《奥德赛》（Odyssey）中的第十一卷，讲述的是特洛伊战争之后的英雄奥德修斯（Odysseus），在返回家乡的海上受尽磨难，在冥界与死去的英雄和亲人的鬼魂相会的故事。第五篇是古罗马著名诗人维吉尔（Virgil）的史诗《埃涅伊德》（Aeneid）的第四卷，讲述的是特洛伊城被毁后，特洛伊王子埃涅阿斯（Aeneas）带着族人逃到了迦太基（Carthage）王国，与迦太基女王狄多（Dido）产生了爱情。但神谕和使命促使他放弃了这段情感，最终带领族人在亚平宁半岛的拉丁姆（Latium）登陆，与当地民族融合，形成了拉丁民族的故事。第六篇选自古希腊著名悲剧作家索福克勒斯（Sophocles）的代表作《俄狄浦斯王》（Oedipus the King），讲述了卡德摩斯的后代俄狄浦斯在命运的捉弄下，发现了自己在不知情的状况下杀父娶母的真相。该作品代表了希腊悲剧的最高成就。

第七篇选自柏拉图（Plato）《理想国》（the Republic）中的第二卷，主要内容是苏格拉底与雅典贵族关于正义和人性的对话讨论，进一步引发出苏格拉底关于理想国家的构想，以及理想国家守护者的教育和培养，人生最终目的的探讨等。第八篇选自柏拉图的《斐多篇》（Phaedo），通过苏格拉底的学生斐多之口，讲述了苏格拉底在临刑前最后一天与自己的学生及哲学家朋友在狱中探讨灵魂是否可以独立于肉体而存在，灵魂是否可以永恒等哲学问题，充分反映了有着坚定信仰的哲学家苏格拉底，面对死亡的坦然和淡定。第九篇选自亚里士多德（Aristotle）的《政治学》（Politics）中的第三卷，亚里士多德从城邦国家的起源，分析国家和政府的终极目标是实现国家的公民最大幸福，第三卷从历史的角度对不同政府形式进行了总结，认为中间阶级（middle class）的宪政（constitutional government）应该是城邦国家的努力目标。

第十篇选自罗马历史传记作家苏维托尼乌斯（Suetonius）的《罗马十二帝王传》（the Twelve Caesars）中的第一篇《尤利乌斯·恺撒》（Julius Caesar）。《罗马十二帝王传》记录了从恺撒到图密善等十二个罗马皇帝的生平事迹及罗马帝国早期发生的大事。

如前所述，本书不仅仅是一个西方古代社会文学和思想的集合，也希望它能成为非英语专业研究生或是其他社科爱好者的一本值得收藏的英文读物。书中的神名、人名、地名都经过作者仔细的鉴别和思考，尽可能做到和传统的译名保持一致，同时又尽量避免不同来源资料的不同译名，至少在全书中保持前后一致的译名，减少阅读中的混淆。为保持英文阅读的流畅性，对于不常出现的神名或人名，会整体在脚注中加以说明，而不是逐字直译。而对于经常出现的神名或人名，则会在脚注中反复注释，但随着读者对材料的逐渐熟悉而降低注释的频次，直至读者完全掌握。所以读者不必在阅读中，去查找其他注释，只需看本页脚注就行，增强了读者顺畅的阅读体验。每篇英文材料之后，有几个可以探讨和思考的问题，本书的最后还有作者的阅读笔记，反映了作者阅读每一本书的个人感受，供读者参考。此外，作者还将书中重要的关系脉络在附录中做了梳理，与读者分享。

  本书还试图成为西方古典文化的精选集合。如果要用一句话来概括所选材料的内容，那就是"在冲突中彰显人性，向死而生的人生态度"，而这恰恰也是西方古典文化之精髓所在。西方的神话传说中从不缺乏冲突的主题，或许这与西方早期文化产生的地理环境有关，地中海文明处于欧亚非三大洲的交汇之处、各民族早期的大迁徙必经之路上，部落和民族之间的冲突必然会经常发生，而这种冲突也必然会反映在早期文字记录之中。赫西俄德的《神谱》将诸神之间的代际冲突跃然纸上，奥维德的《变形记》则将经典的神话故事中的死亡以变形的哲学思维方式表达出来，实现另一种的永恒，荷马史诗《伊利亚特》和《奥德赛》更是用战争表现冲突，其中的英雄为追求荣誉和荣耀，实现向死而生之史诗的永恒。维吉尔的《埃涅伊德》除了描述狄多女王为爱殉情之外，也表达了埃涅阿斯带领一个民族向死求生的艰难历程。索福克勒斯的《俄狄浦斯王》不仅仅是古希腊悲剧之丰碑，也是俄狄浦斯心理煎熬历程中的死亡与重生之路。苏格拉底这位古希腊知识精英面对死亡的坦然与淡定，成就了《理想国》和《斐多篇》之不朽，对真理追求的信仰成为他有价值人生的最好注解。亚里士多德的《政治学》则有预见性地探讨了政治制度的生存与死亡之道，以及其与民情和风俗之间的相互依存关系。古代西方文明不仅仅是希腊和希伯来文明，还应包括古罗马文明。

  或许古希腊罗马神话中对死亡之界已有较多的描述和探讨，死神也和众神一样，只是在坚持自己的职责而已。譬如奥德修斯的祖先西西弗（Sisyphus）因为欺骗了死神，被罚在塔尔塔罗斯深渊里，从山底向山顶反复推石上山之劳苦煎熬，而无法得到解脱。因而，相对于东方人的信念来说，死亡就不再是一个恐惧的过程；或许对死亡的认识与人生的信念和世界观密切相关。如果说苏格拉底是古希腊知识阶层面对死亡仍追求真知的典范，耶稣是坚定的信仰使他义无反顾面死而生的话，那么恺撒则是君王和军人阶层面对死亡的楷模。柏拉图在他的《理想国》中对于三个阶层的划分，实际上也划分了三种不同的向死而生的方式。知识阶层通过认识真理面对死亡，军人阶层通过追求荣誉面对死亡，而普通商贾工匠则通过行善积德来应对死亡恐惧。

　　经典经得住时间的考验，值得反复阅读。尽管选择这十本书的不同部分和章节有个人的主观成分，但它们的确都是西方古代文本之经典，愿读者可以通过本书的学习提高自己的英文阅读欣赏水平和人文社科修养，愿本书成为读者了解西方早期文化和文明史的一块"敲门砖"。

目 录
CONTENTS

第一篇	Theogony	1
第二篇	The Metamorphoses	29
第三篇	The Iliad	63
第四篇	The Odyssey	83
第五篇	The Aeneid	98
第六篇	Oedipus the King	116
第七篇	The Republic	179
第八篇	Phaedo	210
第九篇	Politics	277
第十篇	The Twelve Caesars	308
读书笔记		353
后　记		372
附录1	希腊罗马神名对照表	376
附录2	希腊常见诸神族谱关系图	377
附录3	犹太人十二支族谱关系图	378
主要参考资料		379

第一篇　Theogony

Hesiod

(Translated by Glenn W. Most)

Let us begin to sing from the Heliconian Muses①, who possess the great and holy mountain of Helicon and at dance on their soft feet around the violet-dark fountain and the altar of Cronus' mighty son②. And after they have washed their tender skin in Permessus or Hippocrene or holy Olmeius③, they perform choral dances on highest Helicon, beautiful, lovely ones, and move nimbly with their feet. Starting out from there, shrouded in thick invisibility, by night they walk, sending forth their very beautiful voice, singing of aegis-holding Zeus, and queenly Hera of Argos, who walks in golden sandals, and the daughter of aegis-holding Zeus, bright-eyed Athena, and Phoebus Apollo, and arrow-shooting Artemis, and earth-holding, earth-shaking Poseidon, and venerated Themis (Justice) and quick-glancing Aphrodite, and golden-crowned Hebe (Youth) and beautiful Dione, and Leto and Iapetus and crooked-counseled④ Cronus, and Eos (Dawn) and great Helius (Sun) and gleaming Selene (Moon), and Earth and great Ocean and black Night, and the holy race of the other immortals who always are.

One time, they taught Hesiod beautiful song while he was pasturing lambs under holy Helicon. And this speech the goddesses spoke first of all to me, the Olympian Muses⑤, the daughters of aegis-holding Zeus: "Field-dwelling shepherds, ignoble disgraces, mere bellies: we know how to say many false things similar to genuine ones,

---

① 赫利孔山的缪斯，宙斯有九个主管艺术的女儿都住在赫利孔山上，也统称为九缪斯女神
② 克洛诺斯强大的儿子，指宙斯
③ 河流名称，传说中缪斯在此中沐浴
④ 心思缜密的，狡猾的
⑤ 奥林匹斯山的缪斯女神，即赫利孔山的缪斯

1

but we know, when we wish, how to proclaim true things."

So spoke great Zeus' ready-speaking daughters, and they plucked a staff, a branch of luxuriant laurel, a marvel, and gave it to me; and they breathed a divine voice into me, so that I might glorify what will be and what was before, and they commanded me to sing of the race of the blessed ones who always are, but always to sing of themselves first and last.

But what is this to me, about an oak or a rock①? Come then, let us begin from the Muses, who by singing for their father Zeus give pleasure to his great mind within Olympus, telling of what is and what will be and what was before, harmonizing in their sound. Their tireless voice flows sweet from their mouths; and the house of their father, loud-thundering Zeus②, rejoices at the goddesses' lily-like voice as it spreads out, and snowy Olympus' peak resounds, and the mansions of the immortals. Sending forth their deathless voice, they glorify in their song first the venerated race of the gods from the beginning, those to whom Earth③ and broad Sky④ gave birth, and those who were born from these, the gods givers of good things; second, then, the goddesses, both beginning and ending their song, sing of Zeus, the father of gods and of men, how much he is the best of the gods and the greatest in supremacy; and then, singing of the race of human beings and of the mighty Giants⑤, they give pleasure to Zeus' mind within Olympus, the Olympian Muses, the daughters of aegis-holding Zeus.

Mnemosyne (Memory)⑥ bore them on Pieria, mingling in love with the father, Cronus' son. Mnemosyne, the protectress of the hills of Eleuther as forgetfulness of evils and relief from anxieties. For the counsellor Zeus slept with her for nine nights, apart from the immortals, going up into the sacred bed; and when a year had passed, and the seasons had revolved as the months waned, and many days had been completed, she bore nine maidens-like-minded ones, who in their breasts care for song and have a spirit that knows no sorrow—not far from snowy Olympus' highest peak.

---

① 离题，偏离
② 响雷宙斯，传说中的宙斯以雷电作为他的主要武器。宙斯前通常加一些修辞，表明宙斯拥有不可战胜的力量。如 aegis-holding Zeus，持盾宙斯（宙斯盾级战舰的词源）
③ 大地之母，即盖娅（Gaia or Gaea）
④ 天穹，即乌拉诺斯（Ouranos or Uranus）第一代统治神
⑤ 巨神或巨人，指泰坦（Titan）
⑥ 记忆女神（Mnemosyne），九缪斯女神之母

That is where their bright choral dances and their beautiful mansions are, and beside them the Graces and Desire have their houses, in joyous festivities; and the voice they send forth from their mouths as they sing is lovely, and they glorify the ordinances and the cherished usages of all the immortals, sending forth their lovely voice.

They went towards Olympus at that time, exulting in their beautiful voice, with a deathless song; and around them the black earth resounded as they sang, and from under their feet a lovely din rose up as they traveled to their father, He is king in the sky, holding the thunder and the blazing thunderbolt① himself, since he gained victory in supremacy over his father Cronus; and he distributed well all things alike to the immortals and devised their honors.

These things, then, the Muses sang, who have their mansions on Olympus, the nine daughters born of great Zeus, Clio (Glorifying) and Euterpe (Well Delighting) and Thalia (Blooming) and Melpomene (Singing) and Terpsichore (Delighting in Dance) and Erato (Lovely) and Polymnia (Many Hymning) and Ourania (Heavenly), and Calliope (Beautiful Voiced) —she is the greatest of them all, for she attends upon venerated kings too, Whomever among Zeus-nourished kings the daughters of great Zeus honor and behold when he is born, they pour sweet dew upon his tongue, and his words flow soothingly from his mouth, All the populace look to him as he decides disputes with straight judgments; and speaking publicly without erring, he quickly ends even a great quarrel by his skill, For this is why kings are wise, because when the populace is being harmed in the assembly they easily manage to turn the deeds around, effecting persuasion with mild words; and as he goes up to the gathering they seek his favor like a god with soothing reverence, and he is conspicuous among the assembled people.

Such is the holy gift of the Muses to human beings. For it is from the Muses and far-shooting Apollo② that men are poets upon the earth and lyre-players, but it is from Zeus that they are kings; and that man is blessed, whom-ever the Muses love, for the speech flows sweet from his mouth. Even if someone who has unhappiness in his newly anguished spirit is parched in his heart with grieving, yet when a poet, servant of the

---

① 霹雳，传说中三个独眼巨神为宙斯打造的强大武器，宙斯依靠它打败了父亲克洛诺斯领导的泰坦集团，夺取了世界的统治权
② 射箭之神阿波罗。在希腊神话中，宙斯之子阿波罗既是太阳神，又是射箭之神，还是诗神和竖琴之神

Muses, sings of the glorious deeds of people of old and the blessed gods who possess Olympus, he forgets his sorrows at once and does not remember his anguish at all; for quickly the gifts of the goddesses have turned it aside.

Hail, children of Zeus, and give me lovely song; glorify the sacred race of the immortals who always are, those who were born from Earth and starry Sky, and from dark Night, and those whom salty Pontus (Sea) nourished. Tell how in the first place gods and earth were born, and rivers and the boundless sea seething with its swell, and the shining stars and the broad sky above, and those who were born from them, the gods givers of good things; and how they divided their wealth and distributed their honors, and also how they first took possession of many-folded Olympus. These things tell me from the beginning, Muses who have your mansions on Olympus, and tell which one of them was born first.

In truth, first of all Chasm came to be, and then broad-breasted Earth, the ever immovable seat of all the immortals who possess snowy Olympus' peak and murky Tartarus① in the depths of the broad-pathed earth, and Eros, who is the most beautiful among the immortal gods, the limb-melter-he overpowers the mind and the thoughtful counsel of all the gods and of all human beings in their breasts.

From Chasm, Erebos② and black Night came to be; and then Aether and Day came forth from Night, who conceived and bore them' after mingling in love with Erebos.

Earth first of all bore starry Sky, equal to herself, to cover her on every side, so that she would be the ever immovable seat for the blessed gods; and she bore the high mountains, the graceful haunts of the goddesses, Nymphs who dwell on the wooded mountains. And she also bore the barren sea seething with its swell, Pontus③, without delightful love; and then, having bedded with Sky, she bore deep-eddying Ocean and Coeus and Crius and Hyperion and Iapetus and Theia and Rhea and Themis and

---

① 塔尔塔罗斯之地（Tartarus），希腊神话中用作地牢来惩罚泰坦们的暗无天日的深渊，位于冥界的最底层
② 埃瑞波斯（Erebos），无尽之黑暗，暗夜之神
③ 蓬托斯（Pontus），本都，洪荒之水

4

Mnemosyne and golden-crowned Phoebe and lovely Tethys. After these, Cronus① was born, the youngest of all, crooked-counseled, the most terrible of her children; and he hated his vigorous father.

Then she② bore the Cyclopes③, who have very violent hearts, Brontes (Thunder) arid Steropes (Lightning) and strong-spirited Arges (Bright), those who gave thunder to Zeus and fashioned the thunderbolt These were like the gods in other regards, but only one eye was set in the middle of their foreheads; and they were called Cyclopes (Circle-eyed) by name, since a single circle-shaped eye was set in their foreheads. Strength and force and contrivances were in their works.

Then from Earth and Sky came forth three more sons, great and strong, unspeakable, Cottus and Briareus and Gyges,④ presumptuous children. A hundred arms sprang forth from their shoulders, unapproachable, and upon their massive limbs grew fifty heads out of each one's shoulders; and the mighty strength in their great forms was dreadful.

For all these, who came forth from Earth and Sky as the most terrible of their children, were hated by their own father from the beginning. And as soon as any of them was born, Sky put them all away out of sight in a hiding-place in Earth and did not let them come up into the light, and he rejoiced in his evil deed. But huge Earth groaned within, for she was constricted, and she devised a tricky, evil stratagem. At once she created an offspring, of gray adamant, and she fashioned a big sickle and showed it to her dear sons.

And she spoke, encouraging them while she grieved in her dear heart: "Sons of mine and of a wicked father, obey me, if you wish: we would avenge your father's evil outrage. For he was the first to devise unseemly deeds."

So she spoke, but dread seized them all, and none of them uttered a sound. But great crooked-counseled Cronus took courage and at once addressed his cherished mother in turn with these words: "Mother, I would promise and perform this deed,

---

① 克洛诺斯（Cronus）是第二代统治神，为第一代统治神乌拉诺斯的小儿子，也是第三代统治神宙斯的父亲。而 Ocean, Coeus, Crius, Hyperion, Iapetus, Theia, Rhea, Themis, Mnemosyne, Phoebe, Tethys, Cronus 又被称为十二泰坦，见附录2
② 指地母盖娅
③ 独眼巨神，实际上都属于泰坦
④ 三个百臂巨神

since I do not care at all about our evil-named father. For he was the first to devise unseemly deeds."

So he spoke, and huge Earth rejoiced greatly in her breast. She placed him in an ambush, concealing him from sight, and put into his hands the jagged-toothed sickle, and she explained the whole trick to him. And great Sky came, bringing night with him; and spreading himself out around Earth in his desire for love he lay outstretched in all directions. Then his son reached out from his ambush with his left hand, and with his right hand he grasped the monstrous sickle, long and jagged-toothed, and eagerly he reaped the genitals from his dear father and threw them behind him to be borne away. But not in vain did they fall from his hand: for Earth received all the bloody drops that shot forth, and when the years had revolved she bore the mighty Erinyes and the great Giants, shining in their armor,

holding long spears in their hands, and the Nymphs whom they call the Melian ones on the boundless earth, And when at first he had cut off the genitals with the adamant and thrown them from the land into the strongly surging sea, they were borne along the water for a long time, and a white foam rose up around them from the immortal flesh; and inside this grew a maiden. First she approached holy Cythera, and from there she went on to sea-girt Cyprus. She came forth, a reverend, beautiful goddess, and grass grew up around her beneath her slender feet. Gods and men call her (A) "Aphrodite[①]," the foam-born goddess and (B) the well-garlanded "Cytherea," (a) since she grew in the foam, (b) and also "Cytherea," since she arrived at Cythera, (c) and "Cyprogenea," since she was born on sea-girt Cyprus, (d) and "genial," since she came forth from the genitals, Eros accompanied her and beautiful Desire stayed with her as soon as she was born and when she went to the tribe of the gods; and since the beginning she possesses this honor and has received as her lot this portion among human beings and immortal gods-maidenly whispers and smiles and deceits and sweet delight and fondness and gentleness.

But their father, great Sky, called them Titans[②] (Strainers) as a nickname, rebuking his sons, whom he had begotten himself; for he said that they had strained to

---

① 阿芙洛狄忒，爱与美之女神，即罗马神话中的维纳斯（Venus）。
② 泰坦，天神乌拉诺斯给他的下一代神所起的绰号。因而除了常说的十二泰坦之外，三个独眼巨神和三个百臂巨神均是地母盖娅与天神所生的儿子，同样也被称为泰坦

perform a mighty deed in their wickedness, and that at some later time there would be vengeance for this.

Night bore loathsome Doom and black Fate and Death, and she bore Sleep, and she gave birth to the tribe of Dreams. Second, then, gloomy Night bore Blame and painful Distress, although she① had slept with none of the gods, and the Hesperides,② who care for the golden, beautiful apples beyond glorious Ocean and the trees bearing this fruit. And she bore (a) Destinies and (b) pitilessly punishing Fates, (a) Clotho (Spinner) and Lachesis (Portion) and Atropos (Inflexible),③ who give to mortals when they are born both good and evil to have, and (b) who hold fast to the transgressions of both men and gods; and the goddesses never cease from their terrible wrath until they give evil punishment to whoever commits a crime. Deadly Night gave birth to Nemesis④ (Indignation) too, a woe for mortal human beings; and after her she bore Deceit and Fondness and baneful Old Age, and she bore hard-hearted Strife.

And loathsome Strife bore painful Toil and Forgetfulness and Hunger and tearful Pains, and Combats and Battles and Murders and Slaughters, and Strifes and Lies and Tales and Disputes, and Lawlessness and Recklessness, much like one another, and Oath, who indeed brings most woe upon human beings on the earth, when ever someone willfully swears a false oath.

Pontus begot Nereus⑤, unerring and truthful, the oldest of his sons; they call him the Old Man, because he is infallible and gentle, and does not forget established customs but contrives just and gentle plans. Then, mingling in love with Earth, he begot great Thaumas and manly Phorcys⑥, and beautiful-cheeked Ceto⑦, and Eurybia, who has a heart of adamant in her breast.

And from Nereus and beautiful-haired Doris, the daughter of Ocean the circling river, were born numerous children of goddesses in the barren sea, Protho and

---

① 指夜神
② 赫斯帕里德斯（Hesperides），金苹果树的守护女神，是夜神之女
③ 命运三女神
④ 复仇女神
⑤ 涅柔斯（Nereus），老海神
⑥ 福耳库斯（Phorcys），百怪之父，他是蓬托斯（Pontus）与地母盖娅（Gaia）之子，刻托（Ceto）的哥哥。希腊神话中的许多妖怪皆出自此谱系
⑦ 刻托（Ceto），她与哥哥福耳库斯（Phorcys）结合，生了戈耳工（Gorgons）三姐妹，也是魔兽女神埃凯德娜（Echidna）之母，斯芬克斯（Sphinx）的外婆。

Eucrante and Sao and Amphitrite, and Eudora and Thetis① and Galene and Glauce, Cymothoe and swift Speo and lovely Thalia, and Pasithea and Erato and rosy-armed Eunice, and graceful Melite and Eulimene and Agave, and Doto and Proto and Pherusa and Dynamene, and Nesaea and Actaea and Protomedea, Doris and Panope and fair formed Galatea, and lovely Hippothoe and rosy-armed Hipponoe, and Cymodoce, who together with Cymatolege and fair-ankled Amphitrite easily calms the waves in the murky sea and the blasts of stormy winds, and Cymo and Eone and well-garlanded Halimede, and smile-loving Glauconome and Pontoporea, Leagore and Euagore and Laomedea, Polynoe and Autonoe and Lusianassa, and Euarne, lovely in shape and blameless in form, and Psamathe, graceful in body, and divine Menippe, and Neso and Eupompe and Themisto and Pronoe, and Nemertes (Infallible), who has the disposition of her immortal father. These came forth from excellent Nereus, fifty daughters who know how to do excellent works.

Thaumas married Electra, the daughter of deep flowing Ocean. She bore swift Iris② and the beautiful-haired Harpies, Aello and Ocypete, who with their swift wings keep up with the blasts of the winds and with the birds; for they fly high in the air.

Then to Phorcys Ceto bore beautiful-cheeked old women, gray-haired from their birth, whom both the immortal gods and human beings who walk on the earth call the Graeae, fair-robed Pemphredo and saffron-robed Enyo, and the Gorgons③ who dwell beyond glorious Ocean at the edge towards the night, where the clear-voiced Hesperides are, Sthenno and Euryale, and Medusa④ who suffered woes. She was mortal, but the others⑤ are immortal and ageless, the two of them; with her alone the dark haired one⑥ lay down in a soft meadow among spring flowers. When Perseus⑦ cut her head off from her neck, great Chrysaor and the horse Pegasus sprang forth; the latter received his name from being born beside the waters of Ocean, the former from holding a golden sword in his hands. Pegasus flew off, leaving behind the earth, the

---

① 塞蒂斯（Thetis），又译忒提斯，特洛伊之战中，希腊第一英雄阿喀琉斯的母亲
② 彩虹女神（Iris），信使女神
③ 戈耳工（Gorgons），女海怪，海妖
④ 美杜莎，蛇发女怪
⑤ 指她的两个海怪姐姐
⑥ 指海神波塞冬
⑦ 珀尔修斯（Perseus），传说中的希腊英雄

mother of sheep, and came to the immortals; he dwells in Zeus' house and brings the thunder and lightning to the counsellor Zeus. And Chrysaor, mingling in love with Callirhoe, glorious Ocean's daughter, begot three-headed Geryoneus, who was slain by Heracles' force beside his rolling-footed cattle in sea-girt Erythea on the day when he drove the broad-browed cattle to holy Tiryns, after he crossed over the strait of Ocean and killed Orthus and the cowherd Eurytion in the murky stable beyond glorious Ocean.

She① bore in a hollow cave another monster, intractable, not at all similar to mortal human beings or to the immortal gods: divine, strong-hearted Echidna, half a quick-eyed beautiful-cheeked nymph, but half a monstrous snake, terrible and great, shimmering, eating raw flesh, under the hidden places of the holy earth. That is where she has a cave, deep down under a hollow boulder, far from the immortal gods and mortal human beings; for that is where the gods assigned her to dwell in glorious mansions. She keeps guard among the Arima under the earth, baleful Echidna, an immortal nymph and ageless all her days.

They say that Typhon, terrible, outrageous, lawless, mingled in love with her②, a quick-eyed virgin; and she became pregnant and bore strong-hearted children. First she bore Orthus, the dog, for Geryoneus; second, she then gave birth to something intractable, unspeakable, Cerberus③ who eats raw flesh, the bronze-voiced dog of Hades, fifty-headed, ruthless and mighty; third, she then gave birth to the evil-minded Hydra of Lema, which the goddess, white-armed Hera, raised, dreadfully wrathful against Heracles' force. But Zeus' son, the scion of Amphitryon④, Heracles, slew it with the pitiless bronze, together with warlike Iolaus, by the plans of Athena, leader of the war-host.

She gave birth to Chimaera⑤, who breathed invincible fire, terrible and great and swift-footed and mighty. She had three heads: one was a fierce-eyed lion's, one a she-goat's, one a snake's, a mighty dragon's. [In front a lion, behind a dragon, in the middle a she-goat, breathing forth the terrible strength of burning fire] Pegasus and

---

① 指蓬托斯和地母盖娅之女刻托（Ceto）
② 指埃凯德娜（Echidna）。魔兽女神，刻托之女，斯芬克斯之母
③ 看守冥界之门的恶狗
④ 安菲特里翁（Amphitryon），大力神赫拉克勒斯的养父
⑤ 奇美拉（Chimaera），魔兽女神埃凯德娜之女，三头狮羊蛇合体怪兽

noble Bellerophon killed her. Overpowered by Orthus, she① bore the deadly Sphinx②, destruction for the Cadmeans③, and the Nemean lion, which Hera, Zeus' illustrious consort, raised and settled among the hills of Nemea, a woe for human beings. For dwelling there it destroyed the tribes of human beings and lorded over Tretus in Nemea and Apesas; but the strength of Heracles' force overpowered it.

Ceto mingled in love with Phorcys and gave birth to her youngest offspring, a terrible snake, which guards the all-golden apples in the hidden places of the dark earth at its great limits. This, then, is the progeny of Ceto and Phorcys.

Tethys bore to Ocean④ eddying rivers, the Nile and Alpheius and deep-eddying Eridanus, Strymon and Meander and beautiful-flowing Ister, and Phasis and Rhesus and silver-eddying Achelous, and Nessus and Rhodius and Haliacmon and Heptaporus, and Grenicus and Aesepus and divine Simois, and Peneius and Hennus and fair-flowing Calcus, and great Sangarius and Ladon and Parthenius, and Euenus and Aldescus and divine Scamander. And she gave birth to a holy race of daughters who, together with lord Apollo and the rivers, raise boys so that they become men on the earth, for this is the lot they have from Zeus: Peitho and Admete and Ianthe and Electra, and Doris and Prymno and Ourania of godlike figure, and Hippo and Clymene and Rhodea and Callirhoe, and Zeuxo and Clytia and Idyia and Pasithoe, and Plexaura and Galaxaura and lovely Dione, and Melobosis and Thoe and Polydora of fair figure, and Cerceis, lovely of form, and cow-eyed Pluto, and Perseis and Ianeira and Acaste and Xanthe, and lovely Petraea and Menestho and Europa, and Metis and Eurynome and saffron-robed Telesto, and Chryseis and Asia and lovely Calypso, and Eudora and Tyche and Amphiro and Ocyrhoe, and Styx⑤, who indeed is the greatest of them all. These came forth from Ocean and Tethys as the oldest maidens; but there are many others as well. For there are three thousand long-ankled daughters of Ocean who are widely dispersed and hold fast to the earth and the depths of the waters, everywhere in

---

① 指埃凯德娜

② 斯芬克斯（Sphinx），狮身人面兽

③ 卡德摩斯家族，传说中的卡德摩斯是腓尼基王子，忒拜城的建立者，由于他杀死了战神的大蛇使其后人受到了厄运的诅咒，在这里指斯芬克斯对卡德摩斯后代的伤害

④ 欧申（Ocean）或欧申纳斯（Oceanus）和泰西丝（Tethys）是十二泰坦中的一对夫妻，生了各处的河流。见附录2

⑤ 冥河

the same way, splendid children of goddesses; and there are just as many other loud-flowing rivers, sons of Ocean, to whom queenly Tethys gave birth. The names of them all it is difficult for a mortal man to tell, but each of those who dwell around them knows them.

Theia, overpowered in love by Hyperion①, gave birth to great Helius (Sun) and gleaming Selene (Moon) and Eos (Dawn), who shines for all those on the earth and for the immortal gods who possess the broad sky. Eurybia, revered among goddesses, mingling in love, bore to Crius② great Astraeus and Pallas and 'Perses, who was conspicuous among all for his intelligence. Eos, a goddess bedded in love with a god, bore to Astraeus the strong-spirited winds, clear Zephyrus and swift-pathed Boreas and Notus; and after these the Early-born one③ bore the star, Dawn bringer, and the shining stars with which the sky is crowned.

Styx, Ocean's daughter, mingling with Pallas, bore Zelus (Rivalry) and beautiful-ankled Nike (Victory) in her house, and she gave birth to Cratos (Supremacy) and Bia (Force), eminent children. These have no house apart from Zeus nor any seat, nor any path except that on which the god leads them, but they are always seated next to deep-thundering Zeus. For this is what Styx, Ocean's eternal daughter, planned on the day when the Olympian lightener④ summoned all the immortal gods to high Olym-pus and said that, whoever of the gods would fight together with him against the Titans, him he would not strip of his privileges, but that everyone would have the honor he had had before among the immortal gods; and that whoever had been without honor and without privilege because of Cronus, him he would raise to honor and privileges, as is established right. So eternal Styx came first of all to Olympus with her own children, through the plans of her dear father; and Zeus honored her and gave her exceptional gifts. For he set her to be the great oath of the gods, and her sons to dwell with him for all their days. Just as he promised, so too he fulfilled for all, through and through; and he himself rules mightily and reigns.

---

① 许珀里翁 (Hyperion) 和忒娅 (Theia) 是十二泰坦中的一对夫妻,太阳神赫利俄斯 (Helius) 的父母
② 生长之神克瑞斯 (Crius),十二泰坦之一
③ 指 Eos
④ 指宙斯

Phoebe came to the lovely bed of Coeus;① and the goddess, pregnant in the love of a god, gave birth to dark robed Leto②, always soothing, gentle to human beings and to the immortal gods, soothing from the beginning, the kindliest one within Olympus. She also gave birth to fair-named Asteria, whom Perses once led to his great house to be called his dear wife.

And she became pregnant and bore Hecate③, whom Zeus, Cronus' son, honored above all others: he gave her splendid gifts—to have a share of the earth and of the barren sea, and from the starry sky as well she has a share in honor, and is honored most of all by the immortal gods. For even now, whenever any human on the earth seeks propitiation by performing fine sacrifices according to custom, he invokes Hecate; and much honor very easily stays with that man whose prayers the goddess accepts with gladness, and she bestows happiness upon him, for this power she certainly has. For of all those who came forth from Earth and Sky and received honor, among all of these she has her due share; and neither did Cronus' son use force against her nor did he deprive her of anything that she had received as her portion among the Titans, the earlier gods, but she is still in possession according to the division as it was made at first from the beginning. Nor does the goddess, just because she is an only child, have a lesser share of honor and privileges on earth and in sky and sea, but instead she has far more, since Zeus honors her. She stands mightily at the side of whomever she wishes and helps him. In the assembly, whoever she wishes is conspicuous among the people; and when men arm themselves for man-destroying war, the goddess stands there by the side of whomever she wishes, zealously to grant victory and to stretch forth glory. She sits in judgment beside reverend kings; and again, she is good whenever men are competing in an athletic contest—there the goddess stands by their side too and helps them, and when someone has gained victory by force and supremacy he easily and joyfully carries off a fine prize and grants glory to his parents; and she is good at standing by the side of horsemen, whomever she wishes. And upon those who work the bright, storm-tossed sea and pray to Hecate and the loud sounding

---

① 科俄斯（Coeus）和菲比（Phoebe），十二泰坦中的另一对夫妻，黑袍女神莱托（Leto）之父母
② 黑袍女神莱托（Leto），与宙斯结合，生孪生兄妹太阳神阿波罗（Apollo）和月神阿尔忒弥斯（Artemis）
③ 赫卡忒（Hecate），魔法女神，阿斯忒瑞亚（Asteria）的女儿

Earth-shaker,① the illustrious goddess easily bestows a big haul of fish, and easily she takes it away once it has been seen, if she so wishes in her spirit. And she is good in the stables at increasing the livestock together with Hermes;② and the herds and droves of cattle, and the broad flocks of goats and the flocks of woolly sheep, if in her spirit she so wishes, from a few she strengthens them and from many she makes them fewer. And so, even though she is an only child from her mother, she is honored with privileges among all the immortals. And Cronus' son made her the nurse of all the children who after her see with their eyes the light of much-seeing Dawn. Thus since the beginning she is a nurse, and these are her honors.

Rhea③, overpowered by Cronus, bore him splendid children, Hestia④, Demeter⑤, and golden-sandaled Hera⑥, and powerful Hades⑦, who dwells in mansions beneath the earth and has a pitiless heart, and the loud-sounding Earth-shaker and the counsellor Zeus, the father of gods and of men, by whose thunder the broad earth is shaken. Great Cronus would swallow these down as each one came from his mother's holy womb to her knees, mindful lest anyone else of Sky's illustrious children should have the honor of kingship among the immortals. For he had heard from Earth and starry Sky that, mighty though he was, he was destined to be overpowered by a child of his, through the plans of great Zeus. For this reason, then, he held no unseeing watch, but observed closely, and swallowed down his children; and unremitting grief gripped Rhea. But when she was about to bear Zeus, the father of gods and of men, she beseeched her own dear parents, Earth and starry Sky, to contrive some scheme so that she could bear her dear son without being noticed, and take retribution for the avenging deities of her father and of her children, whom great crooked-counseled Cronus had swallowed down. They listened well to their dear daughter and obeyed her, and they revealed to her everything that was fated to come about concerning Cronus the king and his strong-spirited son. They told her to go to

---

① 指海神波塞冬（Poseidon），宙斯的哥哥，主管海洋与地震，因此也被称为摇晃土地者
② 赫尔墨斯（Hermes），宙斯与迈亚之子，信使与商业之神
③ 瑞娅（Rhea），十二泰坦之一，第二代统治神克洛诺斯的姐姐和妻子，第三代统治神宙斯的母亲
④ 灶神，家务女神
⑤ 农神，主管农业生产
⑥ 赫拉（Hera），宙斯的姐姐和妻子，第三代主神即奥林匹斯山众神之天后
⑦ 哈迪斯（Hades），宙斯的哥哥，后成冥神

Lyctus, to the rich land of Crete①, when she was about to bear the youngest of her children, great Zeus; and huge Earth received him in broad Crete to nurse him and rear him up. There she came first to Lyctus, carrying him through the swift black night; taking him in her hands she concealed him in a deep cave, under the hidden places of the holy earth, in the Aegean mountain, abounding with forests. And she wrapped a great stone in swaddling-clothes and put it into the hand of Sky's son②, the great ruler, the king of the earlier gods. He seized this with his hands and put it down into his belly-cruel one, nor did he know in his spirit that in place of the stone his son remained hereafter, unconquered and untroubled, who would overpower him with force and his own hands, and would soon drive him out from his honor and be king among the immortals.

Swiftly then the king's strength and his splendid limbs grew; and when a year had revolved, great crooked-counselled Cronus, deceived by Earth's very clever suggestions, brought his offspring up again, overcome by his son's devices and force. First he vomited up the stone, since he had swallowed it down last of all; Zeus set it fast in the broad-pathed earth in sacred Pytho③, down in the valleys of Parnassus, to be a sign thereafter, a marvel for mortal human beings.

And he④ freed from their deadly bonds his father's brothers, Sky's sons⑤, whom their father had bound in his folly. And they repaid him in gratitude for his kind deed, giving him the thunder and the blazing thunderbolt and the lightning, which huge Earth had concealed before. Relying on these, he rules over mortals and immortals.

Iapetus married Clymene, Ocean's beautiful ankled daughter, and went up into the same bed with her. She bore him Atlas, a strong-hearted son, and gave birth to the very renowned Menoetius and to Prometheus (Forethought), shifty, quick-scheming, and to mistaken-minded Epimetheus (Afterthought) —he who turned out to be an evil from the beginning for men who live on bread, for he was the one who first accepted

---

① 克里特岛，地中海中岛屿，希腊文明发源地之一
② 乌拉诺斯之子，指克洛诺斯
③ 皮托（Pytho），希腊一地名。也和巨蟒皮同（Python）的名字同源。巨蟒皮同受天后赫拉（Hera）指派追杀黑袍女神莱托（Leto），因为女神莱托怀上了宙斯的孩子。后来，皮同被莱托之子阿波罗（Apollo）杀死。也与编程语言 Python 同词源
④ 指宙斯
⑤ 乌拉诺斯的儿子们，这里指三个独眼巨神

14

Zeus' fabricated woman, the maiden. Far-seeing Zeus hurled down outrageous Menoetius into Erebus, striking him with a smoking thunderbolt because of his wickedness and defiant manhood. And by mighty necessity Atlas① holds up the sky with his head and with his tireless hands, standing at the limits of the earth in front of the clear-voiced Hesperides; for this is the portion which the counsellor Zeus assigned him. And with painful fetters he② bound shifty-planning Prometheus,③ with distressful bonds, driving them through the middle of a pillar; and he set upon him a long-winged eagle which ate his immortal liver, but this grew again on all sides at night just as much as the long-winged bird would eat during the whole day. It was killed by Heracles, the strong son of beautiful-ankled Alcmene④, who warded off the evil plague from Iapetus' son and released him from distress—not against the will of Olympian Zeus, who rules on high, so that the glory of Theban-born Heracles would become even greater than before upon the bounteous earth. With this in mind, he⑤ honored his eminent son; and although he was angry with Prometheus, he ceased from the anger which he had had before because Prometheus had contended in counsels with Cronus' very strong son.

For when the gods and mortal men were reaching a settlement in Mecone, with eager spirit he⑥ divided up a great ox and, trying to deceive Zeus' mind, set it before him. For he set down on the skin before him the meat and the innards, rich with fat, hiding them in the ox's stomach; and then he set down before him in turn the ox's white bones, arranging them with deceptive craft, hiding them with gleaming fat.

Then the father of men and of gods addressed him: "Son of Iapetus, eminent among all rulers, my fine fellow, how unfairly you have divided up the portions!"

So spoke in mockery Zeus, who knows eternal counsels; but crooked-counseled Prometheus addressed him in turn, smiling slightly, and he did not forget his deceptive craft: "Zeus, most renowned, greatest of the eternally living gods, choose from these whichever your spirit in your breast bids you."

---

① 十二泰坦伊阿佩托斯（Iapetus）之子，撑天者阿特拉斯（Atlas），与地图 Atlas 同词源
② 指宙斯
③ 盗火者普罗米修斯（Prometheus），十二泰坦 Iapetus 之子，撑天者 Atlas 的兄弟
④ 阿尔克墨涅（Alcmene），安菲特里翁的妻子，大力神赫拉克勒斯（Heracles）的母亲
⑤ 指宙斯
⑥ 指普罗米修斯

So he spoke, plotting deception. But Zeus, who knows eternal counsels, recognized the deception and did not fail to perceive it; and he saw in his spirit evils for mortal human beings—ones that were going to be fulfilled, too. With both hands he grasped the white fat, and he became enraged in his breast and wrath came upon his spirit when he saw the ox's white bones, the result of the deceptive craft. And ever since then the tribes of human beings upon the earth burn white bones upon smoking altars for the immortals.

Greatly angered, the cloud-gatherer Zeus addressed him: "Son of Iapetus, you who know counsels beyond all others, my fine fellow, so you did not forget your deceptive craft after all!"

So spoke in rage Zeus, who knows eternal counsels. And from then on, constantly mindful of his wrath after that, he did not give the strength of tireless fire to the ash trees for the mortal human beings who live upon the earth. But the good son of Iapetus fooled him by stealing the far-seen gleam of tireless fire in a hollow fennel stalk. It gnawed deeply at high-thundering Zeus' spirit and enraged his dear heart, when he saw the far-seen gleam of fire among human beings. Immediately he contrived an evil for human beings in exchange for fire. For the much renowned Lame One[①] forged from earth the semblance of a reverend maiden by the plans of Cronus' son; and the goddess, bright-eyed Athena, girdled and adorned her with silvery clothing, and with her hands she hung a highly wrought veil from her head, a wonder to see; and around her head Pallas Athena[②] placed freshly budding garlands that arouse desire, the flowers of the meadow; and around her head she placed a golden headband, which the much renowned Lame One made himself, working it with his skilled hands, to do a favor for Zeus the father. On this were contrived many designs, highly wrought, a wonder to see, all the terrible monsters the land and the sea nourish; he put many of these into it, wondrous, similar to living animals endowed with speech, and gracefulness breathed upon them all.

Then, when he had contrived this beautiful evil thing in exchange for that good one,[③] he led her out to where the other gods and the human beings were, while she

---

① Lame One 指火神赫菲斯托斯（Hephaestus），传说中的潘多拉是火神所造的
② 帕拉斯（Pallas），指雅典娜（Athena），是雅典娜的另一个名字
③ 指普罗米修斯所盗之火

exulted in the adornment of the mighty father's bright eyed daughter①; and wonder gripped the immortal gods and the mortal human beings when they saw the steep deception, intractable for human beings. For from her comes the race of female women; for of her is the deadly race and tribe of women, a great woe for mortals, dwelling with men, no companions of baneful poverty but only of luxury. As when bees in vaulted beehives nourish the drones, partners in evil works all day long until the sun goes down, every day, the bees hasten and set up the white honeycombs, while the drones remain inside among the vaulted beehives and gather into their own stomachs the labor of others in just the same way high-thundering Zeus set up women as an evil for mortal men, as partners in distressful works. And he bestowed another evil thing in exchange for that good one: whoever flees marriage and the dire works of women and chooses not to marry arrives at deadly old age deprived of assistance; while he lives he does not lack the means of sustenance, but when he has died his distant relatives divide up his substance. On the other hand, that man to whom the portion of marriage falls as a share, and who acquires a cherished wife, well-fitted in her thoughts, for him evil is balanced continually with good during his whole life. But he who obtains the baneful species lives with incessant woe in his breast, in his spirit and heart, and his evil is incurable.

Thus it is not possible to deceive or elude the mind of Zeus. For not even Iapetus' son, guileful Prometheus, escaped his heavy wrath, but by necessity a great bond holds him down, shrewd though he be.

When first their father② became angry in his spirit with Obriareus③ and Cottus and Gyges,④ he bound them with a mighty bond, for he was indignant at their defiant manhood and their form and size; and he settled them under the broad-pathed earth. Dwelling there, under the earth, in pain, they sat at the edge, at the limits of the great earth, suffering greatly for a long time, with much grief in their hearts. But Cronus' son and the other immortal gods whom beautiful-haired Rhea bore in love with Cronus brought them back up to the light once again, by the prophecies of Earth: for she told

---

① 指雅典娜
② 指 Sky 或 Uranus 乌拉诺斯
③ 百臂巨神 Briareus 的另一个名字
④ 三个百臂巨神

the gods everything from beginning to end, that it was together with these that they would carry off victory and their splendid vaunt. For they battled for a long time, their spirits pained with toil, opposing one another in mighty combats, the Titan gods and all those who were born from Cronus – from lofty Othrys the illustrious Titans, and from Olympus the gods, the givers of good things, those whom beautiful haired Rhea bore after she had bedded with Cronus. They battled continually with one another, their spirits pained with distress, for ten full years; nor was there any resolution for their grievous strife nor an end for either side, but the outcome of the war was evenly balanced.

But when he had offered them① all things fitting, nectar and ambrosia, which the gods themselves eat, and in the breasts of them all their manly spirit was strengthened once they received nectar and lovely ambrosia, the father of men and of gods spoke among them: "Listen to me, splendid children of Earth and Sky, so that I can say what the spirit in my breast bids me. We have already been fighting every day for a very long time, facing one another for the sake of victory and supremacy, the Titan gods and all of us who were born from Cronus. So manifest your great strength and your untouchable hands, facing the Titans in baleful conflict, mindful of our kind friendship, how after so many sufferings you have come up to the light once again out from under a deadly bond, by our plans, out from under the murky gloom."

So he spoke. And at once excellent Cottus answered him in turn: "Really, Sir, it is not something unknown you are telling us. We too know ourselves that your thoughts are supreme and your mind is supreme, and that you have revealed yourself as a protector for the immortals against chilly ruin. It is by your prudent plans that we have once again come back out from under the murky gloom, from implacable bonds – something, Lord, Cronus' son, that we no longer hoped to experience. For that reason, with ardent thought and eager spirit we in turn shall now rescue your supremacy in the dread battle-strife, fighting against the Titans in mighty combats."

So he spoke, and the gods, the givers of good things②, praised his speech when they heard it. Their spirit craved war even more than before, and they all roused up dismal battle, the females and the males, on that day, both the Titan gods and those

---

① 指三个百臂巨神
② 在当时希腊人的信仰中，神是好事情给予者（the givers of good things）

who were born from Cronus, and those whom Zeus sent up towards the light from Erebus, out from under the earth, terrible and mighty, with defiant strength. A hundred arms sprang forth from their shoulders, in the same way for all of them, and upon their massive limbs grew fifty heads out of each one's shoulders. They took up their positions against the Titans in baleful conflict, holding enormous boulders in their massive hands; and on the other side the Titans zealously reinforced their battle-ranks. Both sides. manifested the deed of hands and of strength together. The boundless ocean echoed terribly around them, and the great earth crashed, and the broad sky groaned in response as it was shaken, and high Olympus trembled from its very bottom under the rush of the immortals, and a deep shuddering from their feet reached murky Tartarus[①], and the shrill sound of the immense charge and of the mighty casts. And in this way they hurled their painful shafts against one another; and the noise of both sides reached the starry sky as they shouted encouragement, and they ran towards one another with a great war-cry.

Then Zeus no longer held back his strength, but at once his breast was filled with strength and he manifested his full force. He strode at the same time from the sky and from Olympus, relentlessly hurling lightning bolts, and the thunderbolts, driving forward a sacred flame, flew densely packed, together with the thunder and lightning, all at once from his massive hand. All around, the life-giving earth roared as it burned, and all around the great immense forest crackled; the whole earth boiled, and the streams of Ocean and the barren sea. The hot blast encompassed the earthly Titans, and an immense blaze reached the divine aether, and the brilliant gleam of the lightning bolt and flash blinded their eyes, powerful though they were. A prodigious conflagration took possession of Chasm; and to look upon it with eyes and to hear its sound with ears, it seemed just as when Earth and broad Sky approached from above: for this was the kind of great sound that would rise up as she was pressed down and as he pressed her down from on high-so great a sound was produced as the gods ran together in strife. At the same time, the winds noisily stirred up shuddering and dust and thunder and lightning and the blazing thunderbolt, the shafts of great Zeus, and they brought shouting and screaming into the middle between both sides. A dreadful din of terrifying strife rose up, and the deed of supremacy was made manifest.

---

① 塔尔塔罗斯深渊

And the battle inclined to one side. For earlier, advancing against one another they had battled incessantly in mighty combats. But then among the foremost Cottus and Briareus and Gyges, insatiable of war, roused up bitter battle; and they hurled three hundred boulders from their massive hands one after another and overshadowed the Titans with their missiles. They sent them down under the broad-pathed earth and bound them in distressful bonds after they had gained victory over them with their hands, high-spirited though they were, as far down beneath the earth as the sky is above the earth.

For it is just as far from the earth to murky Tartarus: for a bronze anvil, falling down from the sky for nine nights and days, on the tenth day would arrive at the earth; and again, a bronze anvil, falling down from the earth for nine nights and days, on the tenth would arrive at Tartarus. Around this a bronze barricade is extended, and on both sides of it night is poured out threefold around its neck; and above it grow the roots of the earth and of the barren sea.

That is where the Titan gods are hidden under murky gloom by the plans of the cloud-gatherer Zeus, in a dank place, at the farthest part of huge earth. They cannot get out, for Poseidon has set bronze gates upon it, and a wall is extended on both sides.

That is where Gyges, Cottus, and great-spirited Obriareus dwell, the trusted guards of aegis-holding Zeus.

That is where the sources and limits of the dark earth are, and of murky Tartarus, of the barren sea, and of the starry sky, of everything, one after another, distressful, dank, things which even the gods hate: a great chasm, whose bottom one would not reach in a whole long year, once one was inside the gates, but one would be borne hither and thither by one distressful blast after another—it is terrible for the immortal gods as well, this monstrosity; and the terrible houses of dark Night stand here, shrouded in black clouds.

In front of these, Iapetus' son[①] holds the broad sky with his head and tireless hands, standing immovable, where Night and Day passing near greet one another as they cross the great bronze threshold. The one is about to go in and the other is going out the door, and never does the house hold them both inside, but always the one goes out from the house and passes over the earth, while the other in turn remaining inside

---

① 指阿特拉斯（Atlas）

the house waits for the time of her own departure, until it comes. The one holds much seeing light for those on the earth, but the other holds Sleep in her hands, the brother of Death—deadly Night, shrouded in murky cloud.

That is where the children of dark Night have their houses, Sleep and Death, terrible gods; never does the bright Sun look upon them with his rays when he goes up into the sky nor when he comes back down from the sky. One of them passes gently over the earth and the broad back of the sea and is soothing for human beings. But the other one's temper is of iron, and the bronze heart in his chest is pitiless: once he takes hold of any human, he owns him; and he is hateful even for the immortal gods.

That is where, in front, stand the echoing houses of the earthly god, of powerful Hades and of dread Persephone①, and a terrible dog guards them in front, pitiless. He② has an evil trick: upon those going in he fawns alike with his tail and with both ears, but he does not let them leave again: instead, observing them closely he devours whomever he catches trying to go out from the gates of powerful Hades and dread Persephone.

That is where the goddess dwells who is loathsome for the immortals, terrible Styx, the oldest daughter of backward-flowing Ocean. She lives apart from the gods in a famous mansion vaulted with great crags; it is set fast upon silver pillars on every side reaching towards the sky all around. Seldom does Thaumas' daughter, swift-footed Iris, travel to her with a message upon the broad back of the sea: whenever strife and quarrel arise among the immortals and one of those who have their mansions on Olympus tells a lie, Zeus sends Iris to bring from afar in a golden jug the great oath of the gods, the much renowned water, icy, which pours down from a great, lofty crag. It flows abundantly from under the broad-pathed earth, from the holy river through the black night—a branch of Ocean, and a tenth portion has been assigned to her. For nine-fold around the earth and the broad back of the sea he whirls in silver eddies and falls into the sea, and she as one portion flows forth from the crag, a great woe for the gods. For whoever of the immortals, who possess the peak of snowy Olympus, swears a false oath after having poured a libation from her, he lies breathless for one full year;

---

① 珀尔塞福涅（Persephone），宙斯与农神（Demeter）之女，被冥王哈迪斯（Hades）抢亲成为冥后。宙斯在农神的要求下，让她每年春天回到其母亲农神怀抱，秋天再回冥界。

② 指冥界看门狗（Cerberus），埃凯德娜（Echidna）之子

and he does not go near to ambrosia and nectar for nourishment, but lies there without breath and without voice on a covered bed, and an evil stupor shrouds him. And when he has completed this sickness for a long year, another, even worse trial follows upon this one: for nine years he is cut off from participation with the gods that always are, nor does he mingle with them in their assembly or their feasts for all of nine years; but in the tenth he mingles once again in the meetings of the immortals who have their mansions on Olympus. It is as this sort of oath that the gods have established the eternal water of Styx, primeval; and it pours out through a rugged place.

That is where the sources and limits of the dark earth are, and of murky Tartarus, of the barren sea, and of the starry sky, of everything, one after another, distressful, dank①, things which even the gods hate.

That is where the marble gates are and the bronze threshold, fitted together immovably upon continuous roots, self-generated; and in front, apart from all the gods, live the Titans, on the far side of the gloomy chasm. The celebrated helpers of loud-thundering Zeus live in mansions upon the foundations of Ocean, Cottus and Gyges; but the deep-sounding Earth-shaker② made Briareus, since he was good, his son-in-law, and he gave him Cymopolea, his daughter, to wed.

When Zeus had driven the Titans from the sky, huge Earth bore as her youngest son Typhoeus, in love with Tartarus, because of golden Aphrodite③. His hands are holding deeds upon strength, and tireless the strong god's feet; and from his shoulders there were a hundred heads of a snake, a terrible dragon's, licking with their dark tongues; and on his prodigious heads fire sparkled from his eyes under the eyebrows, and from all of his heads fire burned as he glared. And there were voices in all his terrible heads, sending forth all kinds of sounds, inconceivable: for sometimes they would utter sounds as though for the gods to understand, and at other times the sound of a loud-bellowing, majestic bull, unstoppable in its strength, at other times that of a lion, with a ruthless spirit, at other times like young dogs, a wonder to hear, and at other times he hissed, and the high mountains echoed from below. And on that very day an intractable deed would have been accomplished, and he would have ruled over

---

① 阴冷潮湿的
② 指海神波塞冬（Poseidon）
③ 阿芙洛狄忒（Aphrodite），爱神维纳斯的希腊语名字

mortals and immortals, if the father of men and of gods had not taken sharp notice: he thundered hard and strong, and all around the earth echoed terrifyingly, and the broad sky above, and the sea, and the streams of Ocean, and Tartarus in the earth. As the lord rushed forward, great Olympus trembled under his immortal feet, and the earth groaned in response. The violet-dark sea was enveloped by a conflagration from both of them—of thunder and lightning, and fire from that monster of typhoons and winds, and the blazing thunder-bolt. And all the earth seethed, and the sky and sea; and long waves raged around the shores, around and about, under the rush of the immortals, and an inextinguishable shuddering arose. And Hades, who rules over the dead below, was afraid, and the Titans under Tartarus, gathered around Cronus, at the inextinguishable din and dread battle-strife.

Then when Zeus had lifted up his strength and grasped his weapons, the thunder and lightning and the blazing thunderbolt, he struck him, leaping upon him from Olympus; and all around he scorched all the prodigious heads of the terrible monster. And when he had overpowered him, scourging him with blows, he fell down lamed, and the huge earth groaned; a flame shot forth from that Thunder-bolted lord in the mountain's dark, rugged dales, as he was struck, and the huge earth was much burned by the prodigious blast, and it melted like tin when it is heated with skill by young men in well-perforated melting-pots, or as iron, although it is the strongest thing, melts in the divine earth by the skilled hands of Hephaestus when it is overpowered in a mountain's dales by burning fire. In the same way, the earth melted in the blaze of the burning fire. And he hurled Typhoeus into broad Tartarus, grieving him in his spirit.

From Typhoeus comes the strength of moist blowing winds-apart from Notus[①] and Boreas[②] and clear Zephyrus,[③] for these are from the gods by descent, a great boon for mortals. But the other breezes blow at random upon the sea: falling upon the murky sea, a great woe for mortals, they rage with an evil blast; they blow now one way, now another, and scatter the boats, and destroy the sailors; and there is no safeguard against this evil for men who encounter them upon the sea. And on the boundless, flowering earth too, they destroy the lovely works of earth-born human beings, filling

---

① 南风神
② 北风神
③ 西风神

them with dust and with distressful confusion.

When the blessed gods had completed their toil, and by force had reached a settlement with the Titans regarding honors, then by the prophecies of Earth they urged far-seeing Zeus to become king and to rule over the immortals; and he divided their honors well for them.

Zeus, king of the gods, took as his first wife Metis (Wisdom), she who of the gods and mortal human beings knows the most. But when she was about to give birth to the goddess bright-eyed Athena①. he deceived her mind by craft and with guileful words he put her into his belly, by the prophecies of Earth and of starry Sky: for this was how they had prophesied to him, lest some other one of the eternally living gods hold the kingly honor instead of Zeus. For it was destined that exceedingly wise children would come to be from her: first she would give birth to a maiden, bright-eyed Tritogeneia, possessing strength equal to her father's and wise counsel. and then to a son, a king of gods and of men. possessing a very violent heart. But before that could happen Zeus put her into his belly. so that the goddess would advise him about good and evil.

Second. he married bright Themis. who gave birth to the Horae (Seasons), Eunomia (Lawfulness) and Dike (Justice) and blooming Eirene (Peace), who care for the works of mortal human beings, and the Destinies, upon whom the counsellor Zeus bestowed the greatest honor. Clotho and Lachesis and Atropos, who give to mortal human beings both good and evil to have.

Eurynome, Ocean's daughter, possessing lovely beauty, bore him three beautiful-cheeked Graces, Aglaea (Splendor) and Euphrosyne (Joy) and lovely Thalia (Good Cheer). From their eyes desire, the limb-melter, trickles down when they look; and they look beautifully from under their eyebrows.

Then bounteous Demeter came to his bed; she bore white-armed Persephone②, whom Hades snatched away from her mother–but the counsellor Zeus gave her to him.

Then he desired beautiful-haired Mnemosyne, from whom the Muses with golden headbands came to be, nine of them, who delight in festivities and the pleasure of song.

---

① 雅典娜，宙斯之女，智慧与战争女神，雅典城的保护神
② 珀尔塞福涅，农神与宙斯之女，被冥王劫持娶作冥后

Leto, mingling in love with aegis-holding Zeus, gave birth to Apollo and arrow-shooting Artemis①, children lovely beyond all Sky's descendants.

Last of all he made Hera his vigorous wife; and she, mingling in love with the king of gods and of men, gave birth to Hebe② and Ares③ and Eileithyia④.

He himself gave birth from his head to bright-eyed Athena, terrible, battle-rouser, army-leader, indefatigable, queenly, who delights in din and wars and battles; but Hera was furious and contended with her husband, and without mingling in love gave birth to famous Hephaestus⑤, expert with his skilled hands beyond all of Sky's descendants.

From Amphitrite⑥ and the loud-sounding Earth-shaker was born great, mighty Triton, who possesses the foundations of the sea and dwells in golden mansions beside his dear mother and his lordly father, a terrible god.

To shield-piercing Ares Cytherea⑦ bore Fear and Terror, terrible, who rout the compact battle-lines of men in chilling war together with city-sacking Ares, and also Harmonia⑧, whom high-spirited Cadmus⑨ made his wife.

Maia, Atlas'⑩ daughter, going up into the holy bed, bore Zeus renowned Hermes⑪, the messenger of the immortals.

Semele⑫, Cadmus' daughter, mingling in love, bore him a splendid son, much-cheering Dionysus, a mortal woman giving birth to an immortal son; and now both of them are gods.

---

① 阿尔忒弥斯（Artemis），宙斯与莱托之女，月神、狩猎女神
② 赫柏（Hebe），青青女神，赫拉与宙斯之女，后嫁给赫拉克勒斯（Heracles 大力神）为妻
③ 阿瑞斯（Ares），赫拉与宙斯之子，战神
④ 艾莉西娅（Eileithyia），赫拉与宙斯之女，生育女神
⑤ 赫菲斯托斯（Hephaestus），赫拉之子，火神与兵器之神
⑥ 安菲特里忒，老海神涅柔斯 Nereus 之女，与海神波塞冬结合成为海王后
⑦ 指爱与美之神阿芙洛狄忒，即维纳斯
⑧ 哈尔摩尼娅（Harmonia），战神阿瑞斯和爱神阿芙洛狄忒之女，卡德摩斯之妻
⑨ 卡德摩斯（Cadmus），腓尼基王子，宙斯情人欧罗巴（Europe）的哥哥，忒拜城（Thebes）的建立者，俄狄浦斯王的先祖
⑩ 阿特拉斯，托起地球的泰坦，十二泰坦伊阿佩托斯（Iapetus）的儿子，普罗米修斯（Prometheus）的兄弟
⑪ 赫尔墨斯，迈娅（Maia）与宙斯之子，商业与信使之神
⑫ 塞墨勒（Semele），卡德摩斯的女儿，宙斯的情人，与宙斯生酒神狄奥尼索斯（Dionysus）

Alcmene①, mingling in love with the cloud-gatherer Zeus, gave birth to Heracles' force.

Hephaestus, the very renowned Lame One, made Aglaea, youngest of the Graces, his vigorous wife.

Golden-haired Dionysus made blonde Ariadne, Minos'②daughter, his vigorous wife; Cronus' son③ made her immortal and ageless for his sake.

The strong son of beautiful-ankled Alcmene, Heracles' strength, made Hebe, the daughter of great Zeus and of golden-sandaled Hera, his reverend wife on snowy Olympus, after he had completed his painful tasks, for after having accomplished his great work among the immortals he dwells unharmed and ageless for all his days.

Perseis, Ocean's renowned daughter, bore Circe and king Aeetes④ to tireless Helius. Aeetes, the son of mortal-illumining Helius,⑤ married beautiful-cheeked Idyia, the daughter of the perfect river Ocean, by the plans of the gods; and she, overpowered in love because of golden Aphrodite, gave birth to fair-ankled Medea.⑥

Farewell now to you who dwell in Olympian mansions, and you islands and continents and the salty sea within. And now, sweet-voiced Olympian Muses, daughters of aegis-holding Zeus, sing of the tribe of goddesses, all those who bedded beside mortal men and, immortal themselves, gave birth to children equal to the gods.

Demeter, divine among goddesses, gave birth to Plutus (Wealth), mingling in lovely desire with the hero Iasius in thrice-plowed fallow land in the rich land of Crete-fine Plutus, who goes upon the whole earth and the broad back of the sea, and whoever meets him and comes into his hands, that man he makes rich, and he bestows much wealth upon him.

To Cadmus, Harmonia, golden Aphrodite's daughter, bore Ino and Semele and

---

① 阿尔克墨涅（Alcmene），安菲特律翁（Amphitryon）的妻子，宙斯的情人，与宙斯生大力神赫拉克勒斯（Heracles）

② 米诺斯，欧罗巴（Europa）与宙斯之子，克里特王

③ 克洛诺斯之子，指宙斯

④ 埃厄忒斯（Aeetes），黑海之滨科尔基斯（Colchis）古国之王，美狄亚（Medea）之父，瑟茜（Circe，又译喀耳刻，能将人变成其他动物的女巫）之兄

⑤ 赫利俄斯（Helius），太阳神，十二泰坦 Hyperion 与 Theia 之子

⑥ 美狄亚（Medea），金羊毛故事中的女主角，科尔基斯国王埃厄忒斯（Aeetes）之女，希腊神话传说中个性强烈的女巫。她为了得到伊阿宋（Jason）的爱情，背叛父亲，杀害兄弟。被伊阿宋抛弃后，为报复伊阿宋不惜杀害她与伊阿宋的两个孩子

beautiful-cheeked Agave and Autonoe, whom deep-haired Aristaeus married, and Polydorus, in well-garlanded Thebes.

Callirhoe, Ocean's daughter, mingling in golden Aphrodite's love with strong-spirited Chrysaor, bore a son, the strongest of all mortals, Geryoneus, whom Heracles' force killed on account of rolling-footed cattle in sea-girt Erythea.

To Tithonus, Eos bore bronze-helmeted Memnon, the king of the Ethiopians, and lord Emathion. And to Cephalus she bore a splendid son, powerful Phaethon, a man equal to the gods. While he was young, a delicate spirited child, and still possessed the tender flower of glorious youth, smile-loving Aphrodite snatched him away, and made him her innermost temple-keeper in her holy temples, a divine spirit.

By the plans of the eternally living gods, Aeson's son① led away from Aeetes, that Zeus-nurtured king, Aeetes' daughter,② after completing the many painful tasks imposed upon him by the great overweening king, arrogant and wicked, violent-working Pelias. When Aeson's son had completed these he came to Iolcus, after enduring much toil, upon a swift ship, leading Aeetes' quick-eyed daughter, and he made her his vigorous wife. After she had been overpowered by Jason, the shepherd of the people, she gave birth to a son, Medeus, whom Chiron, Philyra's son, raised upon the mountains—and great Zeus' intention was fulfilled.

As for the daughters of Nereus, the old man of the sea, Psamathe, divine among goddesses, bore Phocus in love with Aeacus because of golden Aphrodite; while Thetis, the silver-footed goddess, overpowered by Peleus, gave birth to Achilles, man-breaker, lion-spirited.

Well-garlanded Cytherea③ bore Aeneas④, mingling in lovely desire with the hero Anchises on the peaks of many-valleyed, windy Ida.

---

① 指伊阿宋（Jason），金羊毛故事中的男主角
② 指美狄亚
③ 指维纳斯，即阿芙洛狄忒（Aphrodite）
④ 埃涅阿斯（Aeneas），特洛伊王子之一，传说中罗马人的早期祖先之一

Circe①, the daughter of Hyperion's son Helius, in love with patient-minded Odysseus②, gave birth to Agrius and Latinus, excellent and strong; and she bore Telegonus because of golden Aphrodite. These ruled over all the much-renowned Tyrrhenians, far away, in the innermost part of holy islands.

Calypso, divine among goddesses, bore Nausithous to Odysseus, and Nausinous, mingling in lovely desire.

These are the goddesses who bedded beside mortal men and, immortal themselves, gave birth to children equal to the gods. And now sing of the tribe of women, sweet-voiced Olympian Muses, daughters of aegis-holding Zeus.

Questions for discussion:

1. Which gods did the Titans include? Who gave them that name? Why are they called that?

2. What other names are there for the goddess Venus? How was she born? Did her birth change your idea of the goddess?

3. Why was Prometheus punished by Zeus? What was his relationship with Zeus like?

4. Why are eastern gods more like "gods" and Western gods more like people?

---

① 瑟茜（Circe，又译喀耳刻），十二泰坦 Hyperion 的儿子赫利俄斯（Helius）与十二泰坦 Ocean 的女儿 Perseis 之女，擅长巫术，在荷马史诗《奥德赛》中，曾将奥德修斯的士兵和水手们变成猪

② 奥德修斯，荷马史诗《奥德赛》中的主要人物，拉丁名尤利西斯（Ulysses），伊萨卡岛领主，特洛伊战争中的爱琴人（the Acheans 亦即希腊联军）主将之一，他足智多谋，能说会道，同时也英勇善战，冷酷无情。参与了十年特洛伊围城之战，又历经十年海上漂泊的磨难，最终回到家乡妻子和儿子的身边

第二篇　The Metamorphoses

Ovid

(Translated by Horace Gregory)

BOOK III

CADMUS

Even now Jove① shed the image of a bull,
Confessed himself a god, and stepped ashore
On the beached mountainside of Crete,
This while Europa's② father, Ignorant
Of what fate fell upon his ravished daughter,
Sent his son Cadmus out to look for her,
Saying if he did not find her, exile
Would be his doom, a warning that was both
Pious and cursed After Agenor's son③
Went up and down the world (who can discover
A secret Jove conceals?) the boy, distraught,
Fearful of Father's anger, strayed from home

---

① 朱庇特，宙斯的拉丁名。在后面出现的文本中，许多作品都是从拉丁文翻译过来的，因此诸神多采用拉丁名称谓
② 欧罗巴，朱庇特变成一头公牛，引诱欧罗巴骑上它，然后带欧罗巴入海，私奔逃离她的家乡
③ Agenor's son 阿基诺的儿子，指卡德摩斯

To be a stranger everywhere he turned.
Cadmus, a pilgrim, came to Phoebus'① shrine
To ask Apollo's spirit where to live,
And Phoebus said, "Go to the countryside,
Where lonely in a field a white ox wanders,
One who has never led the crooked plough
Nor earned the bent yoke across her shoulders.
Go with her till she falls to rest in grass,
And in this place erect your city's walls,
Then to her honor call It Boeotia."②
As soon as Cadmus stepped down from Parnassus③
He saw the wandering ox who strolled alone
Unmarked by plough or halter. Thoughtfully
He kept in step behind her, singing praise
Beneath his breath to Phoebus who had shown
Him where to go. Meanwhile the beast had led him
Through shoals of Cephisus and past deserted
Plains of Panope, where she stood still and
Lifted her fair head up with wide-spread horns
As though they pierced the very veils of heaven,
Then filled the air with her deep cries; she turned
To look behind to see who followed her,
Then kneeled, then sank to rest upon sweet grasses.
Cadmus thanked heaven and bent to kiss the earth,
Such was his praise of unknown fields and mountains.

With piety in mind Cadmus prepared
Duties to Jove and sent his men to look
For running waters, sacred springs and rills.

---

① 福玻斯或腓比斯，太阳神阿波罗的另一个名字
② 皮奥夏（Boeotia），希腊中部一地区，名城忒拜（Thebes，又译底比斯）位于此地区中
③ 希腊中部一山名

<<< 第二篇　The Metamorphoses

The men arrived upon a trackless forest
And deep within it, fast with underbrush,
A cave. There, through a rock-hung arc rushed its
Welled waters; and the place was shared by Mars'
Serpent who wore a golden plume, who as
He rolled his body thick with bile poured fire
From his eyes; flashed from his triple teeth
His three-pronged tongue. When the misfortunate
Tyrians① stumbled here, they dipped their pitchers
Into the cave's well; the silence then became
A plangent darkness and a hissing terror
As sea-blue snake's long head rose from the cave
And into outer air. Water jugs and pitchers
Slipped from men's hands and blood ran chill and limbs
Were taken with cold palsy. Then as the serpent
Wheeled in glittering knots, at once he
Had become a great arc, swung more than half
His length in air, as though his eyes looked down
Over the forest. If It were possible
To see him at a glance, he was as high,
As long, as sky's snake that shines at night
Between twin bears. Nor did he waste his time,
But fell on the Phoenicians,② whether they
Ran or showed fight, stilled or held back by fear.
Some he killed outright with his forked tongue,
And some were crushed within his knotted tail,
Some lost their lives within his tainted breath.

When sun at noon had narrowed shade on earth,

---

① Tyre，推罗，地中海东岸一古城，位于现黎巴嫩南部，腓尼基人（Phoenician）的都城；Tyrians 此处指推罗人或腓尼基人，卡德摩斯是腓尼基的王子
② 腓尼基人，与前文的推罗人（Tyrians）相同，均指卡德摩斯的族人

31

Cadmus began to miss his men and set out
To find where they had gone, or if they'd strayed:
His shield a lion's carcass, his arms a javelin
And iron-tipped spear—and better yet than these,
A hardy spirit-fit to enter deepest woods,
To see about him the poor bodies of his men,
And above them their victorious enemy,
Gorged with their entrails, eating at their wounds
with blood-wet tongue. Then Cadmus cried aloud,
"O naked dead, all friends grown true to me,
Your vengeance mine, or I shall die with you."
And as he spoke, his body swayed with weight
Of the great stone he hurled with his right hand—
A shot (that would have made thick walls collapse
And towers fall) struck the shrewd serpent, yet
The beast rose unharmed; his scales and dark skin
Were like sheets of Iron. But these could not
Endure the javelin-thrust that pierced mid-length
His back, Its iron shaft deep-bedded
In his side. The creature, Wild with pain, reared
Up his head, saw where he suffered, bit at
The shaft, and, writhing as he eased the folds
Around It, drew It out, yet the sharp spear-
Head held fast within his spine, while greater
Heat waked fires in his rage. His throat grew large
With flooded veins, and white foam gushed and bubbled
At his black jaws. And as his scales scraped earth
A tearing sound grew everywhere, and foul
Dark odors like the breath of Hell through air.
The serpent wheeled in green and yellow rings
As high as trees, then rolling into floods
Like springtide rivers, his heavy breast tore down
The forest as he moved. Cadmus stepped back,

<<< 第二篇　The Metamorphoses

Took up the serpent's rushes at his shield,
The lion's skin, but thrust his spear into
The serpent's mouth; the beast in rage clamped down
The Iron bit between his teeth, yet could not
Break It, then his black throat began to bleed
And green grass at his feet grew red with blood.
Because the beast retreated at each spear-
Thrust the wound was shallow, yet hardy Cadmus
Kept the spear forward at the serpent's throat
Until an oak stood at Its back; then with
A last lunge Cadmus followed his stroke home
Through beast and oak. The tree swayed double
With the serpent's weight, its great sides moaned
As the spent monster lashed them with his tail.

While Cadmus, Victor, stared at his great prize,
The conquered beast, a voice came to his ears,
From where he did not know, but heard It say,
"O son of Agenor, why look at ruins
Of monsters you've destroyed? You too shall be
A serpent in men's eyes!" Cold terror came
At him, he pale and trembling stood With hair
As stiff as frost. But look! His good friend Pallas,①
Slipped down beside him from the vault of heaven,
Told him to salt the earth with serpent's teeth
Which were to be the seeds of a new people.
At her command, he steered his deep-forked plough
And sowed the earth with teeth of the dead creature,
The seeds of mortal being Then (as by magic)
The field began to break and from its furrows
First came a line of lances, then gay plumes,

---

① Pallas（帕拉斯），智慧女神，女战神雅典娜（Athena）的另一个名字

Fluttering in air, then helmets, iron shoulders,
Breastplates, swords, Javelins, shields, till earth
Grew heavy with its crowds of men at arms.
As on a feast day when theatres are thrown open
The curtains part and men rise up from trapdoors①
Of the stage-first seen are faces, then slowly
The actors in full dress, their feet In line
Behind the curtain's margin-so was the rise
Of the armed charging army Cadmus saw.

In terror at what seemed new enemies,
Cadmus picked up his Javelin and shield;
"Hands up," one of the earth's progeny called out,
"You have no business in our civil war."
With this his broad sword slashed his earth-born brother,
And as he closed with him he fell, struck by
A javelin thrown from another quarter,
And as his slayer turned, he too was killed,
All dying in the same breath and spirit,
The give and take of war, they spent on each.
These brothers of mutual madness and disaster
Died by their common wounds; the young,
Whose lives were all too short, lay groaning
In warm heart's blood on earth which gave them birth-
All except five, and one was Echion,
Who at Minerva's② orders dropped his sword
And made a truce with his surviving brothers.
These were the friends that homeless Cadmus had
To build the city of Phoebus' oracle.

---

① 舞台的活板门
② Minerva（密涅瓦），雅典娜的拉丁名

<<< 第二篇　The Metamorphoses

Now Thebes① arose, and Cadmus, though exiled,
Would've seemed to be the happiest of men,
His Wife the child of Venus and of Mars,②
His children worthy of their heritage,
O many sons and daughters at his side!
And grandsons grown to men. Yet no man
Is called happy till his death, and all
The taxes at his wake and funeral paid.

ACTAEON

Surrounded by good fortune Cadmus had
A grandson, Actaeon, who was first grief,
Whose forehead wore a most peculiar dress,
A brace of antlers, and whose dogs drank deep
Of his own blood. And these disasters
Were Fortune's③ errors and not his—for how can
Error without intention be called a crime?

On hillside wet with blood of hunted creatures,
When noon had made all shadows thin, and Sun
Was at mid-space between his destinations,
Youthful Actaeon with his fellow sportsmen
Had come upon a place of desolation
And in an easy voice he spoke to them:
"My friends, our traps and spears are stained with blood;
The hunt was good enough; the day was lucky.
When swift Aurora④ in her golden car
Brings us tomorrow there is more to do;

---

① Thebes，希腊中部名城，忒拜城，又译底比斯城
② 指哈尔摩尼娅（Harmonia），爱神阿芙洛狄忒和战神阿瑞斯的女儿
③ 运气女神
④ 黎明女神

35

Phoebus is halfway on his road and rakes
Meadow and plain with his untempered fires.
Call it a day and carry home our traps."
Then men obeyed him and the chase was done.

Within that region was a shaded valley
Grown dense with prickly pine and cypress leaf,
Its name, Gargaphie, sacred to shelter of
Short-clothed Diana①. Hidden within It
Was a cave untouched by art, yet Nature's
Craft had simulated art, had made an arbour
Of moss-grown rock and delicate sandstone,
And from Its side bright waters gushed and glimmered
Into a shallow well where grass came round it.
Here when she wearied of the chase the greenwood
Goddess bathed her pure limbs in streams of dew-
Clear waters. As on this day she came
She dropped her javelin, her unstrung bow,
Her quiver to the safe keeping of her
True maid-at-arms, another girl picked up
The cloak that she let fall, two more undid
The sandals from her feet, then Crocale
Of Thebes, more artful than the rest, caught up
Diana's fallen hair in a swift knot,
Leaving her own hair tossing to the wind.
Meanwhile Nephele, Hyale, and Rhanis,
Psecas and Phiale② poured silver-quick
Streams of pure waters from enormous urns.
But as Diana bathed—and Fate would have it—

---

① 黛安娜，月亮女神也即狩猎女神阿尔忒弥斯（Artemis）的拉丁名
② 传说中狩猎女神黛安娜每次去打猎都会有一些女神作为随从在旁边伺候，文中的
Crocle、Nephele、Hyale、Rhanis、Psecas、Phiale 等均是这样的女神

Actaeon, Cadmus' grandson, at his leisure,
Strolling through unknown ways half-stumbled
Into Diana's arbour: as he stepped through
The raining fountain spray that fell around him
Diana's naked girls beat their small breasts
And filled the cave with sharp, falsetto cries,
And tried to shield her with their nakedness.
They gathered round Diana in a circle
Yet the tall goddess stood head-high above them;
Flushed as the clouds at sunset or rose-colored
As the first hour at dawn, Diana seemed
More naked to the view than all the rest.
Then as her girls closed in the ring around her,
She glanced a sidelong look across her shoulder
As though she wished her arrows were at hand,
But failing these, splashed water, sharp as rain,
In Actaeon's face, and through his streaming hair
Foretold his fate "If you can talk, then speak,
Say that you saw Diana in undress."
And as she spoke his wet hair branched in antlers
Worn by the lively stag; his neck grew long,
Ears pointed, hands were hoofs, arms were thin legs,
And all his body a short-furred, spotted skin.
Diana also placed fear in his heart:
The once heroic son of Autonoe
Ran as he wondered by what miracle
He had become so swift with terror—but when
He saw himself, his face, his branching antlers
In a stream he longed to say, "O miserable
Me" but had no words, nothing but
Animal cries while tears ran down his changed,
Bewildered face. Only his mind remained
What it had been: What could he do? Where could

He turn? Go home where a king's palace waited?
Or make his way into a deeper forest?
Shame unmanned one path and his fears the other.

And while he stood in doubt, he saw his dogs,
His hunters, first Melampus①, then quick-nosed
Ichnobates crying upon his trail,
The first a Spartan, and the next from Crete,
Then swift as wind the other dogs came after,
Pamphagus, Dorceus, Oribasus
Who came from Arcady, sturdy Nebrophonus,
savage Laelaps and Theron, quick-footed
Pterelas, fine-scented Agre, rough Hylaeus
Who had been mauled by a wild hog, the wolf-hound
Nape, and Poemenis the faithful sheep dog,
The bitch Harpyia, with her recent puppies,
Thin-flanked Ladon who came from Sicyon,
Dromas, Canace, Sticte, Tigris, Alce,
Snow-haired Leucon, dark-haired Asbolus,
Powerful Lacon and swiftly running Aello,
Thous and fleetest Cyprio, her brother,
Lycisce and the black Harpalos, well known
The white mark on his mid-forehead,
Melaneus and rough-haired Lachne, and
Two dogs named Agriodus and Labros,
Whose father came from Crete, mother from Sparta,
Sharp-voiced Hylactor and the rest, the list
Too long to set it down in print but all
Were eager for their prey: they leaped high-hanging
Cliffs, crags, rocks, where roads were difficult

---

① 猎狗名，下文的 Ichnobates、Pamphagus、Dorceus、Oribasus、Nebrophonus 等均来自不同地方的狗名

<<< 第二篇 The Metamorphoses

Or else no roads at all, they still sped on.
Actaeon flying where he was once pursuer,
Now pursued, outpacing those who once were
His own creatures. If only he could speak:
"Look at your master, I am Actaeon, I-"
But words were lost to him; the air was filled
With barking and dogs' cries. First Melanchaetes
Thrust leaping Jaws in Actaeon's back, then
Theridamas and Oresitrophus sank
Iron teeth into his shoulder blade, these two
Had taken a late start, but by a short cut,
Spurting across the mountain, outstepped time;
And while they held their master, the entire
Company gathered for assault, snapping
And tearing at their master's body until
No part of It was clear of wounds. He moaned,
And though his voice was scarcely human,
No voice of living deer made such sad cries,
Sounds echoing through valleys he knew well
And filled the mountain air. As If in prayer
He dropped upon his knees, wordless, to plead
In pantomime, open invisible arms
To those who looked at him. Friends of the hunt,
His friends who had come up with the dogs to
Claim their prey. These, innocent of his fate, cry
The dogs at him for the kill, yet seeking him,
Calling out, at each call louder, "Actaeon!
Actaeon!" as though their friend were far away
(And when he heard his name he tossed his head);
They raised objections to his laziness,
Not being there, with a great prize in view.
Himself might well have longed to be away,
Since he was there, might well have wished to see

39

Rather than feel the passion of his hounds,
Jaws deep within his flesh and eating him,
Their master, now misfashioned as a deer.
Some say, not till he died of many wounds
Was angry Goddess of the Arrows① pleased.

SEMELE②

Ambiguous rumours were: the goddess③ was
More violent than Just, others spoke praise
Of how she stood for chastity and both
Extremes found worthy logic for their cause,
But Jove's wife made no public declaration
Of blame or what she thought, yet secretly
She gloried in the ill fortune that had fallen
Upon the house of Agenor, her hate
Had turned from her known rival, young Europa,
To other members of the Tyrian brood.
Added to this was cause for recent pain,
For Juno learned that willing Semele
Had grown big with the seed of generous Jove④.
In injured passion she began to speak:
"What have I gained by all my threats and warnings?
That girl must feel my anger, not my words.
If I'm to keep the name of Empress Juno,
To hold the jewel-wrought sceptre in right hand,
If I am queen of all the world, Jove's sister,
His wife, indeed his sister, I must act.
It seems the girl enjoys adultery,
But this betrayal of my marriage bed

---

① Goddess of the Arrows, 指月亮和狩猎女神黛安娜
② 塞墨勒, 卡德摩斯之女, 酒神狄奥尼索斯 (Dionysus) 的母亲
③ 指天后朱诺 (Juno)
④ 主神朱庇特 (Jupiter) 的另一个名字。后面的文本中多用此名

Is of the moment; she conceived, is pregnant
As though to show how big she is, how proud
Of being made a mother by great Jove,
An honour that has scarcely come to me.
The girl is vain of her good looks; I'll make
Her vanity the cause of her disaster.
My name is not Saturnia① if she fails
To fall in Hell's dark river by Jove's order."

At this decision, Juno went abroad
Wrapped in a golden cloud to Semele;
Yet she took care (before she showed herself)
To simulate old age, take on grey hair,
A wrinkled skin, bent back, and feebleness
As she stepped to the ground. Then she assumed
The voice of Semele's old nurse, Beroe,
An ancient woman from Laconia.②
After much chattering they spoke of Jove;
The ancient sighed, "I hope it's true you were
With Jupiter, but O, I have my doubts;
Many a modest bed has visitors
Who claim that they are gods. To be like Jove
Is not enough. If he is Jove then make him
Prove his love, make him appear before you
In the same fashion as when queen Juno
Takes him in her arms. Tell him to take you
As he is in heaven, dressed in his glory!"

Such was the manner Juno gave advice

---

① 塞坦尼娅（Saturnia）即天后朱诺，因为其父亲克洛诺斯（Cronus）的拉丁名为塞坦（Saturn）
② 希腊南部一地区名

To the untutored mind of Cadmus' daughter.
The girl then asked a secret gift from Jove.
"Take what you will," he said. "Nothing's refused;
And what is more, if you have doubts, I swear
By sacred, boiling torrents of the Styx①
Of which even the greatest gods show fear,
he wish is yours." Pleased with ill luck, damned by
Her lover's promise, the girl replied, "Take me
The way you take Saturnia in your arms."
She spoke too quickly, for Jove would have stopped
Her lips; he groaned, for she could not unsay
What she desired, nor he his promise. High in
His agony he climbed the hills of heaven,
Folded pale dew around him, fogs and clouds,
Lightnings, storms, thunder, inevitable fire.
He tried to make his strenuous powers lighter,
Nor did he take that heavy, fatal bolt
He had sent down to crush Typhoeus,②
The monster of the hundred hands; he took
The lesser bolt, which as the Cyclops made it
Contained less angry vigor and less fire.
The gods called this his "light artillery,"
And bearing it he crossed the threshold into
The House of Agenor, where Cadmus lived,
And Semele's bedroom; nor could her body
Take the full thrust of godly heat and love;
It flamed to ashes In Jove's quick embrace.
The unborn child, ripped from its mother's womb
Was nourished (so some said) until its birth,
Sewn In the hollow of Its father's thigh.

---

① 冥河，任何以它名义起誓的人或神都不可违背其诺言
② 地母盖娅与塔尔塔罗斯之子，宙斯最后的敌人

Discreetly then Ino, Its mother's sister,

Tended the child, and from her girls of Nysa

Took him within a cave and gave him milk.

Book IV

PERSEUS①

Though changed, these two found solace in their grandson

Before whom India bowed, and templed Greece;

Only in Argos, through Acrisius②, son of Abas,

And of his line, was one who shut the gates

Against Lord Bacchus③, he, Acrisius, denied

Bacchus was son of Jove, nor would he say

That Perseus, the spawn of Danae,

Conceived with joy beneath a shower of gold,

Was Jove's creation. Yet the very truth

Has its own strength, and bold Acrisius

Lived to regret denial of the god,

Nor recognized, as all men should, a grandson.

By this time Bacchus earned high rank in heaven

And Perseus carried as a proof of valour

A memorable prize—all that was left

Of a wild snake-haired creature④, fought and won—

Through lucid air on strident, whirling wings,

---

① 珀尔修斯,主神朱庇特(Jupiter 或 Jove)与达那厄(Danae)之子,杀死蛇发女怪美杜莎的希腊英雄

② 阿克瑞斯(Acrisius),阿尔戈斯国王,达那厄(Danae)之父,珀尔修斯(Perseus)的外公

③ 酒神巴克斯,狄奥尼索斯(Dionysus)的拉丁名

④ 指蛇发女怪美杜莎

Sailing for miles across the Libyan desert.
As blood from Gorgon's head① streamed down to earth,
It generated snakes in ancient sands—
And that is why the desert swarmed with serpents.

Light as a cloud that drifts through winds at war,
He tacked to right and left across the skies;
Above the world, he saw its seas and mountains
Unfold beneath him like a map: three times
He saw the frozen Arctic gleam, three times
He saw the open Scissors of the Crab,
He tossed to east, to west, then back again,
And as day faded he feared to sail by night;
He steered to earth close by Hesperides②
Where Atlas③ ruled and hoped to wait until
The morning star took fire from the dawn
And sun-bright chariot made its early start.
Here, tall as any giant, Atlas lived,
The blood of Iapetus in his veins.
He was the captain of World's End, and the master
Of that far sea that opened its cold waters
To cool the horses of the Sun and bring
To rest his well-worn blazing chariot. Atlas
Measured his wealth by several thousand sheep.,
As many heads of steer, and various cattle
Who strayed the grasses of his broad domain,
Nor had he neighbours to contest his rights.
Among his treasures was a golden tree
Whose glancing leaves hid golden fruit and branches.

---

① 指美杜莎的头颅
② 金苹果园
③ 十二泰坦 Iapetus 之子，撑天者阿特拉斯

<<< 第二篇　The Metamorphoses

Said Perseus to him, "If noble heirs
Find glory in your eyes, I am Jove's son;
If you appreciate a man of action,
Whose works are miracles, then look at me;
I ask for shelter and a place to rest."
Atlas recalled an ancient prophecy
Which Themis① of Parnassus told to him:
"Atlas, the day will come when your fine tree
Will lose its gold, and credit for that prize
Will go to no one else but Jove's own son."
Atlas had raised thick walls around his treasure
And set a dragon near the tree to guard it,
And If a traveller wandered past the gate,
The man was warned to go. Then Atlas turned
To Perseus. "Young man, you are invited
To go so far away that all the stories
Which you've been telling me seem true.
So far you'll get protection from your father!"
With this he tried to throw him out of bounds
While Perseus grappling with him tried to hold
Him off, to stay his anger with calm words,
Yet found himself outmatched (for who can stand
Against great Atlas?). Therefore he replied,
"Since you won't give the little that I ask you,
I have a most enduring gift for you."
He then turned round and with his back to Atlas
Lifted with his left hand Medusa's② head
At which the giant turned into a mountain,
His beard and hair were trees, his shoulders, arms
Were mountain trails, plateaus, his very head

---

①　十二泰坦之一，正义女神
②　美杜莎（蛇发女怪）

The frosted mountaintop, his bones were boulders,
Yet he continued growing everywhere
(Such was the will of gods) till heaven Itself
And all its glowing stars had crowned his head.

Meanwhile the son of Hippotas locked up
The winds in their eternal caves and morning
Lucifer, that star that beckons all mankind
To dally rounds, came up the sky. Perseus
Clipped wings to heels and buckled on the curved
Sword that he carried and as quickly leaped,
Sailing at ease full speed through cloudless air.
He travelled over countless multitudes
Until he saw Egyptian shores below him
Where Cepheus① was king, where unjust Ammon②
Had ordered Andromeda③ to be punished
Because the poor girl had a foolish mother
Who talked too much. When Perseus saw her
Fastened to a rock, arms chained above the sea,
But for hot tears that rippled down her face
And swaying hair that fluttered in the wind,
He might have thought the girl a work of art,
Carved out of stone. Dazed by the Sight of her
Fire was lightning in his veins; he could not speak;
Lost as he gazed he almost failed to beat his wings,
Then, as he landed near the girl, remarked,
"O, you should never wear the chains that hold you;
Wear those that lovers cherish as they sleep
In one another's arms. Tell me your name,

---

① 从本文看，西菲乌斯（Cepheus 多译成刻甫斯，仙王座）是埃及国王，也有译者认为他是埃塞俄比亚国王，在古文本中，埃塞俄比亚（Ethiopia）是对非洲的总称
② 原指古埃及的太阳神，本文指海怪阿蒙
③ 安德洛墨达，西菲乌斯（Cepheus）的女儿，后成为珀尔修斯的妻子

Why you are here, the place where you were born."
At first she did not answer, being modest;
She feared to talk to any bold young man,
And If her hands had not been chained behind her
She would have hid her face. Meanwhile her eyes,
Though free to speak, rained down her ceaseless tears.
Then, as he pressed her, to prevent his thinking
That she was guilty of some hopeless crime
She softly said her name, told who she was,
And how her mother bragged of her own beauty.
And as she spoke huge noises lashed the air,
Roaring from waves where a great dragon floated,
Riding the sea, and as it clambered toward her
The girl screamed while her parents, wild and harried,

Raced to her side, and though they beat their breasts,
Weeping their helpless tears, they knew her danger
And clung to her, while the young stranger said,
"There will be time for weeping afterward,
Yet time for rescue is a little space:
If I took to this girl as Perseus,
Jove's son and son of her who in a cell
Received Jove's favor in that golden rain
That filled her veins with life, If you will take me
As one who killed the snake-haired Gorgoness①,
As Perseus who rides the air with wings,
You should be flattered by your daughter's prospects—
A worthy husband as your son-in-law.
With the gods' grace, I'll add to my distinctions
By helping you, and If your daughter's life
Is saved, she's mine" The parents took his terms

---

① 戈耳工女怪，指美杜莎

(As who would not?) and pleaded for the rescue;
And promised him rich lands as daughter's dowry.

Look out to sea! swift as a diving, tossing,
Knife-sharp-nosed ship that cuts the waves, propelled
By sweat-soaked arms of galley slaves, the dragon
Sailed up while churning waters at its breast
Broke into spray, leeside and windward; plunging
It came as near to shore as a Balearic
Sling could send its shot. Perseus, leaping
From earth behind him, vaulted to mid-air;
The dragon saw his shadow on the sea
And plunged to tear at it. Then, as Jove's eagle,
When he has found a snake in a broad meadow
Turning its mottled body to the sun,
Falls on the unseeing creature from the air,
And as the bird, knowing the snake's forked tongue,
Crips its scaled neck and sinks his claws within it,
So Perseus dove upon the raging dragon,
Thrusting, hilt-deep, the sword into Its shoulder.
Burning with Its gaped wound, the dragon reared
Its bulk in air, then dived, veered like a boar
When it has been surrounded by quick hounds,
Loud with the kill. Perseus, dodging, swayed
Past snapping jaws on agile, dancing wings;
Then as the beast rolled Its soft belly open,
Or bared Its neck, his crooked sword struck in:
At back grown tough with sea-wet barnacles,
At flanks, or at the thin and fishlike tail.
The beast began to vomit purple spew,
And Perseus' wings, damp with salt spray, grew heavy;
He saw a rock that pierced the shifting waters
As they stilled, now curtained by the riding

Of the waves, and leaped to safety on it.
With left hand grasping on a ledge of cliff
He struck his sword three times and then again
Into the dragon's bowels. Then all the shores,
Even the highest balconies of heaven,
From which the gods looked down on Perseus,
Rang With great cheers; Cepheus and his Wife,
Cassiope①, called to their hero as a gallant
Bridegroom who saved the glory of their house.
And now the girl, chains dropped away, stepped forward,
The cause for which he fought and his reward.
As sign of victory he washed his hands,
Then, mindful of the snake-haired Gorgon's head,
To keep it free of scars in gravelled sand,
He set it down among sweet ferns and seaweed,
For the Medusa once was Phorcys'② daughter.
At once these grasses drank in magic fluid
Of Gorgon powers; stem, leaf, and tendrils hardened.
Delighted sea nymphs gathered weeds by armfuls,
Throwing them near Medusa, for sight of magic
Where wilted greens turned into filigree
Of semi-precious stones; some tossed these twigs
As seeds to make more grow in distant waters;
Lifted to air the weeds are known as coral.

Then on the grassy shore Perseus raised
His triple altars to his favourite gods:

---

① 卡西欧佩娅（Cassiope），西菲乌斯（Cepheus）的妻子，埃及王后，仙后座。因为吹嘘自己女儿的美貌，得罪了海神尼普顿（Neptune），海神要求她将其女儿安德洛墨达（Andromeda）作为牺牲品供奉给海上怪龙，来换取国家的和平安宁。
② 福耳库斯（Phorcys），蓬托斯（Pontus）和地母盖娅（Gaea）的儿子，与自己的妹妹刻托（Ceto）结合，生海怪美杜莎（Medusa）等姐妹三怪（Gorgons）。

The left to Mercury①, the right a tribute

To the warrior virgin②, and then between them

A shrine to Jove. To his Minerva he

Offered a cow, to the winged god a steer,

And to the greatest of all gods a bull.

And with no mention of a future dowry

He took his Andromeda as his bride.

Hymen③ and Cupid shook the wedding torch,

The fires were lit and incense filled the air,

And through the streets houses were hung with garlands;

Behind each gate and lintel, song echoed to the flute,

All music of the joy that shone within.

Then great doors of the palace were thrown back

Where golden rooms showed gentles to a feast

And Cepheus' court joined in a celebration.

After they'd eaten well and hearts and minds

Grew large with heady draughts of Bacchus'④ vine,

Then Perseus asked his hosts of their own country,

Its habits and the temper of its men.

The prince, who gave him information, said,

"Now that you know us, tell what art you practised,

Bravery and skill, to take that snake-haired head."

Perseus, heir of Agenon, replied

That under freezing Atlas was a shelter

Carved out of rock, where at the open cave,

Two sisters lived, the children of old Phorcys.

These had between them but a single eye;

---

① 信使和商业之神墨丘利，即希腊神话中的赫尔墨斯（Hermes）
② 指密涅瓦（Minerva），即希腊神话中的雅典娜
③ 海蔓（Hymen），婚姻女神
④ 酒神巴克斯，即希腊神话中的狄奥尼索斯（Dionysus）

They loaned it to each other, hand to hand,
And as it passed, Perseus snatched It up
For his own use, then vanished out of reach.
He ran through unknown ways, thick-bearded forests
And tearing rocks and stones, until he found
The Gorgon's home. And as he looked about
From left to right, no matter where he turned,
He saw both man and beast turned into stone,
All creatures who had seen Medusa's face.
Yet he himself glanced only at Its image—
That fatal stare-reflected in the polished
Bronze of the shield he wore on his left arm.
When darkest sleep took hold of dread Medusa,
Even to the writhing serpents of green hair,
He struck her head clean from her collarbone;
From that thick blood, as though it were a mother,
Quick Pegasus and Chrysador① were born.

Then Perseus told the story of his travels,
Their trials and conquests, wonderfully true,
What lands, what oceans he saw under him,
And how his fluttering wings had brushed the stars.
And when he stopped, they waited for still more
Till one prince asked him why only Medusa
Of those three sisters wore snakes in her hair.
Perseus replied, "That too is a good story,
And here it is: Once she was beautiful,
Pursued by many lovers, and best of beauties,
She had glorious hair, as I heard said by one
Who claimed to know her. As the story goes,

---

① 飞马珀伽索斯（Pegasus）和怪兽克莱斯多尔（Chrysador）都是由美杜莎（Medusa）的血生成的，故美杜莎是它们的母亲

Neptune had raped her in Minerva's temple,
A scene that shocked the nerves of Jove's pure daughter①,
Who held her breastplate up to shield her eyes;
As if to warn the girl of carelessness
She turned her hair to snakes. Today Minerva
To keep bold strangers at a proper distance
Wears snakes on the gold shield across her breast."

Book V

PERSEUS' BATTLES

As Perseus, brave son of Danae,
Talked of his famous trials and victories
Before a crowd of African commanders,
The palace halls began to echo turmoil:
Not noise and music of a wedding feast,
But racket that precedes a storm of war,
And, as a hurricane lashes quiet seas
Into a roaring tumult of the waves,
So the gay feast itself became a riot.
The storm was led by raging Phineus②,
King's brother, who thrust a bronze-tipped ash-plant up
And shook It in the air. "I've come," he said,
"To claim my stolen queen. Not even wings,
Nor Jove, nor that faked shower of gold shall save
You now!" He aimed his spear while Cepheus shouted,
"Brother, have you gone mad? Is this your courtesy

---

① 指密涅瓦（Minerva），即希腊神话中的雅典娜
② 菲尼乌斯（Phineus），国王西菲乌斯（Cepheus）的弟弟，欲娶侄女安德洛墨达（Andromeda）为妻

To him, our guest, his earned reward and dowry
For valour and the rescue of his lady?
If you wish truth, It was not Perseus
Who stole her from you, but the scaled and crowned
Ammon, sea-dragon-god of swimming Nereids①
Who'd come to eat the child of my own loins.
You lost your claims when she was left to die—
Perhaps you wished her to, and, sharing in my sorrow,
To ease your own. Since you saw her in peril,
In chains, yet never stirred nor came to help her,
You, her dear uncle and her promised husband,
Sulked, and now envy him who rescued her.
What are you looking for? That girl who seems
So glorious in your eyes? You should have freed
Her from the rocks where she was held; let him who
Saved her take her, who also rescued me
From being childless as I grow old—then have
Him keep what he has won, his bride, his wife
Through his own merit and my word of honour.
And he, your rival, was not favoured here,
He came between you and the choice of death."

And Phineus said no more; his shifting glances
Turned to his brother, and back to Perseus,
Nor did he know at whom to thrust his spear,
Then for a moment gathered breath and charged it
With all the forces of his hate at Perseus;
Yet it went wild and struck a bench near by.
At which, as quick as ever on his feet,
Perseus tossed back the spear so aimed it would
Have pierced his enemy's heart, but Phineus weaved,

---

① 海怪阿蒙是海中仙女们的海龙神，Nereid 指海中仙女

Dodged, turned behind the altar, safe and shameless,
While the swift spear went through young Rhoetus' face;
Flailing the air he fell, and the spear, torn
From joint and skull, released his blood's red fountains
On tablecloth and feast. Then the crowd's temper
Opened in flames: some threw their spears, some said
Cepheus should die as well as Perseus.
Yet the king had vanished to a safer place
Calling on Faith and Justice to look down,
And prayed to gods of hospitality,
Saying the quarrel took fire against his will.
Then war queen Pallas① came to shield Perseus,
And gave her brother② spirit for the battle.

From India there was a boy named Athis
Whom It was said his mother brought to birth—
Since she was creature of the river Ganges③—
Beneath the waves of Ganges' purest waters.
He looked like a young god just turned Sixteen,
Which made him seem much handsomer than ever;
He wore a purple cloak fringed with deep gold
As though he were a king of ancient Tyre,
A gold chain at his throat, a gold tiara
To bind his hair which smelled of sweetest myrrh.
At javelin toss he struck the farthest targets;
Yet as an archer he had greater gifts,
And as he drew an arrow to his bow
Perseus plucked up a heavy smoking torch
From the lit altar and with one quick blow

---

① 智慧女神密涅瓦（Minerva）即希腊神话雅典娜（Athena）的另一个名字
② 这里指珀尔修斯。因为珀尔修斯（Perseus）和帕拉斯（Pallas）都是朱庇特（Jove）的孩子，故以姐弟相称
③ 恒河

Smashed the boy's face into a net of bones.

When Lycabas of the Assyrian kingdom
Saw the boy fall, saw the sweet face of friend,
Bride, lover, changed to a blood-soaked horror
At his feet, he moaned aloud for Athis,
Whose last breath sighed through fissures of his wound.
He then snatched up the bow that Athis dropped
And shouted, "You have me to fight, my friend,
Nor long fame follow murder of this child
Which brings you greater shame than your poor valour."
And as he spoke, his arrow snapped from bowstring,
Yet merely pierced a fold of Perseus' cloak
At which Acrisius' grandson① charged at him,
Waving the sword that brought Medusa's death,
And drove the scimitar into Lycabas' heart.
And yet Lycabas, dying, eyes in darkness,
Sought out his Athis as he fell beside him
Down to death's shades, where they were one forever.

See how Phorbas from Syene, Metion's son,
And Amphimedon of Libya wild to fight,
Rushed, slipped, and fell on blood-wet floors, then, rising,
Met Perseus' sword, which pierced the side of one,
Then, flashing, cut the naked throat of Phorbas.

Yet when Eurytus, son of Actor, swung
His double axe, Perseus had dropped his sword;
He raised above his head a huge wine urn,
Embossed with gold and brass and silver facings,
And flung it at Eurytus, who fell dying

---

① 阿克瑞斯（阿尔戈斯国王）的外孙，即珀尔修斯

To earth in blood, his body throbbing against
The floor. Then in quick order Perseus
Felled Polydaemon of Semiramis,
And of her house Caucasian Abaris,
Lycetus, who had lived near Spercheos,
Then Helices of the long flowing hair—
And Perseus walked over the dead and dying.

Now Phineus feared to close with Perseus,
But with a wild thrust tossed his Javelin,
Which wounded to the quick bystanding Idas
Who did not choose to fight, yet blazed his eyes
At Phineus to say, "O Phineus,
Since I must fight, then you must take me now
As bitterest of all your enemies.
Exchanging wound for wound, I'll come at you!"
But as he raised the spear drawn from his side,
He fell, his veins, his body drained of blood.

Then Hodites, vice-king to Cepheus, fell,
Struck down by Clymenus, while Hypseus
Had cut down Prothoenor, then Lyncides
Hypseus. Yet in that fighting mob was one
Who stood alone, ancient Emathion,
Who also stood for piety and decorum.
Too old to carry arms, he fought with words,
And stepped up to protest unholy warfare.
As trembling with old age he clung at altar,
Chromis struck off his head, which dropped straight down,
The tongue still crying doom among the flames
Until it perished in the altar fires.

Then Phineus chopped down Ammon and Broteas,

Two brothers whose gloved hands had never failed them
At rounds within a ring. But what were gloves
Against the steel that Phineus raised? Then Ampycus,
The kindly devotee of Ceres, perished,
His priestly forehead sealed with a white ribbon.
Even Lampetides, whose voice and lyre
Made him unsuited to the sight of war—
He who'd been called to bless the wedding feast
And lead the marriage choir with his song—
Heard Pettalus shouting as he raised a sword,
"Finish your song among shades of Hell,
Play on, play on!" And as he spoke his blade
Ran through the left side of the singer's face.
Lampetides staggered; as he sank to earth
His dying fingers swept across the strings
And filled the air with deep and deathly music.
Nor was his death in vain: Lycormas,
Frenzied at what he saw, tore out the bar
That held a doorway at the right and crashed it
Against his killer's neck. Pettalus, dazed,
Was struck to earth like a new-butchered bull;
Meanwhile, Pelates, who'd come north from Cinyps,
Leaped up to tear the left side of the lintel
To find his right hand fixed there by a spear
Thrown by Corythus, king of Marmarida,
While Abas plunged a sword into his side;
He could not fall, but rather swung to die.
Of Perseus' company, Melaneus was killed,
And Dorylas, millionaire of Nasamonia,
No one as rich as he in land or spices,
Heaped up in mountains over his estates.
Thrust from one side, a spear pierced through his groin—
A deadly spot. When Halcyoneus, who threw

The spear, heard Dorylas Sigh and saw his eyes
Roll up, he said, "Here where you lie are all
The lands you own," and left the heavy corpse.
Perseus, quick for revenge, drew out the weapon
Warm from the bloody sheath of Dorylas' belly
And thrust It through his killer's nose, as If
It were a hot spit, boiling down his throat and back.
Fortune ran quick with him, he struck down Clytius
And Clanis, brothers of a single mother,
Yet both killed neatly with a different wound,
One with an ash spear through the thigh, the other
with an arrow between his teeth. Then also
Celadon of Mendesia was killed,
And Astreus, got by a Syrian mother,
A nameless father, and Aethion, once apt
At knowing what's to come, now fooled and broken
By false designs, and Thoactes who carried
King's battle-dress to field, and the ill-famed
Agyrtes, known for murder of his father.

Still others pressed on weary Perseus,
All against one and from all quarters rising,
All who denied his loyalty and great valour.
At Perseus' side were ranged his helpless allies;
The father of his bride, his bride, her mother,
Who filled the chamber with their fearful cries
Among the louder crash of shield and spear
And moaning of the men about to die.
Meanwhile Bellona[①], goddess of all wars,
Rained blood on the protectors of the household
And where the fighting ceased restored Its fire.

---

① 贝罗娜，女战神，战神玛尔斯（Mars）之妻

第二篇 The Metamorphoses

When Perseus saw a thousand crowd against him,
Headed by Phineus and a swift storm of spears,
As dense as winter's hail, fly left and right
Past eyes and ears and everywhere around him,
He backed himself against a thick stone column;
Shielded behind, he stood to face the battle.
Then from the left came Molpeus, warrior
Of Chaonia, from the right, full tilt,
Charging the hall, Arabian Ethemon.
Then as a tiger cat, half starved, hears lowing
Of two herds, each within a separate valley,
Can't make her choice, though wild to tear at both,
So Perseus paused to strike on right or left.
Molpeus he crippled with a sharp leg wound
And saw him limp away, but Ethemon
Gave little time for breath, and drove his sword
As If to thrust one blow through Perseus' neck,
Yet too much strength and bad aim splintered it
Against the heavy pillar where Perseus stood;
One edge flew back and lodged In Ethemon's throat,
Yet this was not enough to kill him outright,
Rather he stood with open, helpless, pleading arms
While Perseus hooked him with Cyllenius' scimitar.

When Perseus saw his energy no master
Of the great horde that still came hard against him,
He cried, "You've forced my will, and waked this horror,
The deadliest help of all. If friend is near,
O turn your face away!" Then he swung up
The dreadful Gorgon's head. "Warn others of
Your miracles," cried Thescelus, who raised
A fatal javelin in plangent air,

59

Yet stayed in motion as though carved in stone.
Then Ampyx plunged his sword straight at the breast
Of the great-hearted hero, Perseus, yet
As learning toward the blow, his right hand stiffened
Nor moved at all. Then Nileus, who had falsely
Said he was son of seven-lipped Nile and wore
Its Image bossed In silver and in gold
Across his shield, cried out, "Look, Perseus,
Think who my fathers were—which should be pleasure
To brag of in the silence of Death's shades!
What fame shall greet you to be killed by me!"
Even his words froze as spoke, his lips hung open.
Eryx then shouted at the two who turned to stone,
"It is your fear and not the Gorgon's head
That makes you stand as if you were asleep;
Wake up with me and cut this monster down,
This boy who talks of magic spells and weapons."
He charged, but as he lunged, floor gripped his feet;
He turned to granite in full battle-dress.

All these had earned the treatment they deserved,
Yet there was one, Aconteus, Perseus' man
At arms, who fighting for his hero, glanced
In his direction at the Gorgon's face;
He was himself in stone. Astyages,
Who thought the man alive, raised his long sword
And struck him with it—then he felt the clang
Of iron against rock. Astyages, dazed,
Stood fixed in the same trance, carved with a mask
Of wonder on his face. To tell the names
Of all who died would take too long: two hundred
Came through the battle fearful yet alive;
Two hundred saw the Gorgon and were doomed.

By this time Phineus had his own regrets
Of fighting without reason or just cause.
But what to do? He saw his warriors
All poised for action as he called their names.
Could he believe his eyes? He touched the nearest,
And knew at last that all were monuments.
He turned his face from Perseus, spread his fingers
As if admitting his defeat, and cried,
"O Perseus, you have truly conquered me,
Put that monstrosity away, Medusa-Gorgon
That changes men to stone-whoever she,
Whatever It may be, take it away!
Nor was it hate of you but wild ambition
That made me fight, and fight for her who should
Have been my bride. You have the greater valour,
And I the elder promise she was mine.
Now I want nothing except the right to live,
O powerful and brave! All else is yours."
He feared to look at Perseus, who replied,
"Dear timid Phineus, put aside your worries.
I have a gift, a great gift too, to raise low spirits,
I will not let you perish by the sword,
And you shall be a monument forever,
Here in the palace of my fond in-laws,
Where my young wife can look at you with ease-
The perfect image of a future husband."
At this he swung the Gorgon's head to face
The terror-haunted and averted eyes
Of Phineus, whose neck at once grew rigid,
And tears of onyx hung upon his cheeks.
Here, as if fixed for all eternity,
Were weeping features and a beggar's gaze,
Hands reaching out for mercy in despair.

Though his grandfather scarcely earned that honour,
The conquering Perseus and his new-made wife
Entered the fortress of his native city
To war on Proetus, who usurped his brother
With fire and steel. He held the fort, Acrisius,
Grandpere① of Perseus, was thrown out, yet neither
Armed men nor stone-built walls could hold a siege
Against the deadly stare of snake-crowned Gorgon.

Yet Tyrant Polydectes of Seriphos
Ignored the boy's spectacular successes,
His bravery, his trials, he turned steeled hate
And everlasting anger at the hero.
He could not praise him and he thought aloud
That dread Medusa's death was storytelling.
"We'll give you ample evidence for that,"
Perseus replied. "Now shield your eyes," and wild
Medusa's face turned Tyrant into granite.

Questions for discussion:

1. Cadmus came to Greece from Phoenicia to establish the city of Thebes. The Phoenician alphabet was the predecessor of the Greek alphabet. Are myths and legends a metaphor for recording historical events?

2. Semele, the daughter of Cadmus, becomes the lover of Zeus, how did she set up by Hera? How did Artemis punish Actaeon—the grandson of Cadmus? What are the virtues of god or goddess in Greek mythology?

3. What did Perseus go through to marry Andromeda? When conflict broke out at a wedding reception, why did the majority of those present side with Phineus and not with Perseus?

---

① 外公，即 Grandpa

第三篇　The Iliad

Homer

Translated by Samuel Butler

BOOK XXIV

The assembly now broke up and the people went their ways each to his own ship. There they made ready their supper, and then bethought them of the blessed boon of sleep; but Achilles still wept for thinking of his dear comrade, and sleep, before whom all things bow, could take no hold upon him. This way and that did he turn as he yearned after the might and manfulness of Patroclus①; he thought of all they had done together, and all they had gone through both on the field of battle and on the waves of the weary sea. As he dwelt on these things he wept bitterly and lay now on his side, now on his back, and now face downwards, till at last he rose and went out as one distraught to wander upon the seashore. Then, when he saw dawn breaking over beach and sea, he yoked his horses to his chariot, and bound the body of Hector behind it that he might drag it about. Thrice did he drag it round the tomb of the son of Menoetius②, and then went back into his tent, leaving the body on the ground full length and with its face downwards. But Apollo would not suffer it to be disfigured, for he pitied the man, dead though he now was; therefore he shielded him with his golden aegis continually, that he might take no hurt while Achilles was dragging him.

---

① 帕特洛克勒斯（Patroclus），希腊英雄阿喀琉斯的表弟，被特洛伊王子赫克托（Hector）所杀

② The son of Menoetius 即指帕特洛克勒斯（Patroclus）

Thus shamefully did Achilles in his fury dishonour Hector; but the blessed gods looked down in pity from heaven, and urged Mercury, slayer of Argus①, to steal the body. All were of this mind save only Juno, Neptune, and Jove's grey-eyed daughter②, who persisted in the hate which they had ever borne towards Ilius③ with Priam④ and his people; for they forgave not the wrong done them by Alexandrus⑤ in disdaining the goddesses who came to him when he was in his sheepyards, and preferring her who had offered him a wanton to his ruin.

When, therefore, the morning of the twelfth day had now come, Phoebus Apollo spoke among the immortals saying, "You gods ought to be ashamed of yourselves; you are cruel and hard-hearted. Did not Hector⑥ burn you thigh-bones of heifers and of unblemished goats? And now dare you not rescue even his dead body, for his wife to look upon, with his mother and child, his father Priam, and his people, who would forthwith commit him to the flames, and give him his due funeral rites? So, then, you would all be on the side of mad Achilles, who knows neither right nor ruth⑦? He is like some savage lion that in the pride of his great strength and daring springs upon men's flocks and gorges on them. Even so has Achilles flung aside all pity, and all that conscience which at once so greatly banes yet greatly boons him that will heed it. man may lose one far dearer than Achilles has lost a son, it may be, or a brother born from his own mother's womb; yet when he has mourned him and wept over him he will let him bide, for it takes much sorrow to kill a man; whereas Achilles, now that he has slain noble Hector, drags him behind his chariot round the tomb of his comrade. It were better of him, and for him, that he should not do so, for brave though he be we gods may take it ill that he should vent his fury upon dead clay."

---

① 信使之神墨丘利（Mercury）曾经为了解救朱庇特的情人 Io，逃脱天后朱诺（Juno）的监控，而杀死天后朱诺派去的百眼巨怪阿耳戈斯（Argus），因此 Mercury 也被称为 slayer of Argus
② Jove's grey-eyed daughter，指智慧女神密涅瓦 Minerva（即雅典娜 Athena）
③ Ilius，特洛伊城（Troy）的拉丁名
④ 特洛伊城的国王普里阿姆（Priam）
⑤ 亚历山德鲁斯（Alexandrus），特洛伊小王子帕里斯（Paris）的另一个名字，特洛伊战争因他拐走斯巴达王后海伦而引起
⑥ 赫克托（Hector），特洛伊城大王子，因在战斗中杀死了阿喀琉斯（Achilles）的表弟帕特洛克勒斯（Patroclus），后被阿喀琉斯所杀
⑦ 怜悯

Juno① spoke up in a rage. "This were well," she cried, "O lord of the silver bow②, if you would give like honour to Hector and to Achilles; but Hector was mortal and suckled at a woman's breast, whereas Achilles is the offspring of a goddess whom I myself reared and brought up.

I married her③ to Peleus, who is above measure dear to the immortals; you gods came all of you to her wedding; you feasted along with them yourself and brought your lyre false, and fond of low company, that you have ever been."

Then said Jove④, "Juno, be not so bitter. Their honour shall not be equal, but of all that dwell in Ilius, Hector was dearest to the gods, as also to myself, for his offerings never failed me. Never was my altar stinted of its dues, nor of the drink-offerings and savour of sacrifice which we claim of right. I shall therefore permit the body of mighty Hector to be stolen; and yet this may hardly be without Achilles coming to know it, for his mother keeps night and day beside him. Let some one of you, therefore, send Thetis⑤ to me, and I will impart my counsel to her, namely that Achilles is to accept a ransom from Priam, and give up the body."

On this Iris⑥ fleet as the wind went forth to carry his message. Down she plunged into the dark sea midway between Samos and rocky Imbrus; the waters hissed as they closed over her, and she sank into the bottom as the lead at the end of an ox-horn, that is sped to carry death to fishes. She found Thetis sitting in a great cave with the other sea-goddesses gathered round her; there she sat in the midst of them weeping for her noble son who was to fall far from his own land, on the rich plains of Troy. Iris went up to her and said, "Rise Thetis; Jove, whose counsels fail not, bids you come to him." And Thetis answered, "Why does the mighty god so bid me? I am in great grief, and shrink from going in and out among the immortals. Still, I will go, and the word that he may speak shall not be spoken in vain."

The goddess took her dark veil, than which there can be no robe more sombre, and went forth with fleet Iris leading the way before her. The waves of the sea opened

---

① 天后朱诺（Juno）
② Lord of the silver bow 指太阳神 Apollo
③ 指阿喀琉斯的母亲，海中女神塞蒂斯（Thetis），也译忒提斯
④ 主神朱庇特（Jupiter）的常用名
⑤ 塞蒂斯（Thetis），也译忒提斯，阿喀琉斯的母亲
⑥ 伊里斯（Iris），彩虹女神，亦称信使女神，主要是向诸神传达主神朱庇特的旨意

them a path, and when they reached the shore they flew up into the heavens, where they found the all-seeing son of Saturn① with the blessed gods that live for ever assembled near him. Minerva gave up her seat to her, and she sat down by the side of father Jove. Juno then placed a fair golden cup in her hand, and spoke to her in words of comfort, whereon Thetis drank and gave her back the cup; and the sire of gods and men② was the first to speak.

"So, goddess," said he, "for all your sorrow, and the grief that I well know reigns ever in your heart, you have come hither to Olympus, and I will tell you why I have sent for you. This nine days past the immortals have been quarrelling about Achilles waster of cities and the body of Hector. The gods would have Mercury slayer of Argus steal the body, but in furtherance of our peace and amity henceforward, I will concede such honour to your son as I will now tell you. Go, then, to the host and lay these commands upon him; say that the gods are angry with him, and that I am myself more angry than them all, in that he keeps Hector at the ships and will not give him up. He may thus fear me and let the body go. At the same time I will send Iris to great Priam to bid him go to the ships of the Achaeans③, and ransom his son, taking with him such gifts for Achilles as may give him satisfaction.

Silver-footed Thetis did as the god had told her, and forthwith down she darted from the topmost summits of Olympus. She went to her son's tents where she found him grieving bitterly, while his trusty comrades round him were busy preparing their morning meal, for which they had killed a great woolly sheep. His mother sat down beside him and caressed him with her hand saying, "My son, how long will you keep on thus grieving and making moan? You are gnawing at your own heart, and think neither of food nor of woman's embraces; and yet these too were well, for you have no long time to live, and death with the strong hand of fate are already close beside you. Now, therefore, heed what I say, for I come as a messenger from Jove; he says that the gods are angry with you, and himself more angry than them all, in that you keep Hector at the ships and will not give him up. Therefore let him go, and accept a ransom for his body."

---

① Son of Saturn, 塞坦的儿子,指主神朱庇特。塞坦(Saturn)是第二代主神克洛诺斯(Cronus)的拉丁名
② The sire of gods and men, 神和人共同的先辈,指朱庇特
③ The Achaeans, 亚该亚人,或爱琴人,指希腊联军

And Achilles answered, "So be it. If Olympian Jove of his own motion thus commands me, let him that brings the ransom bear the body away."

Thus did mother and son talk together at the ships in long discourse with one another. Meanwhile the son of Saturn sent Iris to the strong city of Ilius. "Go," said he, "fleet Iris, from the mansions of Olympus, and tell King Priam in Ilius, that he is to go to the ships of the Achaeans and free the body of his dear son. He is to take such gifts with him as shall give satisfaction to Achilles, and he is to go alone, with no other Trojan, save only some honoured servant who may drive his mules and wagon, and bring back the body of him whom noble Achilles has slain. Let him have no thought nor fear of death in his heart, for we will send the slayer of Argus① to escort him, and bring him within the tent of Achilles. Achilles will not kill him nor let another do so, for he will take heed to his ways and sin not, and he will entreat a suppliant with all honourable courtesy."

On this Iris, fleet as the wind, sped forth to deliver her message. She went to Priam's house, and found weeping and lamentation therein. His sons were seated round their father in the outer courtyard, and their raiment was wet with tears: the old man sat in the midst of them with his mantle wrapped close about his body, and his head and neck all covered with the filth which he had clutched as he lay grovelling in the mire. His daughters and his sons' wives went wailing about the house, as they thought of the many and brave men who lay dead, slain by the Argives②. The messenger of Jove stood by Priam and spoke softly to him, but fear fell upon him as she did so. "Take heart," she said, "Priam offspring of Dardanus③, take heart and fear not. I bring no evil tidings, but am minded well towards you. I come as a messenger from Jove, who though he be not near, takes thought for you and pities you. The lord of Olympus bids you go and ransom noble Hector, and take with you such gifts as shall give satisfaction to Achilles. You are to go alone, with no Trojan, save only some honoured servant who may drive your mules and wagon, and bring back to the city the body of him whom noble Achilles has slain. You are to have no thought, nor fear of death, for Jove will send the slayer of Argus to escort you. When he has brought you

---

① 指信使之神墨丘利（Mercury），即赫尔墨斯（Hermes）。
② 阿尔戈斯人（The Argives），阿尔戈斯是希腊南部一地区，这里指希腊联军。
③ 达尔达诺斯（Dardanus），朱庇特之子，特洛伊人的始祖。现在土耳其的恰纳卡莱海峡古称为达达尼尔海峡，名称亦来源于此。

within Achilles' tent, Achilles will not kill you nor let another do so, for he will take heed to his ways and sin not, and he will entreat a suppliant with all honourable courtesy."

Iris went her way when she had thus spoken, and Priam told his sons to get a mule-wagon ready, and to make the body of the wagon fast upon the top of its bed. Then he went down into his fragrant store-room, high-vaulted, and made of cedar-wood, where his many treasures were kept, and he called Hecuba① his wife. "Wife," said he, "a messenger has come to me from Olympus, and has told me to go to the ships of the Achaeans to ransom my dear son, taking with me such gifts as shall give satisfaction to Achilles. What think you of this matter? For my own part I am greatly moved to pass through the bulwark of the Achaeans and go to their ships."

His wife cried aloud as she heard him, and said, "Alas, what has become of that judgement for which you have been ever famous both among strangers and your own people? How can you venture alone to the ships of the Achaeans, and look into the face of him who has slain so many of your brave sons? You must have iron courage, for if the cruel savage sees you and lays hold on you, he will know neither respect nor pity. Let us then weep Hector from afar here in our own house, for when I gave him birth the threads of overruling fate were spun for him that dogs should eat his flesh far from his parents, in the house of that terrible man on whose liver I would fain fasten and devour it. Thus would I avenge my son, who showed no cowardice when Achilles slew him, and thought neither of Right nor of avoiding battle as he stood in defence of Trojan men and Trojan women."

Then Priam said, "I would go, do not therefore stay me nor be as a bird of ill omen in my house, for you will not move me. Had it been some mortal man who had sent me some prophet or priest who divines from sacrifice-I should have deemed him false and have given him no heed; but now I have heard the goddess and seen her face to face, therefore I will go and her saying shall not be in vain. If it be my fate to die at the ships of the Achaeans even so would I have it; let Achilles slay me, if I may but first have taken my son in my arms and mourned him to my heart's comforting."

So saying he lifted the lids of his chests, and took out twelve goodly vestments. He took also twelve cloaks of single fold, twelve rugs, twelve fair mantles, and an equal

---

① 赫克犹巴（Hecuba），特洛伊王后，普里阿姆之妻

number of shirts. He weighed out ten talents of gold, and brought moreover two burnished tripods, four cauldrons, and a very beautiful cup which the Thracians① had given him when he had gone to them on an embassy; it was very precious, but he grudged not even this, so eager was he to ransom the body of his son. Then he chased all the Trojans from the court and rebuked them with words of anger. "Out," he cried, "shame and disgrace to me that you are. Have you no grief in your own homes that you are come to plague me here? Is it a small thing, think you, that the son of Saturn has sent this sorrow upon me, to lose the bravest of my sons? Nay, you shall prove it in person, for now he is gone the Achaeans will have easier work in killing you. As for me, let me go down within the house of Hades, ere② mine eyes behold the sacking and wasting of the city."

He drove the men away with his staff, and they went forth as the old man sped them. Then he called to his sons, upbraiding Helenus, Paris, noble Agathon, Pammon, Antiphonus, Polites of the loud battle-cry, Deiphobus, Hippothous, and Dius③. These nine did the old man call near him. "Come to me at once," he cried, "worthless sons who do me shame; would that you had all been killed at the ships rather than Hector. Miserable man that I am, I have had the bravest sons in all Troy-Noble Nestor, Troilus the dauntless charioteer, and Hector who was a god among men, so that one would have thought he was son to an immortal-yet there is not one of them left. Mars has slain them and those of whom I am ashamed are alone left me. Liars, and light of foot, heroes of the dance, robbers of lambs and kids from your own people, why do you not get a wagon ready for me at once, and put all these things upon it that I may set out on my way?"

Thus did he speak, and they feared the rebuke of their father. They brought out a strong mule-wagon, newly made, and set the body of the wagon fast on its bed. They took the mule-yoke from the peg on which it hung, a yoke of boxwood with a knob on the top of it and rings for the reins to go through. Then they brought a yoke-band eleven cubits long, to bind the yoke to the pole; they bound it on at the far end of the pole, and put the ring over the upright pin making it fast with three turns of the band on

---

① 色雷斯人（Thracians），古代爱琴海北岸一地区，现希腊、保加利亚、土耳其交界地区
② 在……之前
③ 普里阿姆（Priam）剩余的九个儿子

either side the knob, and bending the thong of the yoke beneath it. This done, they brought from the store-chamber the rich ransom that was to purchase the body of Hector, and they set it all orderly on the wagon; then they yoked the strong harness-mules which the Mysians① had on a time given as a goodly present to Priam; but for Priam himself they yoked horses which the old king had bred, and kept for own use.

Thus heedfully did Priam and his servant see to the yoking of their cars at the palace. Then Hecuba came to them all sorrowful, with a golden goblet of wine in her right hand, that they might make a drink-offering before they set out. She stood in front of the horses and said, "Take this, make a drink-offering to father Jove, and since you are minded to go to the ships in spite of me, pray that you may come safely back from the hands of your enemies. Pray to the son of Saturn lord of the whirlwind, who sits on Ida② and looks down over all Troy, pray him to send his swift messenger on your right hand, the bird of omen which is strongest and most dear to him of all birds, that you may see it with your own eyes and trust it as you go forth to the ships of the Danaans③. If all-seeing Jove will not send you this messenger, however set upon it you may be, I would not have you go to the ships of the Argives."

And Priam answered, "Wife, I will do as you desire me; it is well to lift hands in prayer to Jove, if so be he may have mercy upon me."

With this the old man bade the serving-woman pour pure water over his hands, and the woman came, bearing the water in a bowl. He washed his hands and took the cup from his wife; then he made the drink-offering and prayed, standing in the middle of the courtyard and turning his eyes to heaven. "Father Jove," he said, "that rulest from Ida, most glorious and most great, grant that I may be received kindly and compassionately in the tents of Achilles; and send your swift messenger upon my right hand, the bird of omen which is strongest and most dear to you of all birds, that I may see it with my own eyes and trust it as I go forth to the ships of the Danaans."

So did he pray, and Jove the lord of counsel heard his prayer. Forthwith he sent an eagle, the most unerring portent of all birds that fly, the dusky hunter that men also call the Black Eagle. His wings were spread abroad on either side as wide as the well-

---

① 迈西亚人（Mysians）
② 艾达山（Ida）
③ 达纳人（The Danaans），指希腊联军

made and well-bolted door of a rich man's chamber. He came to them flying over the city upon their right hands, and when they saw him they were glad and their hearts took comfort within them. The old man made haste to mount his chariot, and drove out through the inner gateway and under the echoing gatehouse of the outer court. Before him went the mules drawing the four-wheeled wagon, and driven by wise Idaeus①; behind these were the horses, which the old man lashed with his whip and drove swiftly through the city, while his friends followed after, wailing and lamenting for him as though he were on his road to death. As soon as they had come down from the city and had reached the plain, his sons and sons-in-law who had followed him went back to Ilius.

But Priam and Idaeus as they showed out upon the plain did not escape the ken of all-seeing Jove, who looked down upon the old man and pitied him; then he spoke to his son Mercury and said, "Mercury, for it is you who are the most disposed to escort men on their way, and to hear those whom you will hear, go, and so conduct Priam to the ships of the Achaeans that no other of the Danaans shall see him nor take note of him until he reach the son of Peleus②."

Thus he spoke and Mercury, guide and guardian, slayer of Argus, did as he was told. Forthwith he bound on his glittering golden sandals with which he could fly like the wind over land and sea; he took the wand with which he seals men's eyes in sleep, or wakes them just as he pleases, and flew holding it in his hand till he came to Troy and to the Hellespont③. To look at, he was like a young man of noble birth in the heyday of his youth and beauty with the down just coming upon his face.

Now when Priam and Idaeus had driven past the great tomb of Ilius, they stayed their mules and horses that they might drink in the river, for the shades of night were falling, when, therefore, Idaeus saw Mercury standing near them he said to Priam, "Take heed, descendant of Dardanus; here is matter which demands consideration. I see a man who I think will presently fall upon us; let us fly with our horses, or at least embrace his knees and implore him to take compassion upon us?"

When he heard this the old man's heart failed him, and he was in great fear; he

---

① 伊德乌斯（Idaeus），国王的忠实的仆人
② The son of Peleus, 指阿喀琉斯（Achilles）。阿喀琉斯是海中女神塞蒂斯（Thetis）和英雄珀琉斯（Peleus）的儿子
③ 赫勒斯滂（Hellespont），亚欧交界的水域，现在土耳其的恰纳卡莱海峡及附近水域

stayed where he was as one dazed, and the hair stood on end over his whole body; but the bringer of good luck① came up to him and took him by the hand, saying, "Whither, father, are you thus driving your mules and horses in the dead of night when other men are asleep? Are you not afraid of the fierce Achaeans who are hard by you, so cruel and relentless? Should some one of them see you bearing so much treasure through the darkness of the flying night, what would not your state then be? You are no longer young, and he who is with you is too old to protect you from those who would attack you. For myself, I will do you no harm, and I will defend you from any one else, for you remind me of my own father."

And Priam answered, "It is indeed as you say, my dear son; nevertheless some god has held his hand over me, in that he has sent such a wayfarer as yourself to meet me so Opportunely; you are so comely in mien and figure, and your judgement is so excellent that you must come of blessed parents."

Then said the slayer of Argus, guide and guardian, "Sir, all that you have said is right; but tell me and tell me true, are you taking this rich treasure to send it to a foreign people where it may be safe, or are you all leaving strong Ilius in dismay now that your son has fallen who was the bravest man among you and was never lacking in battle with the Achaeans?"

And Priam said, "Who are you, my friend, and who are your parents, that you speak so truly about the fate of my unhappy son?"

The slayer of Argus, guide and guardian, answered him, "Sir, you would prove me, that you question me about noble Hector. Many a time have I set eyes upon him in battle when he was driving the Argives to their ships and putting them to the sword. We stood still and marveled, for Achilles in his anger with the son of Atreus② suffered us not to fight. I am his squire, and came with him in the same ship. I am a Myrmidon③, and my father's name is Polyctor: he is a rich man and about as old as you are; he has six sons besides myself, and I am the seventh. We cast lots, and it fell upon me to sail hither with Achilles. I am now come from the ships on to the plain, for with daybreak the Achaeans will set battle in array about the city. They chafe at doing nothing, and

---

① The bringer of good luck，指信使和商业之神墨丘利（Mercury）
② The son of Atreus，指希腊主帅阿伽门农（Agamemnon）
③ 迈米登人（Myrmidon），阿喀琉斯所带领的士兵的总称

are so eager that their princes cannot hold them back."

Then answered Priam, "If you are indeed the squire of Achilles son of Peleus, tell me now the Whole truth. Is my son still at the ships, or has Achilles hewn him limb from limb, and given him to his hounds?"

"Sir," replied the slayer of Argus, guide and guardian, "neither hounds nor vultures have yet devoured him; he is still just lying at the tents by the ship of Achilles, and though it is now twelve days that he has lain there, his flesh is not wasted nor have the worms eaten him although they feed on warriors. At daybreak Achilles drags him cruelly round the sepulchre of his dear comrade, but it does him no hurt. You should come yourself and see how he lies fresh as dew, with the blood all washed away, and his wounds every one of them closed though many pierced him with their spears. Such care have the blessed gods taken of your brave son, for he was dear to them beyond all measure."

The old man was comforted as he heard him and said, "My son, see what a good thing it is to have made due offerings to the immortals; for as sure as that he was born my son never forgot the gods that hold Olympus, and now they requite it to him even in death. Accept therefore at my hands this goodly chalice; guard me and with heaven's help guide me till I come to the tent of the son of Peleus."

Then answered the slayer of Argus, guide and guardian, "Sir, you are tempting me and playing upon my youth, but you shall not move me, for you are offering me presents without the knowledge of Achilles whom I fear and hold it great guiltless to defraud, lest some evil presently befall me; but as your guide I would go with you even to Argos itself, and would guard you so carefully whether by sea or land, that no one should attack you through making light of him who was with you."

The bringer of good luck then sprang on to the chariot, and seizing the whip and reins he breathed fresh spirit into the mules and horses. When they reached the trench and the wall that was before the ships, those who were on guard had just been getting their suppers, and the slayer of Argus threw them all into a deep sleep. Then he drew back the bolts to open the gates, and took Priam inside with the treasure he had upon his wagon. Ere long they came to the lofty dwelling of the son of Peleus for which the Myrmidons had cut pine and which they had built for their king; when they had built it they thatched it with coarse tussock-grass which they had mown out on the plain, and all round it they made a large courtyard, which was fenced with stakes set close together. The gate was barred with a single bolt of pine which it took three men to force into its place, and three to draw back so as to open the gate, but Achilles could draw it by himself. Mercury opened the gate for the old man, and brought in the treasure that he was taking with him for the son of Peleus. Then he sprang from the chariot on to the ground and said, "Sir, it is I, immortal Mercury, that am come with you, for my father sent me to escort you. I will now leave you, and will not enter into the presence of Achilles, for it might anger him that a god should befriend mortal men thus openly. Go you within, and embrace the knees of the son of Peleus: beseech him by his father, his lovely mother, and his son; thus you may move him."

With these words Mercury went back to high Olympus. Priam sprang from his chariot to the ground, leaving Idaeus where he was, in charge of the mules and horses. The old man went straight into the house where Achilles, loved of the gods, was sitting. There he found him with his men seated at a distance from him: only two, the hero Automedon, and Alcimus of the race of Mars, were busy in attendance about his person, for he had but just done eating and drinking, and the table was still there. King Priam entered without their seeing him, and going right up to Achilles he clasped his knees and kissed the dread murderous hands that had slain so many of his sons.

As when some cruel spite has befallen a man that he should have killed some one in his own country, and must fly to a great man's protection in a land of strangers, and all marvel who see him, even so did Achilles marvel as he beheld Priam. The others looked one to another and marveled also, but Priam besought Achilles saying, "Think of your father, O Achilles like unto the gods, who is such even as I am, on the sad threshold of old age. It may be that those who dwell near him harass him, and there is none to keep war and ruin from him. Yet when he hears of you being still alive, he is glad, and his days are full of hope that he shall see his dear son come home to him from Troy; but I, wretched man that I am, had the bravest in all Troy for my sons, and there is not one of them left. I had fifty sons when the Achaeans came here; nineteen of them were from a single womb, and the others were borne to me by the women of my household. The greater part of them has fierce Mars laid low, and Hector, him who was alone left, him who was the guardian of the city and ourselves, him have you lately slain; therefore I am now come to the ships of the Achaeans to ransom his body from you with a great ransom. Fear, O Achilles, the wrath of heaven; think on your own father and have compassion upon me, who am the more pitiable, for I have steeled myself as no man yet has ever steeled himself before me, and have raised to my lips the hand of him who slew my son."

Thus spoke Priam, and the heart of Achilles yearned as he bethought him of his father. He took the old man's hand and moved him gently away. The two wept bitterly—Priam, as he lay at Achilles' feet, weeping for Hector, and Achilles now for his father and now for Patroclous, till the house was filled with their lamentation. But when Achilles was now sated with grief and had unburthened the bitterness of his sorrow, he left his seat and raised the old man by the hand, in pity for his white hair and beard; then he said, "Unhappy man, you have indeed been greatly daring; how could you venture to come alone to the ships of the Achaeans, and enter the presence of him who has slain so many of your brave sons? You must have iron courage: sit now upon this seat, and for all our grief we will hide our sorrows in our hearts, for weeping will not avail us. The immortals know no care, yet the lot they spin for man is full of sorrow; on the floor of Jove's palace there stand two urns, the one filled with evil gifts, and the other with good ones. He for whom Jove the lord of thunder mixes the gifts he sends, will meet now with good and now with evil fortune; but he to whom Jove sends none but evil gifts will be pointed at by the finger of scorn, the hand of famine will pursue him to the ends of the world, and he will go up and down the face of the earth, respected neither by gods nor men. Even so did it befall Peleus; the gods endowed him with all good things from his birth upwards, for he reigned over the Myrmidons excelling all men in prosperity and wealth, and mortal though he was they gave him a goddess for his bride. But even on him too did heaven send misfortune, for there is no race of royal children born to him in his house, save one son who is doomed to die all untimely; nor may I take care of him now that he is growing old, for I must stay here at Troy to be the bane of you and your children. And you too, O Priam, I have heard that you were aforetime happy. They say that in wealth and plenitude of offspring you surpassed all that is in Lesbos, the realm of Makar to the northward, Phrygia that is more inland, and those that dwell upon the great Hellespont; but from the day when the dwellers in heaven sent this evil upon you, war and slaughter have been about your city continually. Bear up against it, and let there be some intervals in your sorrow. Mourn as you may for your brave son, you will take nothing by it. You cannot raise him from the dead, ere you do so yet another sorrow shall befall you."

And Priam answered, "O king, bid me not be seated, while Hector is still lying uncared for in your tents, but accept the great ransom which I have brought you, and give him to me at once that I may look upon him. May you prosper with the ransom and reach your own land in safety, seeing that you have suffered me to live and to look upon the light of the sun."

Achilles looked at him sternly and said, "Vex me, sir, no longer; I am of myself minded to give up the body of Hector. My mother, daughter of the old man of the sea①, came to me from Jove to bid me deliver it to you. Moreover I know well, O Priam, and you cannot hide it, that some god has brought you to the ships of the Achaeans, for else, no man however strong and in his prime would dare to come to our host; he could neither pass our guard unseen, nor draw the bolt of my gates thus easily; therefore, provoke me no further, lest I sin against the word of Jove, and suffer you not, suppliant though you are, within my tents."

The old man feared him and obeyed. Then the son of Peleus sprang like a lion through the door of his house, not alone, but with him went his two squires Automedon and Alcimus who were closer to him than any others of his comrades now that Patroclus was no more. These unyoked the horses and mules, and bade Priam's herald and attendant be seated within the house. They lifted the ransom for Hector's body from the wagon. but they left two mantles and a goodly shirt, that Achilles might wrap the body in them when he gave it to be taken home. Then he called to his servants and ordered them to wash the body and anoint it, but he first took it to a place where Priam should not see it, lest if he did so, he should break out in the bitterness of his grief, and enrage Achilles, who might then kill him and sin against the word of Jove. When the servants had washed the body and anointed it, and had wrapped it in a fair shirt and mantle, Achilles himself lifted it on to a bier, and he and his men then laid it on the wagon. He cried aloud as he did so and called on the name of his dear comrade, "Be not angry with me, Patroclus," he said, "if you hear even in the house of Hades that I have given Hector to his father for a ransom. It has been no unworthy one, and I will share it equitably with you."

Achilles then went back into the tent and took his place on the richly inlaid seat from which he had risen, by the wall that was at right angles to the one against which

---

① The old man of the sea, 指老海神涅柔斯（Nereus），海中女神塞蒂斯（Thetis）的父亲，阿喀琉斯的外公

Priam was sitting. "Sir," he said, "your son is now laid upon his bier and is ransomed according to desire; you shall look upon him when you take him away at daybreak; for the present let us prepare our supper. Even lovely Niobe① had to think about eating, though her twelve children-six daughters and six lusty sons-had been all slain in her house. Apollo killed the sons with arrows from his silver bow, to punish Niobe, and Diana slew the daughters, because Niobe had vaunted herself against Leto; she said Leto had borne two children only, whereas she had herself borne many-whereon the two killed the many. Nine days did they lie weltering, and there was none to bury them, for the son of Saturn② turned the people into stone; but on the tenth day the gods in heaven themselves buried them, and Niobe then took food, being worn out with weeping. They say that somewhere among the rocks on the mountain pastures of Sipylus, where the nymphs live that haunt the river Achelous, there, they say, she lives in stone and still nurses the sorrows sent upon her by the hand of heaven. Therefore, noble sir, let us two now take food; you can weep for your dear son hereafter as you are bearing him back to Ilius and many a tear will he cost you."

With this Achilles sprang from his seat and killed a sheep of silvery whiteness, which his followers skinned and made ready all in due order. They cut the meat carefully up into smaller pieces, spitted③ them, and drew them off again when they were well roasted. Automedon brought bread in fair baskets and served it round the table, while Achilles dealt out the meat, and they laid their hands on the good things that were before them. As soon as they had had enough to eat and drink, Priam, descendant of Dardanus, marveled at the strength and beauty of Achilles for he was as a god to see, and Achilles marveled at Priam as he listened to him and looked upon his noble presence. When they had gazed their fill Priam spoke first. "And now, O king," he said, "take me to my couch that we may lie down and enjoy the blessed boon of sleep. Never once have my eyes been closed from the day your hands took the life of my son; I have grovelled without ceasing in the mire of my stable-yard, making moan and brooding over my countless sorrows. Now, moreover, I have eaten bread and drunk

---

① 尼俄柏（Niobe），坦塔罗斯（Tantalus）的女儿，生有六男六女，因嘲笑黑袍女神莱托（Leto）只生了一男一女，而后遭到莱托的儿子阿波罗（Apollo）、女儿黛安娜（Diana）的射杀，悲伤欲绝化为顽石
② The son of Saturn，指主神朱庇特（Jove）
③ 用烤肉叉串上

wine; hitherto I have tasted nothing."

As he spoke Achilles told his men and the women-servants to set beds in the room that was in the gatehouse, and make them with good red rugs, and spread coverlets on the top of them with woollen cloaks for Priam and Idaeus to wear. So the maids went out carrying a torch and got the two beds ready in all haste. Then Achilles said laughingly to Priam, "Dear sir, you shall lie outside, lest some counsellor of those who in due course keep coming to advise with me should see you here in the darkness of the flying night, and tell it to Agamemnon①. This might cause delay in the delivery of the body. And now tell me and tell me true, for how many days would you celebrate the funeral rites of noble Hector? Tell me, that I may hold aloof from war and restrain the host."

And Priam answered, "Since, then, you suffer me to bury my noble son with all due rites, do thus, Achilles, and I shall be grateful. You know how we are pent up within our city; it is far for us to fetch wood from the mountain, and the people live in fear. Nine days, therefore, will we mourn Hector in my house; on the tenth day we will bury him and there shall be a public feast in his honour; on the eleventh we will build a mound over his ashes, and on the twelfth, if there be need, we will fight."

And Achilles answered, "All, King Priam, shall be as you have said. I will stay our fighting for as long a time as you have named."

As he spoke he laid his hand on the old man's right wrist, in token that he should have no fear; thus then did Priam and his attendant sleep there in the forecourt, full of thought, while Achilles lay in an inner room of the house, with fair Briseis② by his side.

And now both gods and mortals were fast asleep through the livelong night, but upon Mercury alone, the bringer of good luck, sleep could take no hold for he was thinking all the time how to get King Priam away from the ships without his being seen by the strong force of sentinels. He hovered therefore over Priam's head and said, "Sir, now that Achilles has spared your life, you seem to have no fear about sleeping in the thick of your foes. You have paid a great ransom, and have received the body of your son; were you still alive and a prisoner the sons whom you have left at home would have

---

① 阿伽门农（Agamemnon），迈锡尼国王，希腊军主帅
② 布里塞伊斯（Briseis），阿喀琉斯的战俘美女，曾被阿伽门农（Agamemnon）抢去，为此阿喀琉斯拒绝代表希腊军出战。后阿伽门农将她归还，并向阿喀琉斯道歉

to give three times as much to free you; and so it would be if Agamemnon and the other Achaeans were to know of your being here."

When he heard this the old man was afraid and roused his servant. Mercury then yoked their horses and mules, and drove them quickly through the host so that no man perceived them. When they came to the ford of eddying Xanthus①, begotten of immortal Jove, Mercury went back to high Olympus, and dawn in robe of saffron began to break over all the land. Priam and Idaeus then drove on toward the city lamenting and making moan, and the mules drew the body of Hector. No one neither man nor woman saw them, till Cassandra②, fair as golden Venus standing on Pergamus③, caught sight of her dear father in his chariot, and his servant that was the city's herald with him. Then she saw him that was lying upon the bier, drawn by the mules, and with a loud cry she went about the city saying, "Come hither Trojans, men and women, and look on Hector; if ever you rejoiced to see him coming from battle when he was alive, look now on him that was the glory of our city and all our people."

At this there was not man nor woman left in the city, so great a sorrow had possessed them. Hard by the gates they met Priam as he was bringing in the body. Hector's wife and his mother were the first to mourn him: they flew towards the wagon and laid their hands upon his head, while the crowd stood weeping round them. They would have stayed before the gates, weeping and lamenting the livelong day to the going down of the sun, had not Priam spoken to them from the chariot and said, "Make way for the mules to pass you. Afterwards when I have taken the body home you shall have your fill of weeping."

On this the people stood asunder, and made a way for the wagon. When they had borne the body within the house they laid it upon a bed and seated minstrels round it to lead the dirge, whereon the women joined in the sad music of their lament. Foremost

---

① 特洛伊城外的一条河流
② 卡桑德拉（Cassandra），普里阿姆（Priam）的小女儿，阿波罗神庙的祭司，能够预见未来。特洛伊城破后，被阿伽门农（Agamemnon）娶为小妾。当阿伽门农和卡桑德拉回到希腊后，双双被阿伽门农的妻子克吕泰涅斯特拉（Clytemnestra）及情夫埃吉斯托斯（Aegisthus）所屠杀
③ 帕迦玛斯（Pergamus），特洛伊城的另一个称呼。公元前3世纪，希腊人在小亚细亚建城，也取名帕迦玛斯

among them all Andromache① led their wailing as she clasped the head of mighty Hector in her embrace. "Husband," she cried, "you have died young, and leave me in your house a widow; he② of whom we are the ill-starred parents is still a mere child, and I fear he may not reach manhood. Ere he can do so our city will be razed and overthrown, for you who watched over it are no more-you who were its saviour, the guardian of our wives and children. Our women will be carried away captives to the ships, and I among them; while you, my child, who will be with me will be put to some unseemly tasks, working for a cruel master. Or, may be, some Achaean will hurl you (O miserable death) from our walls, to avenge some brother, son, or father whom Hector slew; many of them have indeed bitten the dust at his hands, for your father's hand in battle was no light one. Therefore do the people mourn him. You have left, O Hector, sorrow unutterable to your parents, and my own grief is greatest of all, for you did not stretch forth your arms and embrace me as you lay dying, nor say to me any words that might have lived with me in my tears night and day for evermore."

　　Bitterly did she weep the while, and the women joined in her lament. Hecuba in her turn took up the strains of woe. "Hector," she cried, "dearest to me of all my children. So long as you were alive the gods loved you well, and even in death they have not been utterly unmindful of you; for when Achilles took any other of my sons, he would sell him beyond the seas, to Samos Imbrus or rugged Lemnos; and when he had slain you too with his sword, many a time did he drag you round the sepulchre of his comrade-though this could not give him life-yet here you lie all fresh as dew, and comely as one whom Apollo has slain with his painless shafts."

　　Thus did she too speak through her tears with bitter moan, and then Helen③ for a third time took up the strain of lamentation. "Hector," said she, "dearest of all my brothers-in-law-for I am wife to Alexandrus④ who brought me hither to Troy-would that I had died ere he did so-twenty years are come and gone since I left my home and came from over the sea, but I have never heard one word of insult or unkindness from

---

① 安德洛玛克（Andromache），特洛伊大王子赫克托（Hector）的妻子。特洛伊城被毁后，她被阿喀琉斯的儿子尼奥托勒摩斯（Neoptolemus）娶为妻
② 指自己和赫克托（Hector）的儿子
③ 海伦（Helen），斯巴达的美女王后，和特洛伊王子帕里斯（Paris）私通，导致了特洛伊战争的爆发
④ 亚历山德鲁斯（Alexandrus），指帕里斯（Paris）

you. When another would chide with me, as it might be one of your brothers or sisters or of your brothers' wives, or my mother-in-law-for Priam was as kind to me as though he were my own father-you would rebuke and check them with words of gentleness and goodwill. Therefore my tears flow both for you and for my unhappy self, for there is no one else in Troy who is kind to me, but all shrink and shudder as they go by me."

She wept as she spoke and the vast crowd that was gathered round her joined in her lament. Then King Priam spoke to them saying, "Bring wood, O Trojans, to the city, and fear no cunning ambush of the Argives, for Achilles when he dismissed me from the ships gave me his word that they should not attack us until the morning of the twelfth day."

Forthwith they yoked their oxen and mules and gathered together before the city. Nine days long did they bring in great heaps wood, and on the morning of the tenth day with many tears they took trave Hector forth, laid his dead body upon the summit of the pile, and set the fire thereto. Then when the child of morning rosy-fingered dawn appeared① on the eleventh day, the people again assembled, round the pyre of mighty Hector. When they were got together, they first quenched the fire with wine wherever it was burning, and then his brothers and comrades with many a bitter tear gathered his white bones, wrapped them in soft robes of purple, and laid them in a golden urn, which they placed in a grave and covered over with large stones set close together. Then they built a barrow hurriedly over it keeping guard on every side lest the Achaeans should attack them before they had finished. When they had heaped up the barrow they went back again into the city, and being well assembled they held high feast in the house of Priam their king.

Thus, then, did they celebrate the funeral of Hector tamer of horses.

Questions for discussion:

1. Why did Achilles stay away from the Battle between the Greeks and the Trojans for a time, and why did he return?

2. How does Homer involve the Olympians in his description of the Trojan War?

---

① When the child of morning rosy-fingered dawn appeared, 荷马对拂晓的习惯性描绘

Which side do they support? How to understand the relationship between man and god in war from the Iliad?

3. How did Priam, the Trojan king, slip into the camp of the Greek Allied forces and enter the tent of Achilles? Why didn't Achilles detain or kill Priam instead of returning Hector's body to him?

4. What are the differences between the Western Achilles hero and the Chinese hero?

第四篇　The Odyssey

Homer

Translated by Samuel Butler

BOOK XI

"Then, when we had got down to the sea shore we drew our ship into the water and got her mast and sails into her; we also put the sheep on board and took our places, weeping and in great distress of mind. Circe①, that great and cunning goddess, sent us a fair wind that blew dead aft and stayed steadily with us keeping our sails all the time well filled; so we did whatever wanted doing to the ship's gear and let her go as the wind and helmsman headed her. All day long her sails were full as she held her course over the sea, but when the sun went down and darkness was over all the earth, we got into the deep waters of the river Oceanus②, where lie the land and city of the Cimmerians who live enshrouded in mist and darkness which the rays of the sun never pierce neither at his rising nor as he goes down again out of the heavens, but the poor wretches live in one long melancholy night. When we got there we beached the ship, took the sheep out of her, and went along by the waters of Oceanus till we came to the place of which Circe had told us.

---

① 瑟茜（Circe）又译喀耳刻，希腊英雄奥德修斯（Odysseus），即尤利西斯（Ulysses）在特洛伊战争后的回家途中（尤利西斯是奥德修斯的拉丁名，本节选从拉丁文译成英文，故用尤利西斯），遇到的女巫，她将尤利西斯（Ulysses）的部下们变成了猪
② The river Oceanus，欧申纳斯河，十二泰坦欧申纳斯（Oceanus）又译俄刻阿诺斯，与同为十二泰坦的泰西丝（Tethys）结合，是所有海洋和江河神之始祖

"Here Perimedes and Eurylochus① held the victims, while I drew my sword and dug the trench a cubit each way. I made a drink-offering to all the dead, first with honey and milk, then with wine, and thirdly with water, and I sprinkled white barley meal over the whole, praying earnestly to the poor feckless ghosts, and promising them that when I got back to Ithaca I would sacrifice a barren heifer for them, the best I had, and would load the pyre with good things. I also particularly promised that Teiresias② should have a black sheep to himself, the best in all my flocks. When I had prayed sufficiently to the dead, I cut the throats of the two sheep and let the blood run into the trench, whereon the ghosts came trooping up from Erebus③-brides, young bachelors, old men worn out with toil, maids who had been crossed in love, and brave men who had been killed in battle, with their armour still smirched with blood; they came from every quarter and flitted round the trench with a strange kind of screaming sound that made me turn pale with fear. When I saw them coming I told the men to be quick and flay the carcasses of the two dead sheep and make burnt offerings of them, and at the same time to repeat prayers to Hades④ and to Proserpine⑤; but I sat where I was with my sword drawn and would not let the poor feckless ghosts come near the blood till Teiresias should have answered my questions.

"The first ghost' that came was that of my comrade Elpenor, for he had not yet been laid beneath the earth. We had left his body unwaked and unburied in Circe's house, for we had had too much else to do. I was very sorry for him, and cried when I saw him: 'Elpenor,' said I, 'how did you come down here into this gloom and darkness? You have here on foot quicker than I have with my ship.'

"'Sir,' he answered with a groan, 'it was all bad luck, and my own unspeakable drunkenness. I was lying asleep on the top of Circe's house, and never thought of coming down again by the great stair-case but fell right off the roof and broke my neck, so my soul down to the house of Hades. And now I beseech you by all

---

① Perimedes and Eurylochus, 尤利西斯的两个部下
② 忒瑞西斯（Teiresias, 又名 Tiresias），希腊著名的瞎子预言家，能预知未来，故尤利西斯到阴间来向他探询自己的命运
③ 黑暗神埃瑞波斯（Erebus）即 Erebus, 混沌之神卡俄斯（Chaos）之子，在这里代表阳间与阴间当中的黑暗界
④ 冥王哈迪斯（Hades）
⑤ 冥后普洛塞尔皮娜（Proserpine），即希神中的珀尔塞福涅（Persephone）

those whom you have left behind you, though they are not here, by your wife, by the father who brought you up when you were a child, and by Telemachus① who is the one hope of your house, do what I shall now ask you. I know that when you leave this limbo you will again hold your ship for the Aeaean island. Do not go thence leaving me unwaked and unburied behind you, or I may bring heaven's anger upon you; but burn me with whatever armour I have, build a barrow for me on the sea shore, that may tell people in days to come what a poor unlucky fellow I was, and plant over my grave the oar I used to row with when I was yet alive and with my messmates.' And I said, 'My poor fellow, I will do all that you have asked of me.'

"Thus, then, did we sit and hold sad talk with one another, I on the one side of the trench with my sword held over the blood, and the ghost of my comrade saying all this to me from the other side. Then came the ghost of my dead mother Anticlea②, daughter to Autolycus. I had left her alive when I set out for Troy and was moved to tears when I saw her, but even so, for all my sorrow I would not let her come near the blood till I had asked my questions of Teiresias. "Then came also the ghost of Theban③ Teiresias, with his golden sceptre in his hand. He knew me and said, 'Ulysses, noble son of Laertes④, why, poor man, have you left the light of day and come down to visit the dead in this sad place? Stand back from the trench and withdraw your sword that I may drink of the blood and answer your questions truly.'

"So I drew back, and sheathed my sword, whereon when he had drank of the blood he began with his prophecy.

"'You want to know,' said he, 'about your return home, but heaven will make this hard for you. I do not think that you will escape the eye of Neptune⑤, who still nurses his bitter grudge against you for having blinded his son. Still, after much suffering you may get home if you can restrain yourself and your companions when your ship reaches the Thrinacian island, where you will find the sheep and cattle belonging to the sun, who sees and gives ear to everything. If you leave these flocks unharmed

---

① 忒勒马科斯（Telemachus），尤利西斯的儿子
② 安蒂克利亚（Anticlea），尤利西斯的母亲
③ 忒拜人（Theban）
④ 雷欧提斯（Laertes），尤利西斯的父亲，son of Laertes 指尤利西斯
⑤ 海神尼普顿（Neptune），即希神中的波塞冬（Poseidon）

and think of nothing but of getting home, you may yet after much hardship reach Ithaca①; but if you harm them, then I forewarn you of the destruction both of your ship and of your men. Even though you may yourself escape, you will return in bad plight after losing all your men, in another man's ship, and you will find trouble in your house, which will be overrun by high‑handed people, who are devouring your substance under the pretext of paying court and making presents to your wife.'

" 'When you get home you will take your revenge on these suitors; and after you have killed them by force or fraud in your own house, you must take a well‑made oar and carry it on and on, till you come to a country where the people have never heard of the sea and do not even mix salt with their food, nor do they know anything about ships, and oars that are as the wings of a ship. I will give you this certain token which cannot escape your notice. A wayfarer will meet you and will say it must be a winnowing shovel that you have got upon your shoulder; on this you must fix the oar in the ground and sacrifice a ram, a bull, and a boar to Neptune. Then go home and offer hecatombs② to the gods in heaven one after the other. As for yourself, death shall come to you from the sea, and your life shall ebb away very gently when you are full of years and peace of mind, and your people shall bless you. All that I have said will come true.'

" 'This,' I answered, 'must be as it may please heaven, but tell me and tell me true, I see my poor mother's ghost close by us; she is sitting by the blood without saying a word, and though I am her own son she does not remember me and speak to me; tell me, Sir, how I can make her know me.'

" 'That,' said he, 'I can soon do Any ghost that you let taste of the blood will talk with you like a reasonable being, but if you do not let them have any blood they will go away again.'

"On this the ghost of Teiresias went back to the house of Hades, for his prophecyings had now been spoken, but I sat still where I was until my mother came up and tasted the blood. Then she knew me at once and spoke fondly to me, saying, 'My son, how did you come down to this abode of darkness while you are still alive? It is a hard thing for the living to see these places, for between us and them there are great

---

① 伊萨卡岛（Ithaca），希腊西北部一岛名，尤利西斯的故乡
② 祭献

and terrible waters, and there is Oceanus, which no man can cross on foot, but he must have a good ship to take him. Are you all this time trying to find your way home from Troy, and have you never yet got back to Ithaca nor seen your wife in your own house?'

"'Mother,' said I, 'I was forced to come here to consult the ghost of the Theban prophet Teiresias. I have never yet been near the Achaean land nor set foot on my native country, and I have had nothing but one long series of misfortunes from the very first day that I set out with Agamemnon for Ilius, the land of noble steeds, to fight the Trojans. But tell me, and tell me true, in what way did you die? Did you have a long illness, or did heaven vouchsafe you a gentle easy passage to eternity? Tell me also about my father, and the son whom I left behind me; is my property still in their hands, or has some one else got hold of it, who thinks that I shall not return to claim it? Tell me again what my wife intends doing, and in what mind she is; does she live with my son and guard my estate securely, or has she made the best match she could and married again?'

"My mother answered, 'Your wife still remains in your house, but she is in great distress of mind and spends her whole time in tears both night and day. No one as yet has got possession of your fine property, and Telemachus still holds your lands undisturbed. He has to entertain largely, as of course he must, considering his position as a magistrate, and how every one invites him; your father remains at his old place in the country and never goes near the town. He has no comfortable bed nor bedding; in the winter he sleeps on the floor in front of the fire with the men and goes about all in rags, but in summer, when the warm weather comes on again, he lies out in the vineyard on a bed of vine leaves thrown anyhow upon the ground. He grieves continually about your never having come home, and suffers more and more as he grows older. As for my own end it was in this wise: heaven did not take me swiftly and painlessly in my own house, nor was I attacked by any illness such as those that generally wear people out and kill them, but my longing to know what you were doing and the force of my affection for you—this it was that was the death of me.'

"Then I tried to find some way of embracing my mother's ghost. Thrice I sprang towards her and tried to clasp her in my arms, but each time she flitted from my embrace as it were a dream or phantom, and being touched to the quick I said to her, 'Mother, why do you not stay still when I would embrace you? If we could throw our arms around one another we might find sad comfort in the sharing of our sorrows even in the house of Hades; does Proserpine want to lay a still further load of grief upon me by mocking me with a phantom only?'

" 'My son,' she answered, 'most ill-fated of all mankind, it is not Proserpine that is beguiling you, but all people are like this when they are dead. The sinews no longer hold the flesh and bones together; these perish in the fierceness of consuming fire as soon as life has left the body, and the soul flits away as though it were a dream. Now, however, go back to the light of day as soon as you can, and note all these things that you may tell them to your wife hereafter.'

"Thus did we converse, and anon Proserpine sent up the ghosts of the wives and daughters of all the most famous men. They gathered in crowds about the blood, and I considered how I might question them severally. In the end I deemed that it would be best to draw the keen blade that hung by my sturdy thigh, and keep them from all drinking the blood at once. So they came up one after the other, and each one as I questioned her told me her race and lineage.

"The first I saw was Tyro. She was daughter of Salmoneus and wife of Cretheus the son of Aeolus. She fell in love with the river Enipeus who is much the most beautiful river in the whole world. Once when she was taking a walk by his side as usual, Neptune, disguised as her lover, lay with her at the mouth of the river, and a huge blue wave arched itself like a mountain over them to hide both woman and god, whereon he loosed her virgin girdle and laid her in a deep slumber. When the god had accomplished the deed of love, he took her hand in his own and said, 'Tyro, rejoice in all good will; the embraces of the gods are not fruitless, and you will have fine twins about this time twelve months. Take great care of them. I am Neptune, so now go home, but hold your tongue and do not tell any one.'

"Then he dived under the sea, and she in due course bore Pelias and Neleus, who both of them served Jove with all their might. Pelias was a great breeder of sheep and lived in Iolcus, but the other lived in Pylos. The rest of her children were by Cretheus, namely, Aeson, Pheres, and Amythaon, who was a mighty warrior and charioteer." Next to her I saw Antiope, daughter to Asopus, who could boast of having slept in the arms of even Jove himself, and who bore him two sons Amphion and Zethus. These founded Thebes with its seven gates, and built a wall all round it; for strong though they were they could not hold Thebes till they had walled it.

第四篇　The Odyssey

"Then I saw Alcmena①, the wife of Amphitryon, who also bore to Jove indomitable Hercules; and Megara who was daughter to great King Creon, and married the redoubtable son of Amphitryon.

"I also saw fair Jocasta② mother of king Oedipus③ whose awful lot it was to marry her own son without suspecting it. He married her after having killed his father, but the gods proclaimed the whole story to the world; whereon he remained king of Thebes, in great grief for the spite the gods had borne him; but Jocasta went to the house of the mighty jailor Hades, having hanged herself for grief, and the avenging spirits haunted him as for an outraged mother-to his ruing bitterly thereafter.

"Then I saw Chloris, whom Neleus married for her beauty, having given priceless presents for her. She was youngest daughter to Amphion son of Iasus and king of Minyan Orchomenus, and was Queen in Pylos. She bore Nestor, Chromius, and Periclymenus, and she also bore that marvellously lovely woman Pero, who was wooed by all the country round; but Neleus would only give her to him who should raid the cattle of Iphicles from the grazing grounds of Phylace, and this was a hard task. The only man who would undertake to raid them was a certain excellent seer, but the will of heaven was against him, for the rangers of the cattle caught him and put him in prison; nevertheless when a full year had passed and the same season came round again, Iphicles set him at liberty, after he had expounded all the oracles of heaven. Thus, then, was the will of Jove accomplished.

"And I saw Leda④ the wife of Tyndarus, who bore him two famous sons, Castor breaker of horses, and Pollux the mighty boxer. Both these heroes are lying under the earth, though they are still alive, for by a special dispensation of Jove, they die and come to life again, each one of them every other day throughout all time, and they have the rank of gods.

"After her I saw Iphimedeia wife of Aloeus who boasted the embrace of Neptune.

---

① 阿尔克墨涅（Alcmena），大力神海格力斯（Hercules）即希神赫拉克勒斯（Heracles）的母亲，安菲特律翁（Amphitryon）的妻子
② 犹卡斯塔（Jocasta），忒拜城（Thebes）的王后，俄狄浦斯王的母亲
③ 俄狄浦斯（Oedipus），因命运的捉弄弑父娶母，希腊悲剧人物
④ 莱达（Leda），廷达柔斯（Tyndarus）之妻，斯巴达王后，双子座卡斯托耳（Castor）和波吕克斯（Pollux）之母，也是美女海伦（Helen）和克吕泰涅斯特拉（Clytemnestra）之母

She bore two sons Otus and Ephialtes, but both were short lived. They were the finest children that were ever born in this world, and the best looking, Orion only excepted; for at nine years old they were nine fathoms high, and measured nine cubits round the chest. They threatened to make war with the gods in Olympus, and tried to set Mount Ossa on the top of Mount Olympus, and Mount Pelion on the top of Ossa, that they might scale heaven itself, and they would have done it too if they had been grown up, but Apollo, son of Leto, killed both of them, before they had got so much as a sign of hair upon their cheeks or chin.

"Then I saw Phaedra, and Procris, and fair Ariadne① daughter of the magician Minos②, whom Theseus③ was carrying off from Crete to Athens, but he did not enjoy her, for before he could do so Diana④ killed her in the island of Dia on account of what Bacchus⑤ had said against her.

"I also saw Maera and Clymene and hateful Eriphyle, who sold her own husband for gold. But it would take me all night if I were to name every single one of the wives and daughters of heroes whom I saw, and it is time for me to go to bed, either on board ship with my crew, or here. As for my escort, heaven and yourselves will see to it."

Here he ended, and the guests sat all of them enthralled and speechless throughout the covered cloister. Then Arete⑥ said to them:

"What do you think of this man, O Phaecians⑦? Is he not tall and good looking, and is he not Clever? True, he is my own guest, but all of you share in the distinction. Do not be a hurry to send him away, nor niggardly in the presents you make to one who is in such great need, for heaven has blessed all of you with great abundance."

Then spoke the aged hero Echeneus who was one of the oldest men among them, "My friends," said he, "what our august queen has just said to us is both reasonable

---

① 阿里阿德涅（Ariadne），克里特岛（Crete）国王米诺斯（Minos）的女儿，曾用线团救雅典王子忒修斯（Theseus）出迷宫。被忒修斯抛弃后，与酒神巴克斯（Bacchus）即希腊神话狄奥尼索斯（Dionysus），结为夫妻

② 米诺斯（Minos），克里特国王，朱庇特（Jove）与欧罗巴（Europa）之子

③ 忒修斯（Theseus），雅典王子，在克里特杀死牛头怪米诺陶（Minotaur）

④ 黛安娜（Diana），月亮和狩猎女神，即希腊神话阿尔忒弥斯（Artemis）

⑤ 酒神巴克斯（Bacchus），朱庇特（Jove）与塞墨涅（Semele）之子

⑥ 阿瑞特（Arete），菲西亚人（Phaecians）的王后。由此看来前面全是尤利西斯所回忆的故事

⑦ 菲西亚人（Phaecians），尤利西斯海上漂泊遇到的海洋民族

and to the purpose, therefore be persuaded by it; but the decision whether in word or deed rests ultimately with King Alcinous①."

"The thing shall be done," exclaimed Alcinous, "as surely as I still live and reign over the Phaeacians. Our guest is indeed very anxious to get home, still we must persuade him to remain with us until to-morrow, by which time I shall be able to get together the whole sum that I mean to give him. As regards-his escort it will be a matter for you all, and mine above all others as the chief person among you."

And Ulysses answered, "King Alcinous, if you were to bid me to stay here for a whole twelve months, and then speed me on my way, loaded with your noble gifts, I should obey you gladly and it would redound greatly to my advantage, for I should return fuller-handed to my own people, and should thus be more respected and beloved by all who see me when I get back to Ithaca."

"Ulysses," replied Alcinous, "not one of us who sees you has any idea that you are a charlatan or a swindler. I know there are many people going about who tell such plausible stories that it is very hard to see through them, but there is a style about your language which assures me of your good disposition. Moreover you have told the story of your own misfortunes, and those of the Argives, as though you were a practised bard; but tell me, and tell me true, whether you saw any of the mighty heroes who went to Troy at the same time with yourself, and perished there. The evenings are still at their longest, and it is not yet bed time-go on, therefore, with your divine story, for I could stay here listening till tomorrow morning, so long as you will continue to tell us of your adventures."

"Alcinous," answered Ulysses, "there is a time for making speeches, and a time for going to bed; nevertheless, since you so desire, I will not refrain from telling you the still sadder tale of those of my comrades who did not fall fighting with the Trojans, but perished on their return, through the treachery of a wicked woman.

"When Proserpine had dismissed the female ghosts in all directions, the ghost of Agamemnon son of Atreus② came sadly up tome, surrounded by those who had

---

① 阿尔申诺斯（Alcinous），菲西亚人的国王
② Son of Atreus, 阿特柔斯之子，即阿伽门农（Agamemnon）

perished with him in the house of Aegisthus①. As soon as he had tasted the blood he knew me, and weeping bitterly stretched out his arms towards me to embrace me; but he had no strength nor substance any more, and I too wept and pitied him as I beheld him. 'How did you come by your death,' said I, 'King Agamemnon? Did Neptune raise his winds and waves against you when you were at sea, or did your enemies make an end of you on the mainland when you were cattle-lifting or sheep-stealing, or while they were fighting in defence of their wives and city?'

"'Ulysses,' he answered, 'noble son of Laertes, was not lost at sea in any storm of Neptune's raising, nor did my foes despatch me upon the mainland, but Aegisthus and my wicked wife were the death of me between them. He asked me to his house, feasted me, and then butchered me most miserably as though I were a fat beast in a slaughter house, while all around me my comrades were slain like sheep or pigs for the wedding breakfast, or picnic, or gorgeous banquet of some great nobleman. You must have seen numbers of men killed either in a general engagement, or in single combat, but you never saw anything so truly pitiable as the way in which we fell in that cloister, with the mixing-bowl and the loaded tables lying all about, and the ground reeking with our-blood. I heard Priam's daughter Cassandra② scream as Clytemnestra③ killed her close beside me. I lay dying upon the earth with the sword in my body, and raised my hands to kill the slut of a murderess, but she slipped away from me; she would not even close my lips nor my eyes when I was dying, for there is nothing in this world so cruel and so shameless as a woman when she has fallen into such guilt as hers was. Fancy murdering her own husband! I thought I was going to be welcomed home by my children and my servants, but her abominable crime has brought disgrace on herself and all women who shall come after-even on the good ones.'

"And I said, 'In truth Jove has hated the house of Atreus from first to last in the matter of their women's counsels. See how many of us fell for Helen's sake, and now it

---

① 埃吉斯托斯（Aegisthus），阿伽门农（Agamemnon）的妻子克吕泰涅斯特拉（Clytemnestra）的情夫，当阿伽门农从特洛伊返回希腊时，他们设计在宴会上将阿伽门农及其随从屠杀
② 卡桑德拉（Cassandra），特洛伊城国王普里阿姆（Priam）的小女儿，后被阿伽门农强娶为妾
③ 克吕泰涅斯特拉（Clytemnestra），迈锡尼王后，莱达（Leda）的女儿，海伦（Helen）的姐姐，阿伽门农的妻子

seems that Clytemnestra hatched mischief against too during your absence.'

" 'Be sure, therefore,' continued Agamemnon, 'and not be too friendly even with your own wife. Do not tell her all that you know perfectly well yourself. Tell her a part only, and keep your own counsel about the rest. Not that your wife, Ulysses, is likely to murder you, for Penelope① is a very admirable woman, and has an excellent nature. We left her a young bride with an infant at her breast when we set out for Troy. This child no doubt is now grown up happily to man's estate, and he and his father will have a joyful meeting and embrace one another as it is right they should do, whereas my wicked wife did not even allow me the happiness of looking upon my son, but killed me ere I could do so. Furthermore I say—and lay my saying to your heart—do not tell people when you are bringing your ship to Ithaca, but steal a march upon them, for after all this there is no trusting women. But now tell me, and tell me true, can you give me any news of my son Orestes②? Is he in Orchomenus, or at Pylos, or is he at Sparta with Menelaus③—for I presume that he is still living.'

"And I said, 'Agamemnon, why do you ask me? I do not know whether your son is alive or dead, and it is not right to talk when one does not know.'

"As we two sat weeping and talking thus sadly with one another the ghost of Achilles came up to us with Patroclus, Antilochus, and Ajax who was the finest and goodliest man of all the Danaans④ after the son of Peleus⑤. The fleet descendant of Aeacus⑥ knew me and spoke piteously, saying, 'Ulysses, noble son of Laertes, what deed of daring will you undertake next, that you venture down to the house of Hades among us silly dead, who are but the ghosts of them that can labour no more?'

"And I said, 'Achilles, son of Peleus, foremost champion of the Achaeans, I came to consult Teiresias, and see if he could advise me about my return home to Ithaca, for I have never yet been able to get near the Achaean land, nor to set foot in my own country, but have been in trouble all the time. As for you, Achilles, no one

---

① 珀涅罗珀（Penelope），尤利西斯的妻子
② 俄瑞斯忒斯（Orestes），阿伽门农之子，长大后杀死母亲和继父，为父报仇，但由于弑母而受到复仇女神追杀
③ 蒙勒劳斯（Menelaus），斯巴达国王，美女海伦（Helen）的丈夫，阿伽门农之弟
④ The Danaans，达纳人，即希腊联军
⑤ The son of Peleus，指阿喀琉斯
⑥ 埃俄科斯（Aeacus），阿喀琉斯的祖父，珀琉斯（Peleus）的父亲

was ever yet so fortunate as you have been, nor ever will be, for you were adored by all us Argives as long as you were alive, and now that you are here you are a great prince among the dead. Do not, therefore, take it so much to heart even if you are dead.'

" 'Say not a word,' he answered, 'in death's favour; I would rather be a paid servant in a poor man's house and be above ground than king of kings among the dead. But give me news about son; is he gone to the wars and will he be a great soldier, or is this not so? Tell me also if you have heard anything about my father Peleus—does he still rule among the Myrmidons, or do they show him no respect throughout Hellas and Phthia now that he is old and his limbs fail him? Could I but stand by his side, in the light of day, with the same strength that I had when I killed the bravest of our foes upon the plain of Troy—could I but be as I then was and go even for a short time to my father's house, anyone who tried to do him violence or supersede him would soon meet it.'

" 'I have heard nothing,' I answered, 'of Peleus, but I can tell you all about your son Neoptolemus①, for I took him in my own ship from Scyros with the Achaeans. In our councils of war before Troy he was always first to speak, and his judgement was unerring. Nestor② and I were the only two who could surpass him; and when it came to fighting on the plain of Troy, he would never remain with the body of his men, but would dash on far in front, foremost of them all in valour. Many a man did he kill in battle—I cannot name every single one of those whom he slew while fighting on the side of the Argives, but will only say how he killed that valiant hero Eurypylus son of Telephus, who was the handsomest man I ever saw except Memnon; many others also of the Ceteians fell around him by reason of a woman's bribes. Moreover, when all the bravest of the Argives went inside the horse that Epeus③ had made, and it was left to me to settle when we should either open the door of our ambuscade, or close it, though all the other leaders and chief men among the Danaans were drying their eyes and quaking in every limb, I never once saw him turn pale nor wipe a tear from his cheek; he was all the time urging me to break out from the horse—grasping the handle of his sword and his bronze-shod spear, and breathing fury against the foe. Yet when we had

---

① 尼奥托勒摩斯（Neoptolemus），阿喀琉斯的儿子
② 内斯托（Nestor），特洛伊战争中，希腊军中老英雄
③ 埃皮乌斯（Epeus），和尤利西斯一起设计木马计的希腊英雄

sacked the city of Priam he got his handsome share of the prize money and went on board (such is the fortune of war) without a wound upon him, neither from a thrown spear nor in close combat, for the rage of Mars is a matter of great chance.'

"When I had told him this, the ghost of Achilles strode off across a meadow full of asphodel, exulting over what I had said concerning the prowess of his son.

"The ghosts of other dead men stood near me and told me each his own melancholy tale; but that of Ajax① son of Telamon alone held aloof-still angry with me for having won the cause in our dispute about the armour of Achilles. Thetis had offered it as a prize, but the Trojan prisoners and Minerva② were the judges. Would that I had never gained the day in such a contest, for it cost the life of Ajax, who was foremost of all the Danaans after the son of Peleus, alike in stature and prowess.

"When I saw him I tried to pacify him and said, 'Ajax, will you not forget and forgive even in death, but must the judgement about that hateful armour still rankle with you? It cost us Argives dear enough to lose such a tower of strength as you were to us. We mourned you as much as we mourned Achilles son of Peleus himself, nor can the blame be laid on anything but on the spite which Jove bore against the Danaans, for it was this that made him counsel your destruction-come hither, therefore, bring your proud spirit into subjection, and hear what I can tell you.'

"He would not answer, but turned away to Erebus and to the other ghosts; nevertheless, I should have made him talk to me in spite of his being so angry, or I should have gone talking to him, only that there were still others among the dead whom I desired to see.

"Then I saw Minos son of Jove with his golden sceptre in his hand sitting in judgement on the dead, and the ghosts were gathered sitting and standing round him in the spacious house of Hades, to learn his sentences upon them.

"After him I saw huge Orion in a meadow full of asphodel driving the ghosts of the wild beasts that he had killed upon the mountains, and he had a great bronze club in his hand, unbreakable for ever and ever.

"And I saw Tityus son of Gaia stretched upon the plain and covering some nine

---

① 阿贾克斯（Ajax），希腊英雄，后因没有争夺到阿喀琉斯的铠甲而情绪失控，最终为保名节而自杀身亡
② 密涅瓦（Minerva），即雅典娜（Athena）

acres of ground. Two vultures on either side of him were digging their beaks into his liver, and he kept on trying to beat them off with his hands, but could not; for he had violated Jove's mistress Leto as she was going through Panopeus on her way to Pytho.

"I saw also the dreadful fate of Tantalus①, who stood in a lake that reached his chin; he was dying to quench his thirst, but could never reach the water, for whenever the poor creature stooped to drink, it dried up and vanished, so that there was nothing but dry ground-parched by the spite of heaven. There were tall trees, moreover, that shed their fruit over his head-pears, pomegranates, apples, sweet figs and juicy olives, but whenever the poor creature stretched out his hand to take some, the wind tossed the branches back again to the clouds.

"And I saw Sisyphus② at his endless task raising his prodigious stone with both his hands. With hands and feet he' tried to roll it up to the top of the hill, but always, just before he could roll it over on to the other side, its weight would be too much for him, and the pitiless stone would come thundering down again on to the plain. Then he would begin trying to push it up hill again, and the sweat ran off him and the steam rose after him.

"After him I saw mighty Hercules, but it was his phantom only, for he is feasting ever with the immortal gods, and has lovely Hebe③ to wife, who is daughter of Jove and Juno. The ghosts were screaming round him like scared birds flying all whithers. He looked black as night with his bare bow in his hands and his arrow on the string, glaring around as though ever on the point of taking aim. About his breast there was a wondrous golden belt adorned in the most marvellous fashion with bears, wild boars, and lions with gleaming eyes; there was also war, battle, and death. The man who made that belt, do what he might, would never be able to make another like it. Hercules knew me at once when he saw me, and spoke piteously, saying, my poor Ulysses, noble son of Laertes, are you too leading the same sorry kind of life that I did

---

① 坦塔罗斯（Tantalus），朱庇特之子，因烹煮自己的儿子招待众神，触犯了天条，被打入塔尔塔罗斯深渊，永受欲望无法满足之折磨。阿伽门农（Agamemnon）和蒙勒劳斯（Menelaus）是其后人

② 西西弗斯（Sisyphus），曾狡猾地愚弄过死神和冥王，触犯了天条，被罚反复推石头上山，受永远无法成功之折磨。尤利西斯是其后人

③ 海格力斯（Hercules）即赫拉克勒斯（Heracles）死后成神，青春女神赫柏（Hebe）与他结为夫妻

when I was above ground? I was son of Jove, but I went through an infinity of suffering, for I became bondsman to one who was far beneath me—a low fellow who set me all manner of labours. He once sent me here to fetch the hell-hound—for he did not think he could find anything harder for me than this, but I got the hound out of Hades and brought him to him, for Mercury and Minerva helped me.'

"On this Hercules went down again into the house of Hades, but I stayed where I was in case some other of the mighty dead should come to me. And I should have seen still other of them that are gone before, whom I would fain have seen—Theseus and Pirithous glorious children of the gods, but so many thousands of ghosts came round me and uttered such appalling cries, that I was panic stricken lest Proserpine should send up from the house of Hades the head of that awful monster Gorgon. On this I hastened back to my ship and ordered my men to go on board at once and loose the hawsers; so they embarked and took their places, whereon the ship went down the stream of the river Oceanus. We had to row at first, but presently a fair wind sprang up.

Questions for discussion:

1. What was Odysseus, the hero of the Odyssey, like? What are his strengths and weaknesses in character?

2. What problem did Odysseus go to the underworld mainly to solve? How would Homer's description of the world after death reflect the Greek outlook on life and the world?

3. Why would Odysseus, dressed as a beggar, plan with his son Telemachus to slaughter all his wife's suitors instead of returning home from Troy fair and square?

第五篇　The Aeneid

Virgil

(Translated by H. R. Fairclough)

Book IV

　　But the queen, long since smitten with a grievous love-pang, feeds the wound with her lifeblood, and is wasted with fire unseen. Oft① to her mind rushes back the hero's valour, oft his glorious stock; his looks and words cling fast to her bosom, and longing withholds calm rest from her limbs.

　　The morrow's dawn was lighting the earth with the lamp of Phoebus②, and had scattered from the sky the dewy shades, when, much distraught, she thus speaks to her sister, sharer of her heart: "Anna, my sister, what dreams thrill me with fears? Who is this stranger guest who has entered our home? How noble his③ mien! How brave in heart and feats of arms! I believe it well-nor is my confidence vain-that he is sprung from gods. It is fear that proves souls base-born. Alas! by what fates is he vexed! What wars, long endured, did he recount! Were the purpose not planted in my mind, fixed and immovable, to ally myself with none in bond of wedlock, since my first love, turning traitor, cheated me by death; were I not tired of the bridal bed and torch, to this one fault, perhaps, I might have yielded! Anna-for I will own it-since the death of my hapless lord Sychaeus④, and the shattering of our home by a brother's murder,

---

①　常常，再三
②　指太阳神阿波罗（Apollo）
③　指埃涅阿斯（Aeneas）
④　女王狄多（Dido）的前夫

he alone has swayed my will and overthrown my tottering soul. I feel again a spark of that former flame. But rather, I would pray, may earth yawn for me to its depths, or may the Almighty Father① hurl me with his bolt to the shades – the pale shades and abysmal night in Erebus② – before, Shame, I violate you or break your laws! He who first linked me to himself has taken away my heart; may he keep it with him, and guard it in the grave!" So saying, she filled her breast with upwelling③ tears.

Anna replies: "O you who are dearer to your sister than the light, are you, lonely and sad, going to pine away all your youth long, and know not sweet children or love's rewards? Do you think that dust or buried shades give heed to that? Grant that until now no wooers moved your sorrow, not in Libya, not before then in Tyre④; that Iarbas⑤ was slighted, and other lords whom the African land, rich in triumphs, rears; will you wrestle also with a love that pleases? And does it not come to your mind whose lands you have settled in? On this side Gaetulian cities, a race invincible in war, unbridled Numidians⑥, and the unfriendly Syrtis hem you in; on that side lies a tract barren with drought, and Barcaeans, raging far and wide. Why speak of the wars rising from Tyre, your brother's threats …? I certainly believe that it was with the gods' favour and Juno's aid that the Ilian⑦ ships held their course hither with the wind. What a city you will see rise here, my sister, what a realm, by reason of such a marriage! With Teucrian⑧ arms beside us, to what heights will Punic⑨ glory soar? Only ask favour of the gods and, with sacrifice duly offered, be lavish with your welcome, and weave pleas for delay, while at sea winter rages fiercely and Orion⑩ is stormy – while the ships are shattered, and the skies intractable!"

With these words she fanned into flame the queen's love – enkindled heart, put

---

① 指朱庇特（Jupiter or Jove）
② 埃瑞波斯（Erebus 即 Erebos），从混乱（Chasm 或 Chaos）中产生的黑暗。见《神谱》中第 9 段
③ 上涌的
④ 推罗（Tyre）
⑤ 非洲国王伊阿尔巴斯（Iarbas），狄多的追求者
⑥ 努米底亚人（Numidians）
⑦ 特洛伊人的
⑧ 特洛伊的另一种称谓
⑨ 布匿人的（Punic），即迦太基人的
⑩ 月神和狩猎女神黛安娜（Diana）所爱的猎人

hope in her wavering mind, and loosed the bonds of shame. First they visit the shrines and sue for peace at every altar; duly they slay chosen sheep to Ceres the lawgiver, to Phoebus and father Lyaeus, above all to Juno, guardian of the bonds of marriage. Dido herself, matchless in beauty, with cup in hand, pours libation midway between the horns of a white heifer, or in presence of the gods moves slowly to the rich altars, and day by day renews her gifts, then, gazing into the opened breasts of victims, consults the quivering entrails. Ah, the blind souls of seers! Of what avail are vows or shrines to one wild with love? All the while the flame devours her tender heartstrings, and deep in her breast lives the silent wound. Unhappy Dido burns, and through the city wanders in frenzy-even as a hind①, smitten by an arrow, which, all unwary, amid the Cretan woods, a shepherd hunting with darts has pierced from afar, leaving in her the winged steel, unknowing: she in flight ranges the Dictaean woods and glades②, but fast to her side clings the deadly shaft. Now through the city's midst she leads Aeneas with her, and displays her Sidonian③ wealth and the city built; she begins to speak and stops with the word half-spoken. Now, as day wanes, she seeks that same banquet, again in her madness craves to hear the sorrows of Ilium④ and again hangs on the speaker's lips. Then when all have gone their ways, and in turn the dim moon sinks her light, and the setting stars invite sleep, alone she mourns in the empty hall, and falls on the couch he has left. Though absent, each from each, she hears him, she sees him, or, captivated by his look of his father, she holds Ascanius⑤ on her lap, in case she may beguile a passion beyond all utterance. No longer rise the towers begun, no longer do the youth exercise in arms, or toil at havens or bulwarks for safety in war; the works are broken off and idle-great menacing walls and cranes that touch the sky.

Soon as the loved wife of Jove saw that Dido was held in a passion so fatal, and that her good name was now no bar to her frenzy, the daughter of Saturn⑥ accosts

---

① 雌鹿
② 林中空地
③ 西顿人的（Sidonian，西顿是古腓尼基的重要港口城市）
④ 特洛伊城
⑤ 阿斯卡尼乌斯（Ascanius），埃涅阿斯之子。从文中看，应是埃涅阿斯与前妻埃莉莎（Elissa）之子。也有另一种说法：阿斯卡尼乌斯（Ascanius）是埃涅阿斯到达亚平宁半岛之后与拉丁王之女拉维尼亚（Lavinia）的儿子。他是罗马城建立者罗慕路斯（Romulus）和雷慕斯（Remus）的先祖
⑥ 塞坦的女儿。塞坦（Saturn）是克罗诺斯（Cronus）的拉丁名，即指天后朱诺（Juno）

Venus thus: "Splendid indeed is the praise and rich the spoils you win, you and your boy; mighty and glorious is the power divine, if one woman is subdued by the guile of two gods! Nay, it escapes me not how, in fear of our city, you have held in suspicion the homes of high Carthage. But what shall be the end? And what is the point of all this contest now? Why do we not rather strive for an enduring peace and a plighted wedlock? What you sought with all your heart you have; Dido is on fire with love and has drawn the madness through her veins. Let us then rule this people jointly with equal sovereignty; let her serve a Phrygian① husband and yield her Tyrians② to your power as dowry!"

To her—for she knew that with feigned purpose she had spoken, to turn the empire from Italy to Libya's shores—Venus thus began in reply: "Who so mad as to refuse such terms, or prefer to strive against you in war, as long as Fortune favour the fulfilment of your word? But the Fates send me adrift, uncertain whether Jupiter wills that there be one city for the Tyrians and the wanderers from Troy, or approves the blending of peoples and the league of union. You are his wife; it is lawful for you to try to persuade his heart with entreaty. Go on; I will follow!" Then queenly Juno thus replied: "With me shall rest that task. Now in what way the present purpose can be achieved, hearken and I will explain in brief. Aeneas and unhappy Dido plan to go hunting together in the forest, as soon as tomorrow's sun shows his rising and with his rays unveils the world. On them, while the hunters run to and fro and gird the glades with nets, I will pour down from above a black rain mingled with hail, and wake the whole welkin③ with thunder. The company shall scatter and be veiled in gloom of night; to the same cave shall come Dido and the Trojan chief. I will be there and, if I can be sure of your good will, will link them in sure wedlock, sealing her for his own; this shall be their bridal!" Yielding to her suit, the Cytherean④ gave assent and smiled at the guile discovered.

Meanwhile Dawn rose and left the ocean. When sunlight has burst forth, there issues from the gates a chosen band of youth; with meshed nets, toils, broad-pointed hunting spears, there stream forth Massylian horsemen and their strong, keen-scented

---

① 佛里吉亚人 (Phrygian), 指埃涅阿斯
② 推罗人 (Tyrians)
③ 天空, 苍穹
④ 维纳斯的另一个名字

101

hounds. As the queen lingers in her bower, the Punic princes await her at the doorway; her prancing steed stands brilliant in purple and gold, and proudly champs the foaming bit. At last she comes forth, attended by a mighty throng, and clad in a Sidonian robe with embroidered border. Her quiver is of gold, her tresses are knotted into gold, a buckle of gold clasps her purple cloak. With her pace a Phrygian train and joyous Iulus①. Aeneas himself, goodly beyond all others, advances to join her and unites his band with hers. As when Apollo quits Lycia, his winter home, and the streams of Xanthus, to visit his mother's Delos②, and renews the dance, while mingling about his altars Cretans and Dryopes and painted Agathyrsians raise their voices—he himself treads the Cynthian ridges, and with soft foliage shapes and binds his flowing locks, braiding it with golden diadem; the shafts rattle on his shoulders: so no less lightly than he went Aeneas, such beauty shines forth from his noble face! When they came to the mountain heights and pathless lairs, wild goats dislodged from the rocky peaks ran down the ridges; in another part stags scurry across the open moors and amid clouds of dust mass their bands in flight, as they leave the hills behind. But in the midst of the valleys the young Ascanius glories in his fiery steed, galloping past now these, now those, and prays that amid the timorous herds a foaming boar may be granted to his vows or a tawny lion come down from the mountain.

Meanwhile in the sky begins the turmoil of a wild uproar; rain follows, mingled with hail. The scattered Tyrian train and the Trojan youth, with the Dardan③ grandson of Venus, in their fear seek shelter here and there over the fields; torrents rush down from the heights. To the same cave come Dido and the Trojan chief. Primal Earth and nuptial Juno give the sign; fires flashed in Heaven, the witness to their bridal, and on the mountaintop screamed the Nymphs. That day the first of death, the first of calamity was cause. For no more is Dido swayed by fair show or fair fame, no more does she dream of a secret love: she calls it marriage and with that name veils her sin.

At once Rumour runs through Libya's great cities—Rumour the swiftest of all evils. Speed lends her strength, and she winds vigour as she goes; small at first through fear, soon she mounts up to heaven, and walks the ground with head hidden in the clouds.

---

① 埃涅阿斯之子阿斯卡尼乌斯（Ascanius）的另一个名字
② 得洛斯岛，传说中太阳神阿波罗（Apollo）和月神阿尔忒弥斯（Artemis）的诞生地
③ 特洛伊人

Mother Earth, provoked to anger against the gods, brought her forth last, they, say as sister to Coeus① and Enceladus, swift of foot and fleet of wing, a monster awful and huge, who for the many feathers in her body has as many watchful eyes beneath – wondrous to tell – as many tongues, as many sounding mouths, as many pricked-up ears. By night, midway between heaven and earth, she flies through the gloom, screeching, and droops not her eyes in sweet sleep; by day she sits on guard on high rooftop or lofty turrets, and affrights great cities, clinging to the false and the wrong, yet heralding truth. Now exulting in manifold gossip, she filled the nations and sang alike of fact and falsehood, how Aeneas is come, one born of Trojan blood, to whom in marriage fair Dido deigns to join herself; now they while away the winter, all its length, in wanton ease together, heed-less of their realms and enthralled by shameless passion. These tales the foul goddess spreads here and there upon the lips of men. Straightway to King Iarbas② she bends her course, and with her words fires his spirit and heaps high his wrath.

He, the son of Hammon by a ravished Garamantian Nymph, set up to Jupiter in his broad realms a hundred vast temples, a hundred altars, and had hallowed the wakeful fire, the eternal sentry of the gods. The ground was fat with the blood of beasts and the portals bloomed with varied garlands. Distraught in mind and fired with the bitter tale, they say, before the altars and amid the divine presences he often besought Jove in prayer with upturned hands: "Almighty Jupiter, to whom now the Moorish③ race, feasting on embroidered couches, pour a Lenaean offering, do you see these things? Is it vainly, father, that we shudder at you, when you hurl your thunderbolts? And do aimless fires amid the clouds terrify our souls and stir murmurs void of purpose? This woman who, straying in our bounds, set up a tiny city at a price, to whom we gave coastland to plough and terms of tenure, has spurned④ my offers of marriage, and welcomed Aeneas into her realm as lord. And now that Paris with his eunuch train, his chin and perfumed locks bound with a Lydian turban, grasps the spoil; while we bring offerings to your temples, yours forsooth, and cherish an idle story."

---

① 科俄斯（Coeus）的妹妹，指谣言女神 Rumour
② 北非国王，狄多的追求者，
③ 摩尔人（北非一民族）的
④ 蔑视

As with such words he pleaded, clasping the altars, the Almighty① gave ear and turned his eyes on the royal city and the lovers forgetful of their nobler fame. Then thus to Mercury② he speaks and gives this charge: "Go forth, my son, call the Zephyrs③, glide on they wings, and speak to the Dardan④ chief, who now at Carthage is looking forward to Tyrian cities, unmindful of those granted him by the Fates; so carry down my words through the swift winds. Not such as this did his lovely mother promise him to us, nor for this twice rescue him from Grecian arms; but he it was who should rule Italy, a land teeming with empire and clamorous with war, hand on a race from Teucer's⑤ noble blood, and bring all the world beneath his laws. If the glory of such a fortune fires him not and for his own fame's sake he shoulders not the burden, does he, the father, grudge Ascanius⑥ the towers of Rome? What is his plan? In what hope does he tarry among a hostile people and pays no heed to Ausonia race and the Lavinian fields? Let him set sail; this is the sum; be this the message from me."

He ceased. The god made ready to obey his mighty father's bidding, and first binds on his feet the golden shoes which carry him upborne on wings over seas or land, swift as the gale. Then he takes his wand; with this he calls pale ghosts from Orcus⑦ and sends others down to gloomy Tartaurs⑧, gives or takes away sleep and unseals eyes in death; relying on this, he drives the winds and skims the stormy clouds. And now in flight he descries the peak and steep sides of toiling Atlas, who props heaven on his peak-Atlas, whose pine-wreathed head is ever girt with black clouds, and beaten with wind and rain; fallen snow mantles his shoulders while rivers plunge down the aged chin and his rough beard is stiff with ice. Here, poised on even wings, the Cyllenian⑨ first halted; hence with his whole frame he sped sheer down to the waves like a bird, which round the shores, round the fish-haunted cliffs, flies low near to the waters. Even thus between earth and sky flew Cyllene's nursling to Libya's sandy shore, and cut

---

① 指主神朱庇特（Jove）
② 信使之神墨丘利，即赫尔墨斯（Hermes）
③ 西风
④ 特洛伊人
⑤ 特洛伊人的
⑥ 埃涅阿斯之子阿斯卡尼乌斯（Ascanius）
⑦ 死神；冥国
⑧ 塔尔塔罗斯深渊（Tartaurs），即 Tartarus
⑨ 信使之神墨丘利（Mercury）的另一个名字

the winds, coming from his mother's sire.

As soon as with winged feet he reached the huts, he sees Aeneas founding towers and building new houses. And his sword was starred with yellow jasper, and a cloak hung from his shoulders ablaze with Tyrian purple – a gift that wealthy Dido had wrought, interweaving the web with thread of gold. At once he assails him: "Are you now laying the foundations of lofty Carthage, and building up a fair city, and all for a woman's whim? Alas! With never a thought of your own realm and fate! The ruler of the gods himself, who sways heaven and earth with his power, sends me down to you from bright Olympus. He himself bids me bring this charge through the swift breezes: What are you planning? In what hope do you waste idle hours in Libyan lands? If the glory of such a fortune does not stir you, and for your own fame's sake you do not shoulder the burden, have regard from growing Ascanius, the promise of Iulus your heir, to whom the kingdom of Italy and the Roman land are due." Such words the Cyllenian① spoke, and while yet speaking left the sight of men and far away from their eyes vanished into thin air.

But in truth Aeneas, aghast at he sight, was struck dumb; his hair stood up in terror and the voice choked in his throat. He burns to flee away and quit that pleasant land, awed by that warning and divine commandment. Ah, what to do? With what speech now dare he approach the frenzied queen? What opening words choose first? And as he casts his swift mind this way and that, takes it in different directions and considers every possibility, this, as he wavered, seemed the better counsel; he calls Mnestheus and Sergestus, bidding them make ready the fleet in silence, gather the crews to the shore, and order the armament, but hide the cause of his altered plans. He meanwhile, since gracious Dido knows nothing, nor expects the breaking of so strong a love, will essay an approach and seek the happiest season for speech, the plan auspicious for his purpose. At once all gladly obey his command and do his bidding. But the queen—who may deceive a lover? —divined his guile, and early caught news of the coming stir, fearful even when all was safe. The same heartless Rumour brought her the maddening news that they are arming the fleet and making ready for sailing. Helpless in mind she rages, and all aflame raves through the city, like some Thyiad②

---

① 指信使之神
② 酒神的女信徒

startled by the shaken emblems, when she has heard the Bacchic cry: the biennial revels fire her and at night Cithaeron① summons her with its din. At length she thus accosts Aeneas first:

"False one! Did you really hope to cloak so foul a crime, and to steal from my land in silence? Does neither our love restrain you, nor the pledge once given, nor the doom of a cruel death for Dido? Even in the winter season do you actually hasten to labour at your fleet, and to journey over the sea in the midst of northern gales, heartless one? What! If you were not in quest of alien lands and homes unknown, were ancient Troy yet standing, would Troy be sought by your ships over stormy seas? Is it from me you are fleeing? By these tears and your right hand, I pray you—since nothing else, alas, have I left myself—by the marriage that is ours, by the nuptial rites begun, if ever I deserved well of you, or if anything of mine has been sweet in your sight, pity a falling house, and if yet there be any room for prayers, put away, I pray, this purpose. Because of you the Libyan tribes and Numidian chiefs② hate me, the Tyrians are my foes; because of you I have also lost my honour and that former fame by which alone I was winning a title to the stars. To whose mercy do you leave me on the point of death, guest—since that alone is left from the name of husband? Why do I linger? Is it till Pygmalion③, my brother, overthrow this city, or the Gaetulian Iarbas lead me captive? At least, if before your flight a child of yours had been born to me, if in my hall a baby Aeneas were playing, whose face, in spite of all, would bring back yours, I should not think myself utterly vanquished and forlorn."

She ceased; he by Jove's command held his eyes steadfast and with a struggle smothered the pain deep within his heart. At last he briefly replies: "I will never deny, Queen, that you have deserved of me the utmost you can set forth in speech, nor shall my memory of Elissa④ be bitter, while I have memory of myself, and while breath governs these limbs. For my conduct few words will I say. I did not hope—think not that—to veil my flight in stealth. I never held out a bridegroom's torch or entered such a compact. Had destiny permitted me to shape my life after my own pleasure and order my sorrows at my own will, my first care would be the city of Troy and the sweet relics

---

① 希腊东南部的一座山
② 指狄多的追求者伊阿尔巴斯 (Iarbas)
③ 狄多的哥哥, 腓尼基国王皮格马利翁 (Pygmalion)
④ 埃莉莎 (Elissa), 埃涅阿斯的前妻

of my king. Priam's high house would still abide and my own hand would have set up a revived Pergamus① for the vanquished. But now of great Italy has Grynean Apollo bidden me lay hold, of Italy the Lycian oracles. There is my love, there my country! If the towers of Carthage and the sight of Libyan city charm you, a Phoenician, why, pray, grudge the Trojans their settling on Ausonian land? We, too, have the right to seek a foreign realm. Each time the night with dewy shades veils the earth, each time the starry fires arise, in my dreams my father Anchises' troubled ghost brings me warning and terror; the thought of young Ascanius comes to me and the wrong done to one so dear, whom I am cheating of a Hesperian kingdom② and predestined lands. Now, too, the messenger of the gods sent from Jove himself—I sear by both our lives— has borne his command down through the swift breezes; my own eyes saw the god in the clear light of day come within our walls and these ears drank in his words. Cease to inflame yourself and me with your complaints. It is not by my wish that I make for Italy … "

As thus he spoke, all the while she gazes on him askance, turning her eyes to and fro, and with silent glances scans the whole man; then thus, inflamed, cries out: "False one, no goddess was your mother, nor was Dardanus③ the founder of your line, but rugged Caucasus④ on his flinty rocks begot you, and Hyrcanian tigresses suckled you. For why hide my feelings? For what greater wrongs do I hold myself back? Did he sigh while I wept? Did he turn on me a glance? Did he yield and shed tears or pity her who loved him? What shall I say first? What next? Now, neither mighty Juno nor the Saturnian sire looks on these things with righteous eyes! Nowhere is faith secure. I welcomed him, a castaway on the shore, a beggar, and madly gave him a share of my throne; his lost fleet I rescued, his crews I saved from death. Alas! I am whirled on the fires of frenzy. Now prophetic Apollo, now the Lycian oracles, now the messenger of the gods sent from Jove himself, brings through the air this dread command. Truly, this is work for gods, this is care to vex their peace! I detain you not; I dispute not your words. Go, make for Italy with the winds; seek your kingdom over the waves. Yet I trust, if the righteous gods have any power, that on the rocks midway you will drain the

---

① 指特洛伊城
② Hesperian kingdom, 西方国家, 指意大利
③ 达尔达诺斯 (Dardanus), 宙斯之子, 特洛伊人的祖先
④ 高加索人 (Caucasus)

cup of vengeance and often call on Dido's name. Though far away, I will chase you with murky brands and, when chill death has severed soul and body, everywhere my shade shall haunt you. Relentless one, you will repay! I shall hear, and the tale will reach me in the depths of the world below!" So saying, she breaks off her speech midway and flees in anguish from the light, turning away, tearing herself from his sight, and leaving him in fear and much hesitance, and ready to say much. Her maids support her, carry her swooning form to her marble bower, and lay her on her bed.

But loyal Aeneas, though longing to soothe and assuage her grief and by his words turn aside her sorrow, with many a sigh, his soul shaken by his mighty love, yet fulfills Heaven's bidding and returns to the fleet. Then, indeed, the Teucrians[①] fall to and all along the shore launch their tall ships. The keels, well-pitched, are set afloat; the sailors, eager for flight, bring from the woods leafy boughs for oars and logs unhewn ... One could see them moving away and streaming forth from all the city. Even as when ants, mindful of winter, plunder a huge heap of corn and store it in their home; over the plain moves a black column, and through the grass they carry the spoil on a narrow track; some strain with their shoulders and heave on the huge grains, some close up the ranks and rebuke the delay; all the path is aglow with work. What feelings then were yours, Dido, at such a sight! or what sighs did you utter, viewing from the top of the fortress the beach aglow far and near, and seeing before your eyes the whole sea astir with loud cries! O relentless Love, to what do you not drive the heats of men. Once more she must needs break into tears, once more assail him with prayer, and humbly bow down her pride to love, lest she leave anything untried and go to death in vain.

"Anna, you see the bustle[②] all along the shore; from all sides they have gathered; already the canvas invites the breeze, and the joyous sailors have crowned the stern with garlands. If I have had strength to foresee this great sorrow, I shall also, sister, have strength to endure it. Yet this one service, Anna, do for me—for you alone that traitor made his friend, to you he confided even his secret thoughts, you alone will know the hour for easy access to him—go, sister, and humbly address our haughty foe. I never conspired with the Danaans[③] at Aulis to root out the Trojan race; I never sent a

---

① 特洛伊人
② 喧闹
③ 希腊联军，希腊人

fleet to Pergamus①, nor tore up the ashes and disturbed the spirit of his father Anchises. Why does he refuse to admit my words to his stubborn ears? Whither does he hasten? This, the last boon, let him grant his poor lover: let him await an easy flight and favouring winds. No more do I plead for the old marriage tie which he forswore, nor that he give up fair Latium② and resign his realm: for empty time I ask, for peace and reprieve for my frenzy, till fortune teach my vanquished soul to grieve. This last grace I crave–pity your sister–which, when he has granted it, I will repay with full interest in my death."

Such was her prayer and such the tearful pleas the unhappy sister bears again and again. But by no tearful pleas is he moved, nor in yielding mood does he pay heed to any words. Fate withstands and heaven seals his kindly, mortal ears. Even as when northern Alpine③ winds, blowing now hence, now thence, emulously strive to uproot an oak strong with the strength of years, there comes a roar, the trunk quivers and the high leafage thickly strews the ground, but the oak clings to the crag, and as far as it lifts its top to the airs of heaven, so far it strikes its roots down towards hell–even so with ceaseless appeals, from this side and from that, the hero is buffeted, and in his mighty heart feels agony: his mind stands steadfast; his tears fall without effect.

Then, indeed, awed by her doom, luckless Dido prays for death; she is weary of gazing on the arch of heaven. And to make her more surely fulfil her purpose and leave the light, she saw, as she laid her gifts on the altars ablaze with incense–fearful to tell–the holy water darken and the out–poured wine change into loathsome gore. Of this sight she spoke to no one–not even her sister. Moreover, there was in the palace a marble chapel to her former lord, which she cherished in wondrous honour, wreathing it with snowy fleeces and festal foliage. Thence she heard, it seemed, sounds and speech as of her husband calling, whenever darkling night held the world; and alone on the housetops with ill–boding song the owl would oft complain, drawing out its lingering notes into a wail; and likewise many a saying of the seers of old terrifies her with fearful boding. In her sleep fierce Aeneas himself drives her in her frenzy; and ever she seems to be left lonely, ever ending, companion–less, an endless way, and seeking her

---

① 指特洛伊城
② 拉丁姆（Latium），意大利东南部，埃涅阿斯族人的目的地，拉丁文化起源地
③ 亚平宁（Alpine）

Tyrians in a land forlorn-even as raving Pentheus sees the Bacchants' bands, and a double sun and two-fold Thebes rise to view; or as when Agamemnon's son, Orestes, hounded by the Furies, flees from his mother, who is armed with brands and black serpents, while at the doorway crouch avenging Fiends.

So when, outworn with anguish, she caught the madness and resolved to die, in her own heart she determines the time and manner, and accosts her sorrowful sister, with mien that veils her plan and on her brow a cloudless hope. "Sister mine, I have found a way-wish your sister joy-to return him to me or release me from my love for him. Near Ocean's bound and the setting sun lies Ethiopia, farthest of lands, where mightiest Atlas on this shoulders turns the sphere, inset with gleaming stars. Thence a priestess of Massylian race has been shown me, warden of the fane of the Hesperides①, who gave dainties to the dragon and guarded the sacred bows on the tree, sprinkling dewy honey and slumberous pop-pies. With her spells she professes to set free the hearts of whom she wills, but on others to bring cruel love pains; to stay the flow of rivers and turn back the stars; she awakes the ghosts of night; and you will see earth rumbling under your feet and ash trees coming down the mountains. I call heaven to witness and you, dear sister mine, and your dear life, that against my will I arm myself with magic arts! Secretly raise up a pyre in the inner court under the sky, and heap up on it's the arms that heartless one left hanging in my bower, and all his attire and the bridal bed that was my undoing. I want to destroy all memorials of the abhorred wretch, and the priestess to directs." Thus she speaks and is silent; pallor the while overspreads her face. Yet Anna thinks not that her sister veils her death under these strange rites; her mind dreams not of such frenzy nor does she fear anything worse than when Sychaeus② died. So she makes ready as bidden …

But the queen, when in the heart of her home the pyre rose heaven-ward, piled high with pine logs and hewn ilex, hangs the place with garlands and crowns it with funeral boughs. On top, upon the couch, she lays the dress he wore, the sword he left, and an image of him, knowing what was to come. Round about stand altars, and with streaming hair the priestess calls in thunder tones on thrice a hundred gods, Erebos and

---

① 赫斯帕里德斯（Hesperides），金苹果树园
② 狄多的前夫

Chaos, and threefold Hecate①, triple-faced maiden Diana. Waters, too, she had sprinkled feigned to be from the spring of Avernus②, and herbs were sought, cut by moonlight with brazen sickles, and juicy with milk of black venom; sought, too, was the love charm, torn from the brow of a colt at birth before the mother snatched it … She herself, with holy meal and holy hands, stood beside the altars, one for unsandalled and girdle loosened; soon to die, she calls on the gods and on the stars, witnesses of her doom; then she prays to whatever power, righteous and mindful, watches over lovers unequally allied.

  It was night, and over the earth weary creatures were tasting the peace of slumber; the woods and wild seas had sunk to rest – the hour when stars roll midway in their gliding course, when all the land is still, and beasts and coloured birds, both those that far and near haut the limpid lakes, and those that dwell in the thorny thickets of the countryside, are couched in sleep beneath the silent night. They were soothing their cares, their hearts oblivious of sorrows. But not so the soul-racked Phoenician queen; she never sinks into sleep, nor draws darkness into eyes or heart. Her pangs redouble, and her love, swelling up, surges afresh, as she heaves with a mighty tide of passion. Thus then she begins, and thus alone revolves her thoughts in her heart: "See, what shall I do? Shall I once more make trial of my old wooers, only to be mocked, and shall I humbly sue for marriage with Numidians, whom I have scorned so often as husbands? Shall I then follow the Ilian ships and the Trojan's uttermost commands? Is it because they are thankful for aid once given, and gratitude for past kindness stands firm in their mindful hearts? But who-suppose that I wished it-will suffer me, or take on so hated on those haughty ships? Ah! lost one, do you not yet understand nor perceive the treason of Laomedon's③ race? What then? Shall I on my own accompany the exultant sailors in their flight? Or, surrounded by all my Tyrian band, shall I pursue, and shall I again drive seaward the men whom I could scarce tear from the Sidonian city, and bid them unfurl their sails to the winds? Nay, die as you deserve, and with the sword end your sorrow. Won over by my tears, you, my sister, you were the first to load my frenzied soul with these ills, and drive me on the foe. Ah, that I could not spend my

---

  ① 赫卡特（Hecate），巫术女神
  ② 阿佛纳斯（Avernus），地狱入口
  ③ 特洛伊城的建立者拉俄墨冬的（Laomedon's），即特洛伊种族的

life apart from wedlock, a blameless life, like some wild creature, and not know such cares! The faith vowed to the ashes of Sychaeus I have not kept." Such were the cries that kept bursting from her heart.

But now that all was duly ordered, and now that he was resolved on going, Aeneas was snatching sleep on his vessel's high stern. In his sleep there appeared to him a vision of the god, as he came again with the same aspect, and once more seemed to warn him thus, in all aspects like Mercury, in voice and colouring, in golden hair and the graceful limbs of youth: "Goddess-born[①], when such hazard threatens, can you still slumber? Do you not see the perils that from henceforth hem you in, madman? Do you not hear the kindly breezes blowing? She, resolved on death, revolves in her heart fell craft and crime, and awakens the swirling surge of passion. Will you not flee hence in haste, while hasty flight is possible? Soon you will see the waters a welter of timbers, see fierce brands ablaze, and soon the shore flashing with flames, if dawn finds you lingering in these lands. Up then, break off delay! A fickle and changeful thing is woman ever." So he spoke and melted into the black night.

Thus indeed Aeneas, scared by the sudden vision, tears himself from sleep and bestirs his comrades. "Make haste, my men, awake and man the benches! Unfurl the sails with speed! A god sent from high heaven again spurs us to hasten our flight and cut the twisted cables. We follow you, holy among gods, whoever you are, and again joyfully obey your command. Oh, be with us, give your gracious aid, and in the sky vouch-safe kindly stars!" He spoke, and from its sheath snatches his flashing sword and strikes the hawser with the drawn blade. The same zeal catches all at once; with hurry and scurry they have quitted the shore; the sea is hidden under their fleets; lustily they churn the foam and sweep the blue waters.

And now early Dawn, leaving the saffron bed of Tithonus[②], was sprinkling her[③] fresh rays upon the earth. Soon as the queen from her watchtower saw the light whiten and the fleet move on with even sails, and knew the shores and harbours were void of oarsmen, thrice and four times she struck her comely breast with her hand, and tearing her golden hair, "O God," she cries, "shall he go? Shall the intruder have made of

---

① 指埃涅阿斯

② 提托诺斯（Tithonus），拉俄墨冬的儿子，黎明女神的情人

③ 指黎明女神（Dawn）

our realm a laughingstock? Will pursuers not fetch arms and give chase from all the city, and some of them speed ships from the docks? Go, haste to bring fire, serve arms, ply oars! What say I? Where am I? What madness turns my brain? Unhappy Dido, do only now your sinful deeds come home to you? Then was the time, when you gave your crown away. Behold the pledge and promise of him who, so they say, carries wit him his ancestral gods and bore his worn-out father on his shoulders! Could I not have seized him, torn him limb from limb, and scattered the pieces on the waves? Could I not have put his men to the sword, and Ascanius himself, and served him up as a meal at his father's table? But perhaps the issue of battle had been doubtful? Suppose it had been: doomed to death, whom had I to fear? I should have carried fire to his camp, filled his decks with flame, blotted out father and son together with the whole race, and immolated myself on top of all. O Sun, whose rays survey all that is done on earth; and Juno, agent and witness of unhappy love; Hecate, whose name is wailed by night in city streets; and Avenging Furies and gods of dying Elissa: hear me now; turn your anger upon the sins that merit it, and listen to my prayers! If that accursed wretch must needs reach harbour and come to shore, if Jove's ordinances so demand and this is the outcome fixed: yet even so, harassed in war by the arms of a fearless nation, expelled from his territory and torn from Iulus' embrace, let him plead for aid an see his friends cruelly slaughtered! Nor yet, when he has submitted to the terms of an unjust peace, may he enjoy his kingship or the life he longs for, but perish before his time and lie unburied on a lonely strand! This is my prayer; this last utterance I pour out with my blood. Then do you, Tyrians, persecute with hate his stock and all the race to come, and to my dust offer this tribute! Let no lover or treaty unite the nations! Arise from my ashes, unknown avenger, to harass the Trojan settlers with fire and sword-today, hereafter, whenever strength be ours! May coast with coast conflict, I pray, and sea with sea, arms with arms; war may they have, themselves and their children's children!" With this curse she turned her mind in every direction, seeking how most quickly to end the life she loathed. Then briefly she addressed Barce, the nurse of Sychaeus, for the pyre's black ashes held her own back in her country of long ago. "Dear nurse, bring my sister Anna here. Bid her hasten to sprinkle her body with river water and bring with her the victims and offerings ordained for atonement. This done, let her come; and veil your brows, too, with a pure chaplet. I am minded to fulfil the rites of Stygian Jove that I have duly ordered and begun, to put an end to my

113

owes, and give over to the flames the pyre of that Dardan wretch." She spoke; the nurse hastened her steps with an old woman's zeal. But Dido, trembling and frantic with her dreadful design, rolling bloodshot eyes, her quivering cheeks flecked with burning spots, and pale at the imminence of death, bursts into the inner courts of the house, climbs the high pyre in a frenzy and unsheathes the Dardan sword, a gift south for no such purpose. Then, as she saw the Trojan garb and the familiar bed, pausing awhile in tearful thought, she threw herself on the couch and spoke her last words: "O relics once dear, while God and Fate allowed, take my spirit, and release me from my woes! My life is done and I have finished the course that Fortune gave; and now in majesty my shade shall pass beneath the earth. A noble city I have built; my own walls I have seen; avenging my husband, I have exacted punishment from my brother and foe – happy, too happy, had but the Dardan keels never touched our shores!" She spoke, and burying her face in the couch, "I shall die unavenged," she cries, "but let me die! Thus, I go gladly into the dark! Let the cruel Dardan's eyes drink in this fire from the deep, and carry with him the omen of my death!"

She ceased; and even as she spoke her handmaids see her fallen on the sword, the blade reeking with blood and her hands bespattered. A scream rises to the lofty roof; Rumour riots through the stricken city. The palace rings with lamentation, with sobbing and women's shrieks, and heaven echoes with loud wails – as though all Carthage or ancient Tyre were falling before the in-rushing foe, and fierce flames were rolling on over the roofs of men, over the roofs of gods.

Swooning, her sister heard, and in dismay rushed through the throng, tearing her face with her nails, and beating her breast with her fists, as she called on the dying woman by name. "Was this your purpose, sister? Did you aim your fraud at me? Was this for me the meaning of your pyre, this the meaning of your altar and fires? Forlorn, what shall I first lament? Did you scorn in death your sister's company? You should have summoned me to share your fate; the same sword stroke, the same moment would have taken us both! Did these hands indeed build the pyre, and did my voice call on our father's gods, in order that, when you were lying thus, I, cruel one, should be far away? You have destroyed yourself and me together, sister, the Sidonian senate and people, and your city! Bring me water to bathe her wounds and catch with my lips whatever last breath may linger!" Thus speaking, she had climbed the high steps, and, throwing her arms round her dying sister, sobbed and clasped her to her bosom, stanching with her dress the dark streams of blood. She, trying to lift her heavy eyes, swoons again, and the deep-set wound gurgles in her breast. Thrice rising, she struggles to prop herself on her elbow, thrice the bed rolled back, with wandering eyes sought high heaven's light, and when she found it, moaned.

Then almighty Juno, pitying her long agony and painful dying, sent Iris down from heaven to release her struggling soul from the prison of her flesh. For since she perished neither in the course of fate nor by a death she had earned, but wretchedly before her day, in the heat of sudden frenzy, not yet had Proserpine taken from head the golden lock and consigned her to the Stygian underworld. So Iris on dewy saffron wings flits down through the sky, trailing athwart the sun a thousand shifting tints, and halted above her head. "This offering, sacred to Dis, I take as bidden, and from your body set you free": so she speaks and with her hand severs the lock; and therewith all the warmth passed away, and the life vanished into the winds.

Questions for discussion:

1. Why did Dido, Queen of Carthage, fall in love with Aeneas, a stranger? If love is the result of having the right person at the right time, why does Dido think Aeneas is the right person at the right time?

2. Why did Dido, ashamed and angry, commit suicide when she learned that Aeneas had fled secretively? Why not abandon Carthage and follow Aeneas on his expedition to Apennine? Or hunt down the Trojans, to prevent a life-or-death conflict in the Mediterranean 600 years later?

3. What other reasons were there for the war between Aeneas and Turnus besides ethnic conflict?

第六篇 Oedipus the King[①]

Sophocles

Translated by Robert Bagg

CHARACTERS

Delegation of Thebans, young, middle-aged, elderly

OEDIPUS, king of Thebes

PRIEST of Zeus

CREON, Jocasta's brother

CHORUS of older Theban men

LEADER of the Chorus

TIRESIAS, blind prophet of Apollo

Boy to lead Tiresias

JOCASTA, Oedipus' wife

MESSENGER from Corinth

Attendants and maids

HERDSMAN, formerly of Laius' house

SERVANT from Oedipus' house

Antigone and Ismene, Oedipus' daughters

The play opens in front of the royal palace in Thebes. The palace has an imposing central double door flanked by two altars: one to Apollo, one to household gods. The

---

[①]《俄狄浦斯王》是索福克勒斯（Sophocles）最伟大的作品，也代表古希腊悲剧的最高成就

Delegation of Thebans enters carrying olive branches wound with wool strips①. They gather by the palace stairs. The light and atmosphere are oppressive. Oedipus enters through the great doors.

OEDIPUS

My children—you are the fresh green life old Cadmus② nurtures and protects. Why do you surge at me like this—with your wool-strung boughs? While the city is swollen with howls of pain, reeking incense, and prayers sung to the Healing God? To have others tell me these things would not be right, my sons. So I've come out myself.

My name is Oedipus—the famous—as everyone calls me. Tell me, old man, yours is the natural voice for the rest, what troubles you? You're terrified? Looking for reassurance? Be certain I'll give you all the help I can. I'd be a hard man if an approach like yours failed to rouse my pity.

PRIEST

You rule our land, Oedipus! You can see who comes to your altars, how varied we are in years: children too weak-winged to fly far, others hunched with age, a few priests—I am a priest of Zeus—joined by the best of our young lads. More of us wait with wool-strung boughs in the markets, and at Athena's two temples. Some, at Ismenos' shrine, are watching ashes for the glow of prophecy. You can see our city going under, too feeble to lift its head clear of the angry murderous waves. Plague blackens our flowering farmland, sickens our cattle where they graze. Our women in labor give birth to nothing. A burning god rakes his fire through our town. He hates us with fever, he empties the House of Cadmus, enriching black Hades with our groans and tears. We haven't come to beg at your hearth because we think you're the gods' equal.

We've come because you are the best man at handling trouble or confronting gods. You came to Thebes, you freed us from the tax we paid with our lives to that rasping Singer. You did it with no help from us. We had nothing to teach you. People say—they believe!—you had a god's help when you restored life to our city. Oedipus, we need

---

① 古希腊人用羊毛裹着棕榈树枝，表示求助
② 卡德摩斯（Cadmus），忒拜城（Thebes）的建立者，俄狄浦斯（Oedipus）的先祖

now the great power men everywhere know you possess.

Find some way to protect us—learn it from a god's intimation, or a man's. This much I know: guidance from men proven right in the past will meet a crisis with the surest force. Act as our greatest man! Act as you did when you first seized fame! We believe your nerve saved us then. Don't let us look back on your rule and say, He lifted us once, but then let us down.

Put us firmly back on our feet, so Thebes will never fall again. You were a bird from god, you brought good luck the day you rescued us. Be that man now! If you want to rule us, it's better to rule the living than a barren waste. Walled cities and ships are worthless—when they've been emptied of people.

OEDIPUS

I do pity you, children. Don't think I'm unaware. I know what need brings you: this sickness ravages all of you. Yet, sick as you are, not one of you suffers a sickness like mine. Yours is a private grief, you feel only what touches you. But my heart grieves for you, for myself, and for our city. You've come to wake me to all this. There was no need. I haven't been sleeping. I have wept tears enough, for long enough. My mind has raced down every twisting path. And after careful thought, I've set in motion

the only cure I could find: I've sent Creon[①], my wife's brother, to Phoebus at Delphi[②], to hear what action or what word of mine will save this town. Already, counting the days, I'm worried: what is Creon doing? He takes too long, more time than he needs. But when he comes, I'll be the guilty one—if I don't do all the gods show me to do.

PRIEST

Well timed! The moment you spoke, your men gave the sign: Creon's arriving.

OEDIPUS

O Lord Apollo may the luck he brings save us! Luck so bright we can see it—just as we see him now.

---

① 克里翁（Creon），忒拜城（Thebes）王后犹卡斯塔（Jocasta）的哥哥
② Phoebus at Delphi，德尔菲的阿波罗神庙，古希腊神谕最准的地方

CREON enters from the countryside, wearing a laurel crown speckled with red.

PRIEST

He must bring pleasing news. If not, why would he wear laurel dense with berries?

OEDIPUS

We'll know very soon. He's within earshot. Prince! Brother kinsman, son of Menoikeos! What kind of answer have you brought from god?

CREON

A good one. No matter how dire, if troubles turn out well, everything will be fine.

OEDIPUS

What did the god say? Nothing you've said so far alarms or reassures me.

CREON

Do you want me to speak in front of these men? If so, I will. If not, let's go inside.

OEDIPUS

Speak here, to all of us. I suffer more for them than for my own life.

CREON

Then I'll report what I heard from Apollo. He made his meaning very clear. He commands we drive out what corrupts us, what sickens our city. We now harbor something incurable. He says: purge it.

OEDIPUS

Tell me the source of our trouble. How do we cleanse ourselves?

CREON

By banishing a man or killing him. It's blood—kin murder—that brings this storm on our city.

OEDIPUS

Who is the man god wants us to punish?

CREON

As you know, King, our city was ruled once by Laius①, before you came to take the helm.

OEDIPUS

I've heard as much. Though I never saw him.

CREON

Well, Laius was murdered. Now god tells you plainly: with your own hands punish the very men whose hands killed Laius.

OEDIPUS

Where do I find these men? How do I track vague footprints from a bygone crime?

CREON

The god said: here, in our own land. What we look for we can capture. What we ignore goes free.

OEDIPUS

Was Laius killed at home? Or in the fields? Or did they murder him on foreign ground?

CREON

He told us his journey would take him into god's presence. He never came back.

---

① 拉伊俄斯（Laius），忒拜前国王

OEDIPUS

Did none of his troop see and report what happened? Isn't there anyone to question whose answers might help?

CREON

All killed but a single terrified survivor, able to tell us but one fact.

OEDIPUS

What was it? One fact might lead to many, if we had one small clue to give us hope.

CREON

They had the bad luck, he said, to meet bandits who struck them with a force many hands strong. This wasn't the violence of one man only.

OEDIPUS

What bandit would dare commit such a crime unless somebody here had hired him?

CREON

That was our thought, but after Laius died, we were mired in new troubles—and no avenger came.

OEDIPUS

But here was your kingship murdered! What kind of trouble could have blocked your search?

CREON

The Sphinx's[①] song. So wily, so baffling! She forced us to forget the dark past, to confront what lay at our feet.

---

① 斯芬克斯的（Sphinx's），狮身人面女妖。

OEDIPUS

Then I'll go back, start fresh, and light up that darkness. Apollo was exactly right, and so were you, to turn our minds back to the murdered man. It's time I joined your search for vengeance. Our country and the god deserve no less. This won't be on behalf of distant kin—I'll banish this plague for my own sake. Laius' killer might one day come for me, exacting vengeance with that same hand. Defending the dead man serves my interest. Rise, children, quick, up from the altar, pick up those branches that appeal to god. Someone go call the people of Cadmus—tell them I'm ready to do anything. With god's help our good luck is assured. Without it we're doomed.

Exit OEDIPUS, into the palace.

PRIEST

Stand up, children. He has proclaimed himself the cure we came to find. May god Apollo, who sent the oracle, be our savior and end this plague!

The Delegation of Thebans leaves; the CHORUS enters.

CHORUS

What will you say to Thebes, Voice from Zeus? What sweet sounds convey your will from golden Delphi to our bright city? We're at the breaking point, our minds are wracked with dread. Our wild cries reach out to you, Healing God from Delos①— in holy fear we ask: does your will bring a new threat, or has an old doom come round again as the years wheel by? Say it, Great Voice, you who answer us always, speak as Hope's golden child. Athena, immortal daughter of Zeus, your help is the first we ask—then Artemis, your sister who guards our land, throned in the heart of our city. And Apollo, whose arrows strike from far off! Our three defenders② against death:

---

① Healing God from Delos, 从得洛斯岛来的治疗之神，指太阳神阿波罗。阿波罗（Apollo）也是治疗之神，并且他和孪生妹妹月亮及狩猎女神阿尔忒弥斯（Artemis）都出生于得洛斯岛

② Our three defenders, 三个保护者。忒拜城的百姓认为阿波罗（Apollo）、阿尔忒弥斯（Artemis）和雅典娜（Athena）三神都是他们的保护者

come now! Once before, when ruin threatened, you drove the flames of fever from our city. Come to us now! The troubles I suffer are endless. The plague attacks our troops. I can think of no weapon that will keep a man safe. Our rich earth shrivels what it grows. Women in labor scream, but no children are born to ease their pain. One life after another flies—you see them pass—like birds driving their strong wings faster than flash-fire to the Death god's western shore. Our city dies as its people die these countless deaths, her children rot in the streets, unmourned, spreading more death. Young wives and gray mothers wash to our altars, their cries carry from all sides, sobbing for help, each lost in her pain. A hymn rings out to the Healer—an oboe answers, keening in a courtyard.

Against all this, Goddess, golden child of Zeus, send us the bright shining face of courage. Force that raging killer, the god Ares①, to turn his back and run from our land. He wields no weapons of war to kill us, but burning with his fever, we shout in the hot blast of his charge. Blow Ares to the vast sea-room of Amphitrite②, banish him under a booming wind to jagged harbors in the roiling seas off Thrace. If night doesn't finish the god's black work, the day will finish it. Lightning lurks in your fiery will, O Zeus, our Father. Blast it into the god who kills us.

Apollo, lord of the morning light, draw back your taut, gold-twined bowstring, fire the sure arrows that rake our attackers and keep them at bay. Artemis, bring your radiance into battle on bright quick feet down through the morning hills. I call on the god whose hair is bound with gold, the god who gave us our name, Bacchus③! —the wine-flushed—who answers the maenads'④ cries, running beside them! Bacchus, come here on fire, pine-torch flaring. Face with us the one god all the gods hate: Ares!

OEDIPUS has entered while the CHORUS was singing.

---

① 战神阿瑞斯（Ares），忒拜城的百姓将死亡归因于战神的杀气太重，因为建城时卡德摩斯（Cadmus）屠杀了战神的巨蟒，故种下了祸根
② 安菲特里忒（Amphitrite），海神波塞冬（Poseidon）的王后
③ 酒神巴克斯（Bacchus）
④ The maenads, 酒神的女祭司们

OEDIPUS

I heard your prayer. It will be answered if you trust and obey my words: pull hard with me, bear down on the one cure that will stop this plague. Help will come, the evils will be gone. I hereby outlaw the killer myself, by my own words, though I'm a stranger both to the crime and to accounts of it. But unless I can mesh some clue I hold with something known of the killer, I will be tracking him alone, on a cold trail. Since I've come late to your ranks, Thebans, and the crime is past history, there are some things that you, the sons of Cadmus, must tell me. If any one of you knows how Laius, son of Labdacus①, died, he must tell me all that he knows. He should not be afraid to name himself the guilty one: I swear he'll suffer nothing worse than exile. Or if you know of someone else—a foreigner—who struck the blow, speak up. I will reward you now. I will thank you always. But if you know the killer and don't speak—out of fear—to shield kin or yourself, listen to what that silence will cost you. I order everyone in my land, where I hold power and sit as king: don't let that man under your roof, don't speak with him, no matter who he is. Don't pray or sacrifice with him, don't pour purifying water for him.

I say this to all my people: drive him from your houses. He is our sickness. He poisons us. This the Pythian god② has shown me. This knowledge makes me an ally—of both the god and the dead king. I pray god that the unseen killer, whoever he is, and whether he killed alone or had help, be cursed with a life as evil as he is, a life of utter human deprivation. I pray this, too: if he's found at my hearth, inside my house, and I know he's there, may the curses I aimed at others punish me. I charge you all—act on my words, for my sake and the god's, for our dead land stripped barren of its harvests, abandoned by its gods. Even if god had not forced the issue, this crime should not have gone uncleansed. You should have looked to it! The dead man was not only noble, he was your king! But as my luck would have it, I have his power, his bed—a wife who shares our seed. And had she borne the children of us both, she might have linked us closer still. But Laius had no luck fathering children, and Fate itself came down on his

---

① 拉布达克斯（Labdacus），卡德摩斯（Cadmus）的孙子，拉伊俄斯（Laius）的父亲，俄狄浦斯（Oedipus）的祖父
② The Pythian god，指太阳神阿波罗（Apollo）。阿波罗射杀大蛇皮同（Python）的地方在德尔菲（Delphi），因而 Pythian 指德尔菲居民，故 the Pythian god 指阿波罗

head. These concerns make me fight for Laius as I would for my own father. I'll stop at nothing to trace his murder back to the killer's hand. I act in this for Labdacus and Polydorus①, for Cadmus and Agenor—all our kings. I warn those who would disobey me: god make their fields harvest dust, their women's bodies harvest death. O you gods, let them die from the plague that kills us now, or die from something worse. As for the rest of you, who are the loyal sons of Cadmus: may Justice fight with us, the gods be always at your side.

CHORUS

King, your curse forces me to speak. None of us is the killer. And none of us can point to him. Apollo ordered us to search. It's up to him to find the killer.

OEDIPUS

So he must. But what man can force the gods to act against their will?

LEADER

May I suggest a second course of action?

OEDIPUS

Don't stop at two. Not if you have more.

LEADER

Tiresias② is the man whose power of seeing shows him most nearly what Apollo sees. If we put our questions to him, King, he could give us the clearest answers.

OEDIPUS

But I've seen to this already. At Creon's urging I've sent for him—twice now. I find it strange that he still hasn't come.

---

① 波吕多洛斯（Polydorus），腓尼基国王阿基诺（Agenor）的孙子，忒拜城建立者卡德摩斯（Cadmus）的儿子，拉布达克斯（Labdacus）的父亲
② 忒瑞西斯（Tiresias），忒拜城的盲人先知，全希腊最著名的预言家

LEADER

There were rumors—too faint and old to be much help.

OEDIPUS

What were they? I'll examine every word.

LEADER

They say Laius was killed by some travelers.

OEDIPUS

That's something even I have heard. But the man who did it—no one sees him.

LEADER

If fear has any hold on him he won't linger in Thebes, not after he hears threats of the kind you made.

OEDIPUS

If murder didn't scare him, my words won't.

LEADER

There's the man who will convict him: god's own prophet, led here at last. God gave to him what he gave no one else: the truth—it's living in his mind.

Enter TIRESIAS, led by a Boy.

OEDIPUS

Tiresias, you are master of the hidden world. You can read earth and sky. You know what knowledge to reveal and what to hide. Though your eyes can't see it, your mind is well aware of the plague that afflicts us. Against it, we have no savior or defense but you, my Lord.

If you haven't heard it from messengers, we now have Apollo's answer: to end this plague we must root out Laius' killers. Find them, then kill or banish them. Help us do this. Don't begrudge us what you divine from bird cries, show us everything prophecy has shown you. Save Thebes! Save yourself! Save me! Wipe out what defiles us, keep the poison of our king's murder from poisoning the rest of us. We're in your hands. The best use a man makes of his powers is to help others.

TIRESIAS

The most terrible knowledge is the kind it pays no wise man to possess. I knew this, but I forgot it. I should never have come here.

OEDIPUS

What? You've come, but with no stomach for this?

TIRESIAS

Let me go home. Your life will then be easier to bear—and so will mine.

OEDIPUS

It's neither lawful nor humane to hold back god's crucial guidance from the city that raised you.

TIRESIAS

What you've said has made matters worse. I won't let that happen to me.

OEDIPUS

For god's sake, if you know something, don't turn your back on us! We're on our knees.

TIRESIAS

You don't understand! If I spoke of my grief, then it would be yours.

OEDIPUS

What did you say? You know and won't help? You would betray us all and destroy Thebes?

TIRESIAS

I'll cause no grief to you or me. Why ask futile questions? You'll learn nothing.

OEDIPUS

So the traitor won't answer. You would enrage a rock. Still won't speak? Are you so thick-skinned nothing touches you?

TIRESIAS

You blame your rage on me? When you don't see how she embraces you, this fury you live with? No, so you blame me.

OEDIPUS

Who wouldn't be enraged? Your refusal to speak dishonors the city.

TIRESIAS

It will happen. My silence can't stop it.

OEDIPUS

If it must happen, you should tell me now.

TIRESIAS

I'd rather not. Rage at that, if you like, with all the savage fury in your heart.

OEDIPUS

That's right. I am angry enough to speak my mind. I think you helped plot the murder. Did everything but kill him with your own hands. Had you eyes, though, I would have said you alone were the killer.

TIRESIAS

That's your truth? Now hear mine: honor the curse your own mouth spoke. From this day on, don't speak to me or to your people here. You are the plague. You poison your own land.

OEDIPUS

So. The appalling charge has been at last flushed out, into the open. What makes you think you'll escape?

TIRESIAS

I have escaped. I nurture truth, so truth guards me.

OEDIPUS

Who taught you this truth? Not your prophet's trade.

TIRESIAS

You did. By forcing me to speak.

OEDIPUS

Speak what? Repeat it so I understand.

TIRESIAS

You missed what I said the first time? Are you provoking me to make it worse?

OEDIPUS

I heard you. But you made no sense. Try again.

TIRESIAS

You killed the man whose killer you now hunt.

OEDIPUS

The second time is even more outrageous. You'll wish you'd never said a word.

TIRESIAS

Shall I feed your fury with more words?

OEDIPUS

Use any words you like. They'll be wasted.

TIRESIAS

I say: you have been living unaware in the most hideous intimacy with your nearest and most loving kin, immersed in evil that you cannot see.

OEDIPUS

You think you can blithely go on like this?

TIRESIAS

I can, if truth has any strength.

OEDIPUS

Oh, truth has strength, but you have none. You have blind eyes, blind ears, and a blind brain.

TIRESIAS

And you're a desperate fool—throwing taunts at me that these men, very soon, will throw at you.

OEDIPUS

You're living in the grip of black unbroken night! You can't harm me or any man who can see the sunlight.

TIRESIAS

I'm not the one who will bring you down. Apollo will do that. You're his concern.

OEDIPUS

Did you make up these lies? Or was it Creon?

TIRESIAS

Creon isn't your enemy. You are.

OEDIPUS

Wealth and a king's power, the skill that wins every time—how much envy, what malice they provoke! To rob me of power—power I didn't ask for, but which this city thrust into my hands—my oldest friend here, loyal Creon, worked quietly against me, aching to steal my throne. He hired for the purpose this fortune-teller—conniving bogus beggar-priest! —a man who knows what he wants but cannot seize it, being but a blind groper in his art. Tell us now, when or where did you ever prove you had the power of a seer?

Why—when the Sphinx who barked black songs was hounding us—why didn't you speak up and free the city? Her riddle wasn't the sort just anyone who happened by could solve: prophetic skill was needed. But the kind you learned from birds or gods failed you. It took Oedipus, the know-nothing, to silence her. I needed no help from the birds. I used my wits to find the answer. I solved it—the same man for whom you plot disgrace and exile, so you can maneuver close to Creon's throne. But your scheme to rid Thebes of its plague will destroy both you and the man who planned it. Were you not so frail, I'd make you suffer exactly what you planned for me.

LEADER

He spoke in anger, Oedipus—but so did you, if you'll hear what we think. We don't need angry words. We need insight—how best to carry out the god's commands.

TIRESIAS

You may be king, but my right to answer makes me your equal. In this respect, I am as much my own master as you are. You do not own my life. Apollo does. Nor am I Creon's man. Hear me out. Since you have thrown my blindness at me I will tell you what your eyes don't see: what evil you are steeped in. You don't see where you live or who shares your house. Do you know your parents? You are their enemy in this life and down there with the dead. And soon their double curse—your father's and your mother's—will lash you out of Thebes on terror-stricken feet. Your eyes, which now see life, will then see darkness. Soon your shriek will burrow in every cave, bellow from every mountain outcrop on Cithaeron, when what your marriage means strikes home, when it shows you the house that took you in. You sailed a fair wind to a most foul harbor. Evils you cannot guess will bring you down to what you are. To what your children are. Go on, throw muck at Creon, and at the warning spoken through my mouth. No man will ever be ground into wretchedness as you will be.

OEDIPUS

Should I wait for him to attack me more? May you be damned. Go. Leave my house now! Turn your back and go.

TIRESIAS

I'm here only because you sent for me.

OEDIPUS

Had I known you would talk nonsense, I wouldn't have hurried to bring you here.

TIRESIAS

I seem a fool to you, but the parents who gave you birth thought I was wise.

OEDIPUS

What parents? Hold on. Who was my father?

TIRESIAS

Today you will be born. Into ruin.

OEDIPUS

You've always got a murky riddle in your mouth.

TIRESIAS

Don't you surpass us all at solving riddles?

OEDIPUS

Go ahead, mock what made me great.

TIRESIAS

Your very luck is what destroyed you.

OEDIPUS

If I could save the city, I wouldn't care.

TIRESIAS

Then I'll leave you to that. Boy, guide me out.

OEDIPUS

Yes, let him lead you home. Here, underfoot, you're in the way. But when you're gone, you'll give us no more grief.

TIRESIAS

I'll go. But first I must finish what you brought me to do—your scowl can't frighten me. The man you have been looking for, the one your curses threaten, the man you have condemned for Laius' death: I say that man is here. You think he's an immigrant, but he will prove himself a Theban native, though he'll find no joy in that news. A blind man who still has eyes, a beggar who's now rich, he'll jab his stick, feeling the road to foreign lands.

OEDIPUS enters the palace.

He'll soon be shown father and brother to his own children, son and husband to the mother who bore him—she took his father's seed and his seed, and he took his own father's life. You go inside. Think through everything I have said. If I have lied, say of me, then—I have failed as a prophet.

Exit TIRESIAS.

CHORUS

What man provokes the speaking rock of Delphi? This crime that sickens speech is the work of his bloody hands. Now his feet will need to outrace a storm of wild horses, for Apollo is running him down, armed with bolts of fire. He and the Fates close in, dread gods who never miss. From snowfields high on Parnassus the word blazes out to us all: track down the man no one can see. He takes cover in thick brush. He charges up the mountain bull-like to its rocks and caves, going his bleak, hunted way, struggling to escape the doom Earth spoke from her sacred mouth. But that doom buzzes low, never far from his ear. Fear is what the man who reads birds makes us feel, fear we can't fight. We can't accept what he says but have no power to challenge him. We thrash in doubt, we can't see even the present clearly, much less the future. And we've heard of no feud embittering the House of Oedipus in Corinth① against the House of Laius here, no past trouble and none now, no proof that would make us blacken our king's fame as he seeks to avenge our royal house for this murder not yet solved. Zeus and Apollo make no mistakes when they predict what people do. But there is no way to tell whether an earthbound prophet sees more of the future than we can—though in knowledge and skill one person may surpass another. But never, not till I see the charges proved against him, will I give credence to a man who blames Oedipus. All of us saw his brilliance prevail when the winged virgin Sphinx came at him: he passed the test that won the people's love. My heart can't find him guilty.

CREON enters.

CREON

Citizens, I hear that King Oedipus has made a fearful charge against me. I'm here to prove it false. If he thinks anything I've said or done has made this crisis worse, or injured him, then I have no more wish to live. This is no minor charge. It's the most deadly I could suffer, if my city, my own people—you! —believe I'm a traitor.

LEADER

He could have spoken in a flash of ill-considered anger.

CREON

Did he say I persuaded the prophet to lie?

---

① 科林斯（Corinth），俄狄浦斯被抚养长大的城邦

LEADER

That's what he said. What he meant wasn't clear.

CREON

When he announced my guilt—tell me, how did his eyes look? Did he seem sane?

LEADER

I can't say. I don't question what my rulers do. Here he comes, now, out of the palace.

OEDIPUS enters.

OEDIPUS

So? You come here? You have the nerve to face me in my own house? When you're exposed as its master's murderer? Caught trying to steal my kingship? In god's name, what weakness did you see in me that led you to plot this? Am I a coward or a fool? Did you suppose I wouldn't notice your subtle moves? Or not fight back? Aren't you attempting something downright stupid—to win absolute power without partisans or even friends? For that you'll need money—and a mob.

CREON

Now you listen to me. You've had your say, now hear mine. Don't judge until you've heard me out.

OEDIPUS

You speak shrewdly, but I'm a poor learner from someone I know is my enemy.

CREON

I'll prove you are mistaken to think that.

OEDIPUS

How can you prove you're not a traitor?

CREON

If you think mindless presumption is a virtue, then you're not thinking straight.

OEDIPUS

If you think attacking a kinsman will bring you no harm, you must be mad.

CREON

I'll grant that. Now, how have I attacked you?

OEDIPUS

Did you, or did you not, urge me to send for that venerated prophet?

CREON

And I would still give you the same advice.

OEDIPUS

How long ago did King Laius ...

CREON

Laius? Did what? Why speak of him?

OEDIPUS

... die in that murderous attack?

CREON

That was far back in the past.

OEDIPUS

Did this seer practice his craft here then?

CREON

With the same skill and respect he has now.

OEDIPUS

Back then, did he ever mention my name?

CREON

Not in my hearing.

OEDIPUS

Didn't you try to hunt down the killer?

CREON

Of course we did. We found out nothing.

OEDIPUS

Why didn't your expert seer accuse me then?

CREON

I don't know. So I'd rather not say.

OEDIPUS

There is one thing you can explain.

CREON

What's that? I'm holding nothing back.

OEDIPUS

Just this. If that seer hadn't conspired with you, he would never have called me Laius' killer.

CREON

If he said that, you heard him, I didn't. I think you owe me some answers.

OEDIPUS

Question me. I have no blood on my hands.

CREON

Did you marry my sister?

OEDIPUS

Do you expect me to deny that?

CREON

You both have equal power in this country?

OEDIPUS

I give her all she asks.

CREON

Do I share power with you both as an equal?

OEDIPUS

You shared our power and betrayed us with it.

CREON

You're wrong. Think it through rationally, as I have. Who would prefer the anxiety-filled life of a king to one that lets him sleep at night— if his share of power still equaled a king's? Nothing in my nature hungers for power—for me it's enough to enjoy a king's rights, enough for any prudent man. All I want, you give me—and it comes with no fear. To be king would rob my life of its ease. How could my share of power be more pleasant than this painless preeminence, this ready influence I have? I'm not so misguided that I would crave honors that are burdens. But as things stand, I'm greeted and wished well on all sides. Those who want something from you come to me, their best hope of gaining it. Should I quit this good life for a worse one? Treason never corrupts a healthy mind. I have no love for such exploits. Nor would I join someone who did. Test me. Go to Delphi yourself. Find out whether I brought back the oracle's exact words. If you find I plotted with that omen-reader, seize me and kill me—not on your authority alone, but on mine, for I'd vote my own death. But don't

138

convict me because of a wild thought you can't prove, one that only you believe. There's no justice in your reckless confusion of bad men with good men, traitors with friends. To cast off a true friend is like suicide—killing what you love as much as your life.

Time will instruct you in these truths, for time alone is the sure test of a just man—but you can know a bad man in a day.

LEADER

That's good advice, my lord—for someone anxious not to fall. Quick thinkers can stumble.

OEDIPUS

When a conspirator moves abruptly and in secret against me, I must outplot him and strike first. If I pause and do nothing, he will take charge, and I will have lost.

CREON

What do you want? My banishment?

OEDIPUS

No. It's your death I want.

CREON

Then start by defining "betrayal" …

OEDIPUS

You talk as though you don't believe me.

CREON

How can I if you won't use reason?

OEDIPUS

I reason in my own interest.

CREON

You should reason in mine as well.

OEDIPUS

In a traitor's interest?

CREON

What if you're wrong?

OEDIPUS

I still must rule.

CREON

Not when you rule badly.

OEDIPUS

Did you hear him, Thebes!

CREON

Thebes isn't yours alone. It's mine as well!

LEADER

My Lords, stop this. Here's Jocasta① leaving the palace—just in time to calm you both. With her help, end your feud.

Enter JOCASTA from the palace.

JOCASTA

Wretched men! Why are you out here so reckless, yelling at each other? Aren't you ashamed? With Thebes sick and dying you two fight out some personal grievance?

---

① 犹卡斯塔（Jocasta），忒拜城（Thebes）的王后，前国王拉伊俄斯（Laius）的妻子

Oedipus. Go inside. Creon, go home. Don't make us all miserable over nothing.

CREON

Sister, it's worse than that. Oedipus, your husband, threatens either to drive me from my own country or to have me killed.

OEDIPUS

That's right. I caught him plotting to kill me, Lady. False prophecy was his weapon.

CREON

I ask the gods to sicken and destroy me if I did anything you charge me with.

JOCASTA

Believe what he says, Oedipus. Accept the oath he just made to the gods. Do it for my sake too, and for these men.

LEADER

Give in to him, Lord, we beg you. With all your mind and will.

OEDIPUS

What do you want me to do?

LEADER

Believe him. This man was never a fool. Now he backs himself up with a great oath.

OEDIPUS

You realize what you're asking?

LEADER

I do.

OEDIPUS

Then say it to me outright.

LEADER

Groundless rumor shouldn't be used by you to scorn a friend who swears his innocence.

OEDIPUS

You know, when you ask this of me you ask for my exile—or my death.

LEADER

No! We ask neither. By the god outshining all others, the Sun—may I die the worst death possible, die godless and friendless, if I want those things. This dying land grinds pain into my soul—grinds it the more if the bitterness you two stir up adds to our misery.

OEDIPUS

Then let him go, though it means my death or my exile from here in disgrace. What moves my pity are your words, not his. He will be hated wherever he goes.

CREON

You are as bitter when you yield as you are savage in your rage. But natures like your own punish themselves the most—which is the way it should be.

OEDIPUS

Leave me alone. Go.

CREON

I'll go. You can see nothing clearly. But these men see that I'm right.

CREON goes off.

LEADER

Lady, why the delay? Take him inside.

JOCASTA

I will, when you tell me what happened.

LEADER

They had words. One drew a false conclusion. The other took offense.

JOCASTA

Both sides were at fault?

LEADER

Both sides.

JOCASTA

What did they say?

LEADER

Don't ask that. Our land needs no more trouble. No more trouble! Let it go.

OEDIPUS

I know you mean well when you try to calm me, but do you realize where it will lead?

LEADER

King, I have said this more than once. I would be mad, I would lose my good sense, if I lost faith in you—you who put our dear country back on course when you found her wandering, crazed with suffering. Steer us straight, once again, with all your inspired luck.

JOCASTA

In god's name, King, tell me, too. What makes your rage so relentless?

OEDIPUS

I'll tell you, for it's you I respect, not the men. Creon brought on my rage by plotting against me.

JOCASTA

Go on. Explain what provoked the quarrel.

OEDIPUS

He says I murdered Laius.

JOCASTA

Does he know this himself? Or did someone tell him?

OEDIPUS

Neither. He sent that crooked seer to make the charge so he could keep his own mouth innocent.

JOCASTA

Then you can clear yourself of all his charges. Listen to me, for I can make you believe no man, ever, has mastered prophecy. This one incident will prove it. A long time back, an oracle reached Laius—I don't say Apollo himself sent it, but the priests who interpret him did. It said that Laius was destined to die at the hands of a son born to him and me. Yet, as rumor had it, foreign bandits killed Laius at a place where three roads meet.

OEDIPUS reacts with sudden intensity to her words.

But the child was barely three days old when Laius pinned its ankle joints together, then had it left, by someone else's hands, high up a mountain far from any roads. That time Apollo failed to make Laius die the way he feared—at the hands of his own son. Doesn't that tell you how much sense prophetic voices make of our lives? You can forget them. When god wants something to happen, he makes it happen. And has no trouble showing what he's done.

OEDIPUS

Just now, something you said made my heart race. Something ... I remember ... wakes up terrified.

JOCASTA

What fear made you turn toward me and say that?

OEDIPUS

I thought you said Laius was struck down where three roads meet.

JOCASTA

That's the story they told. It hasn't changed.

OEDIPUS

Tell me, where did it happen?

JOCASTA

In a place called Phocis, at the junction where roads come in from Delphi and from Daulia.

OEDIPUS

How long ago was it? When it happened?

JOCASTA

We heard the news just before you came to power.

OEDIPUS

O Zeus! What did you will me to do?

JOCASTA

Oedipus, you look heartsick. What is it?

OEDIPUS

Don't ask me yet. Describe Laius to me. Was he a young man, almost in his prime?

JOCASTA

He was tall, with some gray salting his hair. He looked then not very different from you now.

OEDIPUS

Like me? I'm finished! It was aimed at me, that savage curse I hurled in ignorance.

JOCASTA

What did you say, my Lord? Your face scares me.

OEDIPUS

I'm desperately afraid the prophet sees. Tell me one more thing. Then I'll be sure.

JOCASTA

I'm so frightened I can hardly answer.

OEDIPUS

Did Laius go with just a few armed men, or the large troop one expects of a prince?

JOCASTA

There were five only, one was a herald. And there was a wagon, to carry Laius.

OEDIPUS

Ah! I see it now. Who told you this, Lady?

JOCASTA

Our slave. The one man who survived and came home.

OEDIPUS

Is he by chance on call here, in our house?

JOCASTA

No. When he returned and saw that you had all dead Laius' power, he touched my hand and begged me to send him out to our farmlands and sheepfolds, so he'd be far away and out of sight. I sent him. He was deserving—though a slave—of a much larger favor than he asked.

OEDIPUS

Can you send for him right away?

JOCASTA

Of course. But why do you need him?

OEDIPUS

I'm afraid, Lady, I've said too much. That's why I want to see him now.

JOCASTA

I'll have him come. But don't I have the right to know what so deeply disturbs you, Lord?

OEDIPUS

So much of what I dreaded has come true. I'll tell you everything I fear. No one has more right than you do to know the risks to which I'm now exposed. Polybus of Corinth was my father. My mother was Merope[①], a Dorian. I was the leading citizen, when Chance struck me a sudden blow. Alarming as it was, I took it much too hard. At

---

① Polybus and Merope, 即科林斯国王与王后, 俄狄浦斯的养父母

a banquet, a man who had drunk too much wine claimed I was not my father's son. Seething, I said nothing. All that day I barely held it in. But next morning I questioned Mother and Father. Furious, they took their anger out on the man who shot the insult. They reassured me. But the rumor still rankled; it hounded me. So with no word to my parents, I traveled to the Pythian oracle①. But the god would not honor me with the knowledge I craved. Instead, his words flashed other things—horrible, wretched things—at me: I would be my mother's lover. I would show the world children no one could bear to look at. I would murder the father whose seed I am. When I heard that, and ever after, I traced the road back to Corinth only by looking at the stars. I fled to somewhere I'd never see outrages, like those the god promised, happen to me. But my flight carried me to just the place where, you tell me, the king was killed. Oh, woman, here is the truth. As I approached the place where three roads joined, a herald, a colt-drawn wagon, and a man like the one you describe, met me head-on. The man out front and the old man himself began to crowd me off the road. The driver, who's forcing me aside, I smash in anger. The old man watches me, he measures my approach, then leans out lunging with his two-spiked goad dead at my skull. He's more than repaid: I hit him so fast with the staff this hand holds, he's knocked back rolling off the cart. Where he lies, face up. Then I kill them all. But if this stranger and Laius ... were the same blood, whose triumph could be worse than mine? Is there a man alive the gods hate more? Nobody, no Theban, no foreigner, can take me to his home. No one can speak with me. They all must drive me out. I am the man—no one else—who laid this curse on myself. I make love to his wife with hands repulsive from her husband's blood. Can't you see that I'm evil? My whole nature, utter filth?

Look, I must be banished. I must never set eyes on my people, never set foot in my homeland, because ... I'll marry my own mother, kill Polybus, my father, who brought me up and gave me birth. If someone said things like these must be the work of a savage god, he'd be speaking the truth. O you pure and majestic gods! Never, never, let the day such things happen arrive for me. Let me never see it. Let me vanish from men's eyes before that doom comes down on me.

---

① Pythian oracle, 指德尔菲的阿波罗神庙

JOCASTA

What you say terrifies us, Lord. But don't lose hope until you hear from the eyewitness.

OEDIPUS

That is the one hope I have left—to wait for this man to come in from the fields.

JOCASTA

When he comes, what do you hope to hear?

OEDIPUS

This: if his story matches yours, I will have escaped disaster.

JOCASTA

What did I say that would make such a difference?

OEDIPUS

He told you Laius was killed by bandits. If he still claims there were several, then I cannot be the killer. One man cannot be many. But if he says: one man, braving the road alone, did it, there's no more doubt. The evidence will drag me down.

JOCASTA

You can be sure that was the way he first told it. How can he take it back? The entire city heard him, not just me. Even if now he changes his story, Lord, he could never prove that Laius' murder happened as the god predicted. Apollo said plainly: my son would kill Laius. That poor doomed child had no chance to kill his father, for he was killed first. After that, no oracle ever made me look right, then left, in fear.

OEDIPUS

You've thought this out well. Still, you must send for that herdsman. Don't neglect this.

JOCASTA

I'll send for him now. But come inside. Would I do anything to displease you?

OEDIPUS and JOCASTA enter the palace.

CHORUS

Let it be my good luck to win praise all my life for respecting the sky-walking laws, born to stride through the light-filled heavens. Olympus alone was their father. No human mind could conceive them. Those laws neither sleep nor forget—a mighty god lives on in them who does not age. A violent will fathers the tyrant, and violence, drunk on wealth and power, does him no good. He scales the heights—until he's thrown down to his doom, where quick feet are no use. But there's another fighting spirit I ask god never to destroy—the kind that makes our city thrive. That god will protect us I will never cease to believe. But if a man speaks and acts with contempt—flouts the law, sneers at the stone gods in their shrines—let a harsh death punish his doomed indulgence. Even as he wins he cheats—he denies himself nothing—his hand reaches for things too sacred to be touched.

When crimes like these, which god hates, are not punished—but honored—what good man will think his own life safe from god's arrows piercing his soul? Why should I dance to this holy song?

Here the CHORUS stops dancing and speaks the next strophe motionless.

If prophecies don't show the way to events all men can see, I will no longer honor the holy place untouchable: Earth's navel at Delphi.

I will not go to Olympia nor the temple at Abai. You, Zeus who hold power, if Zeus lord of all is really who you are, look at what's happening here: prophecies made to Laius fade; men ignore them; Apollo is nowhere glorified with praise. The gods lose force.

JOCASTA enters from the palace carrying a suppliant's branch and some smoldering incense. She approaches the altar of Apollo near the palace door.

150

JOCASTA

Lords of my country, this thought came to me: to visit the gods' shrines with incense and a bough in my hands. Oedipus lets alarms of every kind inflame his mind. He won't let past experience calm his present fears, as a man of sense would. He's at the mercy of everybody's terrifying words. Since he won't listen to me, Apollo—you're the nearest god—

Enter MESSENGER from the countryside.

I come praying for your good will. Look, here is my branch. Cleanse us, cure our sickness. When we see Oedipus distraught, we all shake, as though sailing with a fearful helmsman.

MESSENGER

Can you point out to me, strangers, the house where King Oedipus lives? Better yet, tell me if you know where he is now.

LEADER

That's the house where he lives, stranger. He's inside. This woman is his wife and mother ... of his children.

MESSENGER

I wish her joy, and the family joy that comes when a marriage bears fruit.

JOCASTA

And joy to you, stranger, for those kind words. What have you to tell us? Or to ask?

MESSENGER

Great news, Lady, for you and your mate.

JOCASTA

What news? Who sent you to us?

MESSENGER

I come from Corinth. You'll rejoice at my news, I'm sure—but it may also make you grieve.

JOCASTA

What? How can it possibly do both?

MESSENGER

They're going to make him king. So say the people who live on the isthmus.

JOCASTA

Isn't old Polybus still in power?

MESSENGER

No longer. Death has laid him in the tomb.

JOCASTA

You're saying, old man, Polybus has died?

MESSENGER

Kill me if that's not the truth.

JOCASTA speaks to a maid, who then runs inside.

JOCASTA

Girl, run to your master with the news. You oracles of the gods! Where are you now? The man Oedipus feared he would kill, the man he ran from, that man's dead. Chance killed him. Not Oedipus. Chance!

OEDIPUS enters quickly from the palace.

OEDIPUS

Darling Jocasta, my loving wife, why did you ask me to come out?

JOCASTA

Listen to what this man has to say. See what it does to god's proud oracle.

OEDIPUS

Where's he from? What's his news?

JOCASTA

From Corinth. Your father isn't ... Polybus ... is no more ... he's dead.

OEDIPUS

Say it, old man. I want to hear it from your mouth.

MESSENGER

If plain fact is what you want first, have no doubt he is dead and gone.

OEDIPUS

Was it treason, or did disease bring him down?

MESSENGER

A slight push tips an old man into stillness.

OEDIPUS

Then some sickness killed him?

MESSENGER

That, and the long years he had lived.

OEDIPUS

Oh, yes, wife! Why should we scour Pythian smoke or fear birds shrieking

153

overhead? If signs like these had been telling the truth, I would have killed my father. But he's dead. He's safely in the ground. And here I am, who didn't lift a spear. Or did he die of longing for me? That might have been what my killing him meant. Polybus' death has dragged all those worthless oracles with him to Hades.

JOCASTA

Didn't I tell you that before?

OEDIPUS

You did. But I was still driven by fear.

JOCASTA

Don't let these things worry you anymore.

OEDIPUS

Not worry that I'll share my mother's bed?

JOCASTA

Why should a human being live in fear? Chance rules our lives! Who has any sure knowledge of the future? It's best to take life as it comes. This marriage with your mother—don't fear it. In their dreams, before now, many men have slept with their mothers. Those who believe such things mean nothing will have an easier time in life.

OEDIPUS

A brave speech! I would like to believe it. But how can I if my mother's still living? While she lives, I will live in fear, no matter how persuasive you are.

JOCASTA

Your father's tomb shines a great light.

OEDIPUS

On him, yes! But I fear her. She's alive.

154

MESSENGER

What woman do you fear?

OEDIPUS

I dread that oracle from the god, stranger.

MESSENGER

Would it be wrong for someone else to know it?

OEDIPUS

No, you may hear it. Apollo told me I would become my mother's lover, that I would have my father's blood on these hands. Because of that, I haven't gone near Corinth. So far, I've been very lucky—and yet, there's no greater pleasure than to look our own parents in the eyes!

MESSENGER

Did this oracle drive you into exile?

OEDIPUS

I didn't want to kill my father, old man.

MESSENGER

Then why haven't I put your fears to rest, King? I came here hoping to be useful.

OEDIPUS

I would give anything to be free of fear.

MESSENGER

I confess I came partly for that reason—to be rewarded when you've come back home.

OEDIPUS

I will never live where my parents live.

MESSENGER

My son, you can't possibly know what you're doing.

OEDIPUS

Why is that, old man? In god's name, tell me.

MESSENGER

Is it because of them you won't go home?

OEDIPUS

I am afraid Apollo spoke the truth.

MESSENGER

Afraid you'd do your parents unforgivable harm?

OEDIPUS

Exactly that, old man. I am in constant fear.

MESSENGER

Your fear is groundless. Do you understand?

OEDIPUS

How can it be groundless if I'm their son?

MESSENGER

But Polybus was no relation to you.

OEDIPUS

What? Polybus was not my father?

MESSENGER

No more than I am. Exactly the same.

OEDIPUS

How the same? He fathered me and you didn't.

MESSENGER

He didn't father you any more than I did.

OEDIPUS

Why did he say, then, that I was his son?

MESSENGER

He took you from my hands as a gift.

OEDIPUS

He loved me so much—knowing I came from you?

MESSENGER

He had no children of his own to love.

OEDIPUS

And you? Did you buy me? Or find me somewhere?

MESSENGER

I found you in the wooded hollows of Cithaeron①.

OEDIPUS

Why were you wandering way out there?

MESSENGER

I had charge of the sheep grazing those slopes.

---

① 希腊东南部的西塞隆山

OEDIPUS

A migrant hired to work our flocks?

MESSENGER

I saved your life that day, my son.

OEDIPUS

When you picked me up, what was wrong with me?

MESSENGER

Your ankles know. Let them tell you.

OEDIPUS

Ahh! Why do you bring up that ancient wound?

MESSENGER

Your ankles had been pinned. I set you free.

OEDIPUS

From birth I've carried the shame of those scars.

MESSENGER

That was the luck that named you, Oedipus.

OEDIPUS

Did my mother or my father do this to me? Speak the truth for god's sake.

MESSENGER

I don't know. The man who gave you to me will know.

OEDIPUS

You took me from someone? You didn't chance on me yourself?

MESSENGER

I took you from another shepherd.

OEDIPUS

Who was he? Tell me plainly as you can.

MESSENGER

He was known as someone who worked for Laius.

OEDIPUS

The same Laius who was once king here?

MESSENGER

The same. This man worked as his shepherd.

OEDIPUS

Is he alive? Can I see him?

MESSENGER

Someone from here could answer that better.

OEDIPUS

Does anyone here know what has become of this shepherd? Has anyone seen him in town or in the fields? Speak up now. The time has come to make everything known.

LEADER

I believe he means that same herdsman you've already sent for. Your wife would be the best one to ask.

OEDIPUS

Lady, do you recall the man we sent for? Is that the man he means?

JOCASTA

Why ask about him? Don't listen to him. Ignore his words. Forget he said them.

OEDIPUS

With clues like these in my hands, how can I fail to solve the mystery of my birth?

JOCASTA

For god's sake, if you care about your life, give up your search. Let my pain be enough!

OEDIPUS

You'll be fine! What if my mother was born from slaves—from three generations of slaves—how could that make you lowborn?

JOCASTA

Listen to me: I beg you. Don't do this.

OEDIPUS

I cannot listen. I must have the truth.

JOCASTA

I'm thinking only of what's best for you.

OEDIPUS

What's best for me exasperates me now.

JOCASTA

You poor child! Never find out who you are.

OEDIPUS

Someone, bring me the herdsman. Let that woman glory in her precious birth.

JOCASTA

Oh you poor doomed child! That is the only name I can call you now. None other, forever!

JOCASTA runs into the palace.

LEADER

Why has she left like that, Oedipus, driven off by a savage grief? I'm afraid something horrendous will break this silence.

OEDIPUS

Let it burst! My seed may well be common! Even so, I still must know who I am. The meanness of my birth may shame her womanly pride. But since, in my own eyes, I am the child of Luck—she is the source of my well-being—never will I be dishonored. Luck is the mother who raised me. The months are my brothers, who've seen me through the low times in my life and the high ones. Those are the powers that made me. I could never betray them now—by calling off the search for the secret of my birth!

CHORUS

By the gods of Olympus, if I have a prophet's range of eye and mind—tomorrow's moonlight will shine on you, Cithaeron.

Oedipus will honor you—his native mountain, his nurse, his mother. Nothing will keep us from dancing then, mountain joyful to our king! We call out to Phoebus Apollo: be the cause of our joy!

CHORUS turns toward OEDIPUS.

My son, who was your mother? Which nymph bore you to Pan①, the mountain rover?

---

① 潘神（Pan），半人半羊的山林和畜牧之神，多数传说中他是赫尔墨斯（Hermes）之子。也有传说他是宙斯之子

Was it Apollo's bride to whom you were born in the grassy highlands? Or did Hermes, Lord of Kyllene, or Bacchus of the mountain peaks, take you—a sudden joy—from nymphs of Helikon,① whose games he often shares?

OEDIPUS

Old men, if it's possible to recognize a man I've never met, I think I see the herdsman we've been waiting for. Our fellow would be old, like the stranger approaching. Those leading him are my own men. But I expect you'll know him better. Some of you will know him by sight.

Enter HERDSMAN, led by OEDIPUS' Attendants.

LEADER

I do know him. He is from Laius' house, a trustworthy shepherd if he ever had one.

OEDIPUS

Corinthian②, I'll ask you to speak first: is this the man you mean?

MESSENGER

You're looking at him.

OEDIPUS

Now you, old man. Look at me. Answer every question I ask you. Did you once come from Laius' house?

HERDSMAN

I did. I wasn't a bought slave. I was born and raised in their house.

---

① 也有一种传说，潘神（Pan）是酒神（Bacchus）与赫利孔山（Helikon）的仙女之子。在这里将俄狄浦斯的身世之迷类比成潘神的身世之迷

② 指送信人（Messenger）

162

OEDIPUS

What was your job? How did you spend your time?

HERDSMAN

My life I have spent tending sheep.

OEDIPUS

In what region did you normally work?

HERDSMAN

Mainly Cithaeron, and the country thereabouts.

OEDIPUS gestures toward the MESSENGER.

OEDIPUS

That man. Do you recall ever seeing him?

HERDSMAN

Recall how? Doing what? Which man?

OEDIPUS goes to the MESSENGER and puts his hand on him.

OEDIPUS

This man right here. Have you ever seen him before?

HERDSMAN

Not that I recognize—not right away.

MESSENGER

It's no wonder, master. His memory's faded, but I'll revive it for him. I'm sure he knows me. We worked the pastures on Cithaeron together—he with his two flocks, me with one—for three whole grazing seasons, from early spring until Arcturos rose. When the weather turned cold I'd drive my flocks home to their winter pens. He'd drive his away to Laius' sheepfolds. Do I describe what happened, old friend? Or don't I?

HERDSMAN

That's the truth, but it was so long ago.

MESSENGER

Do you remember giving me a boy I was to raise as my own son?

HERDSMAN

What? Why ask me that?

MESSENGER

There, my friend, is the man who was that boy.

The MESSENGER nods toward OEDIPUS.

HERDSMAN

Damn you! Shut up and say nothing.

OEDIPUS

Don't attack him for speaking, old man. Your words beg to be punished more than his.

HERDSMAN

Tell me, royal master, what've I done wrong?

OEDIPUS

You didn't answer him about the boy.

HERDSMAN

He's trying to make something out of nothing.

164

OEDIPUS

Speak of your own free will. Or under torture.

HERDSMAN

Dear god! I'm an old man. Don't hurt me.

OEDIPUS

One of you, bind his arms behind his back. Attendants approach the HERDSMAN and start to seize his arms.

HERDSMAN

Why this, you doomed man? What else must you know?

OEDIPUS

Did you give him the child, as he claims you did?

HERDSMAN

I did. I wish that day I had died.

OEDIPUS

You will die if you don't speak the truth.

HERDSMAN

Answering you is what will get me killed.

OEDIPUS

I think this man is deliberately stalling.

HERDSMAN

No! I've said it once. I gave him the boy.

OEDIPUS

Was the boy from your house? Or someone else's?

HERDSMAN

Not from my house. Someone gave him to me.

OEDIPUS

The person! Name him! From what house?

HERDSMAN

Don't ask me that, master. For god's sake, don't.

OEDIPUS

If I have to ask one more time, you'll die.

HERDSMAN

He was a child from the house of Laius.

OEDIPUS

A slave? Or a child born of Laius' blood?

HERDSMAN

Help me! I am about to speak terrible words.

OEDIPUS

And I to hear them. But hear them I must!

HERDSMAN

The child was said to be Laius' own son. Your lady in the house would know that best.

OEDIPUS

She gave the child to you?

HERDSMAN

She gave him, King.

OEDIPUS

To do what?

HERDSMAN

I was to let it die.

OEDIPUS

Kill her own child?

HERDSMAN

She feared prophecies.

OEDIPUS

What prophecies?

HERDSMAN

That this child would kill his father.

OEDIPUS

Why, then, did you give him to this old man?

HERDSMAN

Out of pity, master. I hoped this man would take him back to his own land. But that man saved him for this—the worst grief of all. If the child he speaks of is you, master, now you know: your birth has doomed you.

OEDIPUS

All! All! It has all happened! It was all true. O light! Let this be the last time I look on you. You see now who I am—the child who must not be born! I loved where I must not love! I killed where I must not kill!

OEDIPUS runs into the palace.

CHORUS

Men and women who live and die, I set no value on your lives. Which one of you ever, reaching for blessedness that lasts, finds more than what seems blest? You live in that seeming a while, then it vanishes.

Your fate teaches me this, Oedipus, yours, you suffering man, the story god spoke through you: never call any man fortunate. O Zeus, no man drew a bow like this man! He shot his arrow home, winning power, pleasure, wealth. He killed the virgin Sphinx, who sang the god's dark oracles; her claws were hooked and sharp.

He fought off death in our land; he towered against its threat. Since those times I've called you my king, honoring you mightily, my Oedipus, who wielded the great might of Thebes. But now—nobody's story has the sorrow of yours. O my so famous Oedipus—the same great harbor welcomed you first as child, then as father tumbling upon your bridal bed. How could the furrows your father plowed, doomed man, how could they suffer so long in silence? Time, who sees all, caught you living a life you never willed. Time damns this marriage that is no marriage, where the fathered child fathered children himself. O son of Laius, I wish I'd never seen you! I fill my lungs, I sing with all my power the plain truth in my heart. Once you gave me new breath, O my Oedipus! —but now you close my eyes in darkness.

Enter SERVANT from the palace.

SERVANT

You've always been our land's most honored men. If you still have a born Theban's love for the House of Labdacus, you'll be crushed by what you're about to see and hear. No rivers could wash this house clean— not the Danube①, not the Rion—it hides so much evil that now is coming to light. What happened here was not involuntary evil. It was willed. The griefs that punish us the most are those we've chosen for ourselves.

LEADER

We already knew more than enough to make us grieve. Do you have more to tell?

---

① 多瑙河

SERVANT

It is the briefest news to say or hear. Our royal lady Jocasta is dead.

LEADER

That pitiable woman. How did she die?

SERVANT

She killed herself. You will be spared the worst—since you weren't there to see it. But you will hear, exactly as I can recall it, what that wretched woman suffered. She came raging through the courtyard straight for her marriage bed, the fists of both her hands clenched in her hair. Once in, she slammed the doors shut and called out to Laius, so long dead. She remembered his living sperm① of long ago, who killed Laius, while she lived on to breed with her son more ruined children. She grieved for the bed she had loved in, giving birth to all those doubled lives—husband fathered by husband, children sired by her child. From this point on I don't know how she died— Oedipus burst in shouting, distracting us from her misery. We looked on, stunned, as he plowed through us, raging, asking us for a spear, asking for the wife who was no wife but the same furrowed twice-mothering Earth from whom he and his children sprang. He was frantic, yet some god's hand drove him toward his wife—none of us near him did. As though someone were guiding him, he lunged, with a savage yell, at the double doors, wrenching the bolts from their sockets. He burst into the room. We saw her there: the woman above us, hanging by the neck, swaying there in a noose of tangled cords. He saw. And bellowing in anguish he reached up, loosening the noose that held her. With the poor lifeless woman laid out on the ground this, then, was the terror we saw: he pulled the long pins of hammered gold clasping her gown, held them up, and punched them into his eyes, back through the sockets. He was screaming: "Eyes, now you will not, no, never see the evil I suffered, the evil I caused. You will see blackness—where once were lives you should never have lived to see, yearned-for faces you so long failed to know." While he howled out these tortured words—not once, but many times—his raised hands kept beating his eyes. The blood kept coming,

---

① 指俄狄浦斯

drenching his beard and cheeks. Not a few wet drops, but a black storm of bloody hail lashing his face. What this man and this woman did broke so much evil loose! That evil joins the whole of both their lives in grief. The happiness they once knew was real, but now that happiness is in ruins—wailing, death, disgrace. Whatever misery we have a name for, is here.

LEADER
Has his grief eased at all?

SERVANT
He shouts for someone to open the door bolts: "Show this city its father-killer," he cries, "Show it its mother …" He said the word. I can't. He wants to banish himself from the land, not doom this house any longer by living here, under his own curse. He's so weak, though, he needs to be helped. No one could stand up under a sickness like his. Look! The door bolts are sliding open. You will witness a vision of such suffering even those it revolts will pity.

OEDIPUS emerges from the slowly opening palace doors. He is blinded, with blood on his face and clothes, but the effect should arouse more awe and pity than shock. He moves with the aid of an Attendant.

LEADER
Your pain is terrible to see, pure, helpless anguish, more moving than anything my eyes have ever touched. O man of pain, where did your madness come from? What god would go to such inhuman lengths to savage your defenseless life? (moans) I cannot look at you—though there's so much to ask you, so much to learn, so much that holds my eyes—so strong are the shivers of awe you send through me.

OEDIPUS
Ahhh! My life screams in pain. Where is my misery taking me? How far does my voice fly, fluttering out there on the wind? O god, how far have you thrown me?

170

LEADER

To a hard place. Hard to watch, hard to hear.

OEDIPUS

Darkness buries me in her hate, takes me in her black hold. Unspeakable blackness. It can't be fought off, it keeps coming, wafting evil all over me. Ahhh!

Those goads piercing my eyes, those crimes stabbing my mind, strike through me—one deep wound.

LEADER

It is no wonder you feel nothing but pain now, both in your mind and in your flesh.

OEDIPUS

Ah, friend, you're still here, faithful to the blind man. I know you are near me. Even in my darkness I know your voice.

LEADER

You terrify us. How could you put out your eyes? What god drove you to it?

OEDIPUS

It was Apollo who did this. He made evil, consummate evil, out of my life. But the hand that struck these eyes was my hand. I in my wretchedness struck me, no one else did. What good was left for my eyes to see? Nothing in this world could I see now with a glad heart.

LEADER

That is so.

OEDIPUS

Whom could I look at? Or love? Whose greeting could I answer with fondness, friends? Take me quickly from this place. I am the most ruined, the most cursed, the most god-hated man who ever lived.

LEADER

You're broken by what happened, broken by what's happening in your own mind. I wish I had never even known you.

OEDIPUS

May he die, the man who found me in the pasture, who unshackled my feet, who saved me from that death for a worse life, a life I cannot thank him for. Had I died then, I would have caused no great grief to my people and myself.

LEADER

I wish he had let you die.

OEDIPUS

I wouldn't have come home to kill my father, no one could call me lover of her from whose body I came. I have no god now. I'm son to a fouled mother. I fathered children in the bed where my father once gave me deadly life. If ever an evil rules all other evils it is my evil, the life god gave to Oedipus.

LEADER

I wish I could say you acted wisely. You would have been better off dead than blind.

OEDIPUS

There was no better way than mine. No more advice! If I had eyes, how could they bear to look at my father in Hades? Or at my devastated mother? Not even hanging could right the wrongs I did them both. You think I'd find the sight of my children delightful, born to the life they must live? Never, ever, delightful to my eyes! Nor this town, its wall, gates, and towers—nor the sacred images of our gods. I severed myself from these joys when I banished the vile killer—myself! —totally wretched now, though I was raised more splendidly than any Theban. But now the gods have proven me defiled, and of Laius' own blood.

And once I've brought such disgrace on myself, how could I look calmly on my

172

people? I could not! If I could deafen my ears I would. I'd deaden my whole body, go blind and deaf to shut those evils out. The silence in my mind would be sweet. O Cithaeron, why did you take me in? Or once you had seized me, why didn't you kill me then, leaving no trace of my birth? O Polybus and Corinth, and that palace they called the ancient home of my fathers! I was their glorious boy growing up, but under that fair skin festered a hideous disease. My vile self now shows its vile birth. You, three roads, and you, darkest ravine, you, grove of oaks, you, narrow place where three paths drank blood from my hands, my fathering blood pouring into you: Do you remember what I did while you watched?

And when I came here, what I did then? O marriages! You marriages! You created us, we sprang to life, then from that same seed you burst fathers, brothers, sons, kinsmen shedding kinsmen's blood, brides and mothers and wives—the most loathsome atrocities that strike mankind. I must not name what should not be. If you love the gods, hide me out there, kill me, heave me into the sea, anywhere you can't see me. Come, take me. Don't shy away. Touch this human derelict. Don't fear me, trust me. No other man, only myself, can be afflicted with my sorrows.

LEADER

Here's Creon. He's come when you need him, to take action or to give you advice. He is the only ruler we have left to guard Thebes in your place.

OEDIPUS

Can I say anything he'll listen to? Why would he believe me? I wronged him so deeply. I proved myself so false to him.

CREON enters.

CREON

I haven't come to mock you, Oedipus. I won't dwell on the wrongs you did me.

CREON speaks to the Attendants.

Men, even if you've no respect for a fellow human being, show some for the life-

173

giving flame of the Sun god: don't leave this stark defilement out here. The Earth, the holy rain, the light, can't bear it. Quickly, take him back to the palace. If these sorrows are shared only among the family, that will spare us further impiety.

OEDIPUS

Thank god! I feared much worse from you. Since you've shown me, a most vile man, such noble kindness, I have one request. For your sake, not for mine.

CREON

What is it? Why do you ask me like that?

OEDIPUS

Expel me quickly to some place where no living person will find me.

CREON

I would surely have done that. But first I need to know what the god wants me to do.

OEDIPUS

He's given his command already. I killed my father. I am unholy. I must die.

CREON

So the god said. But given the crisis we're in, we had better be absolutely sure before we act.

OEDIPUS

You'd ask about a broken man like me?

CREON

Surely, by now, you're willing to trust god.

OEDIPUS

I am. But now I must ask for something within your power. I beg you! Bury her—

she's lying inside—as you think proper. Give her the rites due your kinswoman. As for me, don't condemn my father's city to house me while I'm still alive. Let me live out my life on Cithaeron, the very mountain—the one I've made famous—that my father and mother chose for my tomb.

Let me die there, as my parents decreed. And yet, I know this much: no sickness can kill me. Nothing can. I was saved from that death to face an extraordinary evil. Let my fate take me now, where it will. My children, Creon. My sons. They're grown now. They won't need your help. They'll find a way to live anywhere. But my poor wretched girls, who never ate anywhere but at my table, they've never lived apart from me. I fed them with my own hands. Care for them. If you're willing, let me touch them now, let me give in to my grief. Grant it, Creon, from your great heart. If I could touch them, I would imagine them as my eyes once saw them.

The gentle sobbing of Oedipus' two daughters is heard offstage. Soon two small girls enter.

What's this? O gods, are these my children sobbing? Has Creon pitied me? Given me my own dear children? Has he?

CREON

I have. I brought them to you because I knew how much joy, as always, you would take in them.

OEDIPUS

Bless this kindness of yours. Bless your luck. May the gods guard you better than they did me. Children, where are you? Come to me. These are your brother's hands, hands of the man who created you, hands that caused my once bright eyes to go dark. He, children, saw nothing, knew nothing. He fathered you where his own life began, where his own seed grew. Though I can't see you, I can weep for you …

—OEDIPUS takes his daughters in his arms—

when I think how bitter your lives will be. I know the life that men will make you live. What public gatherings, what festivals could you attend? None! You would be sent home in tears, without your share of holy joy. When the time comes to marry, my daughters, what man will risk the revulsion—the infamy!—that will wound you just as it wounded your parents? What evil is missing? Your father killed his father. He had children with the mother who bore him, fathered you at the source of his own life. Those are the insults you will face. Who will marry you? No one, my children. You will grow old unmarried, living a dried-up childless life. Creon, you're all the father they have now. The parents who conceived them are both lost. Keep these two girls from rootless wandering—unmarried and helpless. They are your kin. Don't bring them down to what I am. Pity them. They are so young, and but for you, alone. Touch my hand, kind man, make that touch your promise.

CREON touches him.

Children, had you been old enough to comprehend, I would have taught you more. Now, all I can do is ask you to pray that you live only where you're welcomed, that your lives be happier than mine was—the father from whose seed you were born.

CREON
Enough grief. Go inside now.

OEDIPUS
Bitter words that I must obey.

CREON
Time runs out on all things.

OEDIPUS
Grant my request before I go.

CREON
Speak.

OEDIPUS
Banish me from my homeland.

CREON

Ask god to do that, not me.

OEDIPUS

I am the man the gods hate most.

CREON

Then you will have your wish.

OEDIPUS

You consent?

CREON

I never promise if I can't be sure.

OEDIPUS

Then lead me inside.

CREON

Come. Let go of your children now.

OEDIPUS

Don't take them from me.

CREON

Give up your power, too. You won the power once, but you couldn't keep it to the end of your life.

CREON leads OEDIPUS into the palace.

LEADER

Thebans, that man is the same Oedipus whose great mind solved the famous riddle. He was a most powerful man. Which of us seeing his glory, his prestige, did not wish his luck could be ours? Now look at what wreckage the seas of savage trouble have made of his life. To know the truth of a man, wait till you see his life end. On that day, look at him. Don't claim any man is god's friend until he has passed through life and crossed the border into death—never having been god's victim.

ALL leave.

Questions for discussion:

1. Why did Oedipus suspect Creon of plotting for the throne? How does Creon explain to Oedipus that he has no desire for the throne?

2. Queen Jocasta is one of the typical female representatives in western tragedies. When does she discover the truth in the play?

3. The play emphasizes the insignificance and powerlessness of individuals in the process of changing their fate. It can be seen from the play that although queen Jucasta and Oedipus tried their best to change their fate and prevent the tragedy from happening, the terrible thing still happened. What is the relationship between fatalism and tragedy? To what extent do personality factors, life attitudes, accidents and so on play a role in shaping personal unhappiness?

第七篇　The Republic

Plato

(Translator: Benjamin Jowett)

Book II

Socrates vs. Glaucon

With these words I was thinking that I had made an end of the discussion; but the end, in truth, proved to be only a beginning. For Glaucon①, who is always the most pugnacious of men, was dissatisfied at Thrasymachus'② retirement; he wanted to have the battle out.

So he said to me:

Socrates, do you wish really to persuade us, or only to seem to have persuaded us, that to be just is always better than to be unjust?

I should wish really to persuade you, I replied, if I could.

Then you certainly have not succeeded. Let me ask you now: —How would you arrange goods—are there not some which we welcome for their own sakes, and independently of their consequences, as, for example, harmless pleasures and enjoyments, which delight us at the time, although nothing follows from them?

---

① 格劳孔（Glaucon），雅典贵族，苏格拉底的主要论战对象，他认为"正义"不过是所谓的美德，它是一种社会建构（social construction），一旦维护"自己是'正义'的"声誉的想法不存在时，譬如在没有人会知道你的行为时，"正义"也就不存在了

② 特拉西马库斯（Thrasymachus），雅典贵族。他认为"正义"无非符合强者的利益要求，第一卷结束时，他已退出论战

I agree in thinking that there is such a class, I replied.

Is there not also a second class of goods, such as knowledge, sight, health, which are desirable not only in themselves, but also for their results?

Certainly, I said.

And would you not recognize a third class, such as gymnastic, and the care of the sick, and the physician's art; also the various ways of money-making—these do us good but we regard them as disagreeable; and no one would choose them for their own sakes, but only for the sake of some reward or result which flows from them?

There is, I said, this third class also. But why do you ask?

Because I want to know in which of the three classes you would place justice?

In the highest class, I replied, —among those goods which he who would be happy desires both for their own sake and for the sake of their results.①

Then the many are of another mind; they think that justice is to be reckoned in the troublesome class, among goods which are to be pursued for the sake of rewards and of reputation, but in themselves are disagreeable and rather to be avoided.

I know, I said, that this is their manner of thinking, and that this was the thesis which Thrasymachus was maintaining just now, when he censured justice and praised injustice. But I am too stupid to be convinced by him.

I wish, he said, that you would hear me as well as him, and then I shall see whether you and I agree. For Thrasymachus seems to me, like a snake, to have been charmed by your voice sooner than he ought to have been; but to my mind the nature of justice and injustice have not yet been made clear. Setting aside their rewards and results, I want to know what they are in themselves, and how they inwardly work in the soul. If you, please, then, I will revive the argument of Thrasymachus. And first I will speak of the nature and origin of justice according to the common view of them. Secondly, I will show that all men who practise justice do so against their will, of necessity, but not as a good. And thirdly, I will argue that there is reason in this view, for the life of the unjust is after all better far than the life of the just—if what they say is true, Socrates, since I myself am not of their opinion. But still I acknowledge that I am

---

① 如果将事物分为三种，一种是其本身就给人好处，让人愉悦的；第二种是其本身没法让人愉悦，而其结果和回报会给人好处的；第三种是其本身和结果都会给人好处的。苏格拉底认为正义是属于第三种，而格劳孔认为正义是属于第二种

perplexed when I hear the voices of Thrasymachus and myriads of others dinning in my ears; and, on the other hand, I have never yet heard the superiority of justice to injustice maintained by any one in a satisfactory way. I want to hear justice praised in respect of itself; then I shall be satisfied, and you are the person from whom I think that I am most likely to hear this; and therefore I will praise the unjust life to the utmost of my power, and my manner of speaking will indicate the manner in which I desire to hear you too praising justice and censuring injustice. Will you say whether you approve of my proposal?

Indeed I do; nor can I imagine any theme about which a man of sense would oftener wish to converse.

I am delighted, he replied, to hear you say so, and shall begin by speaking, as I proposed, of the nature and origin of justice.

Glaucon

They say that to do injustice is, by nature, good; to suffer injustice, evil; but that the evil is greater than the good. And so when men have both done and suffered injustice and have had experience of both, not being able to avoid the one and obtain the other, they think that they had better agree among themselves to have neither; hence there arise laws and mutual covenants; and that which is ordained by law is termed by them lawful and just. This they affirm to be the origin and nature of justice; —it is a mean or compromise, between the best of all, which is to do injustice and not be punished, and the worst of all, which is to suffer injustice without the power of retaliation; and justice, being at a middle point between the two, is tolerated not as a good, but as the lesser evil, and honoured by reason of the inability of men to do injustice. For no man who is worthy to be called a man would ever submit to such an agreement if he were able to resist; he would be mad if he did. Such is the received account, Socrates, of the nature and origin of justice.

Now that those who practise justice do so involuntarily and because they have not the power to be unjust will best appear if we imagine something of this kind: having given both to the just and the unjust power to do what they will, let us watch and see whither desire will lead them; then we shall discover in the very act the just and unjust man to be proceeding along the same road, following their interest, which all natures deem to be their good, and are only diverted into the path of justice by the force of law.

181

The liberty which we are supposing may be most completely given to them in the form of such a power as is said to have been possessed by Gyges①, the ancestor of Croesus② the Lydian. According to the tradition, Gyges was a shepherd in the service of the king of Lydia; there was a great storm, and an earthquake made an opening in the earth at the place where he was feeding his flock. Amazed at the sight, he descended into the opening, where, among other marvels, he beheld a hollow brazen horse, having doors, at which he stooping and looking in saw a dead body of stature, as appeared to him, more than human, and having nothing on but a gold ring; this he took from the finger of the dead and reascended. Now the shepherds met together, according to custom, that they might send their monthly report about the flocks to the king; into their assembly he came having the ring on his finger, and as he was sitting among them he chanced to turn the collet of the ring inside his hand, when instantly he became invisible to the rest of the company and they began to speak of him as if he were no longer present. He was astonished at this, and again touching the ring he turned the collet outwards and reappeared; he made several trials of the ring, and always with the same result—when he turned the collet inwards he became invisible, when outwards he reappeared. Whereupon he contrived to be chosen one of the messengers who were sent to the court; whereas soon as he arrived he seduced the queen, and with her help conspired against the king and slew him, and took the kingdom. Suppose now that there were two such magic rings, and the just put on one of them and the unjust the other; no man can be imagined to be of such an iron nature that he would stand fast in justice. No man would keep his hands off what was not his own when he could safely take what he liked out of the market, or go into houses and lie with any one at his pleasure, or kill or release from prison whom he would, and in all respects be like a God among men. Then the actions of the just would be as the actions of the unjust; they would both come at last to the same point. And this we may truly affirm to be a great proof that a man is just, not willingly or because he thinks that justice is any good to him individually, but of necessity, for wherever anyone thinks that he can safely be unjust, there he is unjust. For all men believe in their hearts that injustice is far more profitable to the individual

---

① 盖吉斯（Gyges），古老传说中吕底亚（Lydia）的牧羊人，因为有了隐身戒指而篡位
② 克罗伊索斯（Croesus），吕底亚（Lydia）的国王，盖吉斯的后人。曾认为自己是世界上最幸福的人，然而雅典智者索伦（Solon）告诫他：在离开这个世界之前谁也无法肯定自己是最幸福的。国破后他成为波斯居鲁士大帝（Cyrus the Great）的囚犯

than justice, and he who argues as I have been supposing, will say that they are right. If you could imagine any one obtaining this power of becoming invisible, and never doing any wrong or touching what was another's, he would be thought by the lookers-on① to be a most wretched idiot, although they would praise him to one another's faces, and keep up appearances with one another from a fear that they too might suffer injustice. Enough of this.

Now, if we are to form a real judgment of the life of the just and unjust, we must isolate them; there is no other way; and how is the isolation to be effected? I answer: Let the unjust man be entirely unjust, and the just man entirely just; nothing is to be taken away from either of them, and both are to be perfectly furnished for the work of their respective lives. First, let the unjust be like other distinguished masters of craft; like the skillful pilot or physician, who knows intuitively his own powers and keeps within their limits, and who, if he fails at any point, is able to recover himself. So let the unjust make his unjust attempts in the right way, and lie hidden if he means to be great in his injustice (he who is found out is nobody): for the highest reach of injustice is, to be deemed just when you are not. Therefore I say that in the perfectly unjust man we must assume the most perfect injustice; there is to be no deduction, but we must allow him, while doing the most unjust acts, to have acquired the greatest reputation for justice. If he has taken a false step he must be able to recover himself; he must be one who can speak with effect, if any of his deeds come to light, and who can force his way where force is required by his courage and strength, and command of money and friends. And at his side let us place the just man in his nobleness and simplicity, wishing, as Aeschylus② says, to be and not to seem good. There must be no seeming, for if he seem to be just he will be honoured and rewarded, and then we shall not know whether he is just for the sake of justice or for the sake of honours and rewards; therefore, let him be clothed in justice only, and have no other covering; and he must be imagined in a state of life the opposite of the former. Let him be the best of men, and let him be thought the worst; then he will have been put to the proof; and we shall see whether he will be affected by the fear of infamy and its consequences. And let him continue thus to the hour of death; being just and seeming to be unjust. When both

---

① 旁观者，looker-on 的复数形式
② 埃斯库罗斯（Aeschylus）是古希腊三大悲剧作家之一，代表作《被缚的普罗米修斯》

have reached the uttermost extreme, the one of justice and the other of injustice, let judgment be given which of them is the happier of the two.

Socrates vs. Glaucon

Heavens! my dear Glaucon, I said, how energetically you polish them up for the decision, first one and then the other, as if they were two statues.

I do my best, he said. And now that we know what they are like there is no difficulty in tracing out the sort of life which awaits either of them. This I will proceed to describe; but as you may think the description a little too coarse, I ask you to suppose, Socrates, that the words which follow are not mine. —Let me put them into the mouths of the eulogists of injustice: They will tell you that the just man who is thought unjust will be scourged, racked, bound—will have his eyes burnt out; and, at last, after suffering every kind of evil, he will be impaled: Then he will understand that he ought to seem only, and not to be, just; the words of Aeschylus may be more truly spoken of the unjust than of the just. For the unjust is pursuing a reality; he does not live with a view to appearances—he wants to be really unjust and not to seem only: — "His mind has a soil deep and fertile, Out of which spring his prudent counsels."

In the first place, he is thought just, and therefore bears rule in the city; he can marry whom he will, and give in marriage to whom he will; also he can trade and deal where he likes, and always to his own advantage, because he has no misgivings① about injustice; and at every contest, whether in public or private, he gets the better of his antagonists, and gains at their expense, and is rich, and out of his gains he can benefit his friends, and harm his enemies; moreover, he can offer sacrifices, and dedicate gifts to the gods abundantly and magnificently, and can honour the gods or any man whom he wants to honour in a far better style than the just, and therefore he is likely to be dearer than they are to the gods. And thus, Socrates, gods and men are said to unite in making the life of the unjust better than the life of the just.

Adeimantus vs. Socrates

I was going to say something in answer to Glaucon, when Adeimantus, his brother, interposed: Socrates, he said, you do not suppose that there is nothing more

---

① Misgivings, 担忧, 害怕

to be urged?

Why, what else is there? I answered.

The strongest point of all has not been even mentioned, he replied.

Well, then, according to the proverb, 'Let brother help brother' —if he fails in any part do you assist him; although I must confess that Glaucon has already said quite enough to lay me in the dust, and take from me the power of helping justice.

Adeimantus

Nonsense, he replied. But let me add something more: There is another side to Glaucon's argument about the praise and censure of justice and injustice, which is equally required in order to bring out what I believe to be his meaning. Parents and tutors are always telling their sons and their wards that they are to be just; but why? not for the sake of justice, but for the sake of character and reputation; in the hope of obtaining for him who is reputed just some of those offices, marriages, and the like which Glaucon has enumerated among the advantages accruing to the unjust from the reputation of justice. More, however, is made of appearances by this class of persons than by the others; for they throw in the good opinion of the gods, and will tell you of a shower of benefits which the heavens, as they say, rain upon the pious; and this accords with the testimony of the noble Hesiod[①] and Homer[②], the first of whom says, that the gods make the oaks of the just—

"To bear acorns at their summit, and bees in the middle;

And the sheep are bowed down with the weight of their fleeces,"

and many other blessings of a like kind are provided for them. And Homer has a very similar strain; for he speaks of one whose fame is—

"As the fame of some blameless king who, like a god, Maintains justice; to whom the black earth brings forth Wheat and barley, whose trees are bowed with fruit, And his sheep never fail to bear, and the sea gives him fish."

Still grander are the gifts of heaven which Musaeus[③] and his son vouchsafe to the just; they take them down into the world below, where they have the saints lying on

---

① 赫西俄德，公元前 8 世纪希腊诗人
② 荷马，公元前 9 世纪希腊诗人
③ 缪塞俄斯（Musaeus）是宗教诗词的创始人，传说他是俄耳甫斯（Orpheus）的弟子

couches at a feast, everlastingly drunk, crowned with garlands; their idea seems to be that an immortality of drunkenness is the highest meed① of virtue. Some extend their rewards yet further; the posterity, as they say, of the faithful and just shall survive to the third and fourth generation. This is the style in which they praise justice. But about the wicked there is another strain; they bury them in a slough in Hades, and make them carry water in a sieve; also while they are yet living they bring them to infamy, and inflict upon them the punishments which Glaucon described as the portion of the just who are reputed to be unjust; nothing else does their invention supply. Such is their manner of praising the one and censuring the other.

Once more, Socrates, I will ask you to consider another way of speaking about justice and injustice, which is not confined to the poets, but is found in prose writers. The universal voice of mankind is always declaring that justice and virtue are honourable, but grievous and toilsome; and that the pleasures of vice and injustice are easy of attainment, and are only censured by law and opinion. They say also that honesty is for the most part less profitable than dishonesty; and they are quite ready to call wicked men happy, and to honour them both in public and private when they are rich or in any other way influential, while they despise and overlook those who may be weak and poor, even though acknowledging them to be better than the others. But most extraordinary of all is their mode of speaking about virtue and the gods: they say that the gods apportion calamity and misery to many good men, and good and happiness to the wicked. And mendicant prophets go to rich men's doors and persuade them that they have a power committed to them by the gods of making an atonement for a man's own or his ancestor's sins by sacrifices or charms, with rejoicings and feasts; and they promise to harm an enemy, whether just or unjust, at a small cost; with magic arts and incantations binding heaven, as they say, to execute their will. And the poets are the authorities to whom they appeal, now smoothing the path of vice with the words of Hesiod; — "Vice may be had in abundance without trouble; the way is smooth and her dwelling-place is near. But before virtue the gods have set toil," and a tedious and uphill road: then citing Homer as a witness that the gods may be influenced by men; for he also says: — "The gods, too, may be turned from their purpose; and men pray to them and avert their wrath by sacrifices and soothing entreaties, and by libations and

---

① Meed 即 reward

the odour of fat, when they have sinned and transgressed."

And they produce a host of books written by Musaeus and Orpheus①, who were children of the Moon and the Muses—that is what they say—according to which they perform their ritual, and persuade not only individuals, but whole cities, that expiations and atonements for sin may be made by sacrifices and amusements which fill a vacant hour, and are equally at the service of the living and the dead; the latter sort they call mysteries, and they redeem us from the pains of hell, but if we neglect them no one knows what awaits us.

He proceeded: And now when the young hear all this said about virtue and vice, and the way in which gods and men regard them, how are their minds likely to be affected, my dear Socrates, —those of them, I mean, who are quick-witted, and, like bees on the wing, light on every flower, and from all that they hear are prone to draw conclusions as to what manner of persons they should be and in what way they should walk if they would make the best of life? Probably the youth will say to himself in the words of Pindar②—

"Can I by justice or by crooked ways of deceit ascend a loftier tower which may be a fortress to me all my days?"

For what men say is that, if I am really just and am not also thought just profit there is none, but the pain and loss on the other hand are unmistakeable. But if, though unjust, I acquire the reputation of justice, a heavenly life is promised to me. Since then, as philosophers prove, appearance tyrannizes over truth and is lord of happiness, to appearance I must devote myself. I will describe around me a picture and shadow of virtue to be the vestibule and exterior of my house; behind I will trail the subtle and crafty fox, as Archilochus③, greatest of sages, recommends. But I hear someone exclaiming that the concealment of wickedness is often difficult; to which I answer, Nothing great is easy. Nevertheless, the argument indicates this, if we would be happy, to be the path along which we should proceed. With a view to concealment we will establish secret brotherhoods and political clubs. And there are professors of rhetoric who teach the art of persuading courts and assemblies; and so, partly by

---

① 俄耳甫斯（Orpheus），太阳神阿波罗（Apollo）与司管文艺的缪斯女神卡利俄珀（Calliope）之子，善竖琴、唱歌
② 品达（Pindar），即品达罗斯（Pindarus），公元前5世纪希腊抒情诗人
③ 阿基罗科斯（Archilochus），公元前7世纪希腊抒情诗人

persuasion and partly by force, I shall make unlawful gains and not be punished. Still I hear a voice saying that the gods cannot be deceived, neither can they be compelled. But what if there are no gods? or, suppose them to have no care of human things—why in either case should we mind about concealment? And even if there are gods, and they do care about us, yet we know of them only from tradition and the genealogies of the poets; and these are the very persons who say that they may be influenced and turned by 'sacrifices and soothing entreaties and by offerings. "Let us be consistent then, and believe both or neither. If the poets speak truly, why then we had better be unjust, and offer of the fruits of injustice; for if we are just, although we may escape the vengeance of heaven, we shall lose the gains of injustice; but, if we are unjust, we shall keep the gains, and by our sinning and praying, and praying and sinning, the gods will be propitiated, and we shall not be punished.' But there is a world below in which either we or our posterity will suffer for our unjust deeds." Yes, my friend, will be the reflection, but there are mysteries and atoning deities, and these have great power. That is what mighty cities declare; and the children of the gods, who were their poets and prophets, bear a like testimony. On what principle, then, shall we any longer choose justice rather than the worst injustice? when, if we only unite the latter with a deceitful regard to appearances, we shall fare to our mind both with gods and men, in life and after death, as the most numerous and the highest authorities tell us. Knowing all this, Socrates, how can a man who has any superiority of mind or person or rank or wealth, be willing to honour justice; or indeed to refrain from laughing when he hears justice praised? And even if there should be someone who is able to disprove the truth of my words, and who is satisfied that justice is best, still he is not angry with the unjust, but is very ready to forgive them, because he also knows that men are not just of their own free will; unless, peradventure, there be someone whom the divinity within him may have inspired with a hatred of injustice, or who has attained knowledge of the truth—but no other man. He only blames injustice who, owing to cowardice or age or some weakness, has not the power of being unjust. And this is proved by the fact that when he obtains the power, he immediately becomes unjust as far as he can be.

　　The cause of all this, Socrates, was indicated by us at the beginning of the argument, when my brother and I told you how astonished we were to find that of all the professing panegyrists of justice—beginning with the ancient heroes of whom any memorial has been preserved to us, and ending with the men of our own time—no one has ever blamed injustice or praised justice except with a view to the glories, honours, and benefits which flow from them. No one has ever adequately described either in verse or prose the true essential nature of either of them abiding in the soul, and invisible to any human or divine eye; or shown that of all the things of a man's soul which he has within him, justice is the greatest good, and injustice the greatest evil. Had this been the universal strain, had you sought to persuade us of this from our youth upwards, we should not have been on the watch to keep one another from doing wrong, but everyone would have been his own watchman, because afraid, if he did wrong, of harbouring in himself the greatest of evils. I dare say that Thrasymachus and others would seriously hold the language which I have been merely repeating, and words even stronger than these about justice and injustice, grossly, as I conceive, perverting their true nature. But I speak in this vehement manner, as I must frankly confess to you, because I want to hear from you the opposite side; and I would ask you to show not only the superiority which justice has over injustice, but what effect they have on the possessor of them which makes the one to be a good and the other an evil to him. And please, as Glaucon requested of you, to exclude reputations; for unless you take away from each of them his true reputation and add on the false, we shall say that you do not praise justice, but the appearance of it; we shall think that you are only exhorting us to keep injustice dark, and that you really agree with Thrasymachus in thinking that justice is another's good and the interest of the stronger, and that injustice is a man's own profit and interest, though injurious to the weaker. Now as you have admitted that justice is one of that highest class of goods which are desired indeed for their results, but in a far greater degree for their own sakes—like sight or hearing or knowledge or health, or any other real and natural and not merely conventional good—I would ask you in your praise of justice to regard one point only: I mean the essential good and evil which justice and injustice work in the possessors of them. Let others praise justice and censure injustice, magnifying the rewards and honours of the one and abusing the other; that is a manner of arguing which, coming from them, I am ready to tolerate, but from you who have spent your whole life in the consideration of this question, unless I hear the contrary from your own lips, I expect something better. And therefore, I say, not only prove to us that justice is better than injustice, but show what they either of them do to the possessor of them, which makes the one to be a good and the other an evil, whether seen or unseen by gods and men.

Socrates vs. Adeimantus

I had always admired the genius of Glaucon and Adeimantus, but on hearing these words I was quite delighted, and said: Sons of an illustrious father, that was not a bad beginning of the Elegiac verses which the admirer of Glaucon made in honour of you after you had distinguished yourselves at the battle of Megara: —

'Sons of Ariston,①' he sang, 'divine offspring of an illustrious hero.'

The epithet is very appropriate, for there is something truly divine in being able to argue as you have done for the superiority of injustice, and remaining unconvinced by your own arguments. And I do believe that you are not convinced—this I infer from your general character, for had I judged only from your speeches I should have mistrusted you. But now, the greater my confidence in you, the greater is my difficulty in knowing what to say. For I am in a strait between two; on the one hand I feel that I am unequal to the task; and my inability is brought home to me by the fact that you were not satisfied with the answer which I made to Thrasymachus, proving, as I thought, the superiority which justice has over injustice. And yet I cannot refuse to help, while breath and speech remain to me; I am afraid that there would be an impiety in being present when justice is evil spoken of and not lifting up a hand in her defence. And therefore I had best give such help as I can.

Glaucon and the rest entreated me by all means not to let the question drop, but to proceed in the investigation. They wanted to arrive at the truth, first, about the nature of justice and injustice, and secondly, about their relative advantages. I told them, what I really thought, that the enquiry would be of a serious nature, and would require very good eyes. Seeing then, I said, that we are no great wits, I think that we had better adopt a method which I may illustrate thus: suppose that a short-sighted person had been asked by someone to read small letters from a distance; and it occurred to someone else that they might be found in another place which was larger and in which the letters were larger—if they were the same and he could read the larger letters first, and then proceed to the lesser—this would have been thought a rare piece of good fortune.

---

① Sons of Ariston：此处指格劳孔（Glaucon）和阿德曼托斯（Adeimantus），他们都是阿里斯顿（Ariston）的儿子

Very true, said Adeimantus; but how does the illustration apply to our enquiry?

I will tell you, I replied; justice, which is the subject of our enquiry, is, as you know, sometimes spoken of as the virtue of an individual, and sometimes as the virtue of a State.

True, he replied.

And is not a State larger than an individual?

It is.

Then in the larger the quantity of justice is likely to be larger and more easily discernible. I propose therefore that we enquire into the nature of justice and injustice, first as they appear in the State, and secondly in the individual, proceeding from the greater to the lesser and comparing them.

That, he said, is an excellent proposal.

And if we imagine the State in process of creation, we shall see the justice and injustice of the State in process of creation also.

I dare say.

When the State is completed there may be a hope that the object of our search will be more easily discovered.

Yes, far more easily.

But ought we to attempt to construct one? I said; for to do so, as I am inclined to think, will be a very serious task. Reflect therefore. I have reflected, said Adeimantus, and am anxious that you should proceed.

A State, I said, arises, as I conceive, out of the needs of mankind; no one is self-sufficing, but all of us have many wants. Can any other origin of a State be imagined?

There can be no other.

Then, as we have many wants, and many persons are needed to supply them, one takes a helper for one purpose and another for another; and when these partners and helpers are gathered together in one habitation the body of inhabitants is termed a State.

True, he said.

And they exchange with one another, and one gives, and another receives, under the idea that the exchange will be for their good.

Very true.

Then, I said, let us begin and create in idea a State; and yet the true creator is necessity, who is the mother of our invention.

Of course, he replied.

Now the first and greatest of necessities is food, which is the condition of life and existence.

Certainly.

The second is a dwelling, and the third clothing and the like.

True.

And now let us see how our city will be able to supply this great demand: We may suppose that one man is a husbandman, another a builder, some one else a weaver—shall we add to them a shoemaker, or perhaps some other purveyor to our bodily wants?

Quite right.

The barest notion of a State must include four or five men.

Clearly.

And how will they proceed? Will each bring the result of his labours into a common stock? —the individual husbandman, for example, producing for four, and labouring four times as long and as much as he need in the provision of food with which he supplies others as well as himself; or will he have nothing to do with others and not be at the trouble of producing for them, but provide for himself alone a fourth of the food in a fourth of the time, and in the remaining three fourths of his time be employed in making a house or a coat or a pair of shoes, having no partnership with others, but supplying himself all his own wants?

Adeimantus thought that he should aim at producing food only and not at producing everything.

Probably, I replied, that would be the better way; and when I hear you say this, I am myself reminded that we are not all alike; there are diversities of natures among us which are adapted to different occupations.

Very true.

And will you have a work better done when the workman has many occupations, or when he has only one?

When he has only one.

Further, there can be no doubt that a work is spoilt when not done at the right time?

No doubt.

For business is not disposed to wait until the doer of the business is at leisure; but the doer must follow up what he is doing, and make the business his first object.

He must.

And if so, we must infer that all things are produced more plentifully and easily and of a better quality when one man does one thing which is natural to him and does it at the right time, and leaves other things.

Undoubtedly.

Then more than four citizens will be required; for the husbandman will not make his own plough or mattock, or other implements of agriculture, if they are to be good for anything. Neither will the builder make his tools—and he too needs many; and in like manner the weaver and shoemaker.

True.

Then carpenters, and smiths, and many other artisans, will be sharers in our little State, which is already beginning to grow?

True.

Yet even if we add neatherds, shepherds, and other herdsmen, in order that our husbandmen may have oxen to plough with, and builders as well as husbandmen may have draught cattle, and curriers and weavers fleeces and hides, —still our State will not be very large. That is true; yet neither will it be a very small State which contains all these.

Then, again, there is the situation of the city—to find a place where nothing need be imported is wellnigh① impossible.

Impossible.

Then there must be another class of citizens who will bring the required supply from another city?

There must.

But if the trader goes empty-handed, having nothing which they require who would supply his need, he will come back empty-handed.

That is certain.

And therefore what they produce at home must be not only enough for themselves, but such both in quantity and quality as to accommodate those from whom their wants

---

① 几乎

are supplied.

Very true.

Then more husbandmen and more artisans will be required? They will.

Not to mention the importers and exporters, who are called merchants?

Yes.

Then we shall want merchants?

We shall.

And if merchandise is to be carried over the sea, skillful sailors will also be needed, and in considerable numbers?

Yes, in considerable numbers.

Then, again, within the city, how will they exchange their productions? To secure such an exchange was, as you will remember, one of our principal objects when we formed them into a society and constituted a State.

Clearly they will buy and sell.

Then they will need a market-place, and a money-token for purposes of exchange.

Certainly.

Suppose now that a husbandman, or an artisan, brings some production to market, and he comes at a time when there is no one to exchange with him, — is he to leave his calling and sit idle in the market-place?

Not at all; he will find people there who, seeing the want, undertake the office of salesmen. In well-ordered states they are commonly those who are the weakest in bodily strength, and therefore of little use for any other purpose; their duty is to be in the market, and to give money in ex-change for goods to those who desire to sell and to take money from those who desire to buy.

This want, then, creates a class of retail-traders in our State. Is not 'retailer' the term which is applied to those who sit in the market-place engaged in buying and selling, while those who wander from one city to another are called merchants?

Yes, he said.

And there is another class of servants, who are intellectually hardly on the level of companionship; still they have plenty of bodily strength for labour, which accordingly they sell, and are called, if I do not mistake, hirelings, hire being the name which is given to the price of their labour.

True.

Then hirelings will help to make up our population?

Yes.

And now, Adeimantus, is our State matured and perfected?

I think so.

Where, then, is justice, and where is injustice, and in what part of the State did they spring up?

Probably in the dealings of these citizens with one another. I cannot imagine that they are more likely to be found any where else.

I dare say that you are right in your suggestion, I said; we had better think the matter out, and not shrink from the enquiry.

Let us then consider, first of all, what will be their way of life, now that we have thus established them. Will they not produce corn, and wine, and clothes, and shoes, and build houses for themselves? And when they are housed, they will work, in summer, commonly, stripped and bare-foot, but in winter substantially clothed and shod. They will feed on barley-meal and flour of wheat, baking and kneading them, making noble cakes and loaves; these they will serve up on a mat of reeds or on clean leaves, themselves reclining the while upon beds strewn with yew or myrtle. And they and their children will feast, drinking of the wine which they have made, wearing garlands on their heads, and hymning the praises of the gods, in happy converse with one another. And they will take care that their families do not exceed their means; having an eye to poverty or war.

Socrates vs. Glaucon

But, said Glaucon, interposing, you have not given them a relish to their meal.

True, I replied, I had forgotten; of course they must have a relish—salt, and olives, and cheese, and they will boil roots and herbs such as country people prepare; for a dessert we shall give them figs, and peas, and beans; and they will roast myrtle-berries and acorns at the fire, drinking in moderation. And with such a diet they may be expected to live in peace and health to a good old age, and bequeath a similar life to their children after them.

Yes, Socrates, he said, and if you were providing for a city of pigs, how else would you feed the beasts?

But what would you have, Glaucon? I replied.

Why, he said, you should give them the ordinary conveniences of life. People who are to be comfortable are accustomed to lie on sofas, and dine off tables, and they should have sauces and sweets in the modern style.

Yes, I said, now I understand: the question which you would have me consider is, not only how a State, but how a luxurious State is created; and possibly there is no harm in this, for in such a State we shall be more likely to see how justice and injustice originate. In my opinion the true and healthy constitution of the State is the one which I have described. But if you wish also to see a State at fever-heat, I have no objection. For I suspect that many will not be satisfied with the simpler way of life. They will be for adding sofas, and tables, and other furniture; also dainties, and perfumes, and incense, and courtesans, and cakes, all these not of one sort only, but in every variety; we must go beyond the necessaries of which I was at first speaking, such as houses, and clothes, and shoes: the arts of the painter and the embroiderer will have to be set in motion, and gold and ivory and all sorts of materials must be procured.

True, he said.

Then we must enlarge our borders; for the original healthy State is no longer sufficient. Now will the city have to fill and swell with a multitude of callings which are not required by any natural want; such as the whole tribe of hunters and actors, of whom one large class have to do with forms and colours; another will be the votaries of music—poets and their attendant train of rhapsodists, players, dancers, contractors; also makers of divers kinds of articles, including women's dresses. And we shall want more servants. Will not tutors be also in request, and nurses wet and dry, tirewomen and barbers, as well as confectioners and cooks; and swineherds, too, who were not needed and therefore had no place in the former edition of our State, but are needed now? They must not be forgotten: and there will be animals of many other kinds, if people eat them.

Certainly.

And living in this way we shall have much greater need of physicians than before?

Much greater.

And the country which was enough to support the original inhabitants will be too small now, and not enough?

Quite true.

Then a slice of our neighbours' land will be wanted by us for pasture and tillage, and they will want a slice of ours, if, like ourselves, they exceed the limit of necessity, and give themselves up to the unlimited accumulation of wealth?

That, Socrates, will be inevitable.

And so we shall go to war, Glaucon. Shall we not?

Most certainly, he replied.

Then without determining as yet whether war does good or harm, thus much we may affirm, that now we have discovered war to be derived from causes which are also the causes of almost all the evils in States, private as well as public.

Undoubtedly.

And our State must once more enlarge; and this time the enlargement will be nothing short of a whole army, which will have to go out and fight with the invaders for all that we have, as well as for the things and persons whom we were describing above.

Why? he said; are they not capable of defending themselves?

No, I said; not if we were right in the principle which was acknowledged by all of us when we were framing the State: the principle, as you will remember, was that one man cannot practise many arts with success.

Very true, he said.

But is not war an art?

Certainly.

And an art requiring as much attention as shoemaking?

Quite true.

And the shoemaker was not allowed by us to be a husbandman, or a weaver, or a builder—in order that we might have our shoes well made; but to him and to every other worker was assigned one work for which he was by nature fitted, and at that he was to continue working all his life long and at no other; he was not to let opportunities slip, and then he would become a good workman. Now nothing can be more important than that the work of a soldier should be well done. But is war an art so easily acquired that a man may be a warrior who is also a husbandman, or shoemaker, or other artisan; although no one in the world would be a good dice or draught player who merely took up the game as a recreation, and had not from his earliest years devoted himself to this and nothing else? No tools will make a man a skilled workman, or master of defence, nor be of any use to him who has not learned how to handle them, and has never bestowed any attention upon them. How then will he who takes up a shield or other implement of war become a good fighter all in a day, whether with heavy-armed or any other kind of troops?

Yes, he said, the tools which would teach men their own use would be beyond price.

And the higher the duties of the guardian, I said, the more time, and skill, and art, and application will be needed by him?

No doubt, he replied.

Will he not also require natural aptitude for his calling?

Certainly.

Then it will be our duty to select, if we can, natures which are fitted for the task of guarding the city?

It will.

And the selection will be no easy matter, I said; but we must be brave and do our best.

We must.

Is not the noble youth very like a well-bred dog in respect of guarding and watching?

What do you mean?

I mean that both of them ought to be quick to see, and swift to over-take the enemy when they see him; and strong too if, when they have caught him, they have to fight with him.

All these qualities, he replied, will certainly be required by them. Well, and your guardian must be brave if he is to fight well? Certainly.

And is he likely to be brave who has no spirit, whether horse or dog or any other animal? Have you never observed how invincible and unconquerable is spirit and how the presence of it makes the soul of any creature to be absolutely fearless and indomitable?

I have.

Then now we have a clear notion of the bodily qualities which are required in the guardian.

True.

And also of the mental ones; his soul is to be full of spirit?

198

Yes.

But are not these spirited natures apt to be savage with one another, and with everybody else?

A difficulty by no means easy to overcome, he replied.

Whereas, I said, they ought to be dangerous to their enemies, and gentle to their friends; if not, they will destroy themselves without waiting for their enemies to destroy them.

True, he said.

What is to be done then? I said; how shall we find a gentle nature which has also a great spirit, for the one is the contradiction of the other?

True.

He will not be a good guardian who is wanting in either of these two qualities; and yet the combination of them appears to be impossible; and hence we must infer that to be a good guardian is impossible.

I am afraid that what you say is true, he replied.

Here feeling perplexed I began to think over what had preceded. —My friend, I said, no wonder that we are in a perplexity; for we have lost sight of the image which we had before us.

What do you mean? he said.

I mean to say that there do exist natures gifted with those opposite qualities.

And where do you find them?

Many animals, I replied, furnish examples of them; our friend the dog is a very good one: you know that well-bred dogs are perfectly gentle to their familiars and acquaintances, and the reverse to strangers.

Yes, I know.

Then there is nothing impossible or out of the order of nature in our finding a guardian who has a similar combination of qualities?

Certainly not.

Would not he who is fitted to be a guardian, besides the spirited nature, need to have the qualities of a philosopher?

I do not apprehend your meaning.

The trait of which I am speaking, I replied, may be also seen in the dog, and is remarkable in the animal.

What trait?

Why, a dog, whenever he sees a stranger, is angry; when an acquaintance, he welcomes him, although the one has never done him any harm, nor the other any good. Did this never strike you as curious?

The matter never struck me before; but I quite recognise the truth of your remark.

And surely this instinct of the dog is very charming; —your dog is a true philosopher.

Why?

Why, because he distinguishes the face of a friend and of an enemy only by the criterion of knowing and not knowing. And must not an animal be a lover of learning who determines what he likes and dislikes by the test of knowledge and ignorance?

Most assuredly.

And is not the love of learning the love of wisdom, which is philosophy?

They are the same, he replied.

And may we not say confidently of man also, that he who is likely to be gentle to his friends and acquaintances, must by nature be a lover of wisdom and knowledge?

That we may safely affirm.

Then he who is to be a really good and noble guardian of the State will require to unite in himself philosophy and spirit and swiftness and strength?

Undoubtedly.

Then we have found the desired natures; and now that we have found them, how are they to be reared and educated? Is not this an enquiry which may be expected to throw light on the greater enquiry which is our final end—How do justice and injustice grow up in States? for we do not want either to omit what is to the point or to draw out the argument to an inconvenient length.

Socrates vs. Adeimantus

Adeimantus thought that the enquiry would be of great service to us.

Then, I said, my dear friend, the task must not be given up, even if somewhat long.

Certainly not.

Come then, and let us pass a leisure hour in story-telling, and our story shall be the education of our heroes.

By all means①.

And what shall be their education? Can we find a better than the traditional sort? —and this has two divisions, gymnastic for the body, and music for the soul.

True.

Shall we begin education with music, and go on to gymnastic afterwards?

By all means.

And when you speak of music, do you include literature or not?

I do.

And literature may be either true or false?

Yes.

And the young should be trained in both kinds, and we begin with the false?

I do not understand your meaning, he said.

You know, I said, that we begin by telling children stories which, though not wholly destitute of truth, are in the main fictitious; and these stories are told them when they are not of an age to learn gymnastics.

Very true.

That was my meaning when I said that we must teach music before gymnastics.

Quite right, he said.

You know also that the beginning is the most important part of any work, especially in the case of a young and tender thing; for that is the time at which the character is being formed and the desired impression is more readily taken.

Quite true.

And shall we just carelessly allow children to hear any casual tales which may be devised by casual persons, and to receive into their minds ideas for the most part the very opposite of those which we should wish them to have when they are grown up?

We cannot.

Then the first thing will be to establish a censorship of the writers of fiction, and let the censors receive any tale of fiction which is good, and reject the bad; and we will desire mothers and nurses to tell their children the authorised ones only. Let them fashion the mind with such tales, even more fondly than they mould the body with their hands; but most of those which are now in use must be discarded.

---

① 当然可以

Of what tales are you speaking? he said.

You may find a model of the lesser in the greater, I said; for they are necessarily of the same type, and there is the same spirit in both of them.

Very likely, he replied; but I do not as yet know what you would term the greater.

Those, I said, which are narrated by Homer and Hesiod, and the rest of the poets, who have ever been the great story-tellers of mankind.

But which stories do you mean, he said; and what fault do you find with them?

A fault which is most serious, I said; the fault of telling a lie, and, what is more, a bad lie.

But when is this fault committed?

Whenever an erroneous representation is made of the nature of gods and heroes, —as when a painter paints a portrait not having the shadow of a likeness to the original.

Yes, he said, that sort of thing is certainly very blamable; but what are the stories which you mean?

First of all, I said, there was that greatest of all lies in high places, which the poet told about Uranus①, and which was a bad lie too, —I mean what Hesiod says that Uranus did, and how Cronus② retaliated on him. The doings of Cronus, and the sufferings which in turn his son inflicted upon him, even if they were true, ought certainly not to be lightly told to young and thoughtless persons; if possible, they had better be buried in silence. But if there is an absolute necessity for their mention, a chosen few might hear them in a mystery, and they should sacrifice not a common (Eleusinian) pig, but some huge and unprocurable victim; and then the number of the hearers will be very few indeed.

Why, yes, said he, those stories are extremely objectionable.

Yes, Adeimantus, they are stories not to be repeated in our State; the young man should not be told that in committing the worst of crimes he is far from doing anything outrageous; and that even if he chastises his father when he does wrong, in whatever manner, he will only be following the example of the first and greatest among the gods.

I entirely agree with you, he said; in my opinion those stories are quite unfit to be

---

① 乌拉诺斯
② 克洛诺斯

repeated.

Neither, if we mean our future guardians to regard the habit of quarrelling among themselves as of all things the basest, should any word be said to them of the wars in heaven, and of the plots and fightings of the gods against one another, for they are not true. No, we shall never mention the battles of the giants, or let them be embroidered on garments; and we shall be silent about the innumerable other quarrels of gods and heroes with their friends and relatives. If they would only believe us we would tell them that quarrelling is unholy, and that never up to this time has there been any quarrel between citizens; this is what old men and old women should begin by telling children; and when they grow up, the poets also should be told to compose for them in a similar spirit. But the narrative of Hephaestus① binding Here② his mother, or how on another occasion Zeus sent him flying for taking her part when she was being beaten, and all the battles of the gods in Homer—these tales must not be admitted into our State, whether they are supposed to have an allegorical meaning or not. For a young person cannot judge what is allegorical and what is literal; anything that he receives into his mind at that age is likely to become indelible and unalterable; and therefore it is most important that the tales which the young first hear should be models of virtuous thoughts.

There you are right, he replied; but if any one asks where are such models to be found and of what tales are you speaking—how shall we answer him?

I said to him, You and I, Adeimantus, at this moment are not poets, but founders of a State: now the founders of a State ought to know the general forms in which poets should cast their tales, and the limits which must be observed by them, but to make the tales is not their business.

Very true, he said; but what are these forms of theology which you mean?

Something of this kind, I replied: —God is always to be represented as he truly is, whatever be the sort of poetry, epic, lyric or tragic, in which the representation is given.

Right.

And is he not truly good? and must he not be represented as such? Certainly.

---

① 赫菲斯托斯（Hephaestus），火神、铁器和武器之神，天后赫拉（Hera）之子
② 天后赫拉（Hera），"Here" 可能为译者笔误

And no good thing is hurtful?

No, indeed.

And that which is not hurtful hurts not?

Certainly not.

And that which hurts not does no evil?

No.

And can that which does no evil be a cause of evil?

Impossible.

And the good is advantageous?

Yes.

And therefore the cause of well-being?

Yes.

It follows therefore that the good is not the cause of all things, but of the good only?

Assuredly.

Then God, if he be good, is not the author of all things, as the many assert, but he is the cause of a few things only, and not of most things that occur to men. For few are the goods of human life, and many are the evils, and the good is to be attributed to God alone; of the evils the causes are to be sought elsewhere, and not in him.

That appears to me to be most true, he said.

Then we must not listen to Homer or to any other poet who is guilty of the folly of saying that two casks

'Lie at the threshold of Zeus, full of lots, one of good, the other of evil lots,'

and that he to whom Zeus gives a mixture of the two 'Sometimes meets with evil fortune, at other times with good;' but that he to whom is given the cup of unmingled ill, 'Him wild hunger drives o'er the beauteous earth.' And again— 'Zeus, who is the dispenser of good and evil to us.'

And if any one asserts that the violation of oaths and treaties, which was really the work of Pandarus①, was brought about by Athene② and Zeus, or that the strife and

---

① 潘达罗斯（Pandarus），利西亚人（Lycians）的首领，在特洛伊战争中由于他违背了双方的停战协议，被希腊英雄、阿尔戈斯（Argos）国王狄俄墨德斯（Diomedes）所杀

② Athene 即 Athena，雅典娜

contention of the gods was instigated by Themis① and Zeus, he shall not have our approval; neither will we allow our young men to hear the words of Aeschylus②, that

'God plants guilt among men when he desires utterly to destroy a house.'

And if a poet writes of the sufferings of Niobe③—the subject of the tragedy in which these iambic verses④ occur—or of the house of Pelops⑤, or of the Trojan war or on any similar theme, either we must not permit him to say that these are the works of God, or if they are of God, he must devise some explanation of them such as we are seeking; he must say that God did what was just and right, and they were the better for being punished; but that those who are punished are miserable, and that God is the author of their misery—the poet is not to be permitted to say; though he may say that the wicked are miserable because they require to be punished, and are benefited by receiving punishment from God; but that God being good is the author of evil to any one is to be strenuously denied, and not to be said or sung or heard in verse or prose by any one whether old or young in any well-ordered commonwealth. Such a fiction is suicidal, ruinous, impious.

I agree with you, he replied, and am ready to give my assent to the law.

Let this then be one of our rules and principles concerning the gods, to which our poets and reciters will be expected to conform,—that God is not the author of all things, but of good only.

That will do, he said.

And what do you think of a second principle? Shall I ask you whether God is a magician, and of a nature to appear insidiously now in one shape, and now in another—sometimes himself changing and passing into many forms, sometimes deceiving us with the semblance of such transformations; or is he one and the same immutably fixed in his own proper image?

I cannot answer you, he said, without more thought.

---

① 忒弥斯（Themis），十二泰坦之一，正义女神
② 埃斯库罗斯（Aeschylus），希腊三大悲剧作家之一
③ 尼俄柏（Niobe），坦塔罗斯（Tantalus）之女，因自己生了六男六女而嘲笑黑袍女神莱托（Leto），后遭天谴。十二子女悉数被射杀，尼俄柏悲恸不已，化为顽石
④ 抑扬格的诗（iambic verses）
⑤ 珀罗普斯（Pelops），坦塔罗斯（Tantalus）之子，被坦塔罗斯杀害宴请诸神，后在海神的帮助下复活

Well, I said; but if we suppose a change in anything, that change must be effected either by the thing itself, or by some other thing?

Most certainly.

And things which are at their best are also least liable to be altered or discomposed; for example, when healthiest and strongest, the human frame is least liable to be affected by meats and drinks, and the plant which is in the fullest vigour also suffers least from winds or the heat of the sun or any similar causes.

Of course.

And will not the bravest and wisest soul be least confused or deranged by any external influence?

True.

And the same principle, as I should suppose, applies to all composite things—furniture, houses, garments: when good and well made, they are least altered by time and circumstances.

Very true.

Then everything which is good, whether made by art or nature, or both, is least liable to suffer change from without?

True.

But surely God and the things of God are in every way perfect?

Of course they are.

Then he can hardly be compelled by external influence to take many shapes?

He cannot.

But may he not change and transform himself?

Clearly, he said, that must be the case if he is changed at all.

And will he then change himself for the better and fairer, or for the worse and more unsightly?

If he change at all he can only change for the worse, for we cannot suppose him to be deficient either in virtue or beauty.

Very true, Adeimantus; but then, would anyone, whether God or man, desire to make himself worse?

Impossible.

Then it is impossible that God should ever be willing to change; being, as is supposed, the fairest and best that is conceivable, every God remains absolutely and forever in his own form.

That necessarily follows, he said, in my judgment.

Then, I said, my dear friend, let none of the poets tell us that

'The gods, taking the disguise of strangers from other lands, walk up and down cities in all sorts of forms;'

and let no one slander Proteus① and Thetis②, neither let anyone, either in tragedy or in any other kind of poetry, introduce Here③ disguised in the likeness of a priestess asking an alms 'For the life-giving daughters of Inachus④ the river of Argos;'

—let us have no more lies of that sort. Neither must we have mothers under the influence of the poets scaring their children with a bad version of these myths—telling how certain gods, as they say, 'Go about by night in the likeness of so many strangers and in divers forms;' but let them take heed lest they make cowards of their children, and at the same time speak blasphemy against the gods.

Heaven forbid, he said.

But although the gods are themselves unchangeable, still by witchcraft and deception they may make us think that they appear in various forms?

Perhaps, he replied.

Well, but can you imagine that God will be willing to lie, whether in word or deed, or to put forth a phantom of himself?

I cannot say, he replied.

Do you not know, I said, that the true lie, if such an expression may be allowed, is hated of gods and men?

What do you mean? he said.

I mean that no one is willingly deceived in that which is the truest and highest part of himself, or about the truest and highest matters; there, above all, he is most afraid of a lie having possession of him.

Still, he said, I do not comprehend you.

---

① 普罗透斯（Proteus）和涅柔斯（Nereus）一样，均为早期的海神，一旦被抓，就会变成各种凶猛动物
② 塞蒂斯（Thetis），海中女神，希腊英雄阿喀琉斯（Achilles）的母亲
③ Here 即 Hera，赫拉
④ 伊那科斯（Inachus）一说是河神，一说是滨河部落之王。伊俄（Io）的父亲

The reason is, I replied, that you attribute some profound meaning to my words; but I am only saying that deception, or being deceived or uninformed about the highest realities in the highest part of themselves, which is the soul, and in that part of them to have and to hold the lie, is what mankind least like; —that, I say, is what they utterly detest.

There is nothing more hateful to them.

And, as I was just now remarking, this ignorance in the soul of him who is deceived may be called the true lie; for the lie in words is only a kind of imitation and shadowy image of a previous affection of the soul, not pure unadulterated falsehood. Am I not right?

Perfectly right.

The true lie is hated not only by the gods, but also by men? Yes.

Whereas the lie in words is in certain cases useful and not hateful; in dealing with enemies—that would be an instance; or again, when those whom we call our friends in a fit of madness or illusion are going to do some harm, then it is useful and is a sort of medicine or preventive; also in the tales of mythology, of which we were just now speaking—because we do not know the truth about ancient times, we make falsehood as much like truth as we can, and so turn it to account.

Very true, he said.

But can any of these reasons apply to God? Can we suppose that he is ignorant of antiquity, and therefore has recourse to invention?

That would be ridiculous, he said.

Then the lying poet has no place in our idea of God?

I should say not.

Or perhaps he may tell a lie because he is afraid of enemies? That is inconceivable.

But he may have friends who are senseless or mad? But no mad or senseless person can be a friend of God. Then no motive can be imagined why God should lie? None whatever.

Then the superhuman and divine is absolutely incapable of falsehood? Yes.

Then is God perfectly simple and true both in word and deed; he changes not; he deceives not, either by sign or word, by dream or waking vision.

Your thoughts, he said, are the reflection of my own.

You agree with me then, I said, that this is the second type or form in which we should write and speak about divine things. The gods are not magicians who transform themselves, neither do they deceive mankind in any way.

I grant that.

Then, although we are admirers of Homer, we do not admire the lying dream which Zeus sends to Agamemnon①; neither will we praise the verses of Aeschylus in which Thetis says that Apollo at her nuptials

'Was celebrating in song her fair progeny whose days were to be long, and to know no sickness. And when he had spoken of my lot as in all things blessed of heaven he raised a note of triumph and cheered my soul. And I thought that the word of Phoebus②, being divine and full of prophecy, would not fail. And now he himself who uttered the strain, he who was present at the banquet, and who said this—he it is who has slain my son.'

These are the kind of sentiments about the gods which will arouse our anger; and he who utters them shall be refused a chorus; neither shall we allow teachers to make use of them in the instruction of the young, meaning, as we do, that our guardians, as far as men can be, should be true worshippers of the gods and like them.

I entirely agree, he said, in these principles, and promise to make them my laws.

Questions for discussion:

1. Why do some people think The Republic should be translated into The Idealistic State? What are the similarities and differences between the Republic and The Idealistic State?

2. How did Socrates talk about Justice with the Athenian nobles? Why does the issue of justice become the core issue of state establishment throughout?

3. Why should philosophers be Kings in Plato's The Republic? Where is the logical starting point for the division of the three classes and the supremacy of philosophers?

4. the idealistic state is based on the idealistic life, the idealistic life is based on faith, what is Socrates' belief in life?

---

① 阿伽门农（Agamemnon），迈锡尼王，特洛伊战争中希腊联军主帅
② Phoebus，太阳神阿波罗（Apollo）的另一个名字

第八篇　Phaedo[①]

Plato

（Translator：Benjamin Jowett）

Phaedo, who is the narrator of the dialogue to Echecrates of Phlius[②].

Socrates, Apollodorus[③], Simmias[④], Cebes[⑤], Crito[⑥] and an Attendant of the Prison.

SCENE：The Prison of Socrates.

PLACE OF THE NARRATION：Phlius.

ECHECRATES：Were you yourself, Phaedo, in the prison with Socrates on the day when he drank the poison?

PHAEDO：Yes, Echecrates, I was.

ECHECRATES：I should so like to hear about his death. What did he say in his last hours? We were informed that he died by taking poison, but no one knew anything more; for no Phliasian[⑦] ever goes to Athens now, and it is a long time since any stranger from Athens has found his way hither; so that we had no clear account.

PHAEDO：Did you not hear of the proceedings at the trial?

ECHECRATES：Yes; someone told us about the trial, and we could not understand why, having been condemned, he should have been put to death, not at the

---

[①] 译为《斐多篇》，斐多（Phaedo）亲历了苏格拉底（Socrates）在狱中最后一天与其弟子及慕名而至的学者对灵魂问题的探讨，通过与艾克格拉底（Echecrates）的对话记录了苏格拉底临终的言行

[②] Echecrates of Phlius，弗里乌斯的艾克格拉底，斐多的谈话对象

[③] 阿波罗多鲁斯（Apollodorus），历史学家

[④] 西米亚斯（Simmias），忒拜人，哲学家菲洛劳斯（Philolaus）的学生

[⑤] 齐贝斯（Cebes），忒拜人，哲学家菲洛劳斯（Philolaus）的学生

[⑥] 克里托（Crito），苏格拉底的学生

[⑦] 弗里乌斯人（Phliasian）

time, but long afterwards. What was the reason of this?

PHAEDO: An accident, Echecrates: the stern of the ship which the Athenians send to Delos① happened to have been crowned on the day before he was tried.

ECHECRATES: What is this ship?

PHAEDO: It is the ship in which, according to Athenian tradition, Theseus② went to Crete when he took with him the fourteen youths, and was the saviour of them and of himself. And they were said to have vowed to Apollo at the time, that if they were saved they would send a yearly mission to Delos. Now this custom still continues, and the whole period of the voyage to and from Delos, beginning when the priest of Apollo crowns the stern of the ship, is a holy season, during which the city is not allowed to be polluted by public executions;

and when the vessel is detained by contrary winds, the time spent in going and returning is very considerable. As I was saying, the ship was crowned on the day before the trial, and this was the reason why Socrates lay in prison and was not put to death until long after he was condemned.

ECHECRATES: What was the manner of his death, Phaedo? What was said or done? And which of his friends were with him? Or did the authorities forbid them to be present—so that he had no friends near him when he died?

PHAEDO: No; there were several of them with him.

ECHECRATES: If you have nothing to do, I wish that you would tell me what passed, as exactly as you can.

PHAEDO: I have nothing at all to do, and will try to gratify your wish. To be reminded of Socrates is always the greatest delight to me, whether I speak myself or hear another speak of him.

ECHECRATES: You will have listeners who are of the same mind with you, and I hope that you will be as exact as you can.

PHAEDO: I had a singular feeling at being in his company. For I could hardly believe that I was present at the death of a friend, and therefore I did not pity him, Echecrates; he died so fearlessly, and his words and bearing were so noble and

---

① 得洛斯（Delos），希腊一著名岛屿，太阳神阿波罗的出生地
② 忒修斯（Theseus），古希腊神话传说中的英雄，雅典王子。曾手刃克里特岛（Crete）上的牛头怪米诺陶（Minotaur），为雅典人民免除灾难

gracious, that to me he appeared blessed. I thought that in going to the other world he could not be without a divine call, and that he would be happy, if any man ever was, when he arrived there, and therefore I did not pity him as might have seemed natural at such an hour. But I had not the pleasure which I usually feel in philosophical discourse (for philosophy was the theme of which we spoke). I was pleased, but in the pleasure there was also a strange admixture of pain; for I reflected that he was soon to die, and this double feeling was shared by us all; we were laughing and weeping by turns, especially the excitable Apollodorus—you know the sort of man?

ECHECRATES: Yes.

PHAEDO: He was quite beside himself; and I and all of us were greatly moved.

ECHECRATES: Who were present?

PHAEDO: Of native Athenians there were, besides Apollodorus, Critobulus and his father Crito, Hermogenes, Epigenes, Aeschines, Antisthenes; likewise Ctesippus of the deme of Paeania, Menexenus, and some others; Plato, if I am not mistaken, was ill.

ECHECRATES: Were there any strangers?

PHAEDO: Yes, there were; Simmias the Theban, and Cebes, and Phaedondes; Euclid and Terpison, who came from Megara.

ECHECRATES: And was Aristippus there, and Cleombrotus?

PHAEDO: No, they were said to be in Aegina[①].

ECHECRATES: Anyone else?

PHAEDO: I think that these were nearly all.

ECHECRATES: Well, and what did you talk about?

PHAEDO: I will begin at the beginning, and endeavour to repeat the entire conversation. On the previous days we had been in the habit of assembling early in the morning at the court in which the trial took place, and which is not far from the prison. There we used to wait talking with one another until the opening of the doors (for they were not opened very early); then we went in and generally passed the day with Socrates. On the last morning we assembled sooner than usual, having heard on the day before when we quitted the prison in the evening that the sacred ship had come from Delos, and so we arranged to meet very early at the accustomed place. On our arrival

---

① 埃伊那岛（Aegina），希腊东南部一岛屿，神话传说中阿喀琉斯（Achilles）的故乡

the jailer who answered the door, instead of admitting us, came out and told us to stay until he called us. 'For the Eleven①,' he said, 'are now with Socrates; they are taking off his chains, and giving orders that he is to die to-day.' He soon returned and said that we might come in. On entering we found Socrates just released from chains, and Xanthippe②, whom you know, sitting by him, and holding his child in her arms. When she saw us she uttered a cry and said, as women will: 'O Socrates, this is the last time that either you will converse with your friends, or they with you.' Socrates turned to Crito and said: 'Crito, let some one take her home.' Some of Crito's people accordingly led her away, crying out and beating herself. And when she was gone, Socrates, sitting up on the couch, bent and rubbed his leg, saying, as he was rubbing: How singular is the thing called pleasure, and how curiously related to pain, which might be thought to be the opposite of it; for they are never present to a man at the same instant, and yet he who pursues either is generally compelled to take the other; their bodies are two, but they are joined by a single head. And I cannot help thinking that if Aesop③ had remembered them, he would have made a fable about God trying to reconcile their strife, and how, when he could not, he fastened their heads together; and this is the reason why when one comes the other follows, as I know by my own experience now, when after the pain in my leg which was caused by the chain pleasure appears to succeed.

Upon this Cebes said: I am glad, Socrates, that you have mentioned the name of Aesop. For it reminds me of a question which has been asked by many, and was asked of me only the day before yesterday by Evenus④ the poet—he will be sure to ask it again, and therefore if you would like me to have an answer ready for him, you may as well tell me what I should say to him: —he wanted to know why you, who never before wrote a line of poetry, now that you are in prison are turning Aesop's fables into verse, and also composing that hymn in honour of Apollo.

Tell him, Cebes, he replied, what is the truth—that I had no idea of rivalling him or his poems; to do so, as I knew, would be no easy task. But I wanted to see whether I could purge away a scruple which I felt about the meaning of certain dreams. In the

---

① The Eleven，指苏格拉底案子的十一个法官
② 赞西比（Xanthippe），苏格拉底之妻
③ 伊索，寓言家
④ 艾凡努斯（Evenus），古希腊诗人

course of my life I have often had intimations in dreams 'that I should compose music.' The same dream came to me sometimes in one form, and sometimes in another, but always saying the same or nearly the same words: 'Cultivate and make music,' said the dream. And hitherto I had imagined that this was only intended to exhort and encourage me in the study of philosophy, which has been the pursuit of my life, and is the noblest and best of music. The dream was bidding me do what I was already doing, in the same way that the competitor in a race is bidden by the spectators to run when he is already running. But I was not certain of this, for the dream might have meant music in the popular sense of the word, and being under sentence of death, and the festival giving me a respite, I thought that it would be safer for me to satisfy the scruple, and, in obedience to the dream, to compose a few verses before I departed. And first I made a hymn in honour of the god of the festival, and then considering that a poet, if he is really to be a poet, should not only put together words, but should invent stories, and that I have no invention, I took some fables of Aesop, which I had ready at hand and which I knew—they were the first I came upon—and turned them into verse. Tell this to Evenus, Cebes, and bid him be of good cheer; say that I would have him come after me if he be a wise man, and not tarry; and that to-day I am likely to be going, for the Athenians say that I must.

Simmias said: What a message for such a man! having been a frequent companion of his I should say that, as far as I know him, he will never take your advice unless he is obliged.

Why, said Socrates, —is not Evenus a philosopher?

I think that he is, said Simmias.

Then he, or any man who has the spirit of philosophy, will be willing to die, but he will not take his own life, for that is held to be unlawful.

Here he changed his position, and put his legs off the couch on to the ground, and during the rest of the conversation he remained sitting.

Why do you say, enquired Cebes, that a man ought not to take his own life, but that the philosopher will be ready to follow the dying?

Socrates replied: And have you, Cebes and Simmias, who are the disciples of Philolaus[①], never heard him speak of this?

---

① 菲洛劳斯（Philolaus），古希腊哲学家

Yes, but his language was obscure, Socrates.

My words, too, are only an echo; but there is no reason why I should not repeat what I have heard: and indeed, as I am going to another place, it is very meet for me to be thinking and talking of the nature of the pilgrimage which I am about to make. What can I do better in the interval between this and the setting of the sun?

Then tell me, Socrates, why is suicide held to be unlawful? as I have certainly heard Philolaus, about whom you were just now asking, affirm when he was staying with us at Thebes: and there are others who say the same, although I have never understood what was meant by any of them.

Do not lose heart, replied Socrates, and the day may come when you will understand. I suppose that you wonder why, when other things which are evil may be good at certain times and to certain persons, death is to be the only exception, and why, when a man is better dead, he is not permitted to be his own benefactor, but must wait for the hand of another.

Very true, said Cebes, laughing gently and speaking in his native Boeotian①.

I admit the appearance of inconsistency in what I am saying; but there may not be any real inconsistency after all. There is a doctrine whispered in secret that man is a prisoner who has no right to open the door and run away; this is a great mystery which I do not quite understand. Yet I too believe that the gods are our guardians, and that we are a possession of theirs. Do you not agree?

Yes, I quite agree, said Cebes.

And if one of your own possessions, an ox or an ass, for example, took the liberty of putting himself out of the way when you had given no intimation of your wish that he should die, would you not be angry with him, and would you not punish him if you could?

Certainly, replied Cebes.

Then, if we look at the matter thus, there may be reason in saying that a man should wait, and not take his own life until God summons him, as he is now summoning me.

Yes, Socrates, said Cebes, there seems to be truth in what you say. And yet how

---

① 皮奥夏方言，皮奥夏（Boeotia）地区位于古希腊中部，其中重要的城邦有忒拜城（Thebes）。

can you reconcile this seemingly true belief that God is our guardian and we his possessions, with the willingness to die which we were just now attributing to the philosopher? That the wisest of men should be willing to leave a service in which they are ruled by the gods who are the best of rulers, is not reasonable; for surely no wise man thinks that when set at liberty he can take better care of himself than the gods take of him. A fool may perhaps think so—he may argue that he had better run away from his master, not considering that his duty is to remain to the end, and not to run away from the good, and that there would be no sense in his running away. The wise man will want to be ever with him who is better than himself. Now this, Socrates, is the reverse of what was just now said; for upon this view the wise man should sorrow and the fool rejoice at passing out of life.

The earnestness of Cebes seemed to please Socrates. Here, said he, turning to us, is a man who is always inquiring, and is not so easily convinced by the first thing which he hears.

And certainly, added Simmias, the objection which he is now making does appear to me to have some force. For what can be the meaning of a truly wise man wanting to fly away and lightly leave a master who is better than himself? And I rather imagine that Cebes is referring to you; he thinks that you are too ready to leave us, and too ready to leave the gods whom you acknowledge to be our good masters.

Yes, replied Socrates; there is reason in what you say. And so you think that I ought to answer your indictment as if I were in a court?

We should like you to do so, said Simmias.

Then I must try to make a more successful defence before you than I did when before the judges. For I am quite ready to admit, Simmias and Cebes, that I ought to be grieved at death, if I were not persuaded in the first place that I am going to other gods who are wise and good (of which I am as certain as I can be of any such matters), and secondly (though I am not so sure of this last) to men departed, better than those whom I leave behind; and therefore I do not grieve as I might have done, for I have good hope that there is yet something remaining for the dead, and as has been said of old, some far better thing for the good than for the evil.

But do you mean to take away your thoughts with you, Socrates? said Simmias. Will you not impart them to us? —for they are a benefit in which we too are entitled to share. Moreover, if you succeed in convincing us, that will be an answer to the charge against yourself.

I will do my best, replied Socrates. But you must first let me hear what Crito wants; he has long been wishing to say something to me.

Only this, Socrates, replied Crito: —the attendant who is to give you the poison has been telling me, and he wants me to tell you, that you are not to talk much, talking, he says, increases heat, and this is apt to interfere with the action of the poison; persons who excite themselves are sometimes obliged to take a second or even a third dose.

Then, said Socrates, let him mind his business and be prepared to give the poison twice or even thrice if necessary; that is all.

I knew quite well what you would say, replied Crito; but I was obliged to satisfy him.

Never mind him, he said.

And now, O my judges[①], I desire to prove to you that the real philosopher has reason to be of good cheer when he is about to die, and that after death he may hope to obtain the greatest good in the other world. And how this may be, Simmias and Cebes, I will endeavour to explain. For I deem that the true votary of philosophy is likely to be misunderstood by other men; they do not perceive that he is always pursuing death and dying; and if this be so, and he has had the desire of death all his life long, why when his time comes should he repine at that which he has been always pursuing and desiring?

Simmias said laughingly: Though not in a laughing humour, you have made me laugh, Socrates; for I cannot help thinking that the many when they hear your words will say how truly you have described philosophers, and our people at home will likewise say that the life which philosophers desire is in reality death, and that they have found them out to be deserving of the death which they desire.

And they are right, Simmias, in thinking so, with the exception of the words 'they have found them out'; for they have not found out either what is the nature of that death which the true philosopher deserves, or how he deserves or desires death. But enough of them: —let us discuss the matter among ourselves: Do we believe that there is such a thing as death?

---

① 指西米亚斯（Simmias）和齐贝斯（Cebes）

To be sure, replied Simmias.

Is it not the separation of soul and body? And to be dead is the completion of this; when the soul exists in herself, and is released from the body and the body is released from the soul, what is this but death?

Just so, he replied.

There is another question, which will probably throw light on our present inquiry if you and I can agree about it: —Ought the philosopher to care about the pleasures—if they are to be called pleasures—of eating and drinking?

Certainly not, answered Simmias.

And what about the pleasures of love—should he care for them?

By no means.

And will he think much of the other ways of indulging the body, for example, the acquisition of costly raiment, or sandals, or other adornments of the body? Instead of caring about them, does he not rather despise anything more than nature needs? What do you say?

I should say that the true philosopher would despise them. Would you not say that he is entirely concerned with the soul and not with the body? He would like, as far as he can, to get away from the body and to turn to the soul.

Quite true.

In matters of this sort philosophers, above all other men, may be observed in every sort of way to dissever the soul from the communion of the body.

Very true.

Whereas, Simmias, the rest of the world are of opinion that to him who has no sense of pleasure and no part in bodily pleasure, life is not worth having; and that he who is indifferent about them is as good as dead.

That is also true.

What again shall we say of the actual acquirement of knowledge? —is the body, if invited to share in the enquiry, a hinderer or a helper? I mean to say, have sight and hearing any truth in them? Are they not, as the poets are always telling us, inaccurate witnesses? and yet, if even they are inaccurate and indistinct, what is to be said of the other senses? —for you will allow that they are the best of them?

Certainly, he replied.

Then when does the soul attain truth? —for in attempting to consider anything in company with the body she is obviously deceived.

True.

Then must not true existence be revealed to her in thought, if at all?

Yes.

And thought is best when the mind is gathered into herself and none of these things trouble her—neither sounds nor sights nor pain nor any pleasure,—when she takes leave of the body, and has as little as possible to do with it, when she has no bodily sense or desire, but is aspiring after true being?

Certainly.

And in this the philosopher dishonours the body; his soul runs away from his body and desires to be alone and by herself?

That is true.

Well, but there is another thing, Simmias: Is there or is there not an absolute justice?

Assuredly there is.

And an absolute beauty and absolute good?

Of course.

But did you ever behold any of them with your eyes?

Certainly not.

Or did you ever reach them with any other bodily sense? —and I speak not of these alone, but of absolute greatness, and health, and strength, and of the essence or true nature of everything. Has the reality of them ever been perceived by you through the bodily organs? or rather, is not the nearest approach to the knowledge of their several natures made by him who so orders his intellectual vision as to have the most exact conception of the essence of each thing which he considers?

Certainly.

And he attains to the purest knowledge of them who goes to each with the mind alone, not introducing or intruding in the act of thought sight or any other sense together with reason, but with the very light of the mind in her own clearness searches into the very truth of each; he who has got rid, as far as he can, of eyes and ears and, so to speak, of the whole body, these being in his opinion distracting elements which when they infect the soul hinder her from acquiring truth and knowledge—who, if not he, is likely to attain the knowledge of true being?

What you say has a wonderful truth in it, Socrates, replied Simmias.

And when real philosophers consider all these things, will they not be led to make a reflection which they will express in words something like the following? 'Have we not found,' they will say, 'a path of thought which seems to bring us and our argument to the conclusion, that while we are in the body, and while the soul is infected with the evils of the body, our desire will not be satisfied? and our desire is of the truth. For the body is a source of endless trouble to us by reason of the mere requirement of food; and is liable also to diseases which overtake and impede us in the search after true being: it fills us full of loves, and lusts, and fears, and fancies of all kinds, and endless foolery, and in fact, as men say, takes away from us the power of thinking at all. Whence come wars, and fightings, and factions? whence but from the body and the lusts of the body? wars are occasioned by the love of money, and money has to be acquired for the sake and in the service of the body; and by reason of all these impediments we have no time to give to philosophy; and, last and worst of all, even if we are at leisure and betake ourselves to some speculation, the body is always breaking in upon us, causing turmoil and confusion in our enquiries, and so amazing us that we are prevented from seeing the truth. It has been proved to us by experience that if we would have pure knowledge of anything we must be quit of the body—the soul in herself must behold things in themselves: and then we shall attain the wisdom which we desire, and of which we say that we are lovers, not while we live, but after death; for if while in company with the body, the soul cannot have pure knowledge, one of two things follows—either knowledge is not to be attained at all, or, if at all, after death. For then, and not till then, the soul will be parted from the body and exist in herself alone. In this present life, I reckon that we make the nearest approach to knowledge when we have the least possible intercourse or communion with the body, and are not surfeited with the bodily nature, but keep ourselves pure until the hour when God himself is pleased to release us. And thus having got rid of the foolishness of the body we shall be pure and hold converse with the pure, and know of ourselves the clear light everywhere, which is no other than the light of truth.' For the impure are not permitted to approach the pure. These are the sort of words, Simmias, which the true lovers of knowledge cannot help saying to one another, and thinking. You would agree; would you not?

Undoubtedly, Socrates.

But, O my friend, if this is true, there is great reason to hope that, going whither I go, when I have come to the end of my journey, I shall attain that which has been the pursuit of my life. And therefore I go on my way rejoicing, and not I only, but every other man who believes that his mind has been made ready and that he is in a manner purified.

Certainly, replied Simmias.

And what is purification but the separation of the soul from the body, as I was saying before; the habit of the soul gathering and collecting herself into herself from all sides out of the body; the dwelling in her own place alone, as in another life, so also in this, as far as she can; —the release of the soul from the chains of the body?

Very true, he said.

And this separation and release of the soul from the body is termed death?

To be sure, he said.

And the true philosophers, and they only, are ever seeking to release the soul. Is not the separation and release of the soul from the body their especial study?

That is true.

And, as I was saying at first, there would be a ridiculous contradiction in men studying to live as nearly as they can in a state of death, and yet repining when it comes upon them.

Clearly.

And the true philosophers, Simmias, are always occupied in the practice of dying, wherefore also to them least of all men is death terrible. Look at the matter thus: —if they have been in every way the enemies of the body, and are wanting to be alone with the soul, when this desire of theirs is granted, how inconsistent would they be if they trembled and repined, instead of rejoicing at their departure to that place where, when they arrive, they hope to gain that which in life they desired—and this was wisdom—and at the same time to be rid of the company of their enemy. Many a man has been willing to go to the world below animated by the hope of seeing there an earthly love, or wife, or son, and conversing with them. And will he who is a true lover of wisdom, and is strongly persuaded in like manner that only in the world below he can worthily enjoy her, still repine at death? Will he not depart with joy? Surely he will, O my friend, if he be a true philosopher. For he will have a firm conviction that there and there only, he can find wisdom in her purity. And if this be true, he would be very absurd, as I was saying, if he were afraid of death.

He would, indeed, replied Simmias.

And when you see a man who is repining at the approach of death, is not his reluctance a sufficient proof that he is not a lover of wisdom, but a lover of the body, and probably at the same time a lover of either money or power, or both?

Quite so, he replied.

And is not courage, Simmias, a quality which is specially characteristic of the philosopher?

Certainly.

There is temperance again, which even by the vulgar is supposed to consist in the control and regulation of the passions, and in the sense of superiority to them—is not temperance a virtue belonging to those only who despise the body, and who pass their lives in philosophy?

Most assuredly.

For the courage and temperance of other men, if you will consider them, are really a contradiction.

How so?

Well, he said, you are aware that death is regarded by men in general as a great evil.

Very true, he said.

And do not courageous men face death because they are afraid of yet greater evils?

That is quite true.

Then all but the philosophers are courageous only from fear, and because they are afraid; and yet that a man should be courageous from fear, and because he is a coward, is surely a strange thing.

Very true.

And are not the temperate exactly in the same case? They are temperate because they are intemperate—which might seem to be a contradiction, but is nevertheless the sort of thing which happens with this foolish temperance. For there are pleasures which they are afraid of losing; and in their desire to keep them, they abstain from some pleasures, because they are overcome by others; and although to be conquered by pleasure is called by men intemperance, to them the conquest of pleasure consists in being conquered by pleasure. And that is what I mean by saying that, in a sense, they are made temperate through intemperance.

Such appears to be the case.

Yet the exchange of one fear or pleasure or pain for another fear or pleasure or pain, and of the greater for the less, as if they were coins, is not the exchange of virtue. O my blessed Simmias, is there not one true coin for which all things ought to be exchanged? —and that is wisdom; and only in exchange for this, and in company with this, is anything truly bought or sold, whether courage or temperance or justice. And is not all true virtue the companion of wisdom, no matter what fears or pleasures or other similar goods or evils may or may not attend her? But the virtue which is made up of these goods, when they are severed from wisdom and exchanged with one another, is a shadow of virtue only, nor is there any freedom or health or truth in her; but in the true exchange there is a purging away of all these things, and temperance, and justice, and courage, and wisdom herself are the purgation of them. The founders of the mysteries would appear to have had a real meaning, and were not talking nonsense when they intimated in a figure long ago that he who passes unsanctified and uninitiated into the world below will lie in a slough, but that he who arrives there after initiation and purification will dwell with the gods. For 'many,' as they say in the mysteries, 'are the thyrsus-bearers, but few are the mystics,' —meaning, as I interpret the words, 'the true philosophers.' In the number of whom, during my whole life, I have been seeking, according to my ability, to find a place; —whether I have sought in a right way or not, and whether I have succeeded or not, I shall truly know in a little while, if God will, when I myself arrive in the other world—such is my belief. And therefore I maintain that I am right, Simmias and Cebes, in not grieving or repining at parting from you and my masters in this world, for I believe that I shall equally find good masters and friends in another world. But most men do not believe this saying; if then I succeed in convincing you by my defence better than I did the Athenian judges, it will be well.

Cebes answered: I agree, Socrates, in the greater part of what you say. But in what concerns the soul, men are apt to be incredulous; they fear that when she has left the body her place may be nowhere, and that on the very day of death she may perish and come to an end—immediately on her release from the body, issuing forth dispersed like smoke or air and in her flight vanishing away into nothingness. If she could only be collected into herself after she has obtained release from the evils of which you are speaking, there would be good reason to hope, Socrates, that what you say is true. But surely it requires a great deal of argument and many proofs to show that when the man is dead his soul yet exists, and has any force or intelligence.

True, Cebes, said Socrates; and shall I suggest that we converse a little of the probabilities of these things?

I am sure, said Cebes, that I should greatly like to know your opinion about them.

I reckon, said Socrates, that no one who heard me now, not even if he were one of my old enemies, the Comic poets, could accuse me of idle talking about matters in which I have no concern: —If you please, then, we will proceed with the inquiry.

Suppose we consider the question whether the souls of men after death are or are not in the world below. There comes into my mind an ancient doctrine which affirms that they go from hence into the other world, and returning hither, are born again from the dead. Now if it be true that the living come from the dead, then our souls must exist in the other world, for if not, how could they have been born again? And this would be conclusive, if there were any real evidence that the living are only born from the dead; but if this is not so, then other arguments will have to be adduced.

Very true, replied Cebes.

Then let us consider the whole question, not in relation to man only, but in relation to animals generally, and to plants, and to everything of which there is generation, and the proof will be easier. Are not all things which have opposites generated out of their opposites? I mean such things as good and evil, just and unjust—and there are innumerable other opposites which are generated out of opposites. And I want to show that in all opposites there is of necessity a similar alternation; I mean to say, for example, that anything which becomes greater must become greater after being less.

True.

And that which becomes less must have been once greater and then have become less.

Yes.

And the weaker is generated from the stronger, and the swifter from the slower.

Very true.

And the worse is from the better, and the more just is from the more unjust.

Of course.

And is this true of all opposites? and are we convinced that all of them are generated out of opposites?

Yes.

And in this universal opposition of all things, are there not also two intermediate processes which are ever going on, from one to the other opposite, and back again; where there is a greater and a less there is also an intermediate process of increase and diminution, and that which grows is said to wax, and that which decays to wane?

Yes, he said.

And there are many other processes, such as division and composition, cooling and heating, which equally involve a passage into and out of one another. And this necessarily holds of all opposites, even though not always expressed in words—they are really generated out of one another, and there is a passing or process from one to the other of them?

Very true, he replied.

Well, and is there not an opposite of life, as sleep is the opposite of waking?

True, he said.

And what is it?

Death, he answered.

And these, if they are opposites, are generated the one from the other, and have there their two intermediate processes also?

Of course.

Now, said Socrates, I will analyze one of the two pairs of opposites which I have mentioned to you, and also its intermediate processes, and you shall analyze the other to me. One of them I term sleep, the other waking. The state of sleep is opposed to the state of waking, and out of sleeping waking is generated, and out of waking, sleeping; and the process of generation is in the one case falling asleep, and in the other waking up. Do you agree?

I entirely agree.

Then, suppose that you analyze life and death to me in the same manner. Is not death opposed to life?

Yes.

And they are generated one from the other?

Yes.

What is generated from the living?

The dead.

And what from the dead?

I can only say in answer—the living.

Then the living, whether things or persons, Cebes, are generated from the dead?

That is clear, he replied.

Then the inference is that our souls exist in the world below?

That is true.

And one of the two processes or generations is visible—for surely the act of dying is visible?

Surely, he said.

What then is to be the result? Shall we exclude the opposite process? And shall we suppose nature to walk on one leg only? Must we not rather assign to death some corresponding process of generation?

Certainly, he replied.

And what is that process?

Return to life.

And return to life, if there be such a thing, is the birth of the dead into the world of the living?

Quite true.

Then here is a new way by which we arrive at the conclusion that the living come from the dead, just as the dead come from the living; and this, if true, affords a most certain proof that the souls of the dead exist in some place out of which they come again.

Yes, Socrates, he said; the conclusion seems to flow necessarily out of our previous admissions.

And that these admissions were not unfair, Cebes, he said, may be shown, I think, as follows: If generation were in a straight line only, and there were no compensation or circle in nature, no turn or return of elements into their opposites, then you know that all things would at last have the same form and pass into the same state, and there would be no more generation of them.

What do you mean? he said.

A simple thing enough, which I will illustrate by the case of sleep, he replied. You know that if there were no alternation of sleeping and waking, the tale of the sleeping Endymion① would in the end have no meaning, because all other things would be asleep, too, and he would not be distinguishable from the rest. Or if there were composition only, and no division of substances, then the chaos of Anaxagoras② would come again. And in like manner, my dear Cebes, if all things which partook of life were to die, and after they were dead remained in the form of death, and did not come to life again, all would at last die, and nothing would be alive—what other result could there be? For if the living spring from any other things, and they too die, must not all things at last be swallowed up in death? (But compare Republic.)

There is no escape, Socrates, said Cebes; and to me your argument seems to be absolutely true.

Yes, he said, Cebes, it is and must be so, in my opinion; and we have not been deluded in making these admissions; but I am confident that there truly is such a thing as living again, and that the living spring from the dead, and that the souls of the dead are in existence, and that the good souls have a better portion than the evil.

Cebes added: Your favorite doctrine, Socrates, that knowledge is simply recollection, if true, also necessarily implies a previous time in which we have learned that which we now recollect. But this would be impossible unless our soul had been in some place before existing in the form of man; here then is another proof of the soul's immortality.

But tell me, Cebes, said Simmias, interposing, what arguments are urged in favour of this doctrine of recollection. I am not very sure at the moment that I remember them.

One excellent proof, said Cebes, is afforded by questions. If you put a question to a person in a right way, he will give a true answer of himself, but how could he do this unless there were knowledge and right reason already in him? And this is most clearly shown when he is taken to a diagram or to anything of that sort. (Compare Meno③.)

But if, said Socrates, you are still incredulous, Simmias, I would ask you whether you may not agree with me when you look at the matter in another way; —I mean, if you are still incredulous as to whether knowledge is recollection.

---

① 恩底弥翁（Endymion），卡里亚（Caria）的青年牧羊人，因为在草地熟睡时被月神塞勒涅（Selene）偷吻，宙斯发现后赐他在睡梦中永葆青春
② 阿那克西哥拉斯（Anaxagoras），古希腊哲学家
③ 参见柏拉图对话录的《美诺篇》（Meno）

Incredulous, I am not, said Simmias; but I want to have this doctrine of recollection brought to my own recollection, and, from what Cebes has said, I am beginning to recollect and be convinced; but I should still like to hear what you were going to say.

This is what I would say, he replied: —We should agree, if I am not mistaken, that what a man recollects he must have known at some previous time.

Very true.

And what is the nature of this knowledge or recollection? I mean to ask, whether a person who, having seen or heard or in any way perceived anything, knows not only that, but has a conception of something else which is the subject, not of the same but of some other kind of knowledge, may not be fairly said to recollect that of which he has the conception?

What do you mean?

I mean what I may illustrate by the following instance: —The knowledge of a lyre is not the same as the knowledge of a man?

True.

And yet what is the feeling of lovers when they recognize a lyre, or a garment, or anything else which the beloved has been in the habit of using? Do not they, from knowing the lyre, form in the mind's eye an image of the youth to whom the lyre belongs? And this is recollection. In like manner anyone who sees Simmias may remember Cebes; and there are endless examples of the same thing.

Endless, indeed, replied Simmias.

And recollection is most commonly a process of recovering that which has been already forgotten through time and inattention.

Very true, he said.

Well; and may you not also from seeing the picture of a horse or a lyre remember a man? and from the picture of Simmias, you may be led to remember Cebes?

True.

Or you may also be led to the recollection of Simmias himself?

Quite so.

And in all these cases, the recollection may be derived from things either like or unlike?

It may be.

And when the recollection is derived from like things, then another consideration is sure to arise, which is—whether the likeness in any degree falls short or not of that which is recollected?

Very true, he said.

And shall we proceed a step further, and affirm that there is such a thing as equality, not of one piece of wood or stone with another, but that, over and above this, there is absolute equality? Shall we say so?

Say so, yes, replied Simmias, and swear to it, with all the confidence in life.

And do we know the nature of this absolute essence?

To be sure, he said.

And whence did we obtain our knowledge? Did we not see equalities of material things, such as pieces of wood and stones, and gather from them the idea of an equality which is different from them? For you will acknowledge that there is a difference. Or look at the matter in another way: —Do not the same pieces of wood or stone appear at one time equal, and at another time unequal?

That is certain.

But are real equals ever unequal? or is the idea of equality the same as of inequality?

Impossible, Socrates.

Then these (so-called) equals are not the same with the idea of equality?

I should say, clearly not, Socrates.

And yet from these equals, although differing from the idea of equality, you conceived and attained that idea?

Very true, he said.

Which might be like, or might be unlike them?

Yes.

But that makes no difference; whenever from seeing one thing you conceived another, whether like or unlike, there must surely have been an act of recollection?

Very true.

But what would you say of equal portions of wood and stone, or other material equals? and what is the impression produced by them? Are they equals in the same sense in which absolute equality is equal? or do they fall short of this perfect equality in a measure?

Yes, he said, in a very great measure too.

And must we not allow, that when I or any one, looking at any object, observes that the thing which he sees aims at being some other thing, but falls short of, and cannot be, that other thing, but is inferior, he who makes this observation must have had a previous knowledge of that to which the other, although similar, was inferior?

Certainly.

And has not this been our own case in the matter of equals and of absolute equality?

Precisely.

Then we must have known equality previously to the time when we first saw the material equals, and reflected that all these apparent equals strive to attain absolute equality, but fall short of it?

Very true.

And we recognize also that this absolute equality has only been known, and can only be known, through the medium of sight or touch, or of some other of the senses, which are all alike in this respect?

Yes, Socrates, as far as the argument is concerned, one of them is the same as the other.

From the senses then is derived the knowledge that all sensible things aim at an absolute equality of which they fall short?

Yes.

Then before we began to see or hear or perceive in any way, we must have had a knowledge of absolute equality, or we could not have referred to that standard the equals which are derived from the senses? —for to that they all aspire, and of that they fall short.

No other inference can be drawn from the previous statements.

And did we not see and hear and have the use of our other senses as soon as we were born?

Certainly.

Then we must have acquired the knowledge of equality at some previous time?

Yes.

That is to say, before we were born, I suppose?

True.

And if we acquired this knowledge before we were born, and were born having the use of it, then we also knew before we were born and at the instant of birth not only the equal or the greater or the less, but all other ideas; for we are not speaking only of equality, but of beauty, goodness, justice, holiness, and of all which we stamp with the name of essence in the dialectical process, both when we ask and when we answer questions. Of all this we may certainly affirm that we acquired the knowledge before birth?

We may.

But if, after having acquired, we have not forgotten what in each case we acquired, then we must always have come into life having knowledge, and shall always continue to know as long as life lasts—for knowing is the acquiring and retaining knowledge and not forgetting. Is not forgetting, Simmias, just the losing of knowledge?

Quite true, Socrates.

But if the knowledge which we acquired before birth was lost by us at birth, and if afterwards by the use of the senses we recovered what we previously knew, will not the process which we call learning be a recovering of the knowledge which is natural to us, and may not this be rightly termed recollection?

Very true.

So much is clear—that when we perceive something, either by the help of sight, or hearing, or some other sense, from that perception we are able to obtain a notion of some other thing like or unlike which is associated with it but has been forgotten. Whence, as I was saying, one of two alternatives follows: —either we had this knowledge at birth, and continued to know through life; or, after birth, those who are said to learn only remember, and learning is simply recollection.

Yes, that is quite true, Socrates.

And which alternative, Simmias, do you prefer? Had we the knowledge at our birth, or did we recollect the things which we knew previously to our birth? I cannot decide at the moment.

At any rate you can decide whether he who has knowledge will or will not be able to render an account of his knowledge? What do you say?

Certainly, he will.

But do you think that every man is able to give an account of these very matters about which we are speaking?

Would that they could, Socrates, but I rather fear that tomorrow, at this time, there will no longer be any one alive who is able to give an account of them such as ought to be given.

Then you are not of opinion, Simmias, that all men know these things?

Certainly not.

They are in process of recollecting that which they learned before?

Certainly.

But when did our souls acquire this knowledge? —not since we were born as men?

Certainly not.

And therefore, previously?

Yes.

Then, Simmias, our souls must also have existed without bodies before they were in the form of man, and must have had intelligence.

Unless indeed you suppose, Socrates, that these notions are given us at the very moment of birth; for this is the only time which remains.

Yes, my friend, but if so, when do we lose them? for they are not in us when we are born—that is admitted. Do we lose them at the moment of receiving them, or if not at what other time?

No, Socrates, I perceive that I was unconsciously talking nonsense.

Then may we not say, Simmias, that if, as we are always repeating, there is an absolute beauty, and goodness, and an absolute essence of all things; and if to this, which is now discovered to have existed in our former state, we refer all our sensations, and with this compare them, finding these ideas to be pre-existent and our inborn possession—then our souls must have had a prior existence, but if not, there would be no force in the argument? There is the same proof that these ideas must have existed before we were born, as that our souls existed before we were born; and if not the ideas, then not the souls.

Yes, Socrates; I am convinced that there is precisely the same necessity for the one as for the other; and the argument retreats successfully to the position that the existence of the soul before birth cannot be separated from the existence of the essence of which you speak. For there is nothing which to my mind is so patent as that beauty, goodness, and the other notions of which you were just now speaking, have a most real and absolute existence; and I am satisfied with the proof.

Well, but is Cebes equally satisfied? for I must convince him too.

I think, said Simmias, that Cebes is satisfied: although he is the most incredulous of mortals, yet I believe that he is sufficiently convinced of the existence of the soul before birth. But that after death the soul will continue to exist is not yet proven even to my own satisfaction. I cannot get rid of the feeling of the many to which Cebes was referring—the feeling that when the man dies the soul will be dispersed, and that this may be the extinction of her①. For admitting that she may have been born elsewhere, and framed out of other elements, and was in existence before entering the human body, why after having entered in and gone out again may she not herself be destroyed and come to an end?

Very true, Simmias, said Cebes; about half of what was required has been proven; to wit, that our souls existed before we were born: —that the soul will exist after death as well as before birth is the other half of which the proof is still wanting, and has to be supplied; when that is given the demonstration will be complete.

But that proof, Simmias and Cebes, has been already given, said Socrates, if you put the two arguments together—I mean this and the former one, in which we admitted that everything living is born of the dead. For if the soul exists before birth, and in coming to life and being born can be born only from death and dying, must she not after death continue to exist, since she has to be born again? —Surely the proof which you desire has been already furnished. Still I suspect that you and Simmias would be glad to probe the argument further. Like children, you are haunted with a fear that when the soul leaves the body, the wind may really blow her away and scatter her; especially if a man should happen to die in a great storm and not when the sky is calm.

Cebes answered with a smile: Then, Socrates, you must argue us out of our fears—and yet, strictly speaking, they are not our fears, but there is a child within us to whom death is a sort of hobgoblin; him too we must persuade not to be afraid when he is alone in the dark.

Socrates said: Let the voice of the charmer be applied daily until you have charmed away the fear.

And where shall we find a good charmer of our fears, Socrates, when you are

---

① 指灵魂 (the soul)

gone?

Hellas①, he replied, is a large place, Cebes, and has many good men, and there are barbarous races not a few: seek for him among them all, far and wide, sparing neither pains nor money; for there is no better way of spending your money. And you must seek among yourselves too; for you will not find others better able to make the search.

The search, replied Cebes, shall certainly be made. And now, if you please, let us return to the point of the argument at which we digressed.

By all means, replied Socrates; what else should I please?

Very good.

Must we not, said Socrates, ask ourselves what that is which, as we imagine, is liable to be scattered, and about which we fear? and what again is that about which we have no fear? And then we may proceed further to enquire whether that which suffers dispersion is or is not of the nature of soul—our hopes and fears as to our own souls will turn upon the answers to these questions.

Very true, he said.

Now the compound or composite may be supposed to be naturally capable, as of being compounded, so also of being dissolved; but that which is uncompounded, and that only, must be, if anything is, indissoluble.

Yes; I should imagine so, said Cebes.

And the uncompounded may be assumed to be the same and unchanging, whereas the compound is always changing and never the same.

I agree, he said.

Then now let us return to the previous discussion. Is that idea or essence, which in the dialectical process we define as essence or true existence—whether essence of equality, beauty, or anything else—are these essences, I say, liable at times to some degree of change? or are they each of them always what they are, having the same simple self-existent and unchanging forms, not admitting of variation at all, or in any way, or at any time?

They must be always the same, Socrates, replied Cebes.

And what would you say of the many beautiful—whether men or horses or garments

---

① 指希腊地区

or any other things which are named by the same names and may be called equal or beautiful, —are they all unchanging and the same always, or quite the reverse? May they not rather be described as almost always changing and hardly ever the same, either with themselves or with one another?

The latter, replied Cebes; they are always in a state of change.

And these you can touch and see and perceive with the senses, but the unchanging things you can only perceive with the mind—they are invisible and are not seen?

That is very true, he said.

Well, then, added Socrates, let us suppose that there are two sorts of existences—one seen, the other unseen.

Let us suppose them.

The seen is the changing, and the unseen is the unchanging? That may be also supposed. And, further, is not one part of us body, another part soul?

To be sure.

And to which class is the body more alike and akin? Clearly to the seen—no one can doubt that. And is the soul seen or not seen?

Not by man, Socrates.

And what we mean by 'seen' and 'not seen' is that which is or is not visible to the eye of man?

Yes, to the eye of man.

And is the soul seen or not seen?

Not seen.

Unseen then?

Yes.

Then the soul is more like to the unseen, and the body to the seen?

That follows necessarily, Socrates.

And were we not saying long ago that the soul when using the body as an instrument of perception, that is to say, when using the sense of sight or hearing or some other sense (for the meaning of perceiving through the body is perceiving through the senses) —were we not saying that the soul too is then dragged by the body into the region of the changeable, and wanders and is confused; the world spins round her[①],

---

① 指灵魂 (the soul)

and she is like a drunkard, when she touches change?

Very true.

But when returning into herself she reflects, then she passes into the other world, the region of purity, and eternity, and immortality, and unchangeableness, which are her kindred, and with them she ever lives, when she is by herself and is not let or hindered; then she ceases from her erring ways, and being in communion with the unchanging is unchanging. And this state of the soul is called wisdom?

That is well and truly said, Socrates, he replied.

And to which class is the soul more nearly alike and akin, as far as may be inferred from this argument, as well as from the preceding one?

I think, Socrates, that, in the opinion of every one who follows the argument, the soul will be infinitely more like the unchangeable—even the most stupid person will not deny that.

And the body is more like the changing?

Yes.

Yet once more consider the matter in another light: When the soul and the body are united, then nature orders the soul to rule and govern, and the body to obey and serve. Now which of these two functions is akin to the divine? and which to the mortal? Does not the divine appear to you to be that which naturally orders and rules, and the mortal to be that which is subject and servant?

True.

And which does the soul resemble?

The soul resembles the divine, and the body the mortal—there can be no doubt of that, Socrates.

Then reflect, Cebes: of all which has been said is not this the conclusion? —that the soul is in the very likeness of the divine, and immortal, and intellectual, and uniform, and indissoluble, and unchangeable; and that the body is in the very likeness of the human, and mortal, and unintellectual, and multiform, and dissoluble, and changeable. Can this, my dear Cebes, be denied?

It cannot.

But if it be true, then is not the body liable to speedy dissolution? and is not the soul almost or altogether indissoluble?

Certainly.

And do you further observe, that after a man is dead, the body, or visible part of him, which is lying in the visible world, and is called a corpse, and would naturally be dissolved and decomposed and dissipated, is not dissolved or decomposed at once, but may remain for a for some time, nay even for a long time, if the constitution be sound at the time of death, and the season of the year favourable? For the body when shrunk and embalmed, as the manner is in Egypt, may remain almost entire through infinite ages; and even in decay, there are still some portions, such as the bones and ligaments, which are practically indestructible:—Do you agree?

Yes.

And is it likely that the soul, which is invisible, in passing to the place of the true Hades①, which like her is invisible, and pure, and noble, and on her way to the good and wise God, whither, if God will, my soul is also soon to go,—that the soul, I repeat, if this be her nature and origin, will be blown away and destroyed immediately on quitting the body, as the many say? That can never be, my dear Simmias and Cebes. The truth rather is, that the soul which is pure at departing and draws after her no bodily taint, having never voluntarily during life had connection with the body, which she is ever avoiding, herself gathered into herself;—and making such abstraction her perpetual study—which means that she has been a true disciple of philosophy; and therefore has in fact been always engaged in the practice of dying? For is not philosophy the practice of death?—

Certainly—

That soul, I say, herself invisible, departs to the invisible world—to the divine and immortal and rational: thither arriving, she is secure of bliss and is released from the error and folly of men, their fears and wild passions and all other human ills, and forever dwells, as they say of the initiated, in company with the gods (compare Apol.②). Is not this true, Cebes?

Yes, said Cebes, beyond a doubt.

But the soul which has been polluted, and is impure at the time of her departure, and is the companion and servant of the body always, and is in love with and fascinated by the body and by the desires and pleasures of the body, until she is led to believe

---

① 哈迪斯，冥王
② 参见柏拉图对话录《申辩篇》（Apol. 即 Apology）

that the truth only exists in a bodily form, which a man may touch and see and taste, and use for the purposes of his lusts, —the soul, I mean, accustomed to hate and fear and avoid the intellectual principle, which to the bodily eye is dark and invisible, and can be attained only by philosophy; —do you suppose that such a soul will depart pure and unalloyed?

Impossible, he replied.

She is held fast by the corporeal, which the continual association and constant care of the body have wrought into her nature.

Very true.

And this corporeal element, my friend, is heavy and weighty and earthy, and is that element of sight by which a soul is depressed and dragged down again into the visible world, because she is afraid of the invisible and of the world below—prowling about tombs and sepulchres, near which, as they tell us, are seen certain ghostly apparitions of souls which have not departed pure, but are cloyed with sight and therefore visible.

That is very likely, Socrates.

Yes, that is very likely, Cebes; and these must be the souls, not of the good, but of the evil, which are compelled to wander about such places in payment of the penalty of their former evil way of life; and they continue to wander until through the craving after the corporeal which never leaves them, they are imprisoned finally in another body. And they may be supposed to find their prisons in the same natures which they have had in their former lives.

What natures do you mean, Socrates?

What I mean is that men who have followed after gluttony, and wantonness, and drunkenness, and have had no thought of avoiding them, would pass into asses and animals of that sort. What do you think?

I think such an opinion to be exceedingly probable.

And those who have chosen the portion of injustice, and tyranny, and violence, will pass into wolves, or into hawks and kites; —whither else can we suppose them to go?

Yes, said Cebes; with such natures, beyond question.

And there is no difficulty, he said, in assigning to all of them places answering to their several natures and propensities?

There is not, he said.

Some are happier than others; and the happiest both in themselves and in the place to which they go are those who have practised the civil and social virtues which are called temperance and justice, and are acquired by habit and attention without philosophy and mind. (Compare Republic①.)

Why are they the happiest?

Because they may be expected to pass into some gentle and social kind which is like their own, such as bees or wasps or ants, or back again into the form of man, and just and moderate men may be supposed to spring from them.

Very likely.

No one who has not studied philosophy and who is not entirely pure at the time of his departure is allowed to enter the company of the Gods, but the lover of knowledge only. And this is the reason, Simmias and Cebes, why the true votaries of philosophy abstain from all fleshly lusts, and hold out against them and refuse to give themselves up to them, —not because they fear poverty or the ruin of their families, like the lovers of money, and the world in general; nor like the lovers of power and honour, because they dread the dishonour or disgrace of evil deeds.

No, Socrates, that would not become them, said Cebes.

No indeed, he replied; and therefore they who have any care of their own souls, and do not merely live moulding and fashioning the body, say farewell to all this; they will not walk in the ways of the blind: and when philosophy offers them purification and release from evil, they feel that they ought not to resist her influence, and whither she leads they turn and follow.

What do you mean, Socrates?

I will tell you, he said. The lovers of knowledge are conscious that the soul was simply fastened and glued to the body—until philosophy received her, she could only view real existence through the bars of a prison, not in and through herself; she was wallowing in the mire of every sort of ignorance; and by reason of lust had become the principal accomplice in her own captivity. This was her original state; and then, as I was saying, and as the lovers of knowledge are well aware, philosophy, seeing how terrible was her confinement, of which she was to herself the cause, received and

---

① 参见《理想国》

gently comforted her and sought to release her, pointing out that the eye and the ear and the other senses are full of deception, and persuading her to retire from them, and abstain from all but the necessary use of them, and be gathered up and collected into herself, bidding her trust in herself and her own pure apprehension of pure existence, and to mistrust whatever comes to her through other channels and is subject to variation; for such things are visible and tangible, but what she sees in her own nature is intelligible and invisible. And the soul of the true philosopher thinks that she ought not to resist this deliverance, and therefore abstains from pleasures and desires and pains and fears, as far as she is able; reflecting that when a man has great joys or sorrows or fears or desires, he suffers from them, not merely the sort of evil which might be anticipated—as for example, the loss of his health or property which he has sacrificed to his lusts—but an evil greater far, which is the greatest and worst of all evils, and one of which he never thinks.

What is it, Socrates? said Cebes.

The evil is that when the feeling of pleasure or pain is most intense, every soul of man imagines the objects of this intense feeling to be then plainest and truest: but this is not so, they are really the things of sight.

Very true.

And is not this the state in which the soul is most enthralled by the body?

How so?

Why, because each pleasure and pain is a sort of nail which nails and rivets the soul to the body, until she becomes like the body, and believes that to be true which the body affirms to be true; and from agreeing with the body and having the same delights she is obliged to have the same habits and haunts, and is not likely ever to be pure at her departure to the world below, but is always infected by the body; and so she sinks into another body and there germinates and grows, and has therefore no part in the communion of the divine and pure and simple.

Most true, Socrates, answered Cebes.

And this, Cebes, is the reason why the true lovers of knowledge are temperate and brave; and not for the reason which the world gives.

Certainly not.

Certainly not! The soul of a philosopher will reason in quite another way; she will not ask philosophy to release her in order that when released she may deliver herself up again to the thraldom of pleasures and pains, doing a work only to be undone again, weaving instead of unweaving her Penelope's web①. But she will calm passion, and follow reason, and dwell in the contemplation of her, beholding the true and divine (which is not matter of opinion), and thence deriving nourishment. Thus she seeks to live while she lives, and after death she hopes to go to her own kindred and to that which is like her, and to be freed from human ills. Never fear, Simmias and Cebes, that a soul which has been thus nurtured and has had these pursuits, will at her departure from the body be scattered and blown away by the winds and be nowhere and nothing.

When Socrates had done speaking, for a considerable time there was silence; he himself appeared to be meditating, as most of us were, on what had been said; only Cebes and Simmias spoke a few words to one another. And Socrates observing them asked what they thought of the argument, and whether there was anything wanting?

For, said he, there are many points still open to suspicion and attack, if anyone were disposed to sift the matter thoroughly. Should you be considering some other matter I say no more, but if you are still in doubt do not hesitate to say exactly what you think, and let us have anything better which you can suggest; and if you think that I can be of any use, allow me to help you.

Simmias said: I must confess, Socrates, that doubts did arise in our minds, and each of us was urging and inciting the other to put the question which we wanted to have answered and which neither of us liked to ask, fearing that our importunity might be troublesome under present at such a time.

Socrates replied with a smile: O Simmias, what are you saying? I am not very likely to persuade other men that I do not regard my present situation as a misfortune, if I cannot even persuade you that I am no worse off now than at any other time in my life. Will you not allow that I have as much of the spirit of prophecy in me as the swans? For

---

① 珀涅罗珀之网，珀涅罗珀（Penelope）是奥德修斯（Odysseus）的妻子，在奥德修斯远征特洛伊的20年期间，她面对众多求婚者的纠缠，答应织好一个嫁妆之后，再从求婚者中选择未来的丈夫。为了痴等奥德修斯的归来，她通过白天织布夜晚再拆布的方式来拖延时间。此处苏格拉底借用珀涅罗珀之网，比喻哲学家的灵魂不能等同于普通人之灵魂，不能由情绪和感官欲望所左右而来来回回做无用之功，而应由理性引导认识真理和神圣之事

they①, when they perceive that they must die, having sung all their life long, do then sing more lustily than ever, rejoicing in the thought that they are about to go away to the god whose ministers they are. But men, because they are themselves afraid of death, slanderously affirm of the swans that they sing a lament at the last, not considering that no bird sings when cold, or hungry, or in pain, not even the nightingale, nor the swallow, nor yet the hoopoe; which are said indeed to tune a lay of sorrow, although I do not believe this to be true of them any more than of the swans. But because they are sacred to Apollo, they have the gift of prophecy, and anticipate the good things of another world, wherefore they sing and rejoice in that day more than they ever did before. And I too, believing myself to be the consecrated servant of the same God, and the fellow-servant of the swans, and thinking that I have received from my master gifts of prophecy which are not inferior to theirs, would not go out of life less merrily than the swans. Never mind then, if this be your only objection, but speak and ask anything which you like, while the eleven magistrates of Athens allow.

Very good, Socrates, said Simmias; then I will tell you my difficulty, and Cebes will tell you his. I feel myself, (and I daresay that you have the same feeling), how hard or rather impossible is the attainment of any certainty about questions such as these in the present life. And yet I should deem him a coward who did not prove what is said about them to the uttermost, or whose heart failed him before he had examined them on every side. For he should persevere until he has achieved one of two things: either he should discover, or be taught the truth about them; or, if this be impossible, I would have him take the best and most irrefragable of human theories, and let this be the raft upon which he sails through life—not without risk, as I admit, if he cannot find some word of God which will more surely and safely carry him. And now, as you bid me, I will venture to question you, and then I shall not have to reproach myself hereafter with not having said at the time what I think. For when I consider the matter, either alone or with Cebes, the argument does certainly appear to me, Socrates, to be not sufficient.

Socrates answered: I dare say, my friend, that you may be right, but I should like to know in what respect the argument is insufficient.

In this respect, replied Simmias: —Suppose a person to use the same argument

---

① 指天鹅们 (the swans)

about harmony and the lyre—might he not say that harmony is a thing invisible, incorporeal, perfect, divine, existing in the lyre which is harmonized, but that the lyre and the strings are matter and material, composite, earthy, and akin to mortality? And when someone breaks the lyre, or cuts and rends the strings, then he who takes this view would argue as you do, and on the same analogy, that the harmony survives and has not perished—you cannot imagine, he would say, that the lyre without the strings, and the broken strings themselves which are mortal remain, and yet that the harmony, which is of heavenly and immortal nature and kindred, has perished—perished before the mortal. The harmony must still be somewhere, and the wood and strings will decay before anything can happen to that. The thought, Socrates, must have occurred to your own mind that such is our conception of the soul; and that when the body is in a manner strung and held together by the elements of hot and cold, wet and dry, then the soul is the harmony or due proportionate admixture of them. But if so, whenever the strings of the body are unduly loosened or overstrained through disease or other injury, then the soul, though most divine, like other harmonies of music or of works of art, of course perishes at once, although the material remains of the body may last for a considerable time, until they are either decayed or burnt. And if any one maintains that the soul, being the harmony of the elements of the body, is first to perish in that which is called death, how shall we answer him?

  Socrates looked fixedly at us as his manner was, and said with a smile: Simmias has reason on his side; and why does not some one of you who is better able than myself answer him? for there is force in his attack upon me. But perhaps, before we answer him, we had better also hear what Cebes has to say that we may gain time for reflection, and when they have both spoken, we may either assent to them, if there is truth in what they say, or if not, we will maintain our position. Please to tell me then, Cebes, he said, what was the difficulty which troubled you?

  Cebes said: I will tell you. My feeling is that the argument is where it was, and open to the same objections which were urged before; for I am ready to admit that the existence of the soul before entering into the bodily form has been very ingeniously, and, if I may say so, quite sufficiently proven; but the existence of the soul after death is still, in my judgment, unproven. Now my objection is not the same as that of Simmias; for I am not disposed to deny that the soul is stronger and more lasting than the body, being of opinion that in all such respects the soul very far excels the body.

Well, then, says the argument to me, why do you remain unconvinced? —When you see that the weaker continues in existence after the man is dead, will you not admit that the more lasting must also survive during the same period of time? Now I will ask you to consider whether the objection, which, like Simmias, I will express in a figure, is of any weight. The analogy which I will adduce is that of an old weaver, who dies, and after his death somebody says: —He is not dead, he must be alive; —see, there is the coat which he himself wove and wore, and which remains whole and undecayed. And then he proceeds to ask of someone who is incredulous, whether a man lasts longer, or the coat which is in use and wear; and when he is answered that a man lasts far longer, thinks that he has thus certainly demonstrated the survival of the man, who is the more lasting, because the less lasting remains. But that, Simmias, as I would beg you to remark, is a mistake; any one can see that he who talks thus is talking nonsense. For the truth is, that the weaver aforesaid, having woven and worn many such coats, outlived several of them, and was outlived by the last; but a man is not therefore proved to be slighter and weaker than a coat. Now the relation of the body to the soul may be expressed in a similar figure; and any one may very fairly say in like manner that the soul is lasting, and the body weak and short-lived in comparison. He may argue in like manner that every soul wears out many bodies, especially if a man live many years. While he is alive the body deliquesces and decays, and the soul always weaves another garment and repairs the waste. But of course, whenever the soul perishes, she must have on her last garment, and this will survive her; and then at length, when the soul is dead, the body will show its native weakness, and quickly decompose and pass away. I would therefore rather not rely on the argument from superior strength to prove the continued existence of the soul after death. For granting even more than you affirm to be possible, and acknowledging not only that the soul existed before birth, but also that the souls of some exist, and will continue to exist after death, and will be born and die again and again, and that there is a natural strength in the soul which will hold out and be born many times—nevertheless, we may be still inclined to think that she will weary in the labours of successive births, and may at last succumb in one of her deaths and utterly perish; and this death and dissolution of the body which brings destruction to the soul may be unknown to any of us, for no one of us can have had any experience of it: and if so, then I maintain that he who is confident about death has but a foolish confidence, unless he is able to prove that the soul is altogether immortal and imperishable. But if he cannot prove the soul's immortality, he who is about to die will always have reason to fear that when the body is disunited, the soul also may utterly perish.

All of us, as we afterwards remarked to one another, had an unpleasant feeling at hearing what they said. When we had been so firmly convinced before, now to have our faith shaken seemed to introduce a confusion and uncertainty, not only into the previous argument, but into any future one; either we were incapable of forming a judgment, or there were no grounds of belief.

ECHECRATES: There I feel with you—by heaven I do, Phaedo, and when you were speaking, I was beginning to ask myself the same question: What argument can I ever trust again? For what could be more convincing than the argument of Socrates, which has now fallen into discredit? That the soul is a harmony is a doctrine which has always had a wonderful attraction for me, and, when mentioned, came back to me at once, as my own original conviction. And now I must begin again and find another argument which will assure me that when the man is dead the soul survives. Tell me, I implore you, how did Socrates proceed? Did he appear to share the unpleasant feeling which you mention? or did he calmly meet the attack? And did he answer forcibly or feebly? Narrate what passed as exactly as you can.

PHAEDO: Often, Echecrates, I have wondered at Socrates, but never more than on that occasion. That he should be able to answer was nothing, but what astonished me was, first, the gentle and pleasant and approving manner in which he received the words of the young men, and then his quick sense of the wound which had been inflicted by the argument, and the readiness with which he healed it. He might be compared to a general rallying his defeated and broken army, urging them to accompany him and return to the field of argument.

ECHECRATES: What followed?

PHAEDO: You shall hear, for I was close to him on his right hand, seated on a sort of stool, and he on a couch which was a good deal higher. He stroked my head, and pressed the hair upon my neck—he had a way of playing with my hair; and then he said: Tomorrow, Phaedo, I suppose that these fair locks of yours will be severed.

Yes, Socrates, I suppose that they will, I replied.

Not so, if you will take my advice.

What shall I do with them? I said.

To-day, he replied, and not to-morrow, if this argument dies and we cannot bring it to life again, you and I will both shave our locks; and if I were you, and the argument got away from me, and I could not hold my ground against Simmias and Cebes, I would myself take an oath, like the Argives①, not to wear hair any more until I had renewed the conflict and defeated them.

Yes, I said, but Heracles② himself is said not to be a match for two.

Summon me then, he said, and I will be your Iolaus③ until the sun goes down.

I summon you rather, I rejoined, not as Heracles summoning Iolaus, but as Iolaus might summon Heracles.

That will do as well, he said. But first let us take care that we avoid a danger.

Of what nature? I said.

Lest we become misologists④, he replied, no worse thing can happen to a man than this. For as there are misanthropists or haters of men, there are also misologists or haters of ideas, and both spring from the same cause, which is ignorance of the world. Misanthropy arises out of the too great confidence of inexperience; —you trust a man and think him altogether true and sound and faithful, and then in a little while he turns out to be false and knavish; and then another and another, and when this has happened several times to a man, especially when it happens among those whom he deems to be his own most trusted and familiar friends, and he has often quarreled with them, he at last hates all men, and believes that no one has any good in him at all. You must have observed this trait of character?

I have.

And is not the feeling discreditable? Is it not obvious that such an one having to deal with other men, was clearly without any experience of human nature; for experience would have taught him the true state of the case, that few are the good and few the evil, and that the great majority are in the interval between them.

What do you mean? I said.

I mean, he replied, as you might say of the very large and very small, that nothing is more uncommon than a very large or very small man; and this applies

---

① 阿尔戈斯人，阿尔戈斯是希腊东南部著名古城
② 赫拉克勒斯，大力神
③ 伊俄拉俄斯（Iolaus），赫拉克勒斯的侄子，帮助赫拉克勒斯完成了许多使命
④ 厌恶辩论者，厌恶知识者

generally to all extremes, whether of great and small, or swift and slow, or fair and foul, or black and white: and whether the instances you select be men or dogs or anything else, few are the extremes, but many are in the mean between them. Did you never observe this?

Yes, I said, I have.

And do you not imagine, he said, that if there were a competition in evil, the worst would be found to be very few?

Yes, that is very likely, I said.

Yes, that is very likely, he replied; although in this respect arguments are unlike men—there I was led on by you to say more than I had intended; but the point of comparison was, that when a simple man who has no skill in dialectics believes an argument to be true which he afterwards imagines to be false, whether really false or not, and then another and another, he has no longer any faith left, and great disputers, as you know, come to think at last that they have grown to be the wisest of mankind; for they alone perceive the utter unsoundness and instability of all arguments, or indeed, of all things, which, like the currents in the Euripus①, are going up and down in never-ceasing ebb and flow.

That is quite true, I said.

Yes, Phaedo, he replied, and how melancholy, if there be such a thing as truth or certainty or possibility of knowledge—that a man should have lighted upon some argument or other which at first seemed true and then turned out to be false, and instead of blaming himself and his own want of wit, because he is annoyed, should at last be too glad to transfer the blame from himself to arguments in general: and forever afterwards should hate and revile them, and lose truth and the knowledge of realities.

Yes, indeed, I said; that is very melancholy.

Let us then, in the first place, he said, be careful of allowing or of admitting into our souls the notion that there is no health or soundness in any arguments at all. Rather say that we have not yet attained to soundness in ourselves, and that we must struggle manfully and do our best to gain health of mind—you and all other men having regard to the whole of your future life, and I myself in the prospect of death. For at this moment I am sensible that I have not the temper of a philosopher; like the vulgar, I am

---

① 埃夫里普海峡（Euripus），爱琴海中一条狭长的海峡，海峡中的水流方向一天变换七次

only a partisan. Now the partisan, when he is engaged in a dispute, cares nothing about the rights of the question, but is anxious only to convince his hearers of his own assertions. And the difference between him and me at the present moment is merely this—that whereas he seeks to convince his hearers that what he says is true, I am rather seeking to convince myself; to convince my hearers is a secondary matter with me. And do but see how much I gain by the argument. For if what I say is true, then I do well to be persuaded of the truth, but if there be nothing after death, still, during the short time that remains, I shall not distress my friends with lamentations, and my ignorance will not last, but will die with me, and therefore no harm will be done. This is the state of mind, Simmias and Cebes, in which I approach the argument. And I would ask you to be thinking of the truth and not of Socrates: agree with me, if I seem to you to be speaking the truth; or if not, withstand me might and main, that I may not deceive you as well as myself in my enthusiasm, and like the bee, leave my sting in you before I die.

And now let us proceed, he said. And first of all let me be sure that I have in my mind what you were saying. Simmias, if I remember rightly, has fears and misgivings whether the soul, although a fairer and diviner thing than the body, being as she is in the form of harmony, may not perish first. On the other hand, Cebes appeared to grant that the soul was more lasting than the body, but he said that no one could know whether the soul, after having worn out many bodies, might not perish herself and leave her last body behind her; and that this is death, which is the destruction not of the body but of the soul, for in the body the work of destruction is ever going on. Are not these, Simmias and Cebes, the points which we have to consider?

They both agreed to this statement of them.

He proceeded: And did you deny the force of the whole preceding argument, or of a part only?

Of a part only, they replied.

And what did you think, he said, of that part of the argument in which we said that knowledge was recollection, and hence inferred that the soul must have previously existed somewhere else before she was enclosed in the body?

Cebes said that he had been wonderfully impressed by that part of the argument, and that his conviction remained absolutely unshaken. Simmias agreed, and added that he himself could hardly imagine the possibility of his ever thinking differently.

But, rejoined Socrates, you will have to think differently, my Theban friend, if you still maintain that harmony is a compound, and that the soul is a harmony which is made out of strings set in the frame of the body; for you will surely never allow yourself to say that a harmony is prior to the elements which compose it.

Never, Socrates.

But do you not see that this is what you imply when you say that the soul existed before she took the form and body of man, and was made up of elements which as yet had no existence? For harmony is not like the soul, as you suppose; but first the lyre, and the strings, and the sounds exist in a state of discord, and then harmony is made last of all, and perishes first. And how can such a notion of the soul as this agree with the other?

Not at all, replied Simmias.

And yet, he said, there surely ought to be harmony in a discourse of which harmony is the theme.

There ought, replied Simmias.

But there is no harmony, he said, in the two propositions that knowledge is recollection, and that the soul is a harmony. Which of them will you retain?

I think, he replied, that I have a much stronger faith, Socrates, in the first of the two, which has been fully demonstrated to me, than in the latter, which has not been demonstrated at all, but rests only on probable and plausible grounds; and is therefore believed by the many. I know too well that these arguments from probabilities are impostors, and unless great caution is observed in the use of them, they are apt to be deceptive—in geometry, and in other things too. But the doctrine of knowledge and recollection has been proven to me on trustworthy grounds; and the proof was that the soul must have existed before she came into the body, because to her belongs the essence of which the very name implies existence. Having, as I am convinced, rightly accepted this conclusion, and on sufficient grounds, I must, as I suppose, cease to argue or allow others to argue that the soul is a harmony.

Let me put the matter, Simmias, he said, in another point of view: Do you imagine that a harmony or any other composition can be in a state other than that of the elements, out of which it is compounded?

Certainly not.

Or do or suffer anything other than they do or suffer?

He agreed.

Then a harmony does not, properly speaking, lead the parts or elements which make up the harmony, but only follows them.

He assented.

For harmony cannot possibly have any motion, or sound, or other quality which is opposed to its parts.

That would be impossible, he replied.

And does not the nature of every harmony depend upon the manner in which the elements are harmonized?

I do not understand you, he said.

I mean to say that a harmony admits of degrees, and is more of a harmony, and more completely a harmony, when more truly and fully harmonized, to any extent which is possible; and less of a harmony, and less completely a harmony, when less truly and fully harmonized.

True.

But does the soul admit of degrees? or is one soul in the very least degree more or less, or more or less completely, a soul than another?

Not in the least.

Yet surely of two souls, one is said to have intelligence and virtue, and to be good, and the other to have folly and vice, and to be an evil soul: and this is said truly?

Yes, truly.

But what will those who maintain the soul to be a harmony say of this presence of virtue and vice in the soul? —will they say that here is another harmony, and another discord, and that the virtuous soul is harmonized, and herself being a harmony has another harmony within her, and that the vicious soul is inharmonical and has no harmony within her?

I cannot tell, replied Simmias; but I suppose that something of the sort would be asserted by those who say that the soul is a harmony.

And we have already admitted that no soul is more a soul than another; which is equivalent to admitting that harmony is not more or less harmony, or more or less completely a harmony?

Quite true.

And that which is not more or less a harmony is not more or less harmonized?

True.

And that which is not more or less harmonized cannot have more or less of harmony, but only an equal harmony?

Yes, an equal harmony.

Then one soul not being more or less absolutely a soul than another, is not more or less harmonized?

Exactly.

And therefore has neither more nor less of discord, nor yet of harmony?

She has not.

And having neither more nor less of harmony or of discord, one soul has no more vice or virtue than another, if vice be discord and virtue harmony?

Not at all more.

Or speaking more correctly, Simmias, the soul, if she is a harmony, will never have any vice; because a harmony, being absolutely a harmony, has no part in the inharmonical.

No.

And therefore a soul which is absolutely a soul has no vice?

How can she have, if the previous argument holds?

Then, if all souls are equally by their nature souls, all souls of all living creatures will be equally good?

I agree with you, Socrates, he said.

And can all this be true, think you? he said; for these are the consequences which seem to follow from the assumption that the soul is a harmony?

It cannot be true.

Once more, he said, what ruler is there of the elements of human nature other than the soul, and especially the wise soul? Do you know of any?

Indeed, I do not.

And is the soul in agreement with the affections of the body? or is she at variance with them? For example, when the body is hot and thirsty, does not the soul incline us against drinking? and when the body is hungry, against eating? And this is only one instance out of ten thousand of the opposition of the soul to the things of the body.

Very true.

But we have already acknowledged that the soul, being a harmony, can never utter a note at variance with the tensions and relaxations and vibrations and other affections of the strings out of which she is composed; she can only follow, she cannot lead them?

It must be so, he replied.

And yet do we not now discover the soul to be doing the exact opposite—leading the elements of which she is believed to be composed; almost always opposing and coercing them in all sorts of ways throughout life, sometimes more violently with the pains of medicine and gymnastic; then again more gently; now threatening, now admonishing the desires, passions, fears, as if talking to a thing which is not herself, as Homer in the Odyssee represents Odysseus doing in the words—

'He beat his breast, and thus reproached his heart: Endure, my heart; far worse hast thou endured!'

Do you think that Homer wrote this under the idea that the soul is a harmony capable of being led by the affections of the body, and not rather of a nature which should lead and master them—herself a far diviner thing than any harmony?

Yes, Socrates, I quite think so.

Then, my friend, we can never be right in saying that the soul is a harmony, for we should contradict the divine Homer, and contradict ourselves.

True, he said.

Thus much, said Socrates, of Harmonia①, your Theban goddess, who has graciously yielded to us; but what shall I say, Cebes, to her husband Cadmus②, and how shall I make peace with him?

I think that you will discover a way of propitiating him, said Cebes; I am sure that you have put the argument with Harmonia in a manner that I could never have expected. For when Simmias was mentioning his difficulty, I quite imagined that no answer could be given to him, and therefore I was surprised at finding that his argument could not sustain the first onset of yours, and not impossibly the other, whom you call Cadmus, may share a similar fate.

---

① 和谐女神哈尔摩尼娅（Harmonia），战神阿瑞斯和爱神阿芙洛狄忒之女，后成为忒拜城（Thebes）的建立者卡德摩斯（Cadmus）之妻
② 卡德摩斯（Cadmus）忒拜城的建立者，和谐女神哈尔摩尼娅（Harmonia）的丈夫

Nay, my good friend, said Socrates, let us not boast, lest some evil eye should put to flight the word which I am about to speak. That, however, may be left in the hands of those above, while I draw near in Homeric fashion, and try the mettle of your words. Here lies the point: —You want to have it proven to you that the soul is imperishable and immortal, and the philosopher who is confident in death appears to you to have but a vain and foolish confidence, if he believes that he will fare better in the world below than one who has led another sort of life, unless he can prove this; and you say that the demonstration of the strength and divinity of the soul, and of her existence prior to our becoming men, does not necessarily imply her immortality. Admitting the soul to be longlived, and to have known and done much in a former state, still she is not on that account immortal; and her entrance into the human form may be a sort of disease which is the beginning of dissolution, and may at last, after the toils of life are over, end in that which is called death. And whether the soul enters into the body once only or many times, does not, as you say, make any difference in the fears of individuals. For any man, who is not devoid of sense, must fear, if he has no knowledge and can give no account of the soul's immortality. This, or something like this, I suspect to be your notion, Cebes; and I designedly recur to it in order that nothing may escape us, and that you may, if you wish, add or subtract anything.

But, said Cebes, as far as I see at present, I have nothing to add or subtract: I mean what you say that I mean.

Socrates paused awhile, and seemed to be absorbed in reflection. At length he said: You are raising a tremendous question, Cebes, involving the whole nature of generation and corruption, about which, if you like, I will give you my own experience; and if anything which I say is likely to avail towards the solution of your difficulty you may make use of it.

I should very much like, said Cebes, to hear what you have to say.

Then I will tell you, said Socrates. When I was young, Cebes, I had a prodigious desire to know that department of philosophy which is called the investigation of nature; to know the causes of things, and why a thing is and is created or destroyed appeared to me to be a lofty profession; and I was always agitating myself with the consideration of questions such as these: —Is the growth of animals the result of some decay which the hot and cold principle contracts, as some have said? Is the blood the element with which we think, or the air, or the fire? or perhaps nothing of the kind—but the brain may be the originating power of the perceptions of hearing and sight and smell, and memory and opinion may come from them, and science may be based on memory and opinion when they have attained fixity. And then I went on to examine the corruption of them, and then to the things of heaven and earth, and at last I concluded myself to be utterly and absolutely incapable of these enquiries, as I will satisfactorily prove to you. For I was fascinated by them to such a degree that my eyes grew blind to things which I had seemed to myself, and also to others, to know quite well; I forgot what I had before thought self-evident truths; e. g. such a fact as that the growth of man is the result of eating and drinking; for when by the digestion of food flesh is added to flesh and bone to bone, and whenever there is an aggregation of congenial elements, the lesser bulk becomes larger and the small man great. Was not that a reasonable notion?

Yes, said Cebes, I think so.

Well; but let me tell you something more. There was a time when I thought that I understood the meaning of greater and less pretty well; and when I saw a great man standing by a little one, I fancied that one was taller than the other by a head; or one horse would appear to be greater than another horse: and still more clearly did I seem to perceive that ten is two more than eight, and that two cubits are more than one, because two is the double of one.

And what is now your notion of such matters? said Cebes.

I should be far enough from imagining, he replied, that I knew the cause of any of them, by heaven I should; for I cannot satisfy myself that, when one is added to one, the one to which the addition is made becomes two, or that the two units added together make two by reason of the addition. I cannot understand how, when separated from the other, each of them was one and not two, and now, when they are brought together, the mere juxtaposition or meeting of them should be the cause of their becoming two: neither can I understand how the division of one is the way to make two; for then a different cause would produce the same effect, —as in the former instance the addition and juxtaposition of one to one was the cause of two, in this the separation and subtraction of one from the other would be the cause. Nor am I any longer satisfied that I understand the reason why one or anything else is either generated or destroyed or is at all, but I have in my mind some confused notion of a new method, and can never admit the other.

Then I heard someone reading, as he said, from a book of Anaxagoras, that mind was the disposer and cause of all, and I was delighted at this notion, which appeared quite admirable, and I said to myself: If mind is the disposer, mind will dispose all for the best, and put each particular in the best place; and I argued that if any one desired to find out the cause of the generation or destruction or existence of anything, he must find out what state of being or doing or suffering was best for that thing, and therefore a man had only to consider the best for himself and others, and then he would also know the worse, since the same science comprehended both. And I rejoiced to think that I had found in Anaxagoras a teacher of the causes of existence such as I desired, and I imagined that he would tell me first whether the earth is flat or round; and whichever was true, he would proceed to explain the cause and the necessity of this being so, and then he would teach me the nature of the best and show that this was best; and if he said that the earth was in the centre, he would further explain that this position was the best, and I should be satisfied with the explanation given, and not want any other sort of cause. And I thought that I would then go on and ask him about the sun and moon and stars, and that he would explain to me their comparative swiftness, and their returnings and various states, active and passive, and how all of them were for the best. For I could not imagine that when he spoke of mind as the disposer of them, he would give any other account of their being as they are, except that this was best; and I thought that when he had explained to me in detail the cause of each and the cause of all, he would go on to explain to me what was best for each and what was good for all. These hopes I would not have sold for a large sum of money, and I seized the books and read them as fast as I could in my eagerness to know the better and the worse.

What expectations I had formed, and how grievously was I disappointed! As I proceeded, I found my philosopher altogether forsaking mind or any other principle of order, but having recourse to air, and ether, and water, and other eccentricities. I might compare him to a person who began by maintaining generally that mind is the cause of the actions of Socrates, but who, when he endeavoured to explain the causes of my several actions in detail, went on to show that I sit here because my body is made up of bones and muscles; and the bones, as he would say, are hard and have joints which divide them, and the muscles are elastic, and they cover the bones, which have also a covering or environment of flesh and skin which contains them; and as the bones are lifted at their joints by the contraction or relaxation of the muscles, I am able to bend my limbs, and this is why I am sitting here in a curved posture—that is what he would say, and he would have a similar explanation of my talking to you, which he would attribute to sound, and air, and hearing, and he would assign ten thousand other causes of the same sort, forgetting to mention the true cause, which is, that the Athenians have thought fit to condemn me, and accordingly I have thought it better and more right to remain here and undergo my sentence; for I am inclined to think that these muscles and bones of mine would have gone off long ago to Megara or Boeotia①— by the dog they would, if they had been moved only by their own idea of what was best, and if I had not chosen the better and nobler part, instead of playing truant and running away, of enduring any punishment which the state inflicts. There is surely a strange confusion of causes and conditions in all this. It may be said, indeed, that without bones and muscles and the other parts of the body I cannot execute my purposes. But to say that I do as I do because of them, and that this is the way in which mind acts, and not from the choice of the best, is a very careless and idle mode of speaking. I wonder that they cannot distinguish the cause from the condition, which the many, feeling about in the dark, are always mistaking and misnaming. And thus one man makes a vortex all round and steadies the earth by the heaven; another gives the air as a support to the earth, which is a sort of broad trough. Any power which in arranging them as they are arranges them for the best never enters into their minds; and instead of finding any superior strength in it, they rather expect to discover another Atlas② of the world who is stronger and more everlasting and more containing than the good; —of the obligatory and containing power of the good they think nothing; and yet this is the principle which I would fain learn if anyone would teach me. But as I have failed either to discover myself, or to learn of anyone else, the nature of the best, I will exhibit to you, if you like, what I have found to be the second best mode of enquiring into the cause.

I should very much like to hear, he replied.

Socrates proceeded: —I thought that as I had failed in the contemplation of true existence, I ought to be careful that I did not lose the eye of my soul; as people may injure their bodily eye by observing and gazing on the sun during an eclipse, unless they take the precaution of only looking at the image reflected in the water, or in some similar medium. So in my own case, I was afraid that my soul might be blinded

---

① 迈加拉（Megara）或皮奥夏（Boeotia），古希腊的两个地区
② 撑天泰坦阿特拉斯

altogether if I looked at things with my eyes or tried to apprehend them by the help of the senses. And I thought that I had better have recourse to the world of mind and seek there the truth of existence. I dare say that the simile is not perfect—for I am very far from admitting that he who contemplates existences through the medium of thought, sees them only 'through a glass darkly,' any more than he who considers them in action and operation. However, this was the method which I adopted: I first assumed some principle which I judged to be the strongest, and then I affirmed as true whatever seemed to agree with this, whether relating to the cause or to anything else; and that which disagreed I regarded as untrue. But I should like to explain my meaning more clearly, as I do not think that you as yet understand me.

No indeed, replied Cebes, not very well.

There is nothing new, he said, in what I am about to tell you; but only what I have been always and everywhere repeating in the previous discussion and on other occasions: I want to show you the nature of that cause which has occupied my thoughts. I shall have to go back to those familiar words which are in the mouth of every one, and first of all assume that there is an absolute beauty and goodness and greatness, and the like; grant me this, and I hope to be able to show you the nature of the cause, and to prove the immortality of the soul.

Cebes said: You may proceed at once with the proof, for I grant you this.

Well, he said, then I should like to know whether you agree with me in the next step; for I cannot help thinking, if there be anything beautiful other than absolute beauty should there be such, that it can be beautiful only in as far as it partakes of absolute beauty—and I should say the same of everything. Do you agree in this notion of the cause?

Yes, he said, I agree.

He proceeded: I know nothing and can understand nothing of any other of those wise causes which are alleged; and if a person says to me that the bloom of colour, or form, or any such thing is a source of beauty, I leave all that, which is only confusing to me, and simply and singly, and perhaps foolishly, hold and am assured in my own mind that nothing makes a thing beautiful but the presence and participation of beauty in whatever way or manner obtained; for as to the manner I am uncertain, but I stoutly contend that by beauty all beautiful things become beautiful. This appears to me to be the safest answer which I can give, either to myself or to another, and to this I cling, in the persuasion that this principle will never be overthrown, and that to myself or to anyone who asks the question, I may safely reply, That by beauty beautiful things become beautiful. Do you not agree with me?

I do.

And that by greatness only great things become great and greater greater, and by smallness the less become less?

True.

Then if a person were to remark that A is taller by a head than B, and B less by a head than A, you would refuse to admit his statement, and would stoutly contend that what you mean is only that the greater is greater by, and by reason of, greatness, and the less is less only by, and by reason of, smallness; and thus you would avoid the danger of saying that the greater is greater and the less less by the measure of the head, which is the same in both, and would also avoid the monstrous absurdity of supposing that the greater man is greater by reason of the head, which is small. You would be afraid to draw such an inference, would you not?

Indeed, I should, said Cebes, laughing.

In like manner you would be afraid to say that ten exceeded eight by, and by reason of, two; but would say by, and by reason of, number; or you would say that two cubits exceed one cubit not by a half, but by magnitude? — for there is the same liability to error in all these cases.

Very true, he said.

Again, would you not be cautious of affirming that the addition of one to one, or the division of one, is the cause of two? And you would loudly asseverate that you know of no way in which anything comes into existence except by participation in its own proper essence, and consequently, as far as you know, the only cause of two is the participation in duality—this is the way to make two, and the participation in one is the way to make one. You would say: I will let alone puzzles of division and addition—wiser heads than mine may answer them; inexperienced as I am, and ready to start, as the proverb says, at my own shadow, I cannot afford to give up the sure ground of a principle. And if any one assails you there, you would not mind him, or answer him, until you had seen whether the consequences which follow agree with one another or not, and when you are further required to give an explanation of this principle, you would go on to assume a higher principle, and a higher, until you found a resting-place in the best of the higher; but you would not confuse the principle and the consequences in your reasoning, like the Eristics①—at least if you wanted to discover real existence. Not that this confusion signifies to them, who never care or think about the matter at all, for they have the wit to be well pleased with themselves however great may be the turmoil of their ideas. But you, if you are a philosopher, will certainly do as I say.

What you say is most true, said Simmias and Cebes, both speaking at once.

ECHECRATES: Yes, Phaedo; and I do not wonder at their assenting. Any one who has the least sense will acknowledge the wonderful clearness of Socrates' reasoning.

PHAEDO: Certainly, Echecrates; and such was the feeling of the whole company at the time.

ECHECRATES: Yes, and equally of ourselves, who were not of the company, and are now listening to your recital. But what followed?

PHAEDO: After all this had been admitted, and they had that ideas exist, and that other things participate in them and derive their names from them, Socrates, if I remember rightly, said:—

This is your way of speaking; and yet when you say that Simmias is greater than Socrates and less than Phaedo, do you not predicate of Simmias both greatness and smallness?

Yes, I do.

But still you allow that Simmias does not really exceed Socrates, as the words may seem to imply, because he is Simmias, but by reason of the size which he has; just as Simmias does not exceed Socrates because he is Simmias, any more than because Socrates is Socrates, but because he has smallness when compared with the greatness of Simmias?

True.

And if Phaedo exceeds him in size, this is not because Phaedo is Phaedo, but because Phaedo has greatness relatively to Simmias, who is comparatively smaller?

That is true.

And therefore Simmias is said to be great, and is also said to be small, because he

---

① 诡辩论者

is in a mean between them, exceeding the smallness of the one by his greatness, and allowing the greatness of the other to exceed his smallness. He added, laughing, I am speaking like a book, but I believe that what I am saying is true.

Simmias assented.

I speak as I do because I want you to agree with me in thinking, not only that absolute greatness will never be great and also small, but that greatness in us or in the concrete will never admit the small or admit of being exceeded: instead of this, one of two things will happen, either the greater will fly or retire before the opposite, which is the less, or at the approach of the less has already ceased to exist; but will not, if allowing or admitting of smallness, be changed by that; even as I, having received and admitted smallness when compared with Simmias, remain just as I was, and am the same small person. And as the idea of greatness cannot condescend ever to be or become small, in like manner the smallness in us cannot be or become great; nor can any other opposite which remains the same ever be or become its own opposite, but either passes away or perishes in the change.

That, replied Cebes, is quite my notion.

Hereupon one of the company, though I do not exactly remember which of them, said: In heaven's name, is not this the direct contrary of what was admitted before—that out of the greater came the less and out of the less the greater, and that opposites were simply generated from opposites; but now this principle seems to be utterly denied.

Socrates inclined his head to the speaker and listened. I like your courage, he said, in reminding us of this. But you do not observe that there is a difference in the two cases. For then we were speaking of opposites in the concrete, and now of the essential opposite which, as is affirmed, neither in us nor in nature can ever be at variance with itself: then, my friend, we were speaking of things in which opposites are inherent and which are called after them, but now about the opposites which are inherent in them and which give their name to them; and these essential opposites will never, as we maintain, admit of generation into or out of one another. At the same time, turning to Cebes, he said: Are you at all disconcerted, Cebes, at our friend's objection?

No, I do not feel so, said Cebes; and yet I cannot deny that I am often disturbed by objections.

Then we are agreed after all, said Socrates, that the opposite will never in any case be opposed to itself?

To that we are quite agreed, he replied.

Yet once more let me ask you to consider the question from another point of view, and see whether you agree with me: —There is a thing which you term heat, and another thing which you term cold?

Certainly.

But are they the same as fire and snow?

Most assuredly not.

Heat is a thing different from fire, and cold is not the same with snow?

Yes.

And yet you will surely admit, that when snow, as was before said, is under the influence of heat, they will not remain snow and heat; but at the advance of the heat, the snow will either retire or perish?

Very true, he replied.

And the fire too at the advance of the cold will either retire or perish; and when the fire is under the influence of the cold, they will not remain as before, fire and cold.

That is true, he said.

And in some cases the name of the idea is not only attached to the idea in an eternal connection, but anything else which, not being the idea, exists only in the form of the idea, may also lay claim to it. I will try to make this clearer by an example: — The odd number is always called by the name of odd?

Very true.

But is this the only thing which is called odd? Are there not other things which have their own name, and yet are called odd, because, although not the same as oddness, they are never without oddness? —that is what I mean to ask—whether numbers such as the number three are not of the class of odd. And there are many other examples: would you not say, for example, that three may be called by its proper name, and also be called odd, which is not the same with three? and this may be said not only of three but also of five, and of every alternate number—each of them without being oddness is odd, and in the same way two and four, and the other series of alternate numbers, has every number even, without being evenness. Do you agree?

Of course.

Then now mark the point at which I am aiming: —not only do essential opposites exclude one another, but also concrete things, which, although not in themselves opposed, contain opposites; these, I say, likewise reject the idea which is opposed to that which is contained in them, and when it approaches them they either perish or withdraw. For example; Will not the number three endure annihilation or anything sooner than be converted into an even number, while remaining three?

Very true, said Cebes.

And yet, he said, the number two is certainly not opposed to the number three?

It is not.

Then not only do opposite ideas repel the advance of one another, but also there are other natures which repel the approach of opposites.

Very true, he said.

Suppose, he said, that we endeavour, if possible, to determine what these are.

By all means.

Are they not, Cebes, such as compel the things of which they have possession, not only to take their own form, but also the form of some opposite?

What do you mean?

I mean, as I was just now saying, and as I am sure that you know, that those things which are possessed by the number three must not only be three in number, but must also be odd.

Quite true.

And on this oddness, of which the number three has the impress, the opposite idea will never intrude?

No.

And this impress was given by the odd principle?

Yes.

And to the odd is opposed the even?

True.

Then the idea of the even number will never arrive at three?

No.

Then three has no part in the even?

None.

Then the triad or number three is uneven?

Very true.

To return then to my distinction of natures which are not opposed, and yet do not admit opposites—as, in the instance given, three, although not opposed to the even, does not any the more admit of the even, but always brings the opposite into play on the other side; or as two does not receive the odd, or fire the cold—from these examples (and there are many more of them) perhaps you may be able to arrive at the general conclusion, that not only opposites will not receive opposites, but also that nothing which brings the opposite will admit the opposite of that which it brings, in that to which it is brought. And here let me recapitulate—for there is no harm in repetition. The number five will not admit the nature of the even, any more than ten, which is the double of five, will admit the nature of the odd. The double has another opposite, and is not strictly opposed to the odd, but nevertheless rejects the odd altogether. Nor again will parts in the ratio 3 : 2, nor any fraction in which there is a half, nor again in which there is a third, admit the notion of the whole, although they are not opposed to the whole: You will agree?

Yes, he said, I entirely agree and go along with you in that.

And now, he said, let us begin again; and do not you answer my question in the words in which I ask it: let me have not the old safe answer of which I spoke at first, but another equally safe, of which the truth will be inferred by you from what has been just said. I mean that if any one asks you 'what that is, of which the inherence makes the body hot,' you will reply not heat (this is what I call the safe and stupid answer), but fire, a far superior answer, which we are now in a condition to give. Or if any one asks you 'why a body is diseased,' you will not say from disease, but from fever; and instead of saying that oddness is the cause of odd numbers, you will say that the monad is the cause of them: and so of things in general, as I dare say that you will understand sufficiently without my adducing any further examples.

Yes, he said, I quite understand you.

Tell me, then, what is that of which the inherence will render the body alive?

The soul, he replied.

And is this always the case?

Yes, he said, of course.

Then whatever the soul possesses, to that she comes bearing life?

Yes, certainly.

And is there any opposite to life?

There is, he said.

And what is that?

Death.

Then the soul, as has been acknowledged, will never receive the opposite of what she brings.

Impossible, replied Cebes.

And now, he said, what did we just now call that principle which repels the even? The odd.

And that principle which repels the musical, or the just? The unmusical, he said, and the unjust.

And what do we call the principle which does not admit of death?

The immortal, he said.

And does the soul admit of death?

No.

Then the soul is immortal?

Yes, he said.

And may we say that this has been proven? Yes, abundantly proven, Socrates, he replied.

Supposing that the odd were imperishable, must not three be imperishable?

Of course.

And if that which is cold were imperishable, when the warm principle came attacking the snow, must not the snow have retired whole and unmelted—for it could never have perished, nor could it have remained and admitted the heat?

True, he said.

Again, if the uncooling or warm principle were imperishable, the fire when assailed by cold would not have perished or have been extinguished, but would have gone away unaffected?

Certainly, he said.

And the same may be said of the immortal: if the immortal is also imperishable, the soul when attacked by death cannot perish; for the preceding argument shows that the soul will not admit of death, or ever be dead, any more than three or the odd number will admit of the even, or fire or the heat in the fire, of the cold. Yet a person may say: 'But although the odd will not become even at the approach of the even, why may not the odd perish and the even take the place of the odd?' Now to him who makes this objection, we cannot answer that the odd principle is imperishable; for this has not been acknowledged, but if this had been acknowledged, there would have been no difficulty in contending that at the approach of the even the odd principle and the number three took their departure; and the same argument would have held good of fire and heat and any other thing.

Very true.

And the same may be said of the immortal: if the immortal is also imperishable, then the soul will be imperishable as well as immortal; but if not, some other proof of her imperishableness will have to be given.

No other proof is needed, he said; for if the immortal, being eternal, is liable to perish, then nothing is imperishable.

Yes, replied Socrates, and yet all men will agree that God, and the essential form of life, and the immortal in general, will never perish.

Yes, all men, he said—that is true; and what is more, gods, if I am not mistaken, as well as men.

Seeing then that the immortal is indestructible, must not the soul, if she is immortal, be also imperishable?

Most certainly.

Then when death attacks a man, the mortal portion of him may be supposed to die, but the immortal retires at the approach of death and is preserved safe and sound?

True.

Then, Cebes, beyond question, the soul is immortal and imperishable, and our souls will truly exist in another world!

I am convinced, Socrates, said Cebes, and have nothing more to object; but if my friend Simmias, or any one else, has any further objection to make, he had better speak out, and not keep silence, since I do not know to what other season he can defer the discussion, if there is anything which he wants to say or to have said.

But I have nothing more to say, replied Simmias; nor can I see any reason for doubt after what has been said. But I still feel and cannot help feeling uncertain in my own mind, when I think of the greatness of the subject and the feebleness of man.

Yes, Simmias, replied Socrates, that is well said: and I may add that first principles, even if they appear certain, should be carefully considered; and when they are satisfactorily ascertained, then, with a sort of hesitating confidence in human reason, you may, I think, follow the course of the argument; and if that be plain and clear, there will be no need for any further enquiry.

Very true.

But then, O my friends, he said, if the soul is really immortal, what care should be taken of her, not only in respect of the portion of time which is called life, but of eternity! And the danger of neglecting her from this point of view does indeed appear to be awful. If death had only been the end of all, the wicked would have had a good bargain in dying, for they would have been happily quit not only of their body, but of their own evil together with their souls.

But now, inasmuch as the soul is manifestly immortal, there is no release or salvation from evil except the attainment of the highest virtue and wisdom. For the soul when on her progress to the world below takes nothing with her but nurture and education; and these are said greatly to benefit or greatly to injure the departed, at the very beginning of his journey thither.

For after death, as they say, the genius of each individual, to whom he belonged in life, leads him to a certain place in which the dead are gathered together, whence after judgment has been given they pass into the world below, following the guide, who is appointed to conduct them from this world to the other: and when they have there received their due and remained their time, another guide brings them back again after many revolutions of ages. Now this way to the other world is not, as Aeschylus[①] says in the Telephus[②], a single and straight path—if that were so no guide would be needed, for no one could miss it; but there are many partings of the road, and windings, as I infer from the rites and sacrifices which are offered to the gods below in places where three ways meet on earth. The wise and orderly soul follows in the straight path and is conscious of her surroundings; but the soul which desires the body, and which, as I was relating before, has long been fluttering about the lifeless frame and the world of sight, is after many struggles and many sufferings hardly and with violence carried away by her attendant genius, and when she arrives at the place where the other souls are

---

① 埃斯库罗斯，古希腊悲剧作家
② 《特勒福斯》是埃斯库罗斯的悲剧作品

gathered, if she be impure and have done impure deeds, whether foul murders or other crimes which are the brothers of these, and the works of brothers in crime—from that soul every one flees and turns away; no one will be her companion, no one her guide, but alone she wanders in extremity of evil until certain times are fulfilled, and when they are fulfilled, she is borne irresistibly to her own fitting habitation; as every pure and just soul which has passed through life in the company and under the guidance of the gods has also her own proper home.

Now the earth has divers wonderful regions, and is indeed in nature and extent very unlike the notions of geographers, as I believe on the authority of one who shall be nameless.

What do you mean, Socrates? said Simmias. I have myself heard many descriptions of the earth, but I do not know, and I should very much like to know, in which of these you put faith.

And I, Simmias, replied Socrates, if I had the art of Glaucus① would tell you; although I know not that the art of Glaucus could prove the truth of my tale, which I myself should never be able to prove, and even if I could, I fear, Simmias, that my life would come to an end before the argument was completed. I may describe to you, however, the form and regions of the earth according to my conception of them.

That, said Simmias, will be enough.

Well, then, he said, my conviction is, that the earth is a round body in the centre of the heavens, and therefore has no need of air or any similar force to be a support, but is kept there and hindered from falling or inclining any way by the equability of the surrounding heaven and by her own equipoise. For that which, being in equipoise, is in the centre of that which is equably diffused, will not incline any way in any degree, but will always remain in the same state and not deviate. And this is my first notion.

Which is surely a correct one, said Simmias.

Also I believe that the earth is very vast, and that we who dwell in the region extending from the river Phasis② to the Pillars of Heracles③ inhabit a small portion only about the sea, like ants or frogs about a marsh, and that there are other

---

① 格劳库斯（Glaucus）是希腊神话中的人鱼（merman），具有预言能力
② The river Phasis，斐西斯河，黑海东岸的一条河流
③ The Pillars of Heracles，赫拉克勒斯之柱，即位于西班牙和北非之间的直布罗陀海峡两岸的陡峭岩石

inhabitants of many other like places; for everywhere on the face of the earth there are hollows of various forms and sizes, into which the water and the mist and the lower air collect. But the true earth is pure and situated in the pure heaven—there are the stars also; and it is the heaven which is commonly spoken of by us as the ether, and of which our own earth is the sediment gathering in the hollows beneath. But we who live in these hollows are deceived into the notion that we are dwelling above on the surface of the earth; which is just as if a creature who was at the bottom of the sea were to fancy that he was on the surface of the water, and that the sea was the heaven through which he saw the sun and the other stars, he having never come to the surface by reason of his feebleness and sluggishness, and having never lifted up his head and seen, nor ever heard from one who had seen, how much purer and fairer the world above is than his own. And such is exactly our case: for we are dwelling in a hollow of the earth, and fancy that we are on the surface; and the air we call the heaven, in which we imagine that the stars move. But the fact is, that owing to our feebleness and sluggishness we are prevented from reaching the surface of the air: for if any man could arrive at the exterior limit, or take the wings of a bird and come to the top, then like a fish who puts his head out of the water and sees this world, he would see a world beyond; and, if the nature of man could sustain the sight, he would acknowledge that this other world was the place of the true heaven and the true light and the true earth. For our earth, and the stones, and the entire region which surrounds us, are spoilt and corroded, as in the sea all things are corroded by the brine, neither is there any noble or perfect growth, but caverns only, and sand, and an endless slough of mud: and even the shore is not to be compared to the fairer sights of this world. And still less is this our world to be compared with the other. Of that upper earth which is under the heaven, I can tell you a charming tale, Simmias, which is well worth hearing.

And we, Socrates, replied Simmias, shall be charmed to listen to you.

The tale, my friend, he said, is as follows: —In the first place, the earth, when looked at from above, is in appearance streaked like one of those balls which have leather coverings in twelve pieces, and is decked with various colours, of which the colours used by painters on earth are in a manner samples. But there the whole earth is made up of them, and they are brighter far and clearer than ours; there is a purple of wonderful lustre, also the radiance of gold, and the white which is in the earth is whiter than any chalk or snow. Of these and other colours the earth is made up, and they are more in number and fairer than the eye of man has ever seen; the very hollows (of which I was speaking) filled with air and water have a colour of their own, and are seen like light gleaming amid the diversity of the other colours, so that the whole presents a single and continuous appearance of variety in unity. And in this fair region everything that grows—trees, and flowers, and fruits—are in a like degree fairer than any here; and there are hills, having stones in them in a like degree smoother, and more transparent, and fairer in colour than our highly-valued emeralds and sardonyxes and jaspers, and other gems, which are but minute fragments of them: for there all the stones are like our precious stones, and fairer still (compare Republic). The reason is, that they are pure, and not, like our precious stones, infected or corroded by the corrupt briny elements which coagulate among us, and which breed foulness and disease both in earth and stones, as well as in animals and plants. They are the jewels of the upper earth, which also shines with gold and silver and the like, and they are set in the light of day and are large and abundant and in all places, making the earth a sight to gladden the beholder's eye. And there are animals and men, some in a middle region, others dwelling about the air as we dwell about the sea; others in islands which the air flows round, near the continent: and in a word, the air is used by them as the water and the sea are by us, and the ether is to them what the air is to us. Moreover, the temperament of their seasons is such that they have no disease, and live much longer than we do, and have sight and hearing and smell, and all the other senses, in far greater perfection, in the same proportion that air is purer than water or the ether than air. Also they have temples and sacred places in which the gods really dwell, and they hear their voices and receive their answers, and are conscious of them and hold converse with them, and they see the sun, moon, and stars as they truly are, and their other blessedness is of a piece with this.

Such is the nature of the whole earth, and of the things which are around the earth; and there are divers regions in the hollows on the face of the globe everywhere, some of them deeper and more extended than that which we inhabit, others deeper but with a narrower opening than ours, and some are shallower and also wider. All have numerous perforations, and there are passages broad and narrow in the interior of the earth, connecting them with one another; and there flows out of and into them, as into basins, a vast tide of water, and huge subterranean streams of perennial rivers, and springs hot and cold, and a great fire, and great rivers of fire, and streams of liquid mud, thin or thick (like the rivers of mud in Sicily, and the lava streams which follow them), and the regions about which they happen to flow are filled up with them. And there is a swinging or see-saw in the interior of the earth which moves all this up and down, and is due to the following cause: —There is a chasm which is the vastest of them all, and pierces right through the whole earth; this is that chasm which Homer describes in the words, — 'Far off, where is the inmost depth beneath the earth;' and which he in other places, and many other poets, have called Tartarus①. And the see-saw is caused by the streams flowing into and out of this chasm, and they each have the nature of the soil through which they flow. And the reason why the streams are always flowing in and out, is that the watery element has no bed or bottom, but is swinging and surging up and down, and the surrounding wind and air do the same; they follow the water up and down, hither and thither, over the earth—just as in the act of respiration the air is always in process of inhalation and exhalation; —and the wind swinging with the water in and out produces fearful and irresistible blasts: when the waters retire with a rush into the lower parts of the earth, as they are called, they flow through the earth in those regions, and fill them up like water raised by a pump, and then when they leave those regions and rush back hither, they again fill the hollows here, and when these are filled, flow through subterranean channels and find their way to their several places, forming seas, and lakes, and rivers, and springs. Thence they again enter the earth, some of them making a long circuit into many lands, others going to a few places and not so distant; and again fall into Tartarus, some at a point a good deal lower than that at which they rose, and others not much lower, but all in some degree lower than the point from which they came. And some burst forth again on the opposite side, and some on the same side, and some wind round the earth with one or many folds like the coils of a serpent, and descend as far as they can, but always return and fall into the chasm. The rivers flowing in either direction can descend only to the centre and no further, for opposite to the rivers is a precipice.

Now these rivers are many, and mighty, and diverse, and there are four principal ones, of which the greatest and outermost is that called Oceanus②, which flows round

---

① 塔尔塔罗斯深渊（Tartarus）
② 欧申纳斯河（Oceanus），大洋河

the earth in a circle; and in the opposite direction flows Acheron①, which passes under the earth through desert places into the Acherusian lake②: this is the lake to the shores of which the souls of the many go when they are dead, and after waiting an appointed time, which is to some a longer and to some a shorter time, they are sent back to be born again as animals. The third river passes out between the two, and near the place of outlet pours into a vast region of fire, and forms a lake larger than the Mediterranean Sea, boiling with water and mud; and proceeding muddy and turbid, and winding about the earth, comes, among other places, to the extremities of the Acherusian Lake, but mingles not with the waters of the lake, and after making many coils about the earth plunges into Tartarus at a deeper level. This is that Pyriphlegethon③, as the stream is called, which throws up jets of fire in different parts of the earth. The fourth river goes out on the opposite side, and falls first of all into a wild and savage region, which is all of a dark-blue colour, like lapis lazuli④; and this is that river which is called the Stygian river⑤, and falls into and forms the Lake Styx, and after falling into the lake and receiving strange powers in the waters, passes under the earth, winding round in the opposite direction, and comes near the Acherusian lake from the opposite side to Pyriphlegethon. And the water of this river too mingles with no other, but flows round in a circle and falls into Tartarus over against Pyriphlegethon; and the name of the river, as the poets say, is Cocytus⑥.

Such is the nature of the other world; and when the dead arrive at the place to which the genius of each severally guides them, first of all, they have sentence passed upon them, as they have lived well and piously or not. And those who appear to have lived neither well nor ill, go to the river Acheron, and embarking in any vessels which they may find, are carried in them to the lake, and there they dwell and are purified of their evil deeds, and having suffered the penalty of the wrongs which they have done to others, they are absolved, and receive the rewards of their good deeds, each of them according to his deserts. But those who appear to be incurable by reason of the

---

① 阿切隆河（Acheron），冥界怨河
② 阿切卢西亚湖（Acherusian lake），黄泉湖
③ 皮瑞弗莱盖松河（Pyriphlegethon），冥界火河
④ 天青石（lapis lazuli）
⑤ 冥界怒河（the Stygian river or the Styx river），以此河起誓，即便是神也必须兑现诺言
⑥ 克塞特斯河（Cocytus），冥界悲河

greatness of their crimes—who have committed many and terrible deeds of sacrilege, murders foul and violent, or the like—such are hurled into Tartarus which is their suitable destiny, and they never come out. Those again who have committed crimes, which, although great, are not irremediable—who in a moment of anger, for example, have done violence to a father or a mother, and have repented for the remainder of their lives, or, who have taken the life of another under the like extenuating circumstances—these are plunged into Tartarus, the pains of which they are compelled to undergo for a year, but at the end of the year the wave casts them forth—mere homicides by way of Cocytus, parricides and matricides by Pyriphlegethon—and they are borne to the Acherusian lake, and there they lift up their voices and call upon the victims whom they have slain or wronged, to have pity on them, and to be kind to them, and let them come out into the lake. And if they prevail, then they come forth and cease from their troubles; but if not, they are carried back again into Tartarus and from thence into the rivers unceasingly, until they obtain mercy from those whom they have wronged: for that is the sentence inflicted upon them by their judges. Those too who have been preeminent for holiness of life are released from this earthly prison, and go to their pure home which is above, and dwell in the purer earth; and of these, such as have duly purified themselves with philosophy live henceforth altogether without the body, in mansions fairer still which may not be described, and of which the time would fail me to tell.

Wherefore, Simmias, seeing all these things, what ought not we to do that we may obtain virtue and wisdom in this life? Fair is the prize, and the hope great!

A man of sense ought not to say, nor will I be very confident, that the description which I have given of the soul and her mansions is exactly true. But I do say that, inasmuch as the soul is shown to be immortal, he may venture to think, not improperly or unworthily, that something of the kind is true. The venture is a glorious one, and he ought to comfort himself with words like these, which is the reason why I lengthen out the tale. Wherefore, I say, let a man be of good cheer about his soul, who having cast away the pleasures and ornaments of the body as alien to him and working harm rather than good, has sought after the pleasures of knowledge; and has arrayed the soul, not in some foreign attire, but in her own proper jewels, temperance, and justice, and courage, and nobility, and truth—in these adorned she is ready to go on her journey to the world below, when her hour comes. You, Simmias and Cebes, and all other men, will depart at some time or other. Me already, as the tragic poet would say, the voice of fate calls. Soon I must drink the poison; and I think that I had better repair to the bath first, in order that the women may not have the trouble of washing my body after I am dead.

When he had done speaking, Crito said: And have you any commands for us, Socrates—anything to say about your children, or any other matter in which we can serve you?

Nothing particular, Crito, he replied: only, as I have always told you, take care of yourselves; that is a service which you may be ever rendering to me and mine and to all of us, whether you promise to do so or not. But if you have no thought for yourselves, and care not to walk according to the rule which I have prescribed for you, not now for the first time, however much you may profess or promise at the moment, it will be of no avail.

We will do our best, said Crito: And in what way shall we bury you?

In any way that you like; but you must get hold of me, and take care that I do not run away from you. Then he turned to us, and added with a smile: —I cannot make Crito believe that I am the same Socrates who have been talking and conducting the argument; he fancies that I am the other Socrates whom he will soon see, a dead body—and he asks, How shall he bury me? And though I have spoken many words in the endeavour to show that when I have drunk the poison I shall leave you and go to the joys of the blessed, —these words of mine, with which I was comforting you and myself, have had, as I perceive, no effect upon Crito. And therefore I want you to be surety for me to him now, as at the trial he was surety to the judges for me: but let the promise be of another sort; for he was surety for me to the judges that I would remain, and you must be my surety to him that I shall not remain, but go away and depart; and then he will suffer less at my death, and not be grieved when he sees my body being burned or buried. I would not have him sorrow at my hard lot, or say at the burial, Thus we lay out Socrates, or, Thus we follow him to the grave or bury him; for false words are not only evil in themselves, but they infect the soul with evil. Be of good cheer, then, my dear Crito, and say that you are burying my body only, and do with that whatever is usual, and what you think best.

When he had spoken these words, he arose and went into a chamber to bathe; Crito followed him and told us to wait. So we remained behind, talking and thinking of the subject of discourse, and also of the greatness of our sorrow; he was like a father of whom we were being bereaved, and we were about to pass the rest of our lives as orphans. When he had taken the bath his children were brought to him— (he had two young sons and an elder one); and the women of his family also came, and he talked to them and gave them a few directions in the presence of Crito; then he dismissed them and returned to us.

Now the hour of sunset was near, for a good deal of time had passed while he was within. When he came out, he sat down with us again after his bath, but not much was said. Soon the jailer, who was the servant of the Eleven, entered and stood by him, saying: —To you, Socrates, whom I know to be the noblest and gentlest and best of all who ever came to this place, I will not impute the angry feelings of other men, who rage and swear at me, when, in obedience to the authorities, I bid them drink the poison—indeed, I am sure that you will not be angry with me; for others, as you are aware, and not I, are to blame. And so fare you well, and try to bear lightly what must needs be—you know my errand. Then bursting into tears he turned away and went out.

Socrates looked at him and said: I return your good wishes, and will do as you bid. Then turning to us, he said, How charming the man is: since I have been in prison he has always been coming to see me, and at times he would talk to me, and was as good to me as could be, and now see how generously he sorrows on my account. We must do as he says, Crito; and therefore let the cup be brought, if the poison is prepared: if not, let the attendant prepare some.

Yet, said Crito, the sun is still upon the hill-tops, and I know that many a one has taken the draught late, and after the announcement has been made to him, he has eaten and drunk, and enjoyed the society of his beloved; do not hurry—there is time enough.

Socrates said: Yes, Crito, and they of whom you speak are right in so acting, for they think that they will be gainers by the delay; but I am right in not following their example, for I do not think that I should gain anything by drinking the poison a little later; I should only be ridiculous in my own eyes for sparing and saving a life which is already forfeit. Please then to do as I say, and not to refuse me.

Crito made a sign to the servant, who was standing by; and he went out, and having been absent for some time, returned with the jailer carrying the cup of poison. Socrates said: You, my good friend, who are experienced in these matters, shall give me directions how I am to proceed. The man answered: You have only to walk about until your legs are heavy, and then to lie down, and the poison will act. At the same time he handed the cup to Socrates, who in the easiest and gentlest manner, without the least fear or change of colour or feature, looking at the man with all his eyes, Echecrates, as his manner was, took the cup and said: What do you say about making a libation out of this cup to any god? May I, or not? The man answered: We only prepare, Socrates, just so much as we deem enough. I understand, he said: but I may and must ask the gods to prosper my journey from this to the other world—even so—and so be it according to my prayer. Then raising the cup to his lips, quite readily and cheerfully he drank off the poison. And hitherto most of us had been able to control our sorrow; but now when we saw him drinking, and saw too that he had finished the draught, we could no longer forbear, and in spite of myself my own tears were flowing fast; so that I covered my face and wept, not for him, but at the thought of my own calamity in having to part from such a friend. Nor was I the first; for Crito, when he found himself unable to restrain his tears, had got up, and I followed; and at that moment, Apollodorus, who had been weeping all the time, broke out in a loud and passionate cry which made cowards of us all. Socrates alone retained his calmness: What is this strange outcry? he said. I sent away the women mainly in order that they might not misbehave in this way, for I have been told that a man should die in peace. Be quiet, then, and have patience. When we heard his words we were ashamed, and refrained our tears; and he walked about until, as he said, his legs began to fail, and then he lay on his back, according to the directions, and the man who gave him the poison now and then looked at his feet and legs; and after a while he pressed his foot hard, and asked him if he could feel; and he said, No; and then his leg, and so upwards and upwards, and showed us that he was cold and stiff. And he felt them himself, and said: When the poison reaches the heart, that will be the end. He was beginning to grow cold about the groin, when he uncovered his face, for he had covered himself up, and said—they were his last words—he said: Crito, I owe a cock to Asclepius[①]; will you remember to pay the debt? The debt shall be paid, said Crito; is there anything else? There was no answer to this question; but in a minute or two a

---

① 阿斯克莱庇乌斯（Asclepius），药神。因为药神帮助苏格拉底的灵魂去了另一个世界旅行，所以苏格拉底吩咐弟子克里托（Crito）记得替自己拿一只公鸡作为对药神的祭献

movement was heard, and the attendants uncovered him; his eyes were set, and Crito closed his eyes and mouth.

Such was the end, Echecrates, of our friend; concerning whom I may truly say, that of all the men of his time whom I have known, he was the wisest and justest and best.

Questions for discussion:

1. How did Socrates prove that the Soul exists before the Body? Is there a flaw in the logic of this proof?

2. Socrates did not believe that he was guilty of the two charges against him. Why did his students bribe the warders to let him escape, but he did not agree?

3. Does Socrates prove to others the existence of the soul after death or its immortality? Why does Socrates think philosophers should not fear death?

第九篇　Politics

Aristotle

(Translated by Benjamin Jowett)

BOOK THREE

Part I

He who would inquire into the essence and attributes of various kinds of governments must first of all determine 'What is a state?' At present this is a disputed question. Some say that the state has done a certain act; others, no, not the state, but the oligarchy or the tyrant. And the legislator or statesman is concerned entirely with the state; a constitution or government being an arrangement of the inhabitants of a state. But a state is composite, like any other whole made up of many parts; these are the citizens, who compose it. It is evident, therefore, that we must begin by asking, Who is the citizen, and what is the meaning of the term? For here again there may be a difference of opinion. He who is a citizen in a democracy will often not be a citizen in an oligarchy. Leaving out of consideration those who have been made citizens, or who have obtained the name of citizen any other accidental manner, we may say, first, that a citizen is not a citizen because he lives in a certain place, for resident aliens and slaves share in the place; nor is he a citizen who has no legal right except that of suing and being sued; for this right may be enjoyed under the provisions of a treaty. Nay, resident aliens in many places do not possess even such rights completely, for they are obliged to have a patron, so that they do but imperfectly participate in citizenship, and we call them citizens only in a qualified sense, as we might apply the term to children who are too young to be on the register, or to old men who have been relieved from state duties. Of these we do not say quite simply that they are citizens, but add in the one case that they are not of age, and in the other, that they are past the age, or something of that sort; the precise expression is immaterial, for our meaning is clear. Similar difficulties to those which I have mentioned may be raised and answered about deprived citizens and about exiles. But the citizen whom we are seeking to define is a citizen in the strictest sense, against whom no such exception can be taken, and his special characteristic is that he shares in the administration of justice, and in offices. Now of offices some are discontinuous, and the same persons are not allowed to hold them twice, or can only hold them after a fixed interval; others have no limit of time— for example, the office of a dicast① or ecclesiast②. It may, indeed, be argued that these are not magistrates at all, and that their functions give them no share in the government. But surely it is ridiculous to say that those who have the power do not govern. Let us not dwell further upon this, which is a purely verbal question; what we want is a common term including both dicast and ecclesiast. Let us, for the sake of distinction, call it 'indefinite office,' and we will assume that those who share in such office are citizens. This is the most comprehensive definition of a citizen, and best suits all those who are generally so called.

But we must not forget that things of which the underlying principles differ in kind, one of them being first, another second, another third, have, when regarded in this relation, nothing, or hardly anything, worth mentioning in common. Now we see that governments differ in kind, and that some of them are prior and that others are posterior; those which are faulty or perverted are necessarily posterior to those which are perfect. (What we mean by perversion will be hereafter explained.) The citizen then of necessity differs under each form of government; and our definition is best adapted to the citizen of a democracy; but not necessarily to other states. For in some states the people are not acknowledged, nor have they any regular assembly, but only extraordinary ones; and suits are distributed by sections among the magistrates. At Lacedaemon③, for instance, the Ephors④ determine suits about contracts, which they

---

① 审判官员（dicast）
② 神职人员（ecclesiast）
③ Lacedaemon，指斯巴达，即 Sparta
④ 埃弗斯（Ephors），五长老，斯巴达的权力机构，从全体公民中选举产生

distribute among themselves, while the elders are judges of homicide, and other causes are decided by other magistrates. A similar principle prevails at Carthage; there certain magistrates decide all causes. We may, indeed, modify our definition of the citizen so as to include these states. In them it is the holder of a definite, not of an indefinite office, who legislates and judges, and to some or all such holders of definite offices is reserved the right of deliberating or judging about some things or about all things. The conception of the citizen now begins to clear up.

He who has the power to take part in the deliberative or judicial administration of any state is said by us to be a citizens of that state; and, speaking generally, a state is a body of citizens sufficing for the purposes of life.

Part II

But in practice a citizen is defined to be one of whom both the parents are citizens; others insist on going further back; say to two or three or more ancestors. This is a short and practical definition but there are some who raise the further question: How this third or fourth ancestor came to be a citizen? Gorgias of Leontini, partly because he was in a difficulty, partly in irony, said— 'Mortars are what is made by the mortar-makers, and the citizens of Larissa are those who are made by the magistrates; for it is their trade to make Larissaeans.' Yet the question is really simple, for, if according to the definition just given they shared in the government, they were citizens. This is a better definition than the other. For the words, 'born of a father or mother who is a citizen,' cannot possibly apply to the first inhabitants or founders of a state.

There is a greater difficulty in the case of those who have been made citizens after a revolution, as by Cleisthenes at Athens after the expulsion of the tyrants, for he enrolled in tribes many metics, both strangers and slaves. The doubt in these cases is, not who is, but whether he who is ought to be a citizen; and there will still be a furthering the state, whether a certain act is or is not an act of the state; for what ought not to be is what is false. Now, there are some who hold office, and yet ought not to hold office, whom we describe as ruling, but ruling unjustly. And the citizen was defined by the fact of his holding some kind of rule or office—he who holds a judicial or legislative office fulfills our definition of a citizen. It is evident, therefore, that the citizens about whom the doubt has arisen must be called citizens.

Part III

Whether they ought to be so or not is a question which is bound up with the previous inquiry. For a parallel question is raised respecting the state, whether a certain act is or is not an act of the state; for example, in the transition from an oligarchy or a tyranny to a democracy. In such cases persons refuse to fulfill their contracts or any other obligations, on the ground that the tyrant, and not the state, contracted them; they argue that some constitutions are established by force, and not for the sake of the common good. But this would apply equally to democracies, for they too may be founded on violence, and then the acts of the democracy will be neither more nor less acts of the state in question than those of an oligarchy or of a tyranny. This question runs up into another: on what principle shall we ever say that the state is the same, or different? It would be a very superficial view which considered only the place and the inhabitants (for the soil and the population may be separated, and some of the inhabitants may live in one place and some in another). This, however, is not a very serious difficulty; we need only remark that the word 'state' is ambiguous.

It is further asked: When are men, living in the same place, to be regarded as a single city—what is the limit? Certainly not the wall of the city, for you might surround all Peloponnesus[①] with a wall. Like this, we may say, is Babylon, and every city that has the compass of a nation rather than a city; Babylon, they say, had been taken for three days before some part of the inhabitants became aware of the fact. This difficulty may, however, with advantage be deferred to another occasion; the statesman has to consider the size of the state, and whether it should consist of more than one nation or not.

Again, shall we say that while the race of inhabitants, as well as their place of abode, remain the same, the city is also the same, although the citizens are always dying and being born, as we call rivers and fountains the same, although the water is always flowing away and coming again Or shall we say that the generations of men, like the rivers, are the same, but that the state changes? For, since the state is a partnership, and is a partnership of citizens in a constitution, when the form of government changes, and becomes different, then it may be supposed that the state is

---

① 伯罗奔尼撒半岛（Peloponnesus），位于希腊南部，科林斯地峡将其与希腊中部分开

no longer the same, just as a tragic differs from a comic chorus, although the members of both may be identical. And in this manner we speak of every union or composition of elements as different when the form of their composition alters; for example, a scale containing the same sounds is said to be different, accordingly as the Dorian① or the Phrygian② mode is employed. And if this is true it is evident that the sameness of the state consists chiefly in the sameness of the constitution, and it may be called or not called by the same name, whether the inhabitants are the same or entirely different. It is quite another question, whether a state ought or ought not to fulfill engagements when the form of government changes.

Part IV

There is a point nearly allied to the preceding: Whether the virtue of a good man and a good citizen is the same or not. But, before entering on this discussion, we must certainly first obtain some general notion of the virtue of the citizen. Like the sailor, the citizen is a member of a community. Now, sailors have different functions, for one of them is a rower, another a pilot, and a third a look-out man, a fourth is described by some similar term; and while the precise definition of each individual's virtue applies exclusively to him, there is, at the same time, a common definition applicable to them all. For they have all of them a common object, which is safety in navigation. Similarly, one citizen differs from another, but the salvation of the community is the common business of them all. This community is the constitution; the virtue of the citizen must therefore be relative to the constitution of which he is a member. If, then, there are many forms of government, it is evident that there is not one single virtue of the good citizen which is perfect virtue. But we say that the good man is he who has one single virtue which is perfect virtue. Hence it is evident that the good citizen need not of necessity possess the virtue which makes a good man.

The same question may also be approached by another road, from a consideration of the best constitution. If the state cannot be entirely composed of good men, and yet each citizen is expected to do his own business well, and must therefore have virtue, still inasmuch as all the citizens cannot be alike, the virtue of the citizen and of the

---

① 多利安人（Dorian），多利安人的。多利安在希腊中部
② 佛里吉亚人（Phrygian），佛里吉亚人的。佛里吉亚在小亚西亚

good man cannot coincide. All must have the virtue of the good citizen—thus, and thus only, can the state be perfect; but they will not have the virtue of a good man, unless we assume that in the good state all the citizens must be good.

Again, the state, as composed of unlikes, may be compared to the living being: as the first elements into which a living being is resolved are soul and body, as soul is made up of rational principle and appetite, the family of husband and wife, property of master and slave, so of all these, as well as other dissimilar elements, the state is composed; and, therefore, the virtue of all the citizens cannot possibly be the same, anymore than the excellence of the leader of a chorus is the same as that of the performer who stands by his side. I have said enough to show why the two kinds of virtue cannot be absolutely and always the same.

But will there then be no case in which the virtue of the good citizen and the virtue of the good man coincide? To this we answer that the good ruler is a good and wise man, and that he who would be a statesman must be a wise man. And some persons say that even the education of the ruler should be of a special kind; for are not the children of kings instructed in riding and military exercises? As Euripides① says: "No subtle arts for me, but what the state requires."

As though there were a special education needed by a ruler. If then the virtue of a good ruler is the same as that of a good man, and we assume further that the subject is a citizen as well as the ruler, the virtue of the good citizen and the virtue of the good man cannot be absolutely the same, although in some cases they may; for the virtue of a ruler differs from that of a citizen. It was the sense of this difference which made Jason② say that 'he felt hungry when he was not a tyrant,' meaning that he could not endure to live in a private station. But, on the other hand, it may be argued that men are praised for knowing both how to rule and how to obey, and he is said to be a citizen of approved virtue who is able to do both. Now if we suppose the virtue of a good man to be that which rules, and the virtue of the citizen to include ruling and obeying, it cannot be said that they are equally worthy of praise. Since, then, it is sometimes thought that the ruler and the ruled must learn different things and not the same, but

---

① 欧里庇得斯（Euripides），古希腊悲剧作家
② 古希腊神话中的英雄伊阿宋（Jason），曾率领阿尔戈斯人去黑海之滨的科尔喀斯寻找金羊毛

that the citizen must know and share in them both, the inference is obvious. There is, indeed, the rule of a master, which is concerned with menial offices—the master need not know how to perform these, but may employ others in the execution of them: the other would be degrading; and by the other I mean the power actually to do menial duties, which vary much in character and are executed by various classes of slaves, such, for example, as handicrafts-men, who, as their name signifies, live by the labor of their hands: under these the mechanic is included. Hence in ancient times, and among some nations, the working classes had no share in the government—a privilege which they only acquired under the extreme democracy. Certainly the good man and the statesman and the good citizen ought not to learn the crafts of inferiors except for their own occasional use; if they habitually practice them, there will cease to be a distinction between master and slave.

This is not the rule of which we are speaking; but there is a rule of another kind, which is exercised over freemen and equals by birth—a constitutional rule, which the ruler must learn by obeying, as he would learn the duties of a general of cavalry by being under the orders of a general of cavalry, or the duties of a general of infantry by being under the orders of a general of infantry, and by having had the command of a regiment and of a company. It has been well said that 'he who has never learned to obey cannot be a good commander.' The two are not the same, but the good citizen ought to be capable of both; he should know how to govern like a freeman, and how to obey like a freeman—these are the virtues of a citizen. And, although the temperance and justice of a ruler are distinct from those of a subject, the virtue of a good man will include both; for the virtue of the good man who is free and also a subject, e. g., his justice, will not be one but will comprise distinct kinds, the one qualifying him to rule, the other to obey, and differing as the temperance and courage of men and women differ. For a man would be thought a coward if he had no more courage than a courageous woman, and a woman would be thought loquacious if she imposed no more restraint on her conversation than the good man; and indeed their part in the management of the household is different, for the duty of the one is to acquire, and of the other to preserve. Practical wisdom only is characteristic of the ruler: it would seem that all other virtues must equally belong to ruler and subject. The virtue of the subject is certainly not wisdom, but only true opinion; he may be compared to the maker of the flute, while his master is like the flute-player or user of the flute.

From these considerations may be gathered the answer to the question, whether the virtue of the good man is the same as that of the good citizen, or different, and how far the same, and how far different.

Part V

There still remains one more question about the citizen: Is he only a true citizen who has a share of office, or is the mechanic to be included? If they who hold no office are to be deemed citizens, not every citizen can have this virtue of ruling and obeying; for this man is a citizen And if none of the lower class are citizens, in which part of the state are they to be placed? For they are not resident aliens, and they are not foreigners. May we not reply, that as far as this objection goes there is no more absurdity in excluding them than in excluding slaves and freedmen from any of the above-mentioned classes? It must be admitted that we cannot consider all those to be citizens who are necessary to the existence of the state; for example, children are not citizen equally with grown-up men, who are citizens absolutely, but children, not being grown up, are only citizens on a certain assumption. Nay, in ancient times, and among some nations the artisan class were slaves or foreigners, and therefore the majority of them are so now. The best form of state will not admit them to citizenship; but if they are admitted, then our definition of the virtue of a citizen will not apply to every citizen nor to every free man as such, but only to those who are freed from necessary services. The necessary people are either slaves who minister to the wants of individuals, or mechanics and laborers who are the servants of the community. These reflections carried a little further will explain their position; and indeed what has been said already is of itself, when understood, explanation enough.

Since there are many forms of government there must be many varieties of citizen and especially of citizens who are subjects; so that under some governments the mechanic and the laborer will be citizens, but not in others, as, for example, in aristocracy or the so-called government of the best (if there be such an one), in which honors are given according to virtue and merit; for no man can practice virtue who is living the life of a mechanic or laborer. In oligarchies the qualification for office is high, and therefore no laborer can ever be a citizen; but a mechanic may, for an actual

284

majority of them are rich. At Thebes① there was a law that no man could hold office who had not retired from business for ten years. But in many states the law goes to the length of admitting aliens; for in some democracies a man is a citizen though his mother only be a citizen; and a similar principle is applied to illegitimate children; the law is relaxed when there is a dearth of population. But when the number of citizens increases, first the children of a male or a female slave are excluded; then those whose mothers only are citizens; and at last the right of citizenship is confined to those whose fathers and mothers are both citizens.

Hence, as is evident, there are different kinds of citizens; and he is a citizen in the highest sense who shares in the honors of the state. Compare Homer's② words, 'like some dishonored stranger'; he who is excluded from the honors of the state is no better than an alien. But when his exclusion is concealed, then the object is that the privileged class may deceive their fellow inhabitants.

As to the question whether the virtue of the good man is the same as that of the good citizen, the considerations already adduced prove that in some states the good man and the good citizen are the same, and in others different. When they are the same it is not every citizen who is a good man, but only the statesman and those who have or may have, alone or in conjunction with others, the conduct of public affairs.

Part VI

Having determined these questions, we have next to consider whether there is only one form of government or many, and if many, what they are, and how many, and what are the differences between them.

A constitution is the arrangement of magistracies in a state, especially of the highest of all. The government is everywhere sovereign in the state, and the constitution is in fact the government. For example, in democracies the people are supreme, but in oligarchies, the few; and, therefore, we say that these two forms of government also are different: and so in other cases.

First, let us consider what is the purpose of a state, and how many forms of government there are by which human society is regulated. We have already said, in

---

① 忒拜城（Thebes），希腊一古城，又译底比斯城
② 荷马的，荷马是古希腊著名吟游诗人，著有史诗《伊利亚特》和《奥德赛》

the first part of this treatise, when discussing household management and the rule of a master, that man is by nature a political animal. And therefore, men, even when they do not require one another's help, desire to live together; not but that they are also brought together by their common interests in proportion as they severally attain to any measure of well-being. This is certainly the chief end, both of individuals and of states. And also for the sake of mere life (in which there is possibly some noble element so long as the evils of existence do not greatly overbalance the good) mankind meet together and maintain the political community. And we all see that men cling to life even at the cost of enduring great misfortune, seeming to find in life a natural sweetness and happiness.

There is no difficulty in distinguishing the various kinds of authority; they have been often defined already in discussions outside the school. The rule of a master, although the slave by nature and the master by nature have in reality the same interests, is nevertheless exercised primarily with a view to the interest of the master, but accidentally considers the slave, since, if the slave perish, the rule of the master perishes with him. On the other hand, the government of a wife and children and of a household, which we have called household management, is exercised in the first instance for the good of the governed or for the common good of both parties, but essentially for the good of the governed, as we see to be the case in medicine, gymnastic, and the arts in general, which are only accidentally concerned with the good of the artists themselves. For there is no reason why the trainer may not sometimes practice gymnastics, and the helmsman is always one of the crew. The trainer or the helmsman considers the good of those committed to his care. But, when he is one of the persons taken care of, he accidentally participates in the advantage, for the helmsman is also a sailor, and the trainer becomes one of those in training. And so in politics: when the state is framed upon the principle of equality and likeness, the citizens think that they ought to hold office by turns. Formerly, as is natural, every one would take his turn of service; and then again, somebody else would look after his interest, just as he, while in office, had looked after theirs. But nowadays, for the sake of the advantage which is to be gained from the public revenues and from office, men want to be always in office. One might imagine that the rulers, being sickly, were only kept in health while they continued in office; in that case we may be sure that they would be hunting after places. The conclusion is evident: that governments which have a regard to the common interest are constituted in accordance with strict principles of justice, and are therefore true forms; but those which regard only the interest of the rulers are all defective and perverted forms, for they are despotic, whereas a state is a community of freemen.

Part VII

Having determined these points, we have next to consider how many forms of government there are, and what they are; and in the first place what are the true forms, for when they are determined the perversions of them will at once be apparent. The words constitution and government have the same meaning, and the government, which is the supreme authority in states, must be in the hands of one, or of a few, or of the many. The true forms of government, therefore, are those in which the one, or the few, or the many, govern with a view to the common interest; but governments which rule with a view to the private interest, whether of the one or of the few, or of the many, are perversions. For the members of a state, if they are truly citizens, ought to participate in its advantages. Of forms of government in which one rules, we call that which regards the common interests, kingship or royalty; that in which more than one, but not many, rule, aristocracy; and it is so called, either because the rulers are the best men, or because they have at heart the best interests of the state and of the citizens. But when the citizens at large administer the state for the common interest, the government is called by the generic name—a constitution. And there is a reason for this use of language. One man or a few may excel in virtue; but as the number increases it becomes more difficult for them to attain perfection in every kind of virtue, though they may in military virtue, for this is found in the masses. Hence in a constitutional government the fighting-men have the supreme power, and those who possess arms are the citizens.

Of the above-mentioned forms, the perversions are as follows: of royalty, tyranny; of aristocracy, oligarchy; of constitutional government, democracy. For tyranny is a kind of monarchy which has in view the interest of the monarch only; oligarchy has in view the interest of the wealthy; democracy, of the needy: none of them the common good of all.

Part VIII

But there are difficulties about these forms of government, and it will therefore be necessary to state a little more at length the nature of each of them. For he who would make a philosophical study of the various sciences, and does not regard practice only, ought not to overlook or omit anything, but to set forth the truth in every particular. Tyranny, as I was saying, is monarchy exercising the rule of a master over the political society; oligarchy is when men of property have the government in their hands; democracy, the opposite, when the indigent, and not the men of property, are the rulers. And here arises the first of our difficulties, and it relates to the distinction drawn. For democracy is said to be the government of the many. But what if the many are men of property and have the power in their hands? In like manner oligarchy is said to be the government of the few; but what if the poor are fewer than the rich, and have the power in their hands because they are stronger? In these cases the distinction which we have drawn between these different forms of government would no longer hold good.

Suppose, once more, that we add wealth to the few and poverty to the many, and name the governments accordingly—an oligarchy is said to be that in which the few and the wealthy, and a democracy that in which the many and the poor are the rulers—there will still be a difficulty. For, if the only forms of government are the ones already mentioned, how shall we describe those other governments also just mentioned by us, in which the rich are the more numerous and the poor are the fewer, and both govern in their respective states?

The argument seems to show that, whether in oligarchies or in democracies, the number of the governing body, whether the greater number, as in a democracy, or the smaller number, as in an oligarchy, is an accident due to the fact that the rich everywhere are few, and the poor numerous. But if so, there is a misapprehension of the causes of the difference between them. For the real difference between democracy and oligarchy is poverty and wealth. Wherever men rule by reason of their wealth, whether they be few or many, that is an oligarchy, and where the poor rule, that is a democracy. But as a fact the rich are few and the poor many; for few are well-to-do, whereas freedom is enjoyed by all, and wealth and freedom are the grounds on which the oligarchical and democratical parties respectively claim power in the state.

Part IX

Let us begin by considering the common definitions of oligarchy and democracy, and what is justice oligarchical and democratical. For all men cling to justice of some kind, but their conceptions are imperfect and they do not express the whole idea. For example, justice is thought by them to be, and is, equality, not. however, for however, for but only for equals. And inequality is thought to be, and is, justice; neither is this for all, but only for unequals. When the persons are omitted, then men judge erroneously. The reason is that they are passing judgment on themselves, and most people are bad judges in their own case. And whereas justice implies a relation to persons as well as to things, and a just distribution, as I have already said in the Ethics, implies the same ratio between the persons and between the things, they agree about the equality of the things, but dispute about the equality of the persons, chiefly for the reason which I have just given—because they are bad judges in their own affairs; and secondly, because both the parties to the argument are speaking of a limited and partial justice, but imagine themselves to be speaking of absolute justice. For the one party, if they are unequal in one respect, for example wealth, consider themselves to be unequal in all; and the other party, if they are equal in one respect, for example free birth, consider themselves to be equal in all. But they leave out the capital point. For if men met and associated out of regard to wealth only, their share in the state would be proportioned to their property, and the oligarchical doctrine would then seem to carry the day. It would not be just that he who paid one mina① should have the same share of a hundred minae②, whether of the principal or of the profits, as he who paid the remaining ninety-nine. But a state exists for the sake of a good life, and not for the sake of life only: if life only were the object, slaves and brute animals might form a state, but they cannot, for they have no share in happiness or in a life of free choice. Nor does a state exist for the sake of alliance and security from injustice, nor yet for the sake of exchange and mutual intercourse; for then the Tyrrhenians③ and the Carthaginians④, and all who have commercial treaties with one another, would be

---

① 迈纳（mina），古希腊金额单位
② Minae，迈纳的复数形式
③ 泰勒尼人（Tyrrhenians），即亚平宁半岛上的伊特鲁尼亚人
④ 迦太基人（Carthaginians）

the citizens of one state. True, they have agreements about imports, and engagements that they will do no wrong to one another, and written articles of alliance. But there are no magistrates common to the contracting parties who will enforce their engagements; different states have each their own magistracies. Nor does one state take care that the citizens of the other are such as they ought to be, nor see that those who come under the terms of the treaty do no wrong or wickedness at all, but only that they do no injustice to one another. Whereas, those who care for good government take into consideration virtue and vice in states. Whence it may be further inferred that virtue must be the care of a state which is truly so called, and not merely enjoys the name: for without this end the community becomes a mere alliance which differs only in place from alliances of which the members live apart; and law is only a convention, 'a surety to one another of justice,' as the sophist Lycophron says, and has no real power to make the citizens

  This is obvious; for suppose distinct places, such as Corinth and Megara①, to be brought together so that their walls touched, still they would not be one city, not even if the citizens had the right to intermarry, which is one of the rights peculiarly characteristic of states. Again, if men dwelt at a distance from one another, but not so far off as to have no intercourse, and there were laws among them that they should not wrong each other in their exchanges, neither would this be a state. Let us suppose that one man is a carpenter, another a husbandman, another a shoemaker, and so on, and that their number is ten thousand: nevertheless, if they have nothing in common but exchange, alliance, and the like, that would not constitute a state. Why is this? Surely not because they are at a distance from one another: for even supposing that such a community were to meet in one place, but that each man had a house of his own, which was in a manner his state, and that they made alliance with one another, but only against evil-doers; still an accurate thinker would not deem this to be a state, if their intercourse with one another was of the same character after as before their union. It is clear then that a state is not a mere society, having a common place, established for the prevention of mutual crime and for the sake of exchange. These are conditions without which a state cannot exist; but all of them together do not constitute a state, which is a community of families and aggregations of families in well-being, for the

---

  ① 迈加拉（Megara），希腊中东部地名

sake of a perfect and self-sufficing life. Such a community can only be established among those who live in the same place and intermarry. Hence arise in cities family connections, brotherhoods, common sacrifices, amusements which draw men together. But these are created by friendship, for the will to live together is friendship. The end of the state is the good life, and these are the means towards it. And the state is the union of families and villages in a perfect and self-sufficing life, by which we mean a happy and honorable life.

Our conclusion, then, is that political society exists for the sake of noble actions, and not of mere companionship. Hence they who contribute most to such a society have a greater share in it than those who have the same or a greater freedom or nobility of birth but are inferior to them in political virtue; or than those who exceed them in wealth but are surpassed by them in virtue.

From what has been said it will be clearly seen that all the partisans of different forms of government speak of a part of justice only.

Part X

There is also a doubt as to what is to be the supreme power in the state: Is it the multitude? Or the wealthy? Or the good? Or the one best man? Or a tyrant? Any of these alternatives seems to involve disagreeable consequences. If the poor, for example, because they are more in number, divide among themselves the property of the rich—is not this unjust? No, by heaven (will be the reply), for the supreme authority justly willed it. But if this is not injustice, pray what is? Again, when in the first division all has been taken, and the majority divide anew the property of the minority, is it not evident, if this goes on, that they will ruin the state? Yet surely, virtue is not the ruin of those who possess her, nor is justice destructive of a state; and therefore this law of confiscation clearly cannot be just. If it were, all the acts of a tyrant must of necessity be just; for he only coerces other men by superior power, just as the multitude coerce the rich. But is it just then that the few and the wealthy should be the rulers? And what if they, in like manner, rob and plunder the people—is this just? if so, the other case will likewise be just. But there can be no doubt that all these things are wrong and unjust.

Then ought the good to rule and have supreme power? But in that case everybody else, being excluded from power, will be dishonored. For the offices of a state are posts of honor; and if one set of men always holds them, the rest must be deprived of them. Then will it be well that the one best man should rule? Nay, that is still more oligarchical, for the number of those who are dishonored is thereby increased. Some one may say that it is bad in any case for a man, subject as he is to all the accidents of human passion, to have the supreme power, rather than the law. But what if the law itself be democratical or oligarchical, how will that help us out of our difficulties? Not at all; the same consequences will follow.

Part XI

Most of these questions may be reserved for another occasion. The Principle that the multitude ought to be supreme rather than the few best is one that is maintained, and, though not free from difficulty, yet seems to contain an element of truth. For the many, of whom each individual is but an ordinary person, when they meet together may very likely be better than the few good, if regarded not individually but collectively, just as a feast to which many contribute is better than a dinner provided out of a single purse. For each individual among the many has a share of virtue and prudence, and when they meet together, they become in a manner one man, who has many feet, and hands, and senses; that is a figure of their mind and disposition. Hence the many are better judges than a single man of music and poetry; for some understand one part, and some another, and among them they understand the whole. There is a similar combination of qualities in good men, who differ from any individual of the many, as the beautiful are said to differ from those who are not beautiful, and works of art from realities, because in them the scattered elements are combined, although, if taken separately, the eye of one person or some other feature in another person would be fairer than in the picture. Whether this principle can apply to every democracy, and to all bodies of men, is not clear. Or rather, by heaven, in some cases it is impossible of application; for the argument would equally hold about brutes; and wherein, it will be asked, do some men differ from brutes? But there may be bodies of men about whom our statement is nevertheless true. And if so, the difficulty which has been already raised, and also another which is akin to it—viz.①, what power should be assigned to the mass of freemen and citizens, who are not rich and have no personal merit—are

---

① That is to say 或 namely

both solved.

There is still a danger in allowing them to share the great offices of state, for their folly will lead them into error, and their dishonesty into crime. But there is a danger also in not letting them share, for a state in which many poor men are excluded from office will necessarily be full of enemies. The only way of escape is to assign to them some deliberative and judicial functions. For this reason Solon① and certain other legislators give them the power of electing to offices, and of calling the magistrates to account, but they do not allow them to hold office singly. When they meet together their perceptions are quite good enough, and combined with the better class they are useful to the state (just as impure food when mixed with what is pure sometimes makes the entire mass more wholesome than a small quantity of the pure would be), but each individual, left to himself, forms an imperfect judgment. On the other hand, the popular form of government involves certain difficulties. In the first place, it might be objected that he who can judge of the healing of a sick man would be one who could himself heal his disease, and make him whole—that is, in other words, the physician; and so in all professions and arts. As, then, the physician ought to be called to account by physicians, so ought men in general to be called to account by their peers. But physicians are of three kinds: there is the ordinary practitioner, and there is the physician of the higher class, and thirdly the intelligent man who has studied the art: in all arts there is such a class; and we attribute the power of judging to them quite as much as to professors of the art. Secondly, does not the same principle apply to elections? For a right election can only be made by those who have knowledge; those who know geometry, for example, will choose a geometrician rightly, and those who know how to steer, a pilot; and, even if there be some occupations and arts in which private persons share in the ability to choose, they certainly cannot choose better than those who know. So that, according to this argument, neither the election of magistrates, nor the calling of them to account, should be entrusted to the many. Yet possibly these objections are to a great extent met by our old answer, that if the people are not utterly degraded, although individually they may be worse judges than those who have special knowledge—as a body they are as good or better. Moreover, there are some arts whose products are not judged of solely, or best, by the artists themselves,

---

① 梭仑（Solon），雅典立法者

namely those arts whose products are recognized even by those who do not possess the art; for example, the knowledge of the house is not limited to the builder only; the user, or, in other words, the master, of the house will be even a better judge than the builder, just as the pilot will judge better of a rudder than the carpenter, and the guest will judge better of a feast than the cook.

This difficulty seems now to be sufficiently answered, but there is another akin to it. That inferior persons should have authority in greater matters than the good would appear to be a strange thing, yet the election and calling to account of the magistrates is the greatest of all. And these, as I was saying, are functions which in some states are assigned to the people, for the assembly is supreme in all such matters. Yet persons of any age, and having but a small property qualification, sit in the assembly and deliberate and judge, although for the great officers of state, such as treasurers and generals, a high qualification is required. This difficulty may be solved in the same manner as the preceding, and the present practice of democracies may be really defensible. For the power does not reside in the dicast, or senator, or ecclesiast, but in the court, and the senate, and the assembly, of which individual senators, or ecclesiasts, or dicasts, are only parts or members. And for this reason the many may claim to have a higher authority than the few; for the people, and the senate, and the courts consist of many persons, and their property collectively is greater than the property of one or of a few individuals holding great offices. But enough of this.

The discussion of the first question shows nothing so clearly as that laws, when good, should be supreme; and that the magistrate or magistrates should regulate those matters only on which the laws are unable to speak with precision owing to the difficulty of any general principle embracing all particulars. But what are good laws has not yet been clearly explained; the old difficulty remains. The goodness or badness, justice or injustice, of laws varies of necessity with the constitutions of states. This, however, is clear, that the laws must be adapted to the constitutions. But if so, true forms of government will of necessity have just laws, and perverted forms of government will have unjust laws.

Part XII

In all sciences and arts the end is a good, and the greatest good and in the highest degree a good in the most authoritative of all—this is the political science of which the good is justice, in other words, the common interest. All men think justice to be a sort of equality; and to a certain extent they agree in the philosophical distinctions which have been laid down by us about Ethics. For they admit that justice is a thing and has a relation to persons, and that equals ought to have equality.

But there still remains a question: equality or inequality of what? Here is a difficulty which calls for political speculation. For very likely some persons will say that offices of state ought to be unequally distributed according to superior excellence, in whatever respect, of the citizen, although there is no other difference between him and the rest of the community; for that those who differ in any one respect have different rights and claims. But, surely, if this is true, the complexion or height of a man, or any other advantage, will be a reason for his obtaining a greater share of political rights. The error here lies upon the surface, and may be illustrated from the other arts and sciences. When a number of flute players are equal in their art, there is no reason why those of them who are better born should have better flutes given to them; for they will not play any better on the flute, and the superior instrument should be reserved for him who is the superior artist. If what I am saying is still obscure, it will be made clearer as we proceed. For if there were a superior flute-player who was far inferior in birth and beauty, although either of these may be a greater good than the art of flute-playing, and may excel flute-playing in a greater ratio than he excels the others in his art, still he ought to have the best flutes given to him, unless the advantages of wealth and birth contribute to excellence in flute-playing, which they do not.

Moreover, upon this principle any good may be compared with any other. For if a given height may be measured wealth and against freedom, height in general may be so measured. Thus if A excels in height more than B in virtue, even if virtue in general excels height still more, all goods will be commensurable; for if a certain amount is better than some other, it is clear that some other will be equal. But since no such comparison can be made, it is evident that there is good reason why in politics men do not ground their claim to office on every sort of inequality any more than in the arts. For if some be slow, and others swift, that is no reason why the one should have little and the others much; it is in gymnastics contests that such excellence is rewarded. Whereas the rival claims of candidates for office can only be based on the possession of elements which enter into the composition of a state. And therefore the noble, or free-born, or rich, may with good reason claim office; for holders of offices must be freemen and taxpayers; a state can be no more composed entirely of poor men than entirely of slaves. But if wealth and freedom are necessary elements, justice and valor are equally so; for without the former qualities a state cannot exist at all, without the latter not well.

Part XIII

If the existence of the state is alone to be considered, then it would seem that all, or some at least, of these claims are just; but, if we take into account a good life, then, as I have already said, education and virtue have superior claims. As, however, those who are equal in one thing ought not to have an equal share in all, nor those who are unequal in one thing to have an unequal share in all, it is certain that all forms of government which rest on either of these principles are perversions.

All men have a claim in a certain sense, as I have already admitted, but all have not an absolute claim. The rich claim because they have a greater share in the land, and land is the common element of the state; also they are generally more trustworthy in contracts. The free claim under the same tide as the noble; for they are nearly akin. For the noble are citizens in a truer sense than the ignoble, and good birth is always valued in a man's own home and country. Another reason is, that those who are sprung from better ancestors are likely to be better men, for nobility is excellence of race. Virtue, too, may be truly said to have a claim, for justice has been acknowledged by us to be a social virtue, and it implies all others. Again, the many may urge their claim against the few; for, when taken collectively, and compared with the few, they are stronger and richer and better. But, what if the good, the rich, the noble, and the other classes who make up a state, are all living together in the same city, Will there, or will there not, be any doubt who shall rule? No doubt at all in determining who ought to rule in each of the above-mentioned forms of government. For states are characterized by differences in their governing bodies—one of them has a government of the rich, another of the virtuous, and so on. But a difficulty arises when all these elements coexist. How are we to decide? Suppose the virtuous to be very few in number: may we consider their numbers in relation to their duties, and ask whether they are enough to administer the state, or so many as will make up a state? Objections may be urged against all the aspirants to political power. For those who found their claims on wealth or family might be thought to have no basis of justice; on this principle, if any one person were richer than all the rest, it is clear that he ought to be ruler of them. In like manner he who is very distinguished by his birth ought to have the superiority over all those who claim on the ground that they are freeborn. In an aristocracy, or government of the best, a like difficulty occurs about virtue; for if one citizen be better than the other members of the government, however good they may be, he too, upon the same principle of justice, should rule over them. And if the people are to be supreme because they are stronger than the few, then if one man, or more than one, but not a majority, is stronger than the many, they ought to rule, and not the many.

All these considerations appear to show that none of the principles on which men claim to rule and to hold all other men in subjection to them are strictly right. To those who claim to be masters of the government on the ground of their virtue or their wealth, the many might fairly answer that they themselves are often better and richer than the few—I do not say individually, but collectively. And another ingenious objection which is sometimes put forward may be met in a similar manner. Some persons doubt whether the legislator who desires to make the justest laws ought to legislate with a view to the good of the higher classes or of the many, when the case which we have mentioned occurs. Now what is just or right is to be interpreted in the sense of 'what is equal'; and that which is right in the sense of being equal is to be considered with reference to the advantage of the state, and the common good of the citizens. And a citizen is one who shares in governing and being governed. He differs under different forms of government, but in the best state he is one who is able and willing to be governed and to govern with a view to the life of virtue.

If, however, there be some one person, or more than one, although not enough to make up the full complement of a state, whose virtue is so pre-eminent that the virtues or the political capacity of all the rest admit of no comparison with his or theirs, he or they can be no longer regarded as part of a state; for justice will not be done to the superior, if he is reckoned only as the equal of those who are so far inferior to him in virtue and in political capacity. Such an one may truly be deemed a God among men. Hence we see that legislation is necessarily concerned only with those who are equal in birth and in capacity; and that for men of pre-eminent virtue there is no law—they are themselves a law. Any would be ridiculous who attempted to make laws for them: they would probably retort what, in the fable of Antisthenes①, the lions said to the hares,

---

① 安提西尼（Antisthenes），希腊哲学家，犬儒学派创始人

when in the council of the beasts the latter began haranguing and claiming equality for all. And for this reason democratic states have instituted ostracism①; equality is above all things their aim, and therefore they ostracized and banished from the city for a time those who seemed to predominate too much through their wealth, or the number of their friends, or through any other political influence.

Mythology tells us that the Argonauts② left Heracles behind for a similar reason; the ship Argo would not take him because she feared that he would have been too much for the rest of the crew. Wherefore those who denounce tyranny and blame the counsel which Periander③ gave to Thrasybulus④ cannot be held altogether just in their censure. The story is that Periander, when the herald was sent to ask counsel of him, said nothing, but only cut off the tallest ears of corn till he had brought the field to a level. The herald did not know the meaning of the action, but came and reported what he had seen to Thrasybulus, who understood that he was to cut off the principal men in the state; and this is a policy not only expedient for tyrants or in practice confined to them, but equally necessary in oligarchies and democracies. Ostracism is a measure of the same kind, which acts by disabling and banishing the most prominent citizens. Great powers do the same to whole cities and nations, as the Athenians did to the Samians, Chians, and Lesbians⑤; no sooner had they obtained a firm grasp of the empire, than they humbled their allies contrary to treaty; and the Persian king has repeatedly crushed the Medes, Babylonians⑥, and other nations, when their spirit has been stirred by the recollection of their former greatness.

The problem is a universal one, and equally concerns all forms of government, true as well as false; for, although perverted forms with a view to their own interests may adopt this policy, those which seek the common interest do so likewise. The same thing may be observed in the arts and sciences; for the painter will not allow the figure to have a foot which, however beautiful, is not in proportion, nor will the shipbuilder

---

① 雅典的陶片放逐法，或称贝壳流放法。公民可以在贝壳或陶片上写上权势人物姓名，公民大会通过有姓名贝壳的多少决定是否流放该人，无须审核该人是否有罪
② 阿尔戈号的英雄（Argonauts），阿尔戈号是伊阿宋等希腊英雄寻找金羊毛的船名
③ 佩里安德（Periander），古希腊政治家、哲学家，希腊七贤之一
④ 色拉西布洛斯（Thrasybulus），米利都（Miletus）僭主
⑤ 萨米亚人，基亚人和莱斯宾人
⑥ 米底人和巴比伦人

allow the stem or any other part of the vessel to be unduly large, any more than the chorus-master will allow any one who sings louder or better than all the rest to sing in the choir. Monarchs, too, may practice compulsion and still live in harmony with their cities, if their own governments for the interest of the state. Hence where there is an acknowledged superiority the argument in favor of ostracism is based upon a kind of political justice. It would certainly be better that the legislator should from the first so order his state as to have no need of such a remedy. But if the need arises, the next best thing is that he should endeavor to correct the evil by this or some similar measure. The principle, however, has not been fairly applied in states; for, instead of looking to the good of their own constitution, they have used ostracism for factious purposes. It is true that under perverted forms of government, and from their special point of view, such a measure is just and expedient, but it is also clear that it is not absolutely just.

In the perfect state there would be great doubts about the use of it, not when applied to excess in strength, wealth, popularity, or the like, but when used against some one who is pre-eminent in virtue—what is to be done with him? Mankind will not say that such an one is to be expelled and exiled; on the other hand, he ought not to be a subject—that would be as if mankind should claim to rule over Zeus, dividing his offices among them. The only alternative is that all should joyfully obey such a ruler, according to what seems to be the order of nature, and that men like him should be kings in their state for life.

Part XIV

The preceding discussion, by a natural transition, leads to the consideration of royalty, which we admit to be one of the true forms of government. Let us see whether in order to be well governed a state or country should be under the rule of a king or under some other form of government; and whether monarchy, although good for some, may not be bad for others. But first we must determine whether there is one species of royalty or many. It is easy to see that there are many, and that the manner of government is not the same in all of them.

Of royalties according to law, the Lacedaemonian is thought to answer best to the true pattern; but there the royal power is not absolute, except when the kings go on an expedition, and then they take the command. Matters of religion are likewise committed to them. The kingly office is in truth a kind of generalship, irresponsible and perpetual.

The king has not the power of life and death, except in a specified case, as for instance, in ancient times, he had it when upon a campaign, by right of force. This custom is described in Homer. For Agamemnon① is patient when he is attacked in the assembly, but when the army goes out to battle he has the power even of life and death. Does he not say—'When I find a man skulking apart from the battle, nothing shall save him from the dogs and vultures, for in my hands is death'?

This, then, is one form of royalty—a generalship for life: and of such royalties some are hereditary and others elective. There is another sort of monarchy not uncommon among the barbarians, which nearly resembles tyranny. But this is both legal and hereditary. For barbarians, being more servile in character than Hellenes②, and Asiadics③ than Europeans, do not rebel against a despotic government. Such royalties have the nature of tyrannies because the people are by nature slaves; but there is no danger of their being overthrown, for they are hereditary and legal. Wherefore also their guards are such as a king and not such as a tyrant would employ, that is to say, they are composed of citizens, whereas the guards of tyrants are mercenaries. For kings rule according to law over voluntary subjects, but tyrants over involuntary; and the one are guarded by their fellow-citizens the others are guarded against them.

These are two forms of monarchy, and there was a third which existed in ancient Hellas④, called an Aesymnetia⑤ or dictatorship. This may be defined generally as an elective tyranny, which, like the barbarian monarchy, is legal, but differs from it in not being hereditary. Sometimes the office was held for life, sometimes for a term of years, or until certain duties had been performed. For example, the Mytilenaeans⑥ elected Pittacus⑦ leader against the exiles, who were headed by Antimenides and Alcaeus⑧ the poet. And Alcaeus himself shows in one of his banquet odes that they chose Pittacus tyrant, for he reproaches his fellow-citizens for 'having made the low-born Pittacus tyrant of the spiritless and ill-fated city, with one voice shouting his

---

① 阿伽门农（Agamemnon），特洛伊战争中希腊联军主帅
② 希腊人（Hellenes）
③ 亚洲人（Asiadics）
④ 希腊（Hellas）
⑤ 阿西姆内蒂亚（Aesymnetia），独裁制
⑥ 米蒂利尼人（Mytilenaean）
⑦ 庇塔库斯（Pittacus），政治家，希腊七贤之一
⑧ 阿尔凯奥斯（Alcaeus），古希腊诗人，米蒂利尼人

praises.'

These forms of government have always had the character of tyrannies, because they possess despotic power; but inasmuch as they are elective and acquiesced in by their subjects, they are kingly. There is a fourth species of kingly rule—that of the heroic times—which was hereditary and legal, and was exercised over willing subjects. For the first chiefs were benefactors of the people in arts or arms; they either gathered them into a community, or procured land for them; and thus they became kings of voluntary subjects, and their power was inherited by their descendants. They took the command in war and presided over the sacrifices, except those which required a priest. They also decided causes either with or without an oath; and when they swore, the form of the oath was the stretching out of their sceptre. In ancient times their power extended continuously to all things whatsoever, in city and country, as well as in foreign parts; but at a later date they relinquished several of these privileges, and others the people took from them, until in some states nothing was left to them but the sacrifices; and where they retained more of the reality they had only the right of leadership in war beyond the border.

These, then, are the four kinds of royalty. First the monarchy of the heroic ages; this was exercised over voluntary subjects, but limited to certain functions; the king was a general and a judge, and had the control of religion The second is that of the barbarians, which is a hereditary despotic government in accordance with law. A third is the power of the so-called Aesymnete or Dictator; this is an elective tyranny. The fourth is the Lacedaemonian, which is in fact a generalship, hereditary and perpetual. These four forms differ from one another in the manner which I have described.

There is a fifth form of kingly rule in which one has the disposal of all, just as each nation or each state has the disposal of public matters; this form corresponds to the control of a household. For as household, management is the kingly rule of a house, so kingly rule is the household management of a city, or of a nation, or of many nations.

Part XV

Of these forms we need only consider two, the Lacedaemonian and the absolute royalty; for most of the others he in a region between them, having less power than the last, and more than the first. Thus the inquiry is reduced to two points: first, is it advantageous to the state that there should be a perpetual general, and if so, should the office be confined to one family, or open to the citizens in turn? Secondly, is it well that a single man should have the supreme power in all things? The first question falls under the head of laws rather than of constitutions; for perpetual generalship might equally exist under any form of government, so that this matter may be dismissed for the present. The other kind of royalty is a sort of constitution; this we have now to consider, and briefly to run over the difficulties involved in it. We will begin by inquiring whether it is more advantageous to be ruled by the best man or by the best laws.

The advocates of royalty maintain that the laws speak only in general terms, and cannot provide for circumstances; and that for any science to abide by written rules is absurd. In Egypt the physician is allowed to alter his treatment after the fourth day, but if sooner, he takes the risk. Hence it is clear that a government acting according to written laws is plainly not the best. Yet surely the ruler cannot dispense with the general principle which exists in law; and this is a better ruler which is free from passion than that in which it is innate. Whereas the law is passionless, passion must ever sway the heart of man. Yes, it may be replied, but then on the other hand an individual will be better able to deliberate in particular cases.

The best man, then, must legislate, and laws must be passed, but these laws will have no authority when they miss the mark, though in all other cases retaining their authority. But when the law cannot determine a point at all, or not well, should the one best man or should all decide? According to our present practice assemblies meet, sit in judgment, deliberate, and decide, and their judgments an relate to individual cases. Now any member of the assembly, taken separately, is certainly inferior to the wise man. But the state is made up of many individuals. And as a feast to which all the guests contribute is better than a banquet furnished by a single man, so a multitude is a better judge of many things than any individual.

Again, the many are more incorruptible than the few; they are like the greater quantity of water which is less easily corrupted than a little. The individual is liable to be overcome by anger or by some other passion, and then his judgment is necessarily perverted; but it is hardly to be supposed that a great number of persons would all get into a passion and go wrong at the same moment. Let us assume that they are the freemen, and that they never act in violation of the law, but fill up the gaps which the law is obliged to leave. Or, if such virtue is scarcely attainable by the multitude, we need only suppose that the majority are good men and good citizens, and ask which will be the more incorruptible, the one good ruler, or the many who are all good? Will not the many? But, you will say, there may be parties among them, whereas the one man is not divided against himself. To which we may answer that their character is as good as his. If we call the rule of many men, who are all of them good, aristocracy, and the rule of one man royalty, then aristocracy will be better for states than royalty, whether the government is supported by force or not, provided only that a number of men equal in virtue can be found.

The first governments were kingships, probably for this reason, because of old, when cities were small, men of eminent virtue were few. Further, they were made kings because they were benefactors, and benefits can only be bestowed by good men. But when many persons equal in merit arose, no longer enduring the pre-eminence of one, they desired to have a commonwealth, and set up a constitution. The ruling class soon deteriorated and enriched themselves out of the public treasury; riches became the path to honor, and so oligarchies naturally grew up. These passed into tyrannies and tyrannies into democracies; for love of gain in the ruling classes was always tending to diminish their number, and so to strengthen the masses, who in the end set upon their masters and established democracies. Since cities have increased in size, no other form of government appears to be any longer even easy to establish.

Even supposing the principle to be maintained that kingly power is the best thing for states, how about the family of the king? Are his children to succeed him? If they are no better than anybody else, that will be mischievous. But, says the lover of royalty, the king, though he might, will not hand on his power to his children. That, however, is hardly to be expected, and is too much to ask of human nature. There is also a difficulty about the force which he is to employ; should a king have guards about him by whose aid he may be able to coerce the refractory? If not, how will he administer his kingdom? Even if he be the lawful sovereign who does nothing arbitrarily or contrary to law, still he must have some force wherewith to maintain the law. In the case of a limited monarchy there is not much difficulty in answering this question; the king must have such force as will be more than a match for one or more individuals, but not so great as that of the people. The ancients observe this principle when they have guards to any one whom they appointed dictator or tyrant. Thus, when Dionysius① asked the Syracusans②to allow him guards, somebody advised that they should give him only such a number.

Part XVI

At this place in the discussion there impends the inquiry respecting the king who acts solely according to his own will he has now to be considered. The so-called limited monarchy, or kingship according to law, as I have already remarked, is not a distinct form of government, for under all governments, as, for example, in a democracy or aristocracy, there may be a general holding office for life, and one person is often made supreme over the administration of a state. A magistracy of this kind exists at Epidamnus③, and also at Opus, but in the latter city has a more limited power. Now, absolute monarchy, or the arbitrary rule of a sovereign over all the citizens, in a city which consists of equals, is thought by some to be quite contrary to nature; it is argued that those who are by nature equals must have the same natural right and worth, and that for unequals to have an equal share, or for equals to have an uneven share, in the offices of state, is as bad as for different bodily constitutions to have the same food and clothing. Wherefore it is thought to be just that among equals everyone be ruled as well as rule, and therefore that all should have their turn. We thus arrive at law; for an order of succession implies law. And the rule of the law, it is argued, is preferable to that of any individual. On the same principle, even if it be better for certain individuals to govern, they should be made only guardians and ministers of the law. For magistrates there must be—this is admitted; but then men say that to give authority to any one man when all are equal is unjust. Nay, there may indeed be cases which the law seems unable to determine, but in such cases can a man? Nay, it will be replied, the law trains officers for this express purpose, and appoints them to determine matters which are left undecided by it, to the best of their judgment. Further, it permits them to make any amendment of the existing laws which experience suggests. Therefore he who bids④ the law rule may be deemed to bid God and Reason alone rule, but he who bids man

---

① 狄奥尼斯乌斯（Dionysius），希腊的海外殖民地叙拉古的僭主
② 叙拉古人（Syracusans），又译锡拉库萨人，希腊在西西里岛上的早期殖民城市
③ 埃庇丹努斯（Epidamnus），古希腊西北一地名，现位于阿尔巴尼亚境内
④ 支持，投标

rule adds an element of the beast; for desire is a wild beast, and passion perverts the minds of rulers, even when they are the best of men. The law is reason unaffected by desire. We are told that a patient should call in a physician; he will not get better if he is doctored out of a book. But the parallel of the arts is clearly not in point; for the physician does nothing contrary to rule from motives of friendship; he only cures a patient and takes a fee; whereas magistrates do many things from spite and partiality. And, indeed, if a man suspected the physician of being in league with his enemies to destroy him for a bribe, he would rather have recourse to the book. But certainly physicians, when they are sick, call in other physicians, and training-masters, when they are in training, other training-masters, as if they could not judge judge truly about their own case and might be influenced by their feelings. Hence it is evident that in seeking for justice men seek for the mean or neutral, for the law is the mean. Again, customary laws have more weight, and relate to more important matters, than written laws, and a man may be a safer ruler than the written law, but not safer than the customary law.

Again, it is by no means easy for one man to superintend many things; he will have to appoint a number of subordinates, and what difference does it make whether these subordinates always existed or were appointed by him because he needed them If, as I said before, the good man has a right to rule because he is better, still two good men are better than one: this is the old saying, two going together, and the prayer of Agamemnon, "Would that I had ten such councillors!"

And at this day there are magistrates, for example judges, who have authority to decide some matters which the law is unable to determine, since no one doubts that the law would command and decide in the best manner whatever it could. But some things can, and other things cannot, be comprehended under the law, and this is the origin of the nexted question whether the best law or the best man should rule. For matters of detail about which men deliberate cannot be included in legislation. Nor does anyone deny that the decision of such matters must be left to man, but it is argued that there should be many judges, and not one only. For every ruler who has been trained by the law judges well; and it would surely seem strange that a person should see better with two eyes, or hear better with two ears, or act better with two hands or feet, than many with many; indeed, it is already the practice of kings to make to themselves many eyes and ears and hands and feet. For they make colleagues of those who are the friends of themselves and their governments. They must be friends of the monarch and of his government; if not his friends, they will not do what he wants; but friendship implies likeness and equality; and, therefore, if he thinks that his friends ought to rule, he must think that those who are equal to himself and like himself ought to rule equally with himself. These are the principal controversies relating to monarchy.

Part XVII

But may not all this be true in some cases and not in others? for there is by nature both a justice and an advantage appropriate to the rule of a master, another to kingly rule, another to constitutional rule; but there is none naturally appropriate to tyranny, or to any other perverted form of government; for these come into being contrary to nature. Now, to judge at least from what has been said, it is manifest that, where men are alike and equal, it is neither expedient nor just that one man should be lord of all, whether there are laws, or whether there are no laws, but he himself is in the place of law. Neither should a good man be lord over good men, nor a bad man over bad; nor, even if he excels in virtue, should he have a right to rule, unless in a particular case, at which I have already hinted, and to which I will once more recur. But first of all, I must determine what natures are suited for government by a king, and what for an aristocracy, and what for a constitutional government.

A people who are by nature capable of producing a race superior in the virtue needed for political rule are fitted for kingly government; and a people submitting to be ruled as freemen by men whose virtue renders them capable of political command are adapted for an aristocracy; while the people who are suited for constitutional freedom are those among whom there naturally exists a warlike multitude able to rule and to obey in turn by a law which gives office to the well-to-do according to their desert[①]. But when a whole family or some individual, happens to be so pre-eminent in virtue as to surpass all others, then it is just that they should be the royal family and supreme over all, or that this one citizen should be king of the whole nation. For, as I said before, to give them authority is not only agreeable to that ground of right which the founders of all states, whether aristocratical, or oligarchical, or again democratical, are accustomed to put forward (for these all recognize the claim of excellence, although not the same

---

① 境况

excellence), but accords with the principle already laid down. For surely it would not be right to kill, or ostracize, or exile such a person, or require that he should take his turn in being governed. The whole is naturally superior to the part, and he who has this preeminence is in the relation of a whole to a part. But if so, the only alternative is that he should have the supreme power, and that mankind should obey him, not in turn, but always. These are the conclusions at which we arrive respecting royalty and its various forms, and this is the answer to the question, whether it is or is not advantageous to states, and to which, and how.

Part XVIII

We maintain that the true forms of government are three, and that the best must be that which is administered by the best, and in which there is one man, or a whole family, or many persons, excelling all the others together in virtue, and both rulers and subjects are fitted, the one to rule, the others to be ruled, in such a manner as to attain the most eligible life. We showed at the commencement of our inquiry that the virtue of the good man is necessarily the same as the virtue of the citizen of the perfect state. Clearly then in the same manner, and by the same means through which a man becomes truly good, he will frame a state that is to be ruled by an aristocracy or by a king, and the same education and the same habits will be found to make a good man and a man fit to be a statesman or a king.

Having arrived at these conclusions, we must proceed to speak of the perfect state, and describe how it comes into being and is established.

Questions for discussion:

1. What is the difference between Aristotle's view of the goals of the state, the identity within the state, and the relationship between citizens and Plato's?

2. Aristotle's classification of states and governments comes more from his knowledge and classification of city-states around the world. How many forms of government does he divide into? What's the difference with Plato?

3. How to understand that there are different forms of government in Aristotle's constitutional states?

4. How to understand that a good political system depends on different people's conditions and history, as well as the rational distribution of power among officials?

第十篇　The Twelve Caesars

Gauis Suetonius Tranquillus[①]

Translated by Robert Graves

Julius Caesar

Gaius Julius Caesar lost his father at the age of fifteen. During the next consulship[②], after being nominated to the priesthood of Jupiter, he broke an engagement made for him while he was still a boy to marry one Cossutia; for though rich she came of only equestrian family. Instead, he married Cornelia; daughter of that Cinna who had been Consul four times, and later she bore him a daughter named Julia. The Dictator Sulla[③] tried to make Caesar divorce Cornelia and when he refused stripped him of the priesthood his wife's downy and his own inheritance, treating him as if he were a member of the popular party. Caesar disappeared from public view and, though suffering from a virulent attack of quartan fever was forced to find a new hiding-place almost every night and bribe householders to protect him from Sulla's Secret police. Finally he won Sulla's pardon through the intercession of the Vestal Virgins[④] and his near relatives Mamerius Aemilius and Aurelius Cotta. It is well known that when the most devoted and eminent members of the aristocratic party pleaded Caesar's cause and would not let the matter drop, Sulla at last gave way. Whether he was divinely inspired

---

① 盖乌斯·苏维托尼乌斯·特兰奎鲁斯（Gaius Suetonius Tranquillus），罗马帝国传记史学家，生于公元69年至75年间，卒于公元130之后，常被称为苏维托尼乌斯，代表作为《罗马十二帝王传》
② 罗马执政官（consul），罗马共和国时期，每年选举一次，每次两人担任
③ 独裁者苏拉（the Dictator Sulla）
④ 灶神维斯塔的女祭师（the Vestal Virgins）

or showed peculiar foresight is an arguable point, but these were his words: "Very well then, you win! Take him! But never forget that the man whom you want me to spare will one day prove the ruin of the party which you and I have so long defended. There are many Mariuses① in this fellow Caesar."

Caesar first saw military service in Asia, where he went as aide-de-camp② to Marcus Thermus, the provincial governor-general. When Thermus sent Caesar to raise a fleet in Bithynia③, he wasted so much time at King Nicomedes's④ court that a homosexual relationship between them was suspected, and suspicion gave place to scandal when soon after his return to headquarters, he revisited Bithynia: ostensibly collecting a debt incurred there by one of his freedmen. However Caesar's reputation improved later in the campaign when Thermus awarded him the civic crown of oak-leaves, at the storming of Mytilene, for saving a fellow-soldier's life.

He also campaigned in Cilicia⑤ under Servilius Isauricus, but not for long, because the news of Sulla's death sent him hurrying back to Rome, where a revolt headed by Marcus Lepidus seemed to offer prospects of rapid advancement. Nevertheless, though Lepidus made him very advantageous offers, Caesar turned them down: he had small confidence in Lepidus's capacities, and found the political atmosphere less promising than he had been led to believe.

After this revolt was suppressed, Caesar brought a charge of extortion against Cornelius Dolabella, an ex-consul who had once been awarded a triumph but failed to secure a sentence; so he decided to visit Rhodes⑥ until the resultant ill-feeling had time to die down, meanwhile taking a course in rhetoric from Apollonius Molo⑦, the best living exponent of the art. Winter had already set in when he sailed for Rhodes and was captured by pirates off the island of Pharmacussa. They kept him prisoner for nearly

---

① Marius 指盖乌斯·马略（Gaius Marius），七次当选为罗马执政官。苏拉此话的含义是恺撒将比马略更加独裁
② 营地帮手（aide-de-camp）
③ 比提尼亚（Bithynia），小亚细亚（Asia Minor）西北部的一个地区，欧亚交界处，现土耳其境西北部
④ 尼克美狄斯（Nicomedes），比提尼亚（Bithynia）国王，此处指尼克美狄斯四世（公元前94—公元前74年）
⑤ 西里西亚地区（Cilicia），小亚细亚南部
⑥ 罗德岛（Rhode），爱琴海东南岛屿，靠近土耳其
⑦ 阿波罗尼乌斯·莫洛（Apllonius Molo），演说家，修辞学家

forty days, to his intense annoyance; he had with him only a physician and two valets, having sent the rest of his staff away to borrow the ransom money. As soon as the stipulated fifty talents arrived (which make 12,000 gold pieces) and the pirates duly set him ashore, he raised a fleet and went after them. He had often smilingly sworn, while still in their power that he would soon capture and crucify them; and this is exactly what he did. Then he continued to Rhodes, but Mithridates① was now ravaging the nearby coast of Asia Minor②; so, to avoid the charge of showing inertia while the allies of Rome were in danger, he raised a force of irregulars and drove Mithridates' deputy from the province—which confirmed the timorous and half-hearted cites of Asia in their allegiance.

On Caesar's return to Rome, the commons③ voted him the rank of colonel, and he vigorously helped their leaders to undo Sulla's legislation by restoring the tribunes of the people④ to their ancient powers. Then one Plotius introduced a bill for the recall from exile of Caesar's brother-in-law, Lucius Cinna⑤—who, with other fellow-conspirators, had escaped to Spain after Lepidus's death and joined Sertorius⑥. Caesar himself spoke in support of the bill, which was passed.

During his quaestorship⑦, he made the customary funeral speeches from the Rostra⑧ in honour of his aunt Julia and his wife Cornelia; and while eulogizing Julia's maternal and paternal ancestry, did the same for the Caesars too. 'Her mother,' he said, 'was a descendant of kings, namely the Royal Marcians, a family founded by the Roman King Ancus Marcius; and her father of gods—since the Julians (of which we Caesars are a branch) reckon descent from the Goddess Venus⑨. Thus Julia's stock can

---

① 米特里达梯六世（Mithridates VI），本都（Pontus）国王，曾对罗马共和国发动3次战争，以争取其对安纳托利亚（Anatolia 即小亚细亚）的控制
② 小亚细亚（Asia Minor），爱琴海东部与欧洲相连接的亚洲半岛，古代亦称安纳托利亚（Anatolia），即现在的土耳其的亚洲部分
③ 公民大会（the commons），在罗马共和国时期的权力机构，类似于现代美国的众议院
④ 古罗马保民官（the tribunes of the people）
⑤ 卢修斯·秦纳（Lucius Cinna），公元前86年罗马二执政官（Consuls）之一
⑥ 昆图斯·瑟托瑞乌斯（Quintus Sertorius），西班牙总督
⑦ 古罗马的度支官任期，司库任期（quaestorship）
⑧ 古罗马大讲坛，罗马演说坛（the Rostra）
⑨ 维纳斯女神（the Goddess Venus），罗马贵族认为自己的祖先是来自特洛伊（Troy）的王子埃涅阿斯（Aeneas）的后代，而埃涅阿斯的母亲是维纳斯女神。可参见维吉尔（Virgil）的史诗《埃涅伊德》

claim both the sanctity of kings, who reign supreme among mortals and the reverence due to gods, who hold even kings in their power.'

He next married Pompeia, Quintus Pompey's daughter who was also Sulla's grand-daughter, but divorced her on a suspicion of adultery with Publius Clodius; indeed, so persistent was the rumour of Clodius' having disguised himself as a woman and seduced her at the Feast of the Good Goddess from which all men are excluded, that the Senate ordered a judicial inquiry into the alleged desecration of these sacred rites.

As quaestor Caesar was appointed to Western Spain where the governor-general, who held praetorian① rank, sent him off on an assize-circuit②. At Cadiz, he saw a statue of Alexander the Great in the Temple of Hercules, and was overheard to sigh impatiently: vexed, it seems, that at an age when Alexander had already conquered the whole world, he himself had done nothing in the least epoch-making. Moreover, when on the following night, much to his dismay he had a dream of raping his own mother, the soothsayers greatly encouraged him by their interpretation of it: namely that he was destined to conquer the earth our Universal Mother.

At all events, he laid down his quaestorship at once, bent on performing some notable act at the first opportunity that offered. He visited the Latin colonists beyond the Po③, who were bitterly demanding the same Roman citizenship as that granted to other townsfolk in Italy; and might have persuaded them to revolt, had not the Consuls realized the danger and garrisoned that district with the legions recently raised for the Cilician campaign.

Undiscouraged, Caesar soon made an even more daring attempt at revolution in Rome itself. A few days before taking up his aedileship④, he was suspected of plotting with Marcus Crassus⑤, an ex-consul; also with Publius Sulla and Lucius Autronius, who had jointly been elected to the consulship but found guilty of bribery and corruption. These four had agreed to wait until the New Year and then attack the Senate House, killing as many senators as convenient. Crassus would then proclaim himself

---

① 执政官的，禁卫军长官的（praetorian）
② 各地巡回办案（Assize-circuit）
③ 波河（the Po），意大利北部重要河流
④ 古罗马的市政官任期（aedileship），主管城市的公共建筑、道路、供水、文体活动等
⑤ 马库斯·克拉苏（Marcus Crassus），公元前70年罗马执政官

Dictator, and Caesar his Master of Horse①; the government would be reorganized to suit their pleasure; Sulla and Autronius would be appointed Consuls.

Tanusius Geminus mentions their plot in his History, more information is given in Marcus Bibulus's② Edicts and in the Orations of Gaius Curio the Elder. Another reference to it may be detected in Cicero's③ letter to Axius, where Caesar is said to have 'established in his consulship the monarchy which he had planned while only an aedile'. Tanusius adds that Crassus was prevented, either by scruples or by nervousness, from appearing at the appointed hour and Caesar therefore did not give the agreed signal which according to Curio, was letting his gown fall and expose the shoulder.

Both Curio and Marcus Actorius Naso state that Caesar also plotted with Gnaeus Piso, a young nobleman suspected of raising a City conspiracy and for that reason appointed Governor-general of Spain, although he had neither solicited nor qualified for the position. Caesar apparently was to lead a revolt in Rome as soon as Piso did so in Spain; the Ambranians④ and the Latins who lived beyond the Po would have risen simultaneously. But Piso's death canceled the plan.

During his aedileship, Caesar filled the Comitium⑤, the Forum⑥, its adjacent basilicas⑦, and the Capitol⑧ itself with a display of the material which he meant to use in his public shows; building temporary colonnades for the purpose. He exhibited wild-beast hunts and stage-plays; some at his own expense, some in co-operation with his colleague, Marcus Bibulus—but took all the credit in either case, so that Bibulus remarked openly: 'The Temple of the Heavenly Twins in the Forum is always simply called "Castor's"; and I always play Pollux to Caesar's Castor when we give a public

---

① 骑兵总督（Master of Horse）
② 马库斯·毕布路斯（Marcus Bibulus），恺撒的政治同僚，于公元前59年与恺撒共同担任罗马执政官
③ 马库斯·图利乌斯·西塞罗（Marcus Tullius Cicero），古罗马著名政治家，演说家
④ 安布拉尼人
⑤ 罗马投票大厅（the Comitium）
⑥ 罗马广场（the Forum）
⑦ 廊柱大厅（basilicas）
⑧ 卡皮托（Capitol），即卡皮托利尼山（Capitoline Hill），实指卡皮托利尼山上的朱庇特神庙（the Temple of Jupiter）

entertainment together.' ①

Caesar also put on a gladiatorial show but had collected so immense a troop of combatants that his terrified political opponents rushed a bill through the House, limiting the number of gladiators that anyone might keep in Rome; consequently far fewer pairs fought than had been advertised

After thus securing the good will of the commons and their tribunes, Caesar tried to get himself elected Governor-General of Egypt by popular vote. His excuse for demanding so unusual an appointment was an outcry against the Alexandrians who had just deposed King Ptolemy, although the Senate had recognized him as an ally and friend of Rome. However the aristocratic party opposed the measure; so, as aedile, Caesar took vengeance by replacing the public monuments—destroyed by Sulla many years ago—that had commemorated Marius's victories over Jugurtha② the Cimbrians③, and the Teutons④, Further as Judge of the Senatorial Court of inquiry into Murder, he prosecuted men who had earned public bounties for bringing in the heads of Roman citizens outlawed by the aristocrats; although this rough justice had been expressly sanctioned in the Cornelian Laws.

He also bribed a man to bring a charge of high treason against Gaius Rabirius who, some years previously had earned the Senate's gratitude by checking the seditious activities of Lucius Saturninus, a tribune. Caesar chosen by lot to try Rabirius, pronounced the sentence with such satisfaction that when Rabirius appealed to the people, the greatest argument in his favour was the judge's obvious prejudice.

Obliged to abandon his ambition of governing Egypt, Caesar stood for the office of Chief Pontiff⑤ and used the most flagrant bribery to secure it. The story goes that reckoning up the enormous debts thus contracted, he told his mother as she kissed him goodbye on the morning of the poll, that if he did not return to her as Chief Pontiff he would not return at all. However he defeated his two prominent rivals, both of whom

---

① 卡斯托耳（Castor）和波吕克斯（Pollux）是古希腊神话中一对情同手足、生死与共的孪生英雄，死后升天成为双子星座。马库斯·毕布路斯此处借喻抱怨恺撒总是要唱主角而自己只能做配角
② 朱古达（Jugurtha），非洲努米底亚（Numidian）的国王，现在北非的阿尔及利亚地区
③ 西姆布里亚人（the Cimbrians）
④ 条顿人（the Teutons），即日耳曼人
⑤ 大祭师（Chief Pontiff）

were much older and more distinguished than himself, and the votes he won from their own tribes exceeded those cast for them in the entire poll.

When the Catilinarian conspiracy came to light, the whole House①, with the sole exception of Caesar, then Praetor-elect demanded the death penalty for Catiline and his associates. Caesar proposed merely that they should be imprisoned each in a different town, and their estates confiscated. What was more, he so browbeat those senators who took a sterner line, by suggesting that the commons would conceive an enduring hatred for them if they persisted in this view, that Decimus Silanus, as Consul-elect, felt obliged to interpret his own proposal—which however he could not bring himself to recast—in a more liberal sense, begging Caesar not to misread it so savagely. And Caesar would have gained his point since many senators (including the Consul Cicero's brother) had been won over to his view, had Marcus Cato② not kept the irresolute Senate in line. Caesar continued to block proceedings until a body of Roman knights, serving as a defence force to the House, threatened to kill him unless he ceased his violent opposition. They even unsheathed their swords and made such passes at him that most of his companions fled, and the remainder huddled around, protecting him with their arms or their gowns. He was sufficiently impressed, not only to leave the House, but to keep away from it for the rest of that year.

On the first day of his praetorship, Caesar ordered Quintus Catulus to appear before the commons and explain why he had made so little progress with the restoration of the Capitol; demanding that Catulus' commission should be taken from him and entrusted, instead, to Gnaeus Pompey③. However, the senators of the aristocratic party who were escorting the newly-elected Consuls to their inaugural sacrifice in the Capitol, heard what was afoot and came pouring downhill in a body to offer obstinate resistance, Caesar withdrew his proposal.

Caecilius Metellus, a tribune of the people, then defended his colleagues' veto by bringing in some highly inflammatory bills; and Caesar stubbornly championed them on the floor of the House until at last both Metellus and himself were suspended by a Senatorial decree. Nevertheless, he had the effrontery to continue holding his court,

---

① The House, 指元老院
② 小加图（Marcus Porcius Cato or Cato the Younger），古罗马共和国政治家（公元前95—公元前64年）
③ 格奈乌斯·庞培（Gnaeus Pompey），古罗马政治家、军事家

until warned that he would be removed by force. Thereupon he dismissed the lictors①, took of his praetorian robe, and went quickly home, where he had decided to live in retirement because the times allowed him no other alternative.

On the following day, however the commons made a spontaneous move towards Caesars house, riotously offering to put him back on the tribunal; but he restrained their ardour. The Senate, who had hurriedly met to deal with this demonstration were so surprised by his unexpectedly correct attitude that they sent a deputation of high officials to thank him publicly; then summoned him to the House where, with warm praises, they revoked their decree and confirmed him in his praetorship.

The next danger that threatened Caesar was the inclusion of his name in a list of Catilinarian conspirators handed to the Special Commissioner, Novius Niger, by an informer named Lucius Vettius; and also in another list laid before the Senate by Quintus Curius, who had been voted a public bounty as the first person to betray the plot. Curius claimed that this information came directly from Catiline, and Vettius went so far as to declare that he could produce a letter written to Catiline in Caesar's own hand.

Caesar would not lie down under this insult, and appealed to the Senatorial Records②, which showed that on Cicero's own admission, he had voluntarily come forward to warn him about the plot; and that Curius was not therefore entitled to the bounty. As for Vettius, who had been obliged to produce a bond when he made his revelations, this was declared forfeit and his goods seized; the commons, crowding around the Rostra, nearly tore him in pieces. Caesar thereupon sent Vettius off to goal; and Novius Niger, the Commissioner as well, for having let a magistrat of superior rank to himself be indicted at his tribunal③

The province of Western Spain was now allotted to Caesar. He relieved himself of the creditors who tried to keep him in Rome until he had paid his debts, by providing sureties for their eventual settlement. Then he took the illegal and unprecedented step of hurrying of before the Senate had either formally confirmed his appointment or voted him the necessary funds, He may have been afraid of being impeached while still

---

① 扈从，开道人员 (lictors)
② 元老院记录 (the Senatorial Records)
③ 在法庭上 (at his tribunal)

private citizen or he may have been anxious to respond as quickly as possible to the appeals of our Spanish allies for help against aggression.

At any rate, on his arrival in Spain, he rapidly subdued the Lusitanian① mountaineers, captured Brigantium, the capital of Galicia②, and returned to Rome in the following summer with equal haste—not waiting until he had been relieved—to demand a triumph and stand for the consulship. But the day of the consular elections had already been announced, His candidacy could therefore not be admitted unless he entered the City as a civilian; and when a general outcry arose against his intrigues to be exempted from the regulations governing candidatures he was faced with the alternative of forgoing the triumph or forgoing the consulship.

There were two other candidates: Lucius Lucceius and Marcus Bibulus, Caesar now approached Lucceius and suggested that they should join forces: but since Lucceius had more money and Caesar greater influence, it was agreed that Lucceius should finance their joint candidacy by bribing the voters. The aristocratic party got wind of this arrangement and, fearing that if Caesar were elected Consul, with a pliant colleague by his side, he would stop at nothing to gain his own ends, they authorized Marcus Bibulus to bribe the voters as heavily as Lucceius had done, Many aristocrats contributed to Bibulus' campaign funds, and Cato himself admitted that this was an occasion when even bribery might be excused as legitimate means of preserving the Constitution.

Caesar and Bibulus were elected Consuls, but the aristocrats continued to restrict Caesars influence by ensuring that when he and Bibulus had completed their term, neither should govern a province garrisoned by large forces; they would be sent of somewhere "to guard mountain-pastures and keep forests clear of brigands". infuriated by this sight, Caesar exerted his charm on Gnaeus Pompey who had quarreled with the Senate because they were so slow in approving the steps that he had taken to defeat King Mithridates of Pontus③, He also succeeded in conciliating Pompey and Marcus Crassus—they were still at odds after their failure to agree on matters of policy while sharing the consulship. Pompey, Caesar, and Crassus now formed a triple pact, jointly

---

① 卢西塔尼亚人（Lusitanian）
② 加利西亚（Galicia），西班牙西北部一地区
③ 本都（Pontus）国王，米特里达梯六世（Mithridates VI）

swearing to oppose all legislation of which any one of them might disapprove.①

Caesar's first act as Consul was to rule that a daily record of proceedings in the Senate, and in the People's Court should be taken and published: he also revived the obsolete custom of having an orderly walk before him, during the months in which his colleague held the rods of office, while the lictors marched behind. Next, he introduced an agrarian law, and when Bibulus delayed its passage through the Senate by announcing that the omens were unfavourable, drove him from the Forum by force of arms. On the following day Bibulus lodged a complaint in the House, and when nobody dared move a vote of censure, or make any observation on this scandalous event—though decrees condemning minor breaches of the peace had often been passed—he felt so frustrated that he stayed at home for the rest of the term, satisfying his resentment with further announcements about unfavourable omens.

Caesar was thus enabled to govern alone and do very much as he pleased, it became a joke to sign and seal bogus documents: Executed during the Consulship of Julius and Caesar, rather than: "…during the Consulship of Bibulus and Caesar". And this lampoon went the rounds:

The event occurred, as I recall, when Caesar governed Rome—
Caesar, not Marcus Bibulus, who kept his seat at home②.

The tribune Rullus had proposed to settle a number of poorer citizens on a Campanian plain③ called Stellas; and another agricultural district also in Campania had been declared public territory and farmed on behalf of the government. Caesar partitioned both these districts among fathers of three or more children, appointing a commission to choose the candidates, instead of letting them draw the customary lots. When the Roman tax-farmers asked for relief, he canceled one-third of their obligations, but gave them frank warning not to bid too high for their contracts in future. He freely granted all other pleas, whatsoever and either met with no opposition or

---

① 庞培 (Pompey)、恺撒 (Caesar)、克拉苏 (Crassus) 正式组成元老院中的政治联盟，称为"前三头同盟" (First Triumvirate)
② Keep one's seat at home, 双语，指取得了控制权
③ 坎帕尼亚平原 (Campanian plain)，亚平宁半岛南部平原，坎帕尼亚区 (Campania)

intimidated anyone who dared intervene. Marcus Cato once tried to delay proceedings by talking out the debate, but Caesar had him forcibly ejected by a lictor and led off to prison. Lucius Lucullus went a little too far in opposing Caesar's policy whereupon Caesar so terrified him by threats of prosecution for the part he had supposedly played in the Mithridatic War, that Lucullus fell on his knees and begged Caesars pardon. Hearing that Cicero had been making a doleful speech in court about the evils of his times, Caesar at once granted the long-standing plea of Cicero's enemy Publius Clodius, to be transferred from patrician to plebeian rank; rushing this measure through the House at three o'clock, just before the adjournment. Finally he began an attack on his aristocratic opponents as a body by bribing an informer who appeared on the Rostra and announced that some of them had tried to make him assassinate Pompey. As had been arranged the informer mentioned a few names, but the whole affair was so suspicious that nobody paid much attention and Caesar, realizing that he had been too hasty is said, to have poisoned his agent①.

Caesar then married Calpurnia, daughter of Lucius Piso, his successor in the consulship; and at the same time betrothed Julia to Gnaeus Pompey, thus breaking her previous engagement to Servilius Caepio who had recently given him a great deal of support in the struggle against Bibulus. He now always called on Pompey to open debates in the House, though having hitherto reserved this honour for Crassus; thereby flouting the tradition that a Consul should continue, throughout the year, to preserve the order of precedence established for speakers on New Year's Day.

Having thus secured the good will of his father-in-law Piso and his son-in-law Pompey, Caesar surveyed the many provinces open to him and chose Gaul as being the likeliest to supply him with wealth and triumphs, true, he was at first appointed Governor-General only of Cisalpine Gaul② and Illyria③—the proposal came from Vatinius—but afterwards the Senate added Transalpine Gaul④ to his jurisdiction,

---

① His agent, 即告密者 (the informer)
② 山南高卢 (Cisalpine Gaul), 指阿尔卑斯山 (Alps) 以南至卢比孔河 (Rubicon) 的意大利北部地区
③ 伊利里亚 (Illyria), 亚德里亚海 (Adriatic) 东北岸一古国
④ 山外高卢 (Transalpin Gaul), 指阿尔卑斯山以北、比利牛斯山 (the Pyrenees) 以北、莱茵河 (the Rhine) 以西的罗马占领区, 相当于现在的法国、比利时、荷兰、卢森堡、瑞士、德国西部等地区

fearing that if this were denied him the commons would insist that he should have it.

His elation was such that he could not refrain from boasting to a packed House, some days later, that having now gained his dearest wish, to the annoyance and grief of his opponents, he would proceed to 'stamp upon their persons'. When someone interjected with a sneer that a woman would not find this an easy feat, he answered amicably: 'Why not? Semiramis① was supreme in Syria and the Amazons② once ruled over a large part of Asia.'

At the close of his consulship the praetors Gaius Memmius and Lucius Domitius Ahenobarbus demanded an inquiry into his official conduct during the past year. Caesar referred the matter to the Senate, who would not discuss it so after three days had been wasted in idle recriminations, he left for Gaul. His quaestor was at once charged with various irregularities, as a first step towards his own impeachment. Then Lucius Antistius, a tribune of the people, arraigned Caesar Who, however appealed to the whole college of tribunes, pleading absence on business of national importance; and thus staved of the trial.

To prevent a recurrence of his sort of trouble he made a point of putting the chief magistrates of each new year under some obligation to him, and refusing to support any candidates, or allow them to be elected, unless they promised to defend his cause while he was absent from Rome. He had no hesitation in holding some of them to their promises by an oath or even a written contract.

At last Lucius Domitius Ahenobarbus stood for the consulship and openly threatened that once elected, he would remove Caesar from his military command, having failed to do this while praetor. So Caesar called upon Pompey and Crassus to visit Lucca③, which lay in his province, and there persuaded them to prolong his governorship of Gaul for another five years, and to oppose Domitius' candidature.

This success encouraged Caesar to expand his regular army with legions raised at his own expense: one even recruited in Transalpine Gaul and called Alauda (Gallic for The Crested Lark) which he trained and equipped in Roman style. Later he made every Alauda legionary a full citizen.

---

① 塞米勒米斯（Semiramis），传说中的亚述女王
② 亚马逊部落（the Amazons），传说中的女战士部落
③ 卢卡（Lucca），意大利北部古城

He now lost no opportunity of picking quarrels—however flimsy the pretext—with allies as well as hostile and barbarous tribes, and marching against them the danger of this policy never occurred to him. At first the Seriate set up a commission of inquiry into the state of the Gallic provinces, and some Speakers went so far as to recommend that Caesar should be handed over to the enemy. But the more successful his campaigns, the more frequent he public thanksgivings voted; and the holidays that went with them were longer than any general before him had ever earned.

Briefly his nine years' governorship produced the following results. He reduced to the form of a province the whole of Gaul enclosed by the Pyrenees, the Alps, the Cevennes①, the Rhine②, and the Rhone③—about 640.000 square miles—except for certain allied states which had given him useful support; and exacted an annual tribute of 400,000 gold pieces.

Caesar was the first Roman to build a military bridge across the Rhine and cause the Germans on the farther bank heavy losses. He also invaded Britain a hitherto unknown country and defeated the natives, from whom he exacted a large sum of money as well as hostages for future good behaviour. He met with only three serious reverses: in Britain, when his fleet was all but destroyed by a gale; in Gaul, when one of his legions was routed at Gergovia among the Auvergne mountains; and on the German frontier when his generals Titurius and Aurunculeius were ambushed and killed.

During these nine years Caesar lost, one after the other, his mother, his daughter, and his grandson. Meanwhile, the assassination of Publius Clodius had caused such an outcry that the Senate voted for the appointment in future, of only a single Consul; naming Pompey as their choice, When the tribunes of the people wanted Caesar to stand as Pompey's colleague, Caesar asked whether they would not persuade the commons to let him do so without visiting Rome; His governorship of Gaul he wrote, was nearly at an end, and he preferred not to leave until his conquests had been completed.

Their granting of this concession so fired Caesars ambitions that he neglected no expense in winning popularity, both as a private citizen and as a candidate for his

---

① 塞文山脉 (the Cevennes)
② 莱茵河 (the Rhine)
③ 罗纳河 (the Rhone)

second consulship. He began building a new Forum with the spoils taken in Gaul and paid more than a million gold pieces for the site alone. Then he announced a gladiatorial show and a public banquet in memory of his daughter Julia—an unprecedented event, and, to create as much excitement among the commons as possible, had the banquet catered for party by his own household, party by the market contractors. He also issued an order that any well-known gladiator who failed to win the approval of the Circus should be forcibly rescued from execution and reserved for the coming show. New gladiators were also trained, not by the usual professionals in the schools, but in private houses by Roman knights and even senators who happened to be masters-at-arms. Letters of his survive, begging these trainers to give their pupils individual instruction in the art of fighting, He fixed the daily pay of the regular soldiers at double what it had been. Whenever the granaries were full he would make a lavish distribution to the army, without measuring the amount, and occasionally gave every man a Gallic slave.

To preserve Pompey's friendship and renew the family ties dissolved by Julia's death he offered him the hand of his sister's grand-daughter Octavia, though she had already married Gaius Marcellus, and in return asked leave to marry Pompey's daughter who was betrothed to Faustus Sulla. Having now won all Pompey's friends, and most of the Senate, to his side with loans at a low rate of interest or interest-free, he endeared himself to persons of less distinction too by handing out valuable presents, whether or not they asked for them, His beneficiaries included the favourite slaves or freedmen of prominent men.

Caesar thus became the one reliable source of help to all who were in legal difficulties, or in debt or living beyond their means; and refused help only to those whose criminal record was so black, or whose purse so empty or whose tastes were so expensive, that even he could do nothing for them. He frankly told such people: 'What you need is a civil war.'

Caesar took equal pains to win the esteem of kings and provincial authorities by offering them gifts of prisoners, a thousand at a time, or lending them troops whenever they asked, and without first obtaining official permission from the Senate or people. He also presented the principal cities of Asia and Greece with magnificent public works, and did the same for those of Italy, Gaul, and Spain. Everyone was amazed by his liberality and wondered what the sequel would be.

At last Marcus Claudius Marcellus, the Consul announced in the House that he intended to raise a matter of vital public interest; and then proposed that, since the Gallic War had now ended in victory. Caesar should be relieved of his command before his term as Governor-General expired; that a successor should be appointed; and that the armies in Gaul should be disbanded, He further proposed that Caesar should be forbidden to stand for the consulship without appearing at Rome in person since a decree against irregularities of this sort still appeared on the Statute Book.

Here Marcellus was on firm legal ground. Pompey when he introduced a bill regulating the privileges of state officials, had omitted to make a special exception for Caesar in the clause debarring absentees from candidacy; or to correct this oversight before the bill had been passed, engraved on a bronze tablet, and registered at the Public Treasury. Nor was Marcellus content to oust Caesar from his command and cancel the privilege already voted him: namely to stand for the consulship in absentia. He also asked that the colonists whom Caesar had settled at Como① under the Vatinian Act should lose their citizenship. This award, he said, had been intended to further Caesars political ambitions and lacked legal sanction.

The news infuriated Caesar, but he had often been reported as saying: 'Now that l am the leading Roman of my day, it will be harder to put me down a peg② than degrade me to the ranks.' So he resisted stubbornly persuading the tribunes of the people to veto Marcellus' bills and at the same time enlisting the help of Servius Sulpicius, Marcellus' colleague. When, in the following year, Marcellus was succeeded in office by his cousin Gaius, who adopted a similar policy, Caesar again won over the other Consul—Aemilius Paulus—with a heavy bribe; and also bought Gaius Curio, the most energetic tribune of the people.

Realizing, however that the aristocratic party had made a determined stand, and that both the new Consuls-elect were unfriendly to him, he appealed to the Senate, begging them in a written address not to cancel a privilege voted him by the commons, without forcing all other governors-general to resign their commands at the same time as he did. But this was read as meaning that he counted on mobilizing his veteran troops

---

① 科摩（Como），意大利北部城市

② 使我陷入困境（to put me down a peg）

sooner than Pompey could his raw levies. Next, Caesar offered to resign command of eight legions and quit Transalpine Gaul if he might keep two legions and Cisalpine Gaul or at least lllyricum① and one legion, until he became Consul.

Since the Senate refused to intervene on his behalf in a matter of such national importance, Caesar crossed into Cisalpine Gaul where he held his regular assizes, and halted at Ravenna②. He was resolved to invade Italy if force were used against the tribunes of the people who had vetoed the Senate's decree disbanding his army by a given date. Force was, in effect used and the tribunes fled towards Cisalpine Gaul which became Caesar's pretext for launching the Civil War. Additional motives are suspected, however: Pompey's comment was that, because Caesar had insufficient capital to carry out his grandiose schemes or give the people all that they had been encouraged to expect on his return, he chose to create an atmosphere of political confusion.

Another view is that he dreaded having to account for the irregularities of his first consulship, during which he had disregarded auspices and vetoes and defied the Constitution for Marcus Cato had often sworn to impeach him as soon as the legions were disbanded. Moreover people said at the time, frankly enough that should Caesar return from Gaul as a private citizen, he would be tried in a court ringed around with armed men, as Titus Annius Milo had lately been at Pompey's orders. This sounds plausible enough because Asinius Pollio records in his History that when Caesar at the Battle of Pharsalus,③ saw his enemies forced to choose between massacre and fight, he said, in these very words: 'They brought it on themselves. They would have condemned me to death regardless of all my victories—me, Gaius Caesar—had I not appealed to my army for help.' It has also been suggested that constant exercise of power gave Caesar a love of it; and that after weighing his enemies' strength against his own, he took this chance of fulfilling his youthful dreams by making a bid for the monarchy. Cicero seems to have come to a similar conclusion: in the third book of his

---

① 伊利里库姆省（Illyricum），古罗马重要行省，即伊利里亚（Illyria）地区，现在的斯洛文尼亚、克罗地亚、波斯尼亚等地
② 拉文纳（Ravenna），意大利东北部港口
③ 法萨卢斯战役（the Battle of Pharsalus），公元前48年在希腊的法萨卢斯（Pharsalus）进行的恺撒和庞培的生死决战

Essay on Duty he records that Caesar quoted the following lines from Euripides' Phoenician Women① on several occasions:

Is crime consonant with nobility?
Then noblest is the crime of tyranny —
In all things else obey the laws of Heaven.

Accordingly when news reached him that the tribunes veto had been disallowed, and that they had fled the City. he at once sent a few battalions ahead with all secrecy, and disarmed suspicion by himself attending a theatrical performance, inspecting the plans of a school for gladiators which he proposed to build, and dining as usual among a crowd of guests. But at dusk he borrowed a pair of mules from a bakery near headquarters, harnessed them to a gig, and set off quietly with a few of his staff. His lights went out, he lost his way. and the party wandered about aimlessly for some hours; but at dawn found a guide who led them on foot along narrow lanes, until they came to the right road. Caesar overtook his advanced guard at the river Rubicon②, which formed the frontier between Gaul and Italy. Well aware how critical a decision confronted him, he turned to his staff remarking: 'We may still draw back but once across that little bridge, we shall have to fight it out.'

As he stood, in two minds, an apparition of superhuman size and beauty was seen sitting on the river bank playing a reed pipe. A party of shepherds gathered around to listen and, when some of Caesar's men broke ranks to do the same, the apparition snatched a trumpet from one of them, ran down to the river blew a thunderous blast and crossed over Caesar exclaimed: Let us accept it his as a sign from the Gods, and follow where they beckon, in vengeance on our double-dealing enemies. The die is cast③.

He led his army to the farther bank, where he welcomed the tribunes of the people who had fled to him from Rome. Then he tearfully addressed the troops and, ripping open his tunic to expose his breast begged them to stand faithfully by him. The belief that he then promised to promote every man present to the Equestrian Order④ is based

---

① 欧里庇得斯的悲剧《腓尼基妇女》(Euripides' Phoenician Women)
② 卢比孔河 (the river Rubicon),意大利北部一条河流
③ 木已成舟 (the die is cast)
④ 骑士阶层 (the Equestrian Order)

on a misunderstanding, He had accompanied his pleas with the gesture of pointing to his left-hand, as he declared that he would gladly reward those who championed his honour with the very seal ring from his thumb; but some soldiers on the fringe of the assembly who saw him better than they could hear his words, read too much into the gesture. They put it about that Caesar had promised them all the right to wear a knight's gold ring, and the 4,000 gold pieces required to support a knighthood.

Here follows a brief account of Caesar's subsequent movements. He occupied Unmbria, Picenum, and Tuscany; captured Lucius Domitius Ahenobarbus who had been illegally named as his successor in Gaul and was holding Corfinium① for the Senate; let him go free; and then marched along the Adriatic coast② to Brindisi, where Pompey and the Consuls had fled from Rome on their way to Epirus③. When his efforts to prevent their crossing the straits proved ineffective, he marched on Rome, entered it summoned the Senate to review the political situation, and then hurriedly set off for Spain; Pompey's strongest forces were stationed there under the command of his friends Marcus Petreius, Lucius Afranius, and Marcus Varro. Before leaving, Caesar told his household: 'I am off to meet an army without a leader; when I return I shall meet a leader without an army.' Though delayed by the siege of Marseilles④, which had shut its gates against him, and by a failure of his commissariat he won a rapid and overwhelming victory.

Caesar returned by way of Rome, crossed the Adriatic and, after blockading Pompey near the Illyrian town of Dyrrhachium for nearly four months, behind an immense containing works routed him at Pharsalus⑤ in Thessaly⑥. Pompey fled to Alexandria⑦; Caesar followed, and when he found that King Ptolemy⑧ had murdered Pompey and was planning to murder him as well, declared war. This proved to be a most difficult campaign, fought during winter within the city walls of a well-equipped

---

① 科菲尼乌姆（Corfinium），罗马以东的一个地区
② 亚德里亚海岸（the Adriatic coast）
③ 伊庇鲁斯（Epirus）地区，位于巴尔干半岛，现在的阿尔巴尼亚，与意大利隔着亚德里亚海
④ 马赛（Marseilles），法国南部港口
⑤ 法萨卢斯（Pharsalus），位于希腊中部区
⑥ 色萨利（Thessaly），希腊北部一地区，东接爱琴海，西接伊庇鲁斯（Epirus）地区
⑦ 亚历山大港（Alexandria），位于埃及北部的地中海港口
⑧ 托勒密（Ptolemy）王朝，亚历山大时代之后，由马其顿将军托勒密在埃及建立的统治

and cunning enemy; but though caught off his guard, and without military supplies of any kind, Caesar was victorious, He then handed over the government of Egypt to Queen Cleopatra① and her younger brother; fearing that, if made a Roman province, it might one day be held against his fellow-countrymen by some independent-minded governor-general. From Alexandria he proceeded to Syria②, and from Syria to Pontus③, news having come that Pharnaces, son of the famous Mithridates, had taken advantage of the confused situation and already gained several successes. Five days after his arrival and four hours after catching sight of Pharnaces, Caesar won a crushing victory at Zela; and commented drily on Pompey's good fortune in having built up his reputation for generalship by victories over such poor stuff as this. Then he beat Scipio and King Juba at Thapsus in North Africa, where the remnants of the Pompeian party were being reorganized; and Pompey's two sons at Munda④ in Spain.

Throughout the Civil War Caesar was never defeated himself; but of his generals, Gaius Curio was killed fighting against King Juba; Gaius Antonius was captured off Illyricum; Publius Dolabella lost another fleet off Illyricum; and Gnaeus Domitius Calvinus had his army destroyed in Pontus. Yet, though invariably successful, he twice came close to disaster: at Dyrrhachium, where Pompey broke his blockade and forced him to retreat—Caesar remarked when Pompey failed to pursue him: 'He does not know how to win wars—and in the final battle at Munda, where all seemed lost and he even considered suicide.'

After defeating Scipio, Caesar celebrated four triumphs in one month with a few days' interval between them: and, after defeating young Pompey, a fifth. These triumphs were the Gallic—the first and most magnificent—the Alexandrian, the Pontic, the African, and lasty the Spanish. Each differed completely from the others in its presentation.

As Caesar rode through the Velabrum⑤ on the day of his Gallic triumph, the axle of his triumphal chariot broke and he nearly took a toss; but afterwards ascended to the

---

① 克里奥帕特拉（Queen Cleopatra），埃及艳后
② 叙利亚（Syria），古罗马时代的叙利亚地区，包括现在的巴勒斯坦、以色列、叙利亚、约旦、伊拉克等地区
③ 本都（Pontus），亦译蓬托斯，黑海南岸小亚西亚古国
④ 蒙达（Munda），西班牙南部平原
⑤ 维拉布鲁姆（the Velabrum），古罗马城内的一个区

Capitol between two lines of elephants, forty in all, which acted as his torch-bearers. In the Pontic triumph one of the decorated wagons, instead of a stage-set representing scenes from the war, like the rest, carried a simple three-word inscription:

CAME, SAW, CONQUERED!

This referred to the speed with which the war had been won.

Every infantryman of Caesar's veteran legions earned a war-gratuity of 240 gold pieces in addition to the twenty paid at the outbreak of hostilities and a farm. These farms could not be grouped together without evicting former owners, but were scattered all over the countryside. Every member of the commons received ten pecks of grain and ten pounds of oil as a bounty besides the three gold pieces which Caesar had promised at first and now raised to five, by way of interest on the four years' delay in payment. He added a popular banquet and a distribution of meat; also a dinner to celebrate his victory at Munda, but decided that this had not been splendid enough and, five days later served a second more succulent one.

His pubic shows were of great variety They included a gladiatorial contest, stage-plays for every quarter of Rome performed in several languages, chariot-races in the Circus①, athletic competitions, and a mock naval battle. At the gladiatorial contest in the Forum, a man named Furius Leptinus, of patrician family fought Quintus Calpenus, a barrister and former senator to the death. The sons of petty kings from Asia and Bithynia danced the Pyrrhic② sword dance.

One of the plays was written and acted by Decimus Laberius, a Roman knight who forfeited his rank by so doing: but after the performance he was given five thousand gold pieces and had his gold ring, the badge of equestrian rank restored to him—so that he could walk straight from stage to orchestra where fourteen rows of seats were reserved for his Order. Abroad ditch had been dug around the race-course now extended at either end of the Circus, and the contestants were young noblemen who drove four-horse and two-horse chariots or rode pairs of horses, jumping from back to back. The so-called Troy Game③, a sham fight supposedly introduced by Aeneas④ was

---

① 大竞技场（the Circus）
② 皮洛士的（Pyrrhic），皮洛士（Pyrrhus）是古希腊伊庇鲁斯国王（Epirus），亚历山大时代之后希腊最重要的军事家、政治家
③ 特洛伊游戏（Troy Game）
④ 埃涅阿斯（Aeneas），特洛伊王子，罗马人先祖之一

performed by two troops of boys, one younger than the other.

Wild-beast hunts took place five days running, and the entertainment ended with a battle between two armies, each consisting of 500 infantry, twenty elephants, and thirty cavalry. To let the camps be pitched facing each other, Caesar removed the central barrier of the Circus, around which he chariots ran. Athletic contests were held in a temporary stadium on the Campus Martius and lasted for three days.

The naval battle was fought on an artificial lake dug in the Lesser Codeta, between Tyrian① and Egyptian ships, with two, three, or four banks of oars, and heavily manned. Such huge numbers of visitors flocked to these shows from all directions that many of them had to sleep in tents pitched along the streets or roads, or on roof tops; and often the pressure of the crowd crushed people to death. The victims included two senators.

Caesar next turned his attention to domestic reforms, First he reorganized the Calendar which the Pontiffs had allowed to full into such disorder by intercalating days or months as it suited them, that the harvest and vintage festivals no longer corresponded with the appropriate seasons. He linked the year to the course of the sun by lengthening it from 355 days to 365, abolishing the short extra month intercalated after every second February, and adding an entire day every fourth year. But to make the next first of January fall at the right season, he drew out his particular year by two extra months inserted between November and December So that it consisted of fifteen, including the intercalary one inserted after February in the old style.

He brought the Senate up to strength by creating new patricians, and increased the yearly quota of praetors, aediles, and quaestors,② as well as of minor officials; reinstating those degraded by the Censors or condemned for corruption by a jury. Also, he arranged with the commons that, apart from the Consul, half the magistrates should be popularly elected and half nominated by himself. Allowing even the sons of proscribed men to stand, he circulated brief directions to the voters. For instance: 'Caesar the Dictator to such-and-such a tribe of voters: 1 recommend so-and-so to you for office.' He limited jury service to knights and senators, disqualifying the

---

① 推罗人的（Tyrian），古腓尼基人的重要城市，位于地中海东岸，今巴勒斯坦地区
② 古罗马政府体系中最重要的三种官员：执政官（praetor）、市政官（aedile）、财政官（quaetor）

Treasury tribunes—these were commoners who collected the tribute and paid the army.

Caesar changed the old method of registering voters: he made the City landlords help him to complete the list, street by street, and reduced from 320,000 to 150,000 the number of householders who might draw free grain. To do away with the nuisance of having to summon everyone for enrolment periodically, he made the praetors keep their register up to date by replacing the names of dead men with those of others not yet listed.

Since the population of Rome had been considerably diminished by the transfer of 80,000 men to overseas colonies, he forbade any citizen between the ages of twenty and forty to absent himself from Italy for more than three years in succession. Nor might any senator's son travel abroad unless as member of some magistrate's household or staff; and at least a third of the cattlemen employed by grazers had to be freeborn. Caesar also granted the citizenship to all medical practitioners and professors of liberal arts resident in Rome, thus inducing them to remain and tempting others to follow suit.

He disappointed popular agitators by cancelling no debts, but in the end decreed that every debtor should have his property assessed according to pre-war valuation and, after deducting the interest already paid directly or by way of a banker's guarantee, should satisfy his creditors with whatever sum that might represent. Since prices had risen steeply, this left debtors with perhaps a fourth part of their property. Caesar dissolved all workers' guilds except the ancient ones, and increased the penalties for crime; and since wealthy men had less compunction about committing major offences, because the worst that could happen to them was a sentence of exile, he punished murderers of fellow-citizens (as Cicero records) by the seizure of either their entire property or half of it.

In his administration of justice he was both conscientious and severe, and went so far as to degrade senators found guilty of extortion. Once, when an ex-praetor married a woman on the day after her divorce from another man, he annulled the union, although adultery between them was not suspected.

He imposed a tariff on foreign manufactures; forbade the use, exception stated occasions, of litters, and the wearing of either scarlet robes or pearls by those below a certain rank and age, To implement his laws against luxury he placed inspectors in different parts of the market to seize delicacies offered for sale in violation of his orders; sometimes he even sent lictors and guards into dining rooms to remove illegal dishes, already served which his watchmen had failed to intercept.

Caesar continually undertook great new works for the embellishment of the City, or for the Empire's protection and enlargement. His first projects were a temple of Mars①, the biggest in the world, to build which he would have had to fill up and pave the lake where the naval sham-fight had been staged: and an enormous theatre sloping down from the Tarpeian Rock② on the Capitoline Hill.

Another task he set himself was the reduction of the Civil Code③ to manageable proportions, by selecting from the unwieldy mass of statutes only the most essential, and publishing them in a few volumes. Still another was to provide public libraries, by Commissioning Marcus Varro④ to collect and classify Greek and Latin books on a comprehensive scale. His engineering schemes included the draining of the Pomptine Marshes and of Lake Fucinus; also a highway running from the Adriatic⑤ across the Apennines⑥ to the Tiber⑦ and a canal to be cut through the isthmus of Corinth⑧. In the military field he planned an expulsion of the Dacians⑨ from Pontus and Thrace⑩, which they had recently occupied and then an attack on Parthia⑪ by way of Lesser Armenia⑫; but decided not to risk a pitched battle until he had familiarized himself with Parthian tactics.

All these schemes were canceled by his assassination before describing that, I should perhaps give a brief description of his appearance, personal habits, dress,

---

① 战神庙（a temple of Mars）
② 塔尔皮亚岩石（the Tarpeian Rock），在此岩石下处死了一个叫塔尔皮亚的叛国罪犯人，此岩石由此得名
③ 《民法典》（the Civil Code）
④ 马库斯·瓦罗（Marcus Varro），古罗马语言学家，学识渊博，著述甚丰。代表作有25卷的《拉丁语研究》
⑤ 亚德里亚海（Adriatic），地中海北部现在的意大利和克罗地亚、波黑、阿尔巴尼亚之间的海域
⑥ 亚平宁山脉（Apennies），现意大利中部顺着半岛走向的山脉
⑦ 台伯河（Tiber），穿过罗马市区流入地中海的一条河流
⑧ 科林斯地峡（the isthmus of Corinth），连接伯罗奔尼撒（Peloponnese）半岛和希腊中部的狭长地带，古城科林斯所在地
⑨ 达西亚（Dacians），古地名，现罗马尼亚
⑩ 色雷斯（Thrace），古地名，现保加利亚南部、土耳其西部、希腊北部地区
⑪ 帕提亚（Parthia）又称安息，现伊朗、伊拉克等地，原古代里海东南的一游牧部落，亚历山大之后消灭了塞琉古帝国，成为西亚第一帝国，帕提亚人的（Parthian）
⑫ 小亚美尼亚（Lesser Armenia），高加索山南麓古国，现土耳其东部

character, and conduct in peace and war.

Caesar is said to have been tall, fair, and well-built, with a rather broad face and keen, dark-brown eyes. His health was sound, apart from sudden comas and a tendency to nightmares which troubled him towards the end of his life; but he twice had epileptic fits while on campaign, He was something of a dandy, always keeping his head carefully trimmed and shaved: and has been accused of having certain other hairy parts of his body depilated with tweezers. His baldness was a disfigurement which his enemies harped upon, much to his exasperation; but he used to comb the thin strands of hair forward from his poll and of all the honours voted him by the Senate and People, none pleased him so much as the privilege of wearing a laurel wreath on all occasions— he constantly took advantage of it.

His dress was, it seems, unusual: he had added wrist-length sleeves with fringes to his purple-striped senatorial tunic and the belt which he wore over it was never tightly fastened—hence Sulla's warning to the aristocratic party: 'Beware of that boy with the loose clothes!'

Caesars first home was a modest house in the Subura quarter, but later, as Chief Pontiff, he used the official residence on the Sacred Way. Contemporary literature contains frequent references to his fondness for luxurious living. Having built a country mansion at Nervi from the foundations up, one story goes, he found so many features in it to dislike that, although poor at the time and heavily in debt, he tore the whole place down. It is also recorded that he carried tessellated and mosaic pavements with him on his campaigns.

Fresh-water pearls seem to have been the lure that prompted his invasion of Britain; he would sometimes weigh them in the palm of his hand to judge their value, and was also a keen collector of gems, cravings, statues, and Old Masters①, so high were the prices he paid for slaves of good character and attainments that he became ashamed of his extravagance and would not allow the sums to be entered in his accounts.

I find also that, while stationed abroad, he always had dinner served in two separate rooms: one for his officers and Greek friends, the other for Roman citizens and the more important provincials, He paid such strict attention to his domestic economy,

---

① 古代的画作（Old Masters）

however small the detail, that he once put his baker in irons for giving him a different sort of bread from that served to his guests; and executed a favourite freedman for committing adultery with a knights' wife, although no complaint had been lodged by the husband.

The only specific charge of unnatural practices ever brought against him was that he had been King Nicomedes' catamite—always a dark stain on his reputation and frequently quoted by his enemies. Licinius Calvus published the notorious verses:

The riches of Bithynias' King
Who Caesar on his couch abused.

Dolabella called him 'the Queen's rival and inner partner of the royal bed', and Curio the Elder: 'Nicomedes' Bithynian brothel.'

Bibulus, Caesar's colleague in the consulship, described him in an edict as 'the Queen of Bithynia... who once wanted to sleep with a monarch, but now wants to be one'. And Marcus Brutus recorded that about the same time, one Octavius, a scatterbrained creature who would say the first thing that came into his head, walked into a packed assembly where he saluted Pompey as 'King' and Caesar as 'Queen'. These can be discounted as mere insults, but Gaius Memmius directly charges Caesar with having joined a group of Nicomedes' debauched young friends at a banquet where he acted as the royal cup-bearer; and adds that certain Roman merchants, whose names he supplies, were present as guests. Cicero too, not only wrote in several letters:

Caesar was led by Nicomedes' attendants to the royal bedchamber, where he lay on a golden couch, dressed in a purple shift... So this descendant of Venus lost his virginity in Bithynia, but also once interrupted Caesar while he was addressing the House in defence of Nicomedes' daughter Nysa and listing his obligations to Nicomedes himself. 'Enough of that,' Cicero shouted, 'if you please! We all know what he gave you, and what you gave him in return.' Lastly when Caesar's own soldiers followed his decorated chariot in the Gallic triumph, chanting ribald songs, as they were privileged to do, this was one of them:

Gaul was brought to shame by Caesar,
By King Nicomedes, he.

Here comes Caesar wreathed in triumph
For his Gallic victory!
Nicomedes wears no laurels,
Though the greatest of the three.

His affairs with women are commonly described as numerous and extravagant: among those of noble birth whom he is said to have seduced were Servius Sulpicius' wife Postumia; Aulus Gabinius' wife Lollia; Marcus Crassus' wife Tertulla; and even Gnaeus Pompey's wife Mucia. Be this how it may both Curio the Elder and Curio the Younger reproached Pompey for having married Caesar's daughter Julia, when it was because of Caesar whom he had often despairingly called 'Aegisthus'①, that he divorced Mucia, mother of his three children. This Aegisthus had been the lover of Agamemnon's wife Clytaemnestra.②

But Marcus Brutus' mother Servilia was the woman whom Caesar loved best and in is first consulship he brought her a pearl worth 60,000 gold pieces. He gave her many presents during the Civil War③, is well as knocking down certain valuable estates to her at a public auction for a song. When surprise was expressed at the low price, Cicero made a neat remark: 'it was even cheaper than you think because a third (tertia) had been discounted.' Servilia, you see, was also suspected at the time of having prostituted her daughter Tertia to Caesar④.

That he had love-affairs in the provinces, too, is suggested by other of the ribald verses sung during the Gallic triumph:

Home we bring our bald whoremonger,
Romans, lock your wives away!
All the bags of gold you lent him

---

① 埃吉斯托斯（Aegisthus），古希腊迈锡尼城（Mycenae）的贵族，勾搭迈锡尼王后克吕泰涅斯特拉（Clytemnestra）成奸，在特洛伊战争后与王后一起，设计屠杀希腊主帅阿伽门农（Agamemnon）及其随从，后被阿伽门农之子俄瑞斯忒斯（Orestes）复仇所杀
② 克吕泰涅斯特拉（Clytaemnestra 即 Clytemnestra），迈锡尼王后，阿伽门农之妻
③ 罗马内战（the Civil War）指恺撒与庞培之间，为争夺罗马共和国控制权而进行的战争
④ Tertia 是双关语，有三分之一的意思，指塞维利亚（Servilia）为控制恺撒，而将自己的女儿特西娅（Tertia）出卖给他

Went his Gallic tarts to pay.

Among his mistresses were several queens—including Eunoe, wife of Bogudes the Moor[①] whom, according to Marcus Actorius Naso, he loaded with presents; Bogudes is said to have profited equally. The most famous of these queens was Cleopatra[②] of Egypt. He often feasted with her until dawn; and they would have sailed together in her state barge nearly to Ethiopia had his soldiers consented to follow him. He eventually Summoned Cleopatra to Rome, and would not let her return to Alexandria without high titles and rich presents. He even allowed her to call the son whom she had borne him 'Caesarion'. Some Greek historians say that the boy close resembled Caesar in features as well as in gait. Mark Antony informed the Senate that Caesar had, in fact, acknowledged Caesarion's paternity and that other friends of Caesar's, including Gaius Matius and Gaius Oppius, were aware of this. Oppius, however, seems to have felt the need of clearing his friend's reputation; because he published a book to prove that the boy whom Cleopatra had fathered on Caesar was not his at all.

A tribune of the people named Helvius Cinna informed a number of people that, following instructions he had drawn up a bill for the commons to pass during Caesar's absence from Rome, legitimizing his marriage with any woman or women he pleased—'for the procreation of children'. And to emphasize the bad name Caesar had won alike for unnatural and natural vice, I may here record that the Elder Curio referred to him in a speech as: 'Every woman's husband and every man's wife'.

Yet not even his enemies denied that he drank abstemiously. An epigram of Marcus Cato's survives: 'Caesar was the only sober man who ever tried to wreck the Constitution'; and Gaius Oppius relates that he cared so little for good food that when once he attended a dinner party where rancid oil had been served by mistake, and all the other guests refused it, Caesar helped himself more liberally than usual, to show that he did not consider his host either careless or boorish.

He was not particularly honest in money matters, either while a provincial governor or while holding office at Rome. Several memoirs record that as Governor-General of Western Spain, he not only begged his allies for money to settle his debts,

---

① 摩尔人 (the Moor), 北非土著部落居民
② 克里奥帕特拉 (Cleopatra), 埃及艳后

but wantonly sacked several Lusitanian towns, though they had accepted his terms and opened their gates to welcome him.

In Gaul he plundered large and small temples of their votive offerings, and more often gave towns over to pillage because their inhabitants were rich than because they had offended him. As a result he collected larger quantities of gold than he could handle, and began selling it for silver, in Italy and the provinces, at 750 denarii to the pound—which was about two-thirds of the official exchange rate.

In the course of his first consulship he stole 3000 lb. of gold from the Capitol and replaced it with the same weight of gilded bronze. He sold alliances and thrones for cash, making King Ptolemy XII of Egypt give him and Pompey nearly 1,500,000 gold pieces; and later paid his Civil War army, and the expenses of his triumphs and entertainments, by open extortion and sacrilege.

Caesar equalled, if he did not surpass, the greatest orators and generals the world had ever known. His prosecution of Dolabella unquestionably placed him in the first rank of advocates; and Cicero, discussing the matter in his Brutus, confessed that he knew no more eloquent speaker than Caesar 'whose style is chaste, pellucid, and grand, not to say noble'. Cicero also wrote to Cornelius Nepos:

'very well, then! Do you know any man who, even if he has concentrated on the art of oratory to the exclusion of all else, can speak batter than Caesar? Or anyone who makes so many witty remarks? Or whose vocabulary is so varied and yet so exact?'

Caesar seems to have modelled his style, at any rate when a beginner, on Caesar Strabo[①]—part of whose Defence of the Sardinians he borrowed verbatim for use in a trial oration of his own; he was then competing with other advocates for the right to plead a cause. It is said that he pitched his voice high in speaking, and used impassioned gestures which far from displeased his audience.

Several of Caesars undoubted speeches survive; and he is credited with others that

---

① 恺撒·斯特拉波（Caesar Strabo），恺撒的亲戚，曾在公元前 90 年担任罗马市政官（aedile）

may or may not have been his. Augustus① said that the 'Defence of Quintus Metellus' could hardly have been published by Caesar himself, and that it appeared to be a version taken down by shorthand writers who could not keep up with his rapid delivery. He was probably right, because on examining several manuscripts of the speech I find that even the title is given as 'A Speech Composed for Metellus' —although Caesar intended to deliver it in defence of Metellus and himself against a joint accusation.

Augustus also doubled the authenticity of Caesars 'Address to my Soldiers in Spain'. It is written in two parts, one speech supposedly delivered before the first battle, the other before the second—though on the later occasion, at least according to Asinius Pollio, the enemy's attack gave Caesar no time to address his troops at all.

He left memoirs of his war in Gaul, and of his civil war against Pompey; but no one knows who wrote those of the Alexandrian, African, and Spanish campaigns. Some say that it was his friend Oppius; others that it was Hirtius, who also finished 'The Gallic War', left incomplete by Caesar, adding a final book. Cicero also in the Brutus, observes: 'Caesar wrote admirably his memoirs are cleanly directly and gracefully composed, and divested of all rhetorical trappings. And while his sole intention was to supply historians with factual material, the result has been that several fools have been pleased to primp up his narrative for their own glorification; but every writer of sense has given the subject a wide berth.

Hirtius says downrightly: 'These memoirs are so highly rated by all judicious critics that the opportunity of enlarging and improving on them, which he purports to offer historians, seems in fact withheld from them. And, as his friends, we admire this feat even more than strangers can: they appreciate the faultless grace of his style, we know how rapidly and easily he wrote.'

Asinius Pollio, however believes that the memoirs show signs of carelessness and inaccuracy: Caesar, he holds, did not always check the truth of the reports that came in, and was either disingenuous or forgetful in describing his own actions. Pollio adds that Caesar must have planned a revision.

Among his literary remains are two books of An Essay on Analogy, two more of

---

① 奥古斯都（Augustus），罗马帝国的第一个皇帝，全名盖乌斯·屋大维乌斯·图里努斯（Gaius Octavius Thurinus），恺撒的侄孙子和遗嘱继承人，通常简称为屋大维或奥古斯都皇帝

Answers to Cato, and a poem, The Journey. He wrote An Essay on Analogy while coming back over the Alps after holding assizes in Cisalpine Gaul; Answers to Cato in the year that he won the battle of Munda①; and The Journey during the twenty-four days he spent on the road between Rome and Western Spain.

Many of the letters and dispatches sent by him to the Senate also survive, and he seems to have been the first statesman who reduced such documents to book form; previously, Consuls and governor-generals had written right across the page, not in neat columns. Then there are his letters to Cicero; and his private letters to friends, the more confidential passages of which he wrote in cypher: to understand their apparently incomprehensible meaning one must number the letters of the alphabet from 1 to 22, and then replace each of the letters that Caesar has used with the one which occurs four numbers lower—for instance, D stands for A.

It is said that in his boyhood and early youth he also wrote pieces called In Praise of Hercules and The Tragedy of Oedipus and Collected Sayings; but nearly a century later the Emperor Augustus② sent Pompeius Macer, his Surveyor of Libraries, a brief, frank letter forbidding him to circulate these minor works.

Caesar was a most skillful swordsman and horseman, and showed surprising powers of endurance. He always led his army, more often on foot than in the saddle, went bareheaded in sun and rain alike, and could travel for long distances at incredible speed in a gig, taking very little luggage. If he reached an unfordable river he would either swim or propel himself across it on an inflated skins and often arrived at his destination before the messengers whom he had sent ahead to announce his approach.

It is a disputable point which was the more remarkable when he went to war: his caution or his daring. He never exposed his army to ambushes, but made careful reconnaissances; and refrained from crossing over into Britain until he had collected reliable information (from Gaius Volusenus) about the harbours there, the best course to steer, and the navigational risks. On the other hand, when news reached him that his camp in Germany was being besieged, he disguised himself as a Gaul and picked his

---

① 蒙达之战（the battle of Munda），恺撒在打败庞培之后，在西班牙南部蒙达平原歼灭庞培残余势力的战争
② 奥古斯都皇帝（the Emperor Augustus），恺撒的遗嘱继承人、养子、侄孙子屋大维（Octavius）在公元前44年恺撒遇刺后，打败了政治对手马克·安东尼（Mark Antony），于公元前27年称帝奥古斯都，改罗马共和国为罗马帝国

way through the enemy outposts to take command on the spot.

He ferried his troops across the Adriatic from Brindisi to Dyrrhachium in the winter season, running the blockade of Pompey's fleet. And one night, when Mark Antony had delayed the supply of reinforcements, despite repeated pleas, Caesar muffled his head with a cloak and secretly put to sea in a small boat, alone and incognito; forced the helmsman to steer into the teeth of a gale, and narrowly escaped shipwreck

Religious scruples never deterred him for a moment. At the formal sacrifice before he launched his attack on Scipio and King Juba①, the victim escaped; but he paid no heed to this most unlucky sign and marched off at once. He had also slipped and fallen as he disembarked on the coast of Africa, but turned an unfavorable omen into a favorable one by clasping the ground and shouting: 'Africa, I have tight hold of you!' Then, to ridicule the prophecy according to which it was the Scipios' fate to be perpetually victorious in Africa, he took about with him a contemptible member of the Cornelian branch of the Scipio family nicknamed 'Salvito' —or 'Greetings! but off with him' —the 'Greetings!' being an acknowledgement of his distinguished birth, the 'off with him' a condemnation of his disgusting habits.

Sometimes he fought after careful tactical planning, sometimes on the spur of the moment—at the end of a march, often; or in miserable weather, when he would be least expected to make a move. Towards the end of his life, however, he took fewer chances; having come to the conclusion that his unbroken run of victories ought to sober him, now that he could not possibly gain more by winning yet another battle than he would be loss by a defeat. It was his rule never let enemy troops rally when he had routed them, and always therefore to assault their camp at once. If the fight were a hard-fought one he used to send the chargers away—his own among the first—as a warning that those who feared to stand their ground need not hope to escape on horseback.

This charger of his, an extraordinary animal with feet that looked almost human—each of its hoofs was cloven in five parts, resembling human toes—had been foaled on his private estate. When the soothsayers pronounced that its master would one day rule the world, Caesar carefully reared, and was the first to ride, the beast; nor would it allow anyone else to do so. Eventually he raised a statue to it before the Temple of

---

① 朱巴王（King Juba），努米底亚（Numidia）国王朱巴一世，公元前85—公元前46年

Mother Venus.①

If Caesars' troops gave ground he would often rally them in person, catching individual fugitives by the throat and forcing them round to face the enemy again; even if they were panic-stricken—as when one standard-bearer threatened him with the sharp butt of his Eagle and another, whom he tried to detain, ran off leaving the Eagle in his hand.

Caesar's reputation for presence of mind is fully borne out by the instances quoted. After Pharsalus, he had sent his legions ahead of him into Asia and was crossing the Hellespont② in a small ferry-boat, when Lucius Cassius with ten naval vessels approached. Caesar made no attempt to escape but rowed towards the flagship and demanded Cassius' surrender; Cassius gave it and stepped aboard Caesars' craft.

Again while attacking a bridge at Alexandria, Caesar was forced by a sudden enemy sortie to jump into a rowboat. So many of his men followed him that he dived into the sea and swam 200 yards until he reached the nearest Caesarean ship—holding his left hand above water the whole way to keep certain documents dry; and towing his purple cloak behind him with his teeth, to save this trophy from the Egyptians.

He judged his men by their fighting record, not by their morals or social position, treating them all with equal severity and equal indulgence; since it was only in the presence of the enemy that he insisted on strict discipline. He never gave forewarning of a march or a battle, but kept his troops always on the alert for sudden orders to go wherever he directed. Often he made them turn out when there was no need at all, especially in wet weather or on public holidays. Sometimes he would say: 'Keep a close eye on me!' and then steal away from camp at any hour of the day or night expecting them to follow. It was certain to be a particularly long march, and hard on stragglers③.

If rumors about the enemy's strength were causing alarm, his practice was to

---

① 母亲维纳斯的神庙（the Temple of Mother Venus），罗马人认为自己的先祖之一是特洛伊王子埃涅阿斯（Aeneas），而神话传说中埃涅阿斯是女神维纳斯的儿子，故罗马人称女神维纳斯为母亲神
② 赫勒斯滂（the Hellespont），即达尼尔海峡，连接爱琴海和马尔马拉海之间的一片水域，传说中赫勒（Helle）与她的哥哥受到后母的迫害，他们骑着一只会飞的金羊，去寻找远方的亲生母亲。赫勒不小心落入这一片水域中而遭遇不幸，人们为了纪念她称此水域为赫勒斯滂
③ 落伍士兵（stragglers）

heighten morale, not by denying or belittling the danger, but on the contrary by further exaggerating it. For instance, when his troops were in panic before the battle of Thapsus① at the news of King Juba's approach, he called them together and announced: 'You may take it from me that the King will be here within a few days, at the head of ten infantry legions, thirty thousand cavalry, a hundred thousand lightly armed troops, and three hundred elephants. This being the case, you may as well stop asking questions and making guesses. I have given you the facts, with which I am familiar. Any of you who remain unsatisfied will find themselves aboard a leaky hulk and being carried across the sea wherever the winds may decide to blow them.'

Though turning a blind eye to much of their misbehaviour and never laying down any fixed scale of penalties he allowed no deserter or mutineer to escape severe punishment. Sometimes, if a victory had been complete enough, he relieved the troops of all military duties and let them carry on as wildly as they pleased. One of his boasts was: 'My men fight just as well when they are stinking of perfume.' He always addressed them not with 'My men', but with 'Comrades. ...', which put them into a better humour; and he equipped them splendidly. The silver and gold inlay of their weapons both improved their appearance on parade and made them more careful not to get disarmed in battle. these being objects of great value. Caesar loved his men dearly; when news came that Titurius' command had been massacred, he swore neither to cut his hair nor to trim his beard until they had been avenged.

By these means he won the devotion of his army as well as making it extraordinary gallant. At the outbreak of the Civil War every centurion in every legion volunteered to equip a cavalryman from his savings; and the private soldiers unanimously offered to serve under him without pay or rations; pooling their money so that nobody should go short. Throughout the entire struggle not a single Caesarean deserted, and many of them, when taken prisoners, preferred death to the alternative of serving with the Pompeians. Such was their fortitude in facing starvation and other hardships, both as besiegers and as besieged, that when Pompey was shown at Dyrrhachium② the substitute for bread, made of grass, on which they were feeding, he exclaimed: 'I am

---

① 萨普索斯战役 (the battle of Thapsus), 恺撒与庞培的残余在北非进行的一场战役。庞培的岳父西庇阿 (Quintus Metellus Scipio) 战败被俘之后自杀, 小加图 (Cato the Younger) 拒绝向恺撒投降, 也自杀身亡

② 底耳哈琴 (Dyrrhachium), 即现在阿尔巴尼亚的都拉索 (Durazzo)

fighting wild beasts!' Then he ordered the loaf to be hidden at once, not wanting his men to find out how tough and resolute the enemy were, and so lose heart.

Here the Caesareans suffered their sole reverse, but proved their stout-heartedness by begging to be punished for the lapse; whereupon he felt called upon to console rather than upbraid them. in other battles, they beat enormously superior forces. Shortly before the defeat at Dyrrhachium, a single company of the Sixth Legion held a redoubt against four Pompeian legions, though almost every man had been wounded by arrow-shot—130,000 arrows were afterwards collected on the scene of the engagement. This high level of courage is less surprising when individual examples are considered: for the centurion Cassius Scaeva, blinded in one eye, wounded in thigh and shoulder, and with no less than 120 holes in his shield, continued to defend the approaches to the redoubt. Nor was his by any means an exceptional case. At the naval battle of Marseilles, a private soldier named Gaius Acilius grasped the stern of an enemy ship and, when someone lopped off his right hand, nevertheless boarded her and drove the enemy back with the boss of his shield only—a feat rivalling that of the Athenian Cynaegeirus① (brother of the poet Aeschylus②), who showed similar courage when maimed in trying to detain a Persian ship after the victory at Marathon.

Caesar's men did not mutiny once during the Gallic War, which lasted thirteen years. In the Civil Wars they were less dependable, but whenever they made insubordinate demands he faced them boldly, and always brought them to heel again—not by appeasement but by sheer exercise of personal authority. At Piacenza③, although Pompey's armies were as yet undefeated, he disbanded the entire Ninth Legion with ignominy, later recalling them to the Colours in response to their abject pleas; this with great reluctance and only after executing the ringleaders.

At Rome, too, when the Tenth Legion agitated for their discharge and bounty and were terrorizing the City, Caesar defied the advice of his friends and at once confronted the mutineers in person. Again he would have disbanded them ignominiously, though the African war was still being hotly fought; but by addressing them as 'Citizens' he readily regained their affections. A shout went up: 'We are your soldiers, Caesar, not

---

① 塞纳吉罗斯（Cynaegeirus），马拉松战役之后，雅典人塞纳吉罗斯在严重受伤之后，仍然试图阻止波斯的战船，激励了希腊联军抵抗波斯军团入侵的勇气
② 埃斯库罗斯（Aeschylus），希腊著名悲剧作家
③ 皮亚琴察（Piacenza），意大利北部城市

civilians!' and they clamoured to serve under him in Africa: a demand which he nevertheless disdained to grant. He showed his contempt for the more disaffected soldiers by withholding a third part of the prize-money and land which had been set aside for them.

Even as a young man Caesar was well known for the loyalty he showed his dependants. While praetor in Africa he protected a nobleman's son named Masintha against the tyranny of Hiempsal, King of Numidia; with such devotion that in the course of the quarrel he caught Juba, the Numidian heir-apparent, by the beard. Masintha, being then declared the King's vassal, was arrested: but Caesar immediately rescued him from the Numidian guards and harboured him in his own quarters for a long while. At the close of his praetorship Caesar sailed for Spain taking Masintha with him. The lictors carrying their rods of office, and the crowds who had come to say goodbye, acted as a screen; nobody realized that Masintha was hidden in Caesar's litter.

He showed consistent affection to his friends. Gaius Oppius, traveling by his side once through a wild forest, suddenly fell sick; but Caesar insisted on his using the only shelter that offered—a woodcutter's hut, hardly large enough for a single occupant—while he and the rest of his staff slept outside on the bare ground. Having attained supreme power he raised some of his friends, including men of humble birth, to high office and brushed aside criticism by saying: 'If bandits and cut-throats had helped to defend my honour, I should have shown them gratitude in the same way.'

Yet when given the chance, he would always cheerfully come to terms with his bitterest enemies. He supported Gaius Memmius' candidature for the consulship, though they had both spoken most damagingly against each other. When Gaius Calvus, after his cruel lampoons of Caesar, made a move towards reconciliation through mutual friends, Caesar met him more than half way by writing him a friendly letter. Valerius Catullus had also libeled him in his verse about Mamurra, yet Caesar while admitting that these were a permanent blot on his name, accepted Catullus' apology and invited him to dinner that same afternoon and never interrupted is friendship with Catullus' father.

Caesar was not naturally vindictive; and if he crucified the pirates who had held him to ransom, this was only because he had sworn in their presence to do so; and he first mercifully cut their throats. He could never bring himself to take vengeance on Cornelius Phagites, even though in his early days, while he was sick and a fugitive from Sulla, Cornelius had tracked him down night after night and demanded large sums of hush-money. On discovering that Philemon his slave-secretary, had been induced to poison him, Caesar ordered a simple execution, without torture. When Publius Clodius was accused of adultery with Caesar's wife Pompeia, in sacrilegious circumstances, and both her mother-in-law Aurelia and her sister-in-law Julia had given the court a detailed and truthful account of the affair, Caesar himself refused to offer any evidence, The Court then asked him why, in that case, he had divorced Pompeia. He replied: 'Because I cannot have members of my household suspected, even if they are innocent.'

Nobody can deny that during the Civil War, and after, he behaved with wonderful restraint and clemency. Whereas Pompey declared that all who were not actively with him were against him and would be treated as public enemies, Caesar announced that all who were not actively against him were with him. He allowed every centurion whom he had appointed on Pompey's recommendation to join the Pompeian forces if he pleased. At Lerida, in Spain, the articles of capitulation were being discussed between Caesar and the Pompeian generals Afranius and Petreius, and the rival armies were fraternizing, when Afranius suddenly decided not to surrender and massacred every Caesarean soldier found in his camp. Yet after capturing both generals a few days later, Caesar could not bring himself to pay Afranius back in the same coin; but let him go free. During the battle of Pharsalus he shouted to his men: 'Spare your fellow-Romans!' and then allowed them to save one enemy soldier apiece, whoever he might be. My researches show that not a single Pompeian was killed at Pharsalus, once the fighting had ended, except Afranius and Faustus and young Lucius Caesar. It is thought that not even these three fell victims to his vengeance, though Afranius and Faustus had taken up arms again after he had spared their lives, and Lucius Caesar had cruelly cut the throats of his famous relative's slaves and freedmen, even butchering the wild beasts brought by him to Rome for a public show! Eventually, towards the end of his career, Caesar invited back to Italy all exiles whom he had not yet pardoned, permitting them to hold magistracies and command armies; and went so far as to restore the statues of Sulla and Pompey, which the City crowds had thrown down and smashed. He also preferred to discourage rather than punish any plots against his life, or any slanders on his name. All that he would do when he detected such plots, or became aware of secret nocturnal meetings, was to announce openly that: he knew about them, As for

343

slanderers, he contented himself with warning them in public to keep their mouths shut; and good-naturedly took no action either against Aulus Caecina for his most libelous pamphlet or against Pitholaus for his scurrilous verses.

Yet other deeds and sayings of Caesar's may be set to the debit account and justify the conclusion that he deserved assassination. Not only did he accept unconstitutional honours, such as a life-consulship, a life-dictatorship, a perpetual Censorship, the title 'Emperor' put before his name, and the title 'Father of his Country' appended to it, also a statue standing among those of the ancient kings, and a raised couch placed in the orchestra at the Theatre; but took other honours which, as a mere mortal, he should certainly have refused. These included a golden throne in the Senate House, and another on the tribunal; a ceremonial chariot and litter for carrying his statue in the religious procession around the Circus; temples, altars and divine images; a priest of his own cult; a new college of Lupercals① to celebrate his divinity; and the renaming of the seventh month as 'July'. Few in fact were the honours which he was not pleased to accept or assume.

His third and fourth consulships were merely titular; the dictatorship conferred on him at the same time supplied all the authority he needed. And in both years he substituted two new Consuls for himself during the last quarter, meanwhile letting only tribunes and aediles of the people be elected, and appointing prefects② instead of praetors③ to govern the City during his absence.

One of the Consuls died suddenly on New Year's Eve and, when someone asked to hold office for the remaining few hours, Caesar granted his request. He showed equal scorn of constitutional precedent by choosing magistrates several years ahead, decorating ten former praetors with the emblems of consular rank, and admitting to the Senate men of foreign birth, including semi-civilized Gauls who had been granted Roman citizenship. He placed his own slaves in charge of the Mint and the public revenues and sent one of his favourites, a freedman's son to command the three legions stationed at Alexandria.

Titus Ampius has recorded some of Caesar's public statements which reveal a

---

① 古罗马的牧神节（Lupercals）
② 督监（prefect），高级行政长官
③ 执政官（praetor），长官

similar presumption: that the Republic was nothing—a mere name without form or substance; that Sulla had proved himself a dunce by resigning his dictatorship; and that now his own word was law, people ought to be more careful how they approached him. Once, when a soothsayer reported that a sacrificial beast had been found to have no heart—an unlucky omen indeed—Caesar told him arrogantly: 'The omens will be as favourable as I wish them to be; meanwhile I am not at all surprised that a beast should lack the organ which inspires our finer feelings.'

What made the Romans hate him so bitterly was that when, one day, the entire Senate armed with an imposing list of honours that they had just voted him, came to where he sat in front of the Temple of Mother Venus, he did not rise to greet them. According to some accounts he would have risen had not Cornelius Balbus prevented him; according to others, he made no such move and grimaced angrily at Gaius Trebatius who suggested this courtesy. The case was aggravated by a memory of Caesar's behaviour during one of his triumphs: he had ridden past the benches reserved for the tribunes of the people, and shouted in fury at a certain Pontius Aquila, who had kept his seat: 'Hey, there, Aquila the tribune! Do you want me to restore the Republic?' For several days after this incident he added to every undertaking he gave: 'With the kind consent of Pontius Aquila.'

This open insult to the Senate was emphasized by an even worse example of his scorn for the Constitution. As he returned to Rome from the Alban Hill,① where the Latin Festival had been celebrated, a member of the crowd set a laurel wreath bound with a royal white fillet on the head of his statue. Two tribunes of the people, Epidius Marullus and Caesetius Flavus, ordered the fillet to be removed at once and the offender imprisoned. But Caesar reprimanded and summarily degraded them both: either because the suggestion that he should be crowned King had been so rudely rejected, or else because—this was his own version—they had given him no chance to reject it himself and so earn deserved credit. From that day forward, however, he lay under the odious suspicion of having tied to revive the title of King; though, indeed, when the commons greeted him with 'Long live the King!' he now protested: 'No, I am Caesar, not King'; and though, again, when he was addressing the crowd from the

---

① 阿尔班山（the Alban Hill），罗马东南的一座小山

Rostra at the Lupercalian Festival①, and Mark Antony, the Consul made several attempts to crown him, he refused the offer each time and at last sent the crown away for dedication to Capitoline Jupiter. What made matters worse was a persistent rumour that Caesar intended to move the seat of government to Troy or Alexandria, carrying off all the national resources, drafting every available man in Italy for military service, and letting his friends govern what was left of the City. At the next meeting of the House (it was further whispered), Lucius Cotta would announce a decision of the Fifteen who had charge of the Sibylline Books, that since these prophetic writings stated clearly: 'Only a king can conquer the Parthians,②' the title of King must be conferred on Caesar.

Because his enemies shrank from agreeing to this proposal, they pressed on with their plans for is assassination. Several groups, each consisting of two or three malcontents, now united in a general conspiracy. Even the commons had come to disapprove of how things were going, and no longer hid their disgust at Caesar's tyrannical rule but openly demanded champions③ to protect their ancient liberties. When foreigners were admitted to the Senate someone put up a poster which read: 'Long live the Constitution; but if any newly-appointed senator inquires the way to the Senate House, let nobody direct him there!' And the following popular song was sung everywhere:

> Caesar led the Gauls in triumph,
> Led them uphill, led them down,
> To the Senate House he took them,
> Once the glory of our town.
> 'Pull those breeches off,' he shouted,
> 'Change into a purple gown!'

As Quintus Maximus, one of the three-months' Consuls, entered the Theatre, the lictor called out as usual: 'Make way for the Consul!' Cries of protest went up: 'What? For him? He is no Consul!' The deposition of Caesetius and Marullus caused

---

① 卢波卡尔神的节日 (Lupercalian Festival)，即古罗马的牧神节
② 帕提亚人 (the Parthians)，即安息人
③ 捍卫者，拥护者 (champions)

such widespread annoyance that at the next Consular elections the commons cast a great many votes in their favour. Someone then wrote on the pedestal of Lucius Brutus① ' statue: 'If only you were alive now!' and on that of Caesar himself:

'Brutus was elected Consul
When he sent the Kings away;
Caesar sent the Consuls packing,
Caesar is our King to-day.'

More than sixty conspirators banded together against him, led by Gaius Cassius② and his lieutenants Marcus and Decimus Brutus. A suggested plan was to wait until the Consular elections, when Caesar would take his stand on the wooden bridge along which voters walked to the poll; one group of conspirators would then topple him over, while another waited underneath with daggers drawn. An alternative was to attack him in the Sacred Way or at the entrance to the Theatre. The conspirators wavered between these plans until Caesar called a meeting of the Senate in the Pompeian Assembly Room for the Ides of March③, which fall on the fifteenth day; they then decided at once that this would be by far the most convenient time and place.

Unmistakable signs forewarned Caesar of his assassination. A few months previously the veterans who had been sent to colonize Capua under the Julian Law were breaking up some ancient tombs in search of stone for their new farm-houses—all the more eagerly when they came across a large hoard of ancient vases. One of these tombs proved to be that of Capys, the legendary founder of the city, and here they found a bronze tablet with a Greek inscription to this effect: 'Disturb the bones of Capys, and a man of Trojan stock will be murdered by his kindred, and later avenged at great cost to Italy.' This story should not be dismissed as idle fiction, or a lie, because our authority for it is none other than Cornelius Balbus, a close friend of Caesar's. Soon afterwards news reached Caesar that a herd of horses which he had dedicated to the river Rubicon,

---

① 卢修斯·布鲁图斯（Lucius Brutus），古罗马传奇人物，罗马共和国的缔造者。公元前509年他驱逐了伊特鲁斯坎（Etruscan）最后一个君主塔昆（Lucius Tarquinius Superbus），建立了罗马共和国
② 盖乌斯·卡西乌斯（Gaius Cassius），刺杀恺撒的主谋之一
③ 3月15日（the Ides of March），Ides指古罗马历中的3月、5月、7月、10月的第15日

after fording it, and allowed to roam untended in the valley, were beginning to show a repugnance for the pasture and shedding bucketfuls of tears. Again, during a sacrifice, the augur Spurinna warned Caesar that the danger threatening him would not pass until the ides of March; and on the day before the ides a little bird, called the King Wren, flew into the Pompeian Assembly Room with a sprig of laurel in its beak—pursued by a swarm of different birds from a nearby copse, which tore it to pieces there and then. And on his last night Caesar dreamed that he was soaring above the clouds, and then shaking hands with Jupiter; while his wife Calpurnia dreamed that the gable ornament, resembling that of a temple, which had been one of the honours voted him by the Senate, collapsed, and there he lay stabbed in her arms! She awoke suddenly and the bedroom door burst open of its own accord.

These warnings, and a touch of ill-health, made him hesitate for some time whether to go ahead with his plans, or whether to postpone the meeting. Finally Decimus Brutus persuaded him not to disappoint the Senate, who had been in full session for an hour or more, waiting for him to arrive. it was about ten o'clock when he set off for the House. As he went, someone handed him a note containing details of the plot against his life, but he merely added it to the bundle of petitions in his left hand, which he intended to read later. Several victims were then sacrificed, and despite consistently unfavourable omens, he entered the House, deriding Spurinna as a false prophet. 'The ides of March have come,' he said. 'Ay, they have come,' replied Spurinna, 'but they have not yet gone.'

As soon as Caesar took his seat the conspirators crowded around him as if to pay their respects. Tillius Cimber, who had taken the lead, came up close, pretending to ask a question. Caesar made a gesture of postponement, but Cimber caught hold of his shoulders. 'This is violence!' Caesar cried, and at that moment one of the Casca brothers slipped behind and with a sweep of his dagger stabbed him just below the throat. Caesar grasped Casca's arm and ran it through with his stylus; he was leaping away when another dagger caught him in the breast. Confronted by a ring of drawn daggers, he drew the top of his gown over his face, and at the same time ungirded the lower part, letting it fall to his feet so that he would die with both legs decently covered. Twenty-three dagger thrusts went home as he stood there. Caesar did not utter a sound after Casca's blow had drawn a groan from him; though some say that when he saw Marcus Brutus about to deliver the second blow, he reproached him in Greek with:

<<< 第十篇 The Twelve Caesars

'You, too, my son?'

The entire Senate then dispersed in confusion, and Caesar was left lying dead for some time until three of his household slaves carried him home in a litter, with one arm hanging over the side. His physician Antistius conducted the post mortem① and came to the conclusion that none of the wounds had been mortal except the second one, in the breast. It had been decided to drag the dead man down to the Tiber, confiscate his property, and revoke all his edicts; but fear of Mark Antony②, the Consul, and Lepidus, the Master of Horse③, kept the assassins from making their plans good.

At the request of Lucius Piso, Calpurnia's father, Caesar's will, which he had drafted six months before at his villa near Lavicum, and entrusted to the safekeeping of the Chief Vestal④, was unsealed and read in Antony's house. From the time of his first consulship until the outbreak of the Civil War (according to Quintus Tubero) Caesar's principal heir had been his son-in-law Pompey, and he used to read out this part of his will to the assembled troops. Later, however, he cancelled the bequest and left three-quarters of his estate, after certain legacies had been deducted, to Gaius Octavius⑤, afterwards Augustus, and one-eighth each to Lucius Pinarius and Quintus Pedius⑥. These were his three sororal grand-nephews. At the close of the will he also adopted Gaius Octavius into the Caesar family, but provided for the possibility of a son being subsequently born to himself and appointed several of the assassins as guardians to the boy. Decimus Brutus⑦ even figured among his heirs in the second degree—that is to say those who would inherit if the heirs in the first degree were prevented by death or scruple from accepting the legacy. Caesar left the commons his gardens on the banks of the Tiber for use as a recreation ground, and three gold pieces a man.

---

① 尸检（post mortem）
② 马克·安东尼（Mark Antony）罗马执政官，在与恺撒刺杀者集团的斗争中，与屋大维（Gaius Octavius）、雷庇达（Lepidus）组成了"后三头同盟"（the Second Triumvirate）
③ 骑兵总督（Master of Horse）雷庇达（Marcus Aemilius Lepidus），罗马共和国"后三头同盟"（the Second Triumvirate）之一
④ 首席宣誓人（the Chief Vestal）
⑤ 盖乌斯·屋大维（Gaius Octavius），恺撒的侄孙子，后来的奥古斯都大帝
⑥ 昆特乌斯·佩狄乌斯（Quintus Pedius），恺撒的侄孙子，后来佩丁法（the Pedian Law）的提出者
⑦ 德西摩斯·布鲁图斯（Decimus Brutus），据传是恺撒的私生子，也是刺杀恺撒的凶手之一

When the funeral arrangements had been announced, his friends raised a pyre on the Campus Martius near his daughter Julia's tomb, and a gilded shrine on the Rostra resembling that of Mother Venus. In it they set an ivory couch, spread with purple and gold cloth, and from a pillar at its head hung the gown in which he had been murdered. Since a procession of mourners, filing past the pyre in orderly fashion and laying funeral gifts on it, would probably take more than a day to organize, everyone was invited to come there by whatever route he pleased, regardless of precedence. Emotions of pity and indignation were aroused at the funeral games by a line from Pacuvius' play Contest for the Arms of Achilles①:

What, did l save these men that they might murder me?

and by a similar sentiment from Atilius' Electra②. Mark Antony③ dispensed with a formal eulogy; instead, he instructed a herald to read, first, the recent decree simultaneously voting Caesar all divine and human honours, and then the oath by which the entire Senate had pledged themselves to watch over his safety. Antony added a few short words of comment. When the ivory funeral couch had been carried down into the Forum by a group of magistrates and ex-magistrates, and a dispute arose as to whether the body should be cremated in the Temple of Capitoline Jupiter④ or in Pompey's Assembly Hall, two divine forms (perhaps the Twin Brethren) suddenly appeared, javelin in hand and sword at thigh, and set fire to the couch with torches. immediately the spectators assisted the blaze by heaping on it dry branches and the judges' chairs, and the court benches, with whatever else came to hand. Thereupon the musicians and the masked professional mourners who had walked in the funeral train wearing the robes that he had himself worn at his four triumphs, tore these in pieces and flung them on the flames—to which veterans who had assisted at his triumphs added the arms they had

---

① 争夺阿喀琉斯的盔甲 (Contest for the Arms of Achilles)
② 厄勒克特拉 (Electra), 古希腊著名悲剧, 厄勒克特拉是阿伽门农 (Agamemnon) 和王后克吕泰涅斯特拉 (Clytemnestra) 的女儿, 后与其弟俄瑞斯忒斯 (Orestes) 一起杀母及继父为其父报仇
③ 马克·安东尼 (Mark Antony), 恺撒遇刺时任罗马的执政官, "后三头同盟" (the Second Triumvirate) 之一
④ 卡皮托利尼山上的朱庇特神庙 (the Temple of Capitoline Jupiter), 卡皮托利尼山 (Capitoline) 是罗马七丘中最重要的一座, 也是首都 (capital) 一词的来源

then borne, Many women in the audience similarly sacrificed their jewellery together with their children's golden buttons and embroidered tunics. Public grief was enhanced by crowds of foreigners lamenting in their own fashion, especially Jews who loved Caesar for the friendship he had shown them, and came flocking to the Forum for several nights in succession.

As soon as the funeral was over, the commons, snatching firebrands from the pyre, ran to burn down the houses of Brutus and Cassius, and were repelled with difficulty. Mistaking Helvius Cinna for the Cornelius Cinna who had delivered a bitter speech against Caesar on the previous day, and whom they were out to kill, they murdered him and paraded the streets with his head stuck on the point of a spear. Later they raised twenty-foot-high column of Numidian marble in the Forum, and inscribed on it: 'To the Father of His Country.' For a long time afterwards they used to offer sacrifices at the foot of this column, make vows there and settle disputes by oaths taken in Caesar's name.

Some of his friends suspected that having no desire to live much longer because of his failing health, he had taken no precautions against the conspiracy and neglected the warnings of soothsayers and well-wishers. It has also been suggested that he placed such confidence in the Senate's last decree and in their oath of loyalty, that he dispensed even with the armed Spaniards who had hitherto acted as his permanent escort. A contrary view is that as a relief from taking constant precautions, he deliberately exposed himself, just this once, to all the plots against his life which he knew had been formed. Also, he is quoted as having often said: 'It is more important for Rome than for myself that I should survive. I have long been sated with power and glory; but, should anything happen to me, Rome will enjoy no peace. A new Civil War will break out under far worse conditions than the last.'

Almost all authorities, at any rate believe that he welcomed the manner of his death. He had once read in Xenophon's Boyhood of Cyrus[①] the paragraph about the funeral instructions given by Cyrus on his deathbed, and said how much he loathed the prospect of a lingering end—he wanted a sudden one. And on the day before his murder he had dined at Marcus Lepidus' house, where the topic discussed happened to be 'the best sort of death'—and 'Let it come swiftly and unexpectedly,' cried Caesar.

---

① 色诺芬的著作《居鲁士的童年》(*Xenophon's Boyhood of Cyrus*)

He was fifty-five years old when he died, and his immediate deification, formally decreed by the loyalists in the Senate, convinced the City as a whole; if only because, on the first day of the Games given by his successor Augustus in honour of this apotheosis, a comet appeared about an hour before sunset and shone for seven days running. This was held to be Caesar's soul, elevated to Heaven; hence the star, now placed above the forehead of his divine image.

The Senate voted that the Assembly hall where he fell should be walled up: that they should never again meet in it; and that the ides of March should be known ever afterwards as 'The Day of Parricide'.

Very few indeed, of the assassins outlived Caesar for more than three years, or died naturally. All were condemned to death under the Pedian Law[①], and all met it in different ways—some in shipwreck, some in battle, some using the very daggers with which they had treacherously murdered Caesar to take their own lives.

Questions for discussion:

1. What are the strengths and weaknesses of Julius Caesar's character from Suetonius' biography of him?

2. Why did he insist on going to the Senate for a meeting on the morning of March 15, despite all signs and even warnings of ominous signs?

3. Why was it that even though the Roman senators risked their lives to assassinate Caesar, they could not stop Rome from becoming a republic into an empire? What was the root cause of the Roman Empire's rise to greatness?

---

① 佩丁法（the Pedian Law），恺撒遇刺后，昆特乌斯·佩狄乌斯（Quintus Pedius）向元老院（the Senate）提出了所谓佩丁法（the Pedian Law），即惩处所有谋杀恺撒并导致其死亡的人员，获元老院通过。刚开始佩狄乌斯提出了一个17人死刑的名单，但名单很快被"后三头同盟"增加和扩大，且不受控制。

读书笔记

第一篇 《神谱》读书笔记

从《神谱》（Theogony）的第一句话我们可以看到，赫西俄德（Hesiod）称是宙斯（Zeus）的女儿们缪斯（the Muses）赋予了他写诗的本领，荷马在《奥德赛》中也不例外。那个时代的诗人都有一个共同点——为了说明自己的看法对所编故事的权威性，都称是缪斯给了他们如此的能力和思想。

本书记述了希腊诸神的起源，主要有两条主线：一条是朴素的宇宙起源与自然演化观；另一条是人类社会的秩序和进化观。自然世界万物起源于混沌之神卡俄斯（Chaos），混沌产生地神盖娅（Gaia 或 Gaea）、塔尔塔罗斯（Tartarus，深渊）和厄洛斯（Eros，老爱神）。同时混沌产生原始的黑暗之神埃瑞波斯（Erebos）和黑夜之神（Night），黑暗和黑夜生出以太（Aether）和白昼（Day）。属于此列的还有被地神所生的天神乌拉诺斯（Uranus）、蓬托斯（Pontus，洪荒之水）以及由黑夜之神所衍生的命运系列和复仇系列女神，由蓬托斯之子涅柔斯（Nereus，海之老人）所衍生的各种海怪和海妖系列（如蛇发女怪美杜莎），由蓬托斯之女刻托（Ceto）所衍生出的各种妖怪系列（如狮身人面兽斯芬克斯）。如果从宇宙起源和自然演化的视角，看诸神之间关系，便不会有"乱伦"之困惑。因为神际之间无伦理，人伦评判只存在于人类社会之中。

人类社会的秩序与进化主线，反映在三代主神之间权力的更迭和神际关系之上。子辈对父辈的反叛与超越，诸神之间的爱恨情仇，无不是人类社会的反映。第一代主神天与地结合，生了三个独眼巨神和三个百臂巨神。同时生了十二泰坦（Titans），其中六个为阳性（Male，后面标注 M），六个为阴性（Female，后面标注 F）。这十二泰坦中最小的克洛诺斯［Cronus（M）］和他姐姐泰坦瑞娅［Rhea（F）］结合，成为第二代主神。这十二位泰坦中除了克洛诺斯和瑞娅之外，另外十个泰坦中还有三对夫妻：欧申［Ocean（M）］或［欧申纳斯，Oceanus（M）］与泰西丝［Tethys（F）］结合，是所有江河湖海之源；许珀里翁［Hyperion（M）］与忒娅［Theia（F）］结合，是太阳神赫利俄斯（Helius）的父母；科俄斯［Coeus（M）］与菲比［Phoebe（F）］结合，是黑袍女神莱托（Leto）之父母；另外两个阳性泰坦分别是普罗米修斯（Prometheus）和阿特拉斯（Atlas）的父亲伊阿佩托斯［Iapetus（M）］，生长之神克瑞斯［Crius（M）］，两个女性泰坦分别是正义女神忒弥斯［Themis（F）］和记忆女神尼莫西妮［Mnemosyne（F）］。十二泰坦承上启下，是了解古希腊诸神关系的关键纽带。

克洛诺斯在地神盖娅的帮助下，反抗乌拉诺斯的统治，将乌拉诺斯的生殖器用镰刀割了下来，扔到大海中，而从浪花里生出了爱与美之女神阿芙洛狄忒（Aphrodite），即维纳斯（Venus）。

克洛诺斯和瑞娅生了灶神赫斯提娅（Hestia）、农神德墨忒尔（Demeter）、宙斯（Zeus）、天后赫拉（Hera）、冥神哈迪斯（Hades）和海神波塞冬（Poseidon），为了防止他们造反，克洛诺斯将他们都吃到肚子里。但瑞娅却将一块巨石替代宙斯（Zeus），并成功欺骗了克洛诺斯，还把宙斯交给地神盖娅藏了起来。宙斯长大之后，在盖娅的帮助下，将自己的哥哥、姐姐们从克洛诺斯肚子中解救了出来，将独眼巨人和百臂巨人也从塔尔塔罗斯深渊中解救了出来，并领导他们和部分泰坦与克洛诺斯领导的泰坦们进行了生死之战，终于打败了克洛诺斯阵营，成为第三代主神。

得到了权力后的宙斯在哥哥、姐姐们之间进行了新的权力分配，最终娶了姐姐赫拉（Hera）为妻。众主神在奥林匹斯山上长期居住，宙斯开始了他的统治。宙斯的第一任妻子是智慧女神墨提斯（Metis），后来担心墨提斯（Metis）怀着的女儿造反，干脆将墨提斯（Metis）吞入自己的腹中，然而墨提斯（Metis）的女儿雅典娜（Athena）最终还是从他的脑袋里诞生了。与第二任妻子正义女神忒弥斯（Themis 为十二泰坦之一，宙斯的姑姑），生了时序女神荷莱（Horae）等。与第三任妻子欧律诺墨（Eurynome，十二泰坦欧申的女儿），生了美惠三女神（Graces）等。与第四任妻子农神德墨忒尔（Demeter，他的姐姐），生了珀尔塞福涅（Persephone，被冥神 Hades 抢亲成婚，成为冥后）。与第五任妻子尼莫西妮（Mnemosyne 为十二泰坦之一，记忆女神），生了9个女儿缪斯（Muses，奥林匹斯山上主管文艺的女神）。与第六任妻子黑袍女神莱托（Leto，为十二泰坦 Coeus 和 Phoebe 之女），生了太阳神（Apollo）和月神（Artemis）。与最后一任妻子姐姐赫拉（Hera），生了青春女神赫柏（Hebe）、战神阿瑞斯

（Ares）和火神赫菲斯托斯（Hephaestus）等。

此外，宙斯还在神界和人间处处留情。其中，在希腊神话传说中经常遇到的还有：与阿特拉斯（Atlas）的女儿迈娅（Maia），生了信息和商业之神赫尔墨斯（Hermes）。与阿特拉斯的另一个女儿埃勒克特拉（Electra），生了特洛伊人的先祖达尔达诺斯（Dardanus）。与情人欧罗巴（Europe），生了克里特国王米诺斯（Minos）。与情人斯巴达王后莱达（Leda），生了美女海伦（Helen）、克吕泰涅斯特拉（Clytemnestra）、卡斯托耳（Castor）、波吕克斯（Pollux），其中特洛伊战争因海伦（Helen）而起。与卡德摩斯（Cadmus）的女儿塞墨勒（Semele），即欧罗巴（Europe）的侄女，生了酒神狄奥尼索斯（Dionysus）。与情人阿尔克墨涅（Alcmene），生了大力神赫拉克勒斯（Heracles）。

宙斯与情人伊娥（Io），生了厄帕福斯（Epaphus）。见第二篇奥维德（Ovid）《变形记》（*the Metamorphoses*）中的第一章倒数第三节。十二泰坦之一欧申（Ocean）的漂亮孙女伊娥（Io）被朱庇特（Jupiter 或 Jove，宙斯的拉丁名）看上了，为了防止被天后朱诺（Juno，赫拉的拉丁名）发现，他将伊娥变成了一头白母牛，但还是被朱诺识破了，朱诺从朱庇特那里要了这头母牛，并用一个不睡觉的百眼怪兽阿耳戈斯（Argus）看管她，不让她变回人形与亲人相认，并不断恐吓她，用牛牤烦扰她。但她最终在墨丘利（Mercury）的帮助下逃到了埃及，生下了朱庇特的儿子厄帕福斯（Epaphus）。

宙斯与情人卡里斯托（Callisto），生了阿尔卡斯（Arcas）。见奥维德（Ovid）《变形记》（*the Metamorphoses*）中的第二章第二节，月神黛安娜（Diana）的女侍从、阿卡迪亚地区的女神卡里斯托（Callisto）被朱庇特看上了，并怀上了朱庇特的孩子阿尔卡斯（Arcas），愤怒的朱诺（Juno）将她变成了一只大熊，后来卡里斯托（Callisto）和阿尔卡斯（Arcas）升天成了大熊座和小熊座。

宙斯与情人达那厄（Danae），生了珀尔修斯（Perseus）。见奥维德（Ovid）《变形记》（*the Metamorphoses*）中的第四章最后一节，Jove 化作金雨使达那厄（Danae）怀孕，生出珀尔修斯（Perseus）。

宙斯与情人安提俄珀（Antiope），生了安菲翁（Amphion）和仄忒斯（Zethus）。他们给忒拜城（Thebes）设置了七个城门，并建设城墙将其围起来。可参见荷马（Homer）《奥德赛》（*the Odyssey*）中的第 11 卷。

由于在希腊神话传说中，一方面，人类出于对自然的敬畏，赋予了诸神超越人类的力量，认为神无所不能；另一方面，又用人类自己的思维方式去想象神与神、神与人之间的关系。所以，在实际的故事中，人们更多地描述了神的人性方面，认为神也会像人一样有着七情六欲，有着江湖情仇。其神性逐渐被淡忘，而神与人之间的差别仅仅是神有超人的神力，对神的美德和善恶却没有了要求。而东方的神话故事首先会将美德和善恶作为神的第一标准。

神话和传说是人类最早期的宗教和信仰体系，赫西俄德在公元前 700 年左右，将地中海地区各部落、各氏族的历史传说做了一个梳理，不但要保持前后的一致性，调和各地崇拜之神，还要避免各地传说之间的矛盾，实属不易。神话和传说故事背后的隐喻或许更值得人们去思考，譬如美和爱欲之神维纳斯（即阿芙洛狄忒，Venus 是她的拉丁名）是天神乌拉诺斯（Uranus）的生殖能力的体现，反映了早期塞浦路斯人的生殖崇拜，暗喻着性爱是上天赋予人类的权利。神名、人名或地名，也许是某一民族或氏族的名字。因而，神与神的结合、神与人的结合的故事，也暗示着不同民族或氏族之间融合的历史过程，而地中海不同民族、氏族、家族都设法与主神宙斯扯上关系，或是为了证明本族的神圣性，抑或为了证明其统治的合法性。从这个意义上说，赫西俄德可被视为古代西方的人种学和文化人类学先驱。

第二篇 《变形记》读书笔记

奥维德（Ovid）——古罗马著名诗人，全名 Publius Ovidius Naso，生于公元前 43 年 3 月 20 日（即恺撒死后一年。恺撒于公元前 44 年 3 月 15 日在罗马元老院被刺杀）。他与古罗马著名诗人维吉尔（Virgil）在同一时代，比维吉尔年纪小近 30 岁。

奥维德的《变形记》（the Metamorphoses）的确可以被称为不朽杰作，它将荷马之前和荷马之后的希腊罗马神话通过自己强大的想象力串联起来，也将优美的文字描述发挥到极高水平。这本由贺拉斯·格里高利（Horace Gregory）翻译的版本，值得收藏。

对于奥维德为何要用"变形记"作为书名，读后有了进一步的了解。作者认为世间所有的动植物，甚至岩石、泉水、河流均有灵魂，而人和这些动植物等其他自然界的物品都是灵魂的一种外在表现形式，这种外在表现形式是可以转化和改变的，即变形。但灵魂则是不变和永恒的，所以阿克特翁（Actaeon）在误撞见月神沐浴后，被月神变成了一只鹿，原来自己是猎人，现在自己却成了朋友和家人狩猎的对象，自己豢养的猎犬也扑上来撕咬，完全无法认出原来的主人。

神话也只是外在的故事，而神话背后的隐喻是什么才更有意义。人类不同文化下有不同的神话传说，这些神话故事背后是否暗示着某种文明起源所经历的事件？譬如，雅典城王子忒修斯（Theseus）杀死了克里特岛（Crete）的米诺斯王（Minos）牛头怪米诺陶（Minotaur）是否暗示着雅典文明与克里特文明之间曾经发生了一场战争，最终雅典文明消灭了克里特文明？再譬如腓尼基（Phoenicia，现在的巴勒斯坦地区）国王的女儿欧罗巴（Europa，欧洲的意思），被变成一头白色公牛的宙斯（Zeus）诱拐，是否暗示了欧洲文明起源于西亚地区？《变形记》中第二章最后一节反复提到的地名西顿（Sidon）和推罗（Tyre）均是腓尼基重要的城市。实际上的考古证据已经表明希腊字母就是从腓尼基字母演化而来的。而希腊神话中克里特岛的米诺斯王（Minos），就是宙斯和欧罗巴的儿子，暗示着地中海地区文明的路径是从西亚的腓尼基传到克里特岛，再传到雅典和希腊本土的。

本书第三章讲了由于欧罗巴失踪后，欧罗巴的哥哥卡德摩斯（Cadmus）受父之命寻找妹妹，如果找不到妹妹就不能再回腓尼基了（古代殖民也需要理由）。卡德摩斯后来就带着自己的族人在希腊本土建立了忒拜城（Thebes，也译成底比斯城），因为他在建城之初杀死了一条巨蛇，而这条巨蛇是战神阿瑞斯（Ares 也即 Mars）的儿子，所以忒拜城建城之后战乱不断，卡德摩斯的家族也遭到了诅咒。卡德摩斯的女儿塞墨勒（Semele）被宙斯看上，天后赫拉（Hera）非常妒忌，设计让塞墨勒被宙斯的炙热烧死，不幸中的万幸是塞墨勒腹中的胎儿存活了下来，就是后来的酒神狄奥尼索斯（Dionysus 或称 Bacchus）。卡德摩斯的孙子阿克特翁（Actaeon）误撞见月神沐浴，月神将他变成一只鹿，他最终被自己的猎狗群杀。卡德摩斯的后代俄狄浦斯（Oedipus）无法改变自己杀父娶母的命运，最终选择刺瞎双眼自我放逐，客死他乡，他的两个儿子也在后来继承忒拜城王位的争夺战中双双战亡。

第四章最后一节讲到了英雄珀尔修斯（Perseus）的来历：宙斯化作一场金雨，让珀尔修斯（Perseus）的母亲达那厄（Danae）受孕，最终生下了珀尔修斯。在砍下了蛇发女怪美杜莎（Medusa）的头颅后，美杜莎的血滴到非洲利比亚沙漠中，就变成蛇。任何人只要看到美杜莎的脸就会被石化，因而美杜莎的头颅也就成了珀尔修斯的秘密核武器。珀尔修斯先是想找个地方休息，与背负地球的阿特拉斯（Atlas）发生争执，然后用美杜莎的头颅让阿特拉斯（Atlas）变成地球上的山脉河流、森林巨石，所以现在的地图还用 Atlas 来代表。然后在埃及海岸上看到了被缚在海边峭壁上的美女安德洛墨达（Andromeda），姑娘在珀尔修斯的反复恳求下，道出了事情的真相。原来安德洛墨达是国王西菲乌斯

357

(Cepheus) 的女儿，因为母后吹嘘说她比海神的女儿们更漂亮，而遭到海神的惩罚。若想避免国难，必须将女儿祭献给海怪。正说话期间，海怪从海中升起，珀尔修斯抓住时机向国王提出救出安德洛墨达（Andromeda）之后，要娶安德洛墨达，国王不但同意了珀尔修斯的提婚，而且承诺将国土作为嫁妆让给珀尔修斯统治。于是珀尔修斯演绎了一场英雄救美的经典故事，杀死了海怪，救出了安德洛墨达。

珀尔修斯为国家除了一害，拯救人民出灾难，自己也要迎娶心爱的安德洛墨达，国王和王后也如愿救出了自己的女儿，举国一片欢腾。珀尔修斯带着自己的随从和朋友们来到王宫，参加国王举办的盛大婚宴，眼看一切都是完美的结局。第五章第一节讲到了婚宴中的情节：国王的弟弟菲尼乌斯（Phineus）突然跳出来，说安德洛墨达是他的新娘，而且带着士兵进入了王宫，转眼婚宴变战场。国王无法制止自己弟弟的政变，被国王请来赴宴的各国客人们也分成了两派，支持菲尼乌斯的多数派和支持珀尔修斯的少数派。一阵血雨腥风之后，珀尔修斯周围只剩下国王的一家和少数朋友了，眼看菲尼乌斯的人越来越多，不得已的情况下，珀尔修斯让自己的朋友转过脸去，他从布袋中掏出了秘密核武器——美杜莎的头颅，菲尼乌斯的人瞬间石化，连在空中飞行的标枪也变成石屑，散落到地上。菲尼乌斯看到前面的人都石化了，想向珀尔修斯表示屈服，话刚到嘴边，但一切都太晚了，他变成了一尊满脸惊惧的石头雕像……

看来在古代的地中海地区，尽管王族的联姻会壮大自己的实力和统治，但也会遭到强大的反抗力量，如果没有足够的实力征服这种力量，又没有珀尔修斯的秘密核武器，很可能在与外族通婚的过程中死于阴谋和暗算，尤其是在继承统治权这样的联姻中，收益越大，风险就越大。也许亚历山大大帝的父亲、马其顿王菲利浦遇害就是这样的一个例子。

在古希腊罗马神话传说中，很多国王声称自己是宙斯的后代，无非有四个原因：①想向世人表明自己统治的合法性。如塞浦路斯国王皮格马利翁（Pygmalion）声称自己是宙斯的儿子，特洛伊国王普里阿姆（Priam）也声称自己的先祖达尔达诺斯（Dardanus）是宙斯的儿子。一个地区的王族，如果要说明自己统治的合法性，必然会与民族所信仰的神扯上关系。②凝聚民众的需要。小到一个部落、一个氏族，大到一个民族，必然会有自己的图腾和神。本民族或部落具有神圣性，便可以更好地凝聚民众的力量，对付外来的敌人，和解决内部的民事纠纷。③对王族中丑闻的一种掩盖方式，对受到伤害王族妇女和儿童的一种保护。现代人的常识是：没有精子和卵子的结合，是不可能怀孕的。但在古代，被强暴的王族妇女或是不伦之恋的结果，最好的解释是神的临幸，而这也是对未婚先孕的母亲和私生子最有力的舆论保护了。④文化整合需要的反映。神与神的结合,神与人的结合,很有可能暗示着一个氏族与另一个氏族的结合,或是一个民族与另一个民族的融合,这种融合也必然伴随着文化的整合。从这些神话中所涉及的地理位置上看,地中海周边的欧亚非三大洲全部都提到过。意味着文化是一种流动的现象,只要不同的人群之间有沟通交流,文化就会如水般流动和融合。

第三篇 《伊利亚特》读书笔记

《伊利亚特》(Iliad)是荷马(Homer)的第一部史诗,记录了公元前12世纪爱琴人(the Achaeans)攻打特洛伊城(Troy)的过程。历史上是否真的有一个伟大的盲目诗人荷马存在过,在学界一直有不同看法(有些学者认为荷马的作品是由一群吟游诗人共同创作的结果),但荷马最著名的两部史诗《伊利亚特》和《奥德赛》是真实地流传了下来。相信荷马存在过的学者认为:荷马应该是生活在公元前9世纪至公元前8世纪的爱琴海地区的希腊人。随着考古学家1871年在土耳其的希沙利克(Hissarlik)发现特洛伊城遗址后,荷马所记录的历史上特洛伊战争的真实性便不再受到怀疑。当然,任何文学作品都有作者的创作加工和想象成分,也不乏虚构的故事情节。理性的读者能够区分事实描述的真伪,感性的读者懂得欣赏作品的情感和产生共鸣。

伊利乌斯(Ilius)或伊利乌姆(Ilium)均是特洛伊(Troy)的拉丁名,伊利亚特(Iliad)的意思是指特洛伊城发生的事情,即特洛伊战争。荷马的《伊利亚特》并没有将特洛伊战争的来龙去脉平铺直叙地告诉读者,而是从希腊联军(Achaeans 或 Danaans)围攻特洛伊城第九年十个月开始的,从希腊第一英雄阿喀琉斯(Achilles)与希腊人主帅阿伽门农(Agamemnon)之间的矛盾总爆发开始。全书共24卷,本书选摘了第24卷的内容。

希腊联军中出现了瘟疫,连续9天在与特洛伊军作战时被弓箭射杀的希腊军死伤无数,阿喀琉斯(Achilles)召集各希腊军事首领召开紧急会议,随军占卜师卡尔克斯(Calchas)认为:太阳神阿波罗(Apollo)降灾于希腊大军,是因为希腊军主帅阿伽门农(Agamemnon)霸占了阿波罗神庙大祭司克莱西斯(Chryses)的女儿为妾,当克莱西斯(Chryses)带着赎金向阿伽门农(Agamemnon)要回自己的女儿时,阿伽门农不但没有将女儿还给他,还将他羞辱了一番,因而克莱西斯向阿波罗哭诉了自己的遭遇,阿波罗便降灾惩罚希腊大军。只有将克莱西斯的女儿送还给他，并向阿波罗献祭才能平复太阳神的愤怒。

阿伽门农听后大怒，骂 Calchas 是个邪恶的巫师。但阿喀琉斯和众将领都觉得卡尔克斯（Calchas）领会了神意，劝阿伽门农将克莱西斯的女儿送还。阿喀琉斯对阿伽门农说："等破了特洛伊城，你可以分得我们每个将领3倍多的女俘和战利品。"阿伽门农对众将说："我可以将克莱西斯的女儿送还，但阿喀琉斯的女俘布里塞伊斯（Briseis）必须作为补偿送到我的帐下。"阿喀琉斯说："我们希腊英雄豪杰为了你们兄弟两人的利益，死了那么多战士，你怎么一点都不能控制一下自己的贪婪呢！"两人剑拔弩张，准备干将起来。老英雄 Nestor 只好出面说话，充当和事佬。一方面要求阿伽门农遵从神意，归还克莱西斯的女儿；另一方面，规劝阿喀琉斯不要顶撞主帅。阿喀琉斯说："女俘布里塞伊斯（Briseis）是我的战利品，是希腊将领们已经决定过的事情。如果阿伽门农将她要走，这是对我的轻慢，我和我的部属将不再代表希腊出战。"

最终阿伽门农还是派人要走了布里塞伊斯（Briseis），阿喀琉斯及其部属也固守本营，不再主动出战，阿喀琉斯也向自己的女神母亲塞蒂斯（Thetis）哭诉阿伽门农的无礼与傲慢，塞蒂斯（Thetis）原本是宙斯的旧相好，便一状告到宙斯那里。从此胜利的天秤倒向了特洛伊人，特洛伊大王子赫克托（Hector）带领特洛伊军出城主动袭击希腊联军，尽管希腊联军各路首领带领自己的人马拼力抵抗，但缺了阿喀琉斯的希腊人不敌特洛伊军的凶猛进攻，各首领包括阿伽门农都有不同程度的受伤，最终都被逼回海滩战船附近防守。阿喀琉斯的战友和表弟帕特洛克勒斯（Patroclus）实在看不下去，便偷了阿喀琉斯的盔甲，冒阿喀琉斯之名出战，被赫克托（Hector）所杀。消息传到阿喀琉斯耳中，阿喀琉斯大怒，便带着自己的 Myrmidons 军出战，将赫克托（Hector）斩杀于城门之下，并将赫克托（Hector）的尸首用马拖着绕城三圈，城中无人敢出来抢尸首。

本书选择的是《伊利亚特》的第 24 卷，也是最后一卷。特洛伊国王普里阿姆（Priam）在信使之神墨丘利（Mercury）的帮助下，深夜潜入阿喀琉斯营中，向阿喀琉斯讨回大儿子赫克托（Hector）的尸首，看到普里阿姆（Priam）满目的悲痛，阿喀琉斯终于动了恻隐之心，让他运回了赫克托的尸体，两军暂时休战，特洛伊城火化了英雄王子赫克托。在本卷中可以看到战争除了给人类带来毁灭之外，还有参与者无尽的痛苦和悲伤，所有的荣耀终将归于虚无。《伊利亚特》并未讲述阿喀琉斯之死、奥德修斯（Odysseus）的木马计、特洛伊城大祭司拉奥孔和他的两个儿子被雅典娜派的两条巨蛇缠死，以及特洛伊城的陷落等内容。在《奥德赛》《埃涅伊德》以及索福克勒斯、欧里庇得斯的悲剧著作中，这些内容均有记述。

第四篇 《奥德赛》读书笔记

  《奥德赛》是荷马最为著名的史诗，描写的是特洛伊战役之后的希腊英雄奥德修斯（*Odysseus*，拉丁名为尤利西斯 *Ulysses*），历经10年的海上漂泊和磨难，重新回到自己的故土伊萨卡（*Ithaca*），面对向他妻子珀涅罗泊（*Penelope*）纠缠不休的众多求婚者（这些求婚者们以为尤利西斯已死于归乡的途中，便成天赖在他的家里，买通他家的仆人，日日纵歌酗酒，欺侮他的妻小，觊觎他的家产，甚至设计谋害他的儿子）。奥德修斯便和儿子忒勒马科斯（*Telemachus*）一起，在女神雅典娜（*Athena*，拉丁名为 *Minerva* 或 *Pallas*）的帮助下，屠杀了众多的无赖求婚者的故事。

  全书分为24卷，分两条主线进行，一条是儿子忒勒马科斯（*Telemachus*）在女神雅典娜的帮助下，摆脱母亲求婚者的控制，从伊萨卡（*Ithaca*）岛出发到希腊本土的皮洛斯（*Pylos*）和斯巴达（*Sparta*），向安全回家的希腊将领内斯托（*Nestor*）和蒙勒劳斯（*Menelaus*）那里打听父亲的生死信息，前4卷均是以忒勒马科斯为主角；另一条主线从第5卷开始，以英雄奥德修斯为主角，采取正叙、倒叙相结合的方式展开故事。阿特拉斯（*Atlas*）的女儿——女神卡吕普索（*Calypso*），让奥德修斯和她在一个孤岛上一起生活了七年，在主神宙斯的干预下，女神终于答应让奥德修斯返回自己的家乡。奥德修斯在海上再次遇到风暴，被海浪冲到菲西亚人（*Phaeacian*）人居住的地方，奥德修斯向国王阿尔申诺斯（*Alcinous*）和众人讲述了自己在海上漂泊的种种遭遇和苦难，然后是冥界之行，终于在太阳神的报复下再遇海难，丧失了所有的部下，孤身一人被女神卡吕普索（*Calypso*）收留。

  最后两条主线合而为一。从第14卷开始，奥德修斯在国王阿尔申诺斯和菲西亚人的帮助下，终于回到伊萨卡岛；儿子忒勒马科斯也在女神雅典娜的帮助下，从斯巴达回归伊萨卡岛。父子两人终于在忠心耿耿仆人猪倌欧迈俄斯（*Eumaeus*）家中秘密相认，他们一起策划针对求婚者的复仇计划，又是一场血雨腥风在等着他们……

  本书收录的是第11卷，奥德修斯在女巫瑟茜（*Circe*）的建议下，去冥界向忒拜城盲人预言家忒瑞西斯（*Teiresias*）的鬼魂了解自己未来归乡的命运。在这一卷里，奥德修斯除了了解到自己归乡之路依然充满艰难与困苦以及归乡后与家乡的无赖求婚者有一场恶战之外，也遇到因为对自己的思念和担忧而逝去的母亲的亡灵、特洛伊战争中已故英雄阿伽门农（Agamemnon）和阿喀琉斯（Achilles）等的亡灵，以及神话传说中逝去的许多英雄的妻女之鬼魂，甚至是早期先祖的鬼魂。鬼魂的范围超出了特洛伊战争期间的死去人物，反映了古希腊人的世界观和生死观，反映了当时爱琴海地区的风土民情，也反映了荷马对人类发动愚蠢的战争行为的反思。

古希腊罗马神话主要可以分为三类：第一类为天神的传说，包括第一代、第二代主神，十二泰坦，奥林匹斯主神，普罗米修斯与宙斯之间的故事等。主要参考书目为《Theogony》《The Metamorphoses》。第二类为希腊各地英雄传说，包括雅典王子忒修斯（Theseus）、杀死蛇发女妖的珀尔修斯（Perseus）、阿戈斯英雄伊阿宋（Jason）、大力神赫拉克勒斯（Heracles）、忒拜王子俄狄浦斯（Oedipus）等。主要参考书目为《the Metamorphoses》《Euripides Ten Plays》《Sophocles the Complete Plays》。第三类为与特洛伊战争相关的神话传说。主要参考书目为荷马和维吉尔的史诗《the Iliad》《the Odyssey》《the Aeneid》。

当然，这三类神话主要是为了方便区分主题，每一类神话故事与其他类或多或少有一定的联系，英雄的成就都依赖于奥林匹斯诸神的帮助，人类的战争也就是诸神的战争，所谓"神仙打架，百姓遭殃"。譬如在特洛伊战争中，赫拉和雅典娜支持希腊联军，而阿波罗、马尔斯和维纳斯支持特洛伊人。人付出了生命的代价，而起因却是神之间争风吃醋的一个小纷争。在希腊神话中，神被人性化了。看上去讲的是神的故事，实际上都是人的故事。神与人最大的差别在于神有非常大的力量（Power），譬如宙斯有闪电霹雳，也有强大的自卫能力——宙斯盾。尽管宙斯标榜自己是公正的化身，但实际上也在神之间的各种矛盾中寻找平衡。从这个角度来看，现代社会的游戏规则和古希腊神话世界并无差别。古希腊的神就相当于现代社会的特权阶层，他们在社会中有着很高的地位和很大的权力，他们的不和决定了战争的发生。在他们看来只是利益的再平衡，甚至只是地位和面子的纷争，对普通百姓却是灾难。故事说的是神话，实际上说的全是人和人之间的关系，譬如希腊联军的第一英雄阿喀琉斯（Achilles）为了向主帅阿伽门农（Agamemnon）证明没有自己的希腊联军不堪一击，在特洛伊人进攻时，不但不出阵杀敌，任凭联军的希腊同胞被特洛伊人宰杀，居然还向其女神母亲塞蒂斯（Thetis）哭诉阿伽门农（Agamemnon）对他的轻视，塞蒂斯（Thetis）为了给自己的儿子赚回荣耀，向"最高权力机构"宙斯求情，宙斯便下令暂时不让赫拉和雅典娜支持希腊联军，阿喀琉斯（Achilles）因其母亲是宙斯眷顾的女神，也就是有了通天的社会关系。由此看来，在君主制下的人治社会里，任何法律和政策的颁布和实施，都是在保护和提升一些人的利益，而损害另一些人罢了，君主为了统治的需要，会不断地变动特权阶层的组成，这也是旧时朝代更迭背后的基本逻辑。因此，法治社会和共和国成了公民社会的共识和现代国家的一种基本特征。我们将荷马对于人类社会中人与人之间关系的细致观察和思考，与吴承恩的《西游记》故事的隐喻做一比较对照，就会发现他们有着基本相同的社会认知。

第五篇 《埃涅伊德》读书笔记

帕布留斯·维吉留斯·马罗（*Publius Vergilius Maro*），通常简称维吉尔（*Virgil*），古罗马著名诗人，生于公元前 70 年，死于公元前 19 年。维吉尔比罗马第一任皇帝屋大维（*Octavian*）长 7 岁，代表作史诗《埃涅伊德》（*Aenied*）。故事讲的是特洛伊城被希腊人攻破之后，特洛伊王子埃涅阿斯（*Aeneas*）带领自己的族人逃出特洛伊城，在海上辗转漂泊 7 年之久，途经色雷斯、克里特、西西里、北非迦太基，最终登陆亚平宁半岛的拉丁姆（*Latium*，意大利语为 *Lazio*）海滩。在经过几次与特努斯（*Turnus*）领导的茹图力人（*Rutulian*）的战争之后，埃涅阿斯杀死了特努斯。特洛伊人也终于与当地人和平融合，最终形成了统一的拉丁民族，埃涅阿斯也就成了罗马城（*Rome*）建立时的两狼孩兄弟罗慕路斯（*Romulus*）和雷穆斯（*Remus*）的先祖。

本书通过埃涅阿斯之口，将希腊人木马计的实施、特洛伊城被焚毁、国王及众王子被杀的经过都叙述清楚了。希腊人将木马放在沙滩上，英雄们隐藏在木马的肚子里，其他的军队乘船离开了海滩，佯装打道回府了。特洛伊城大祭司拉奥孔（*Laocoon*）力劝民众不要将木马拉入城内，结果自己和两个儿子惨遭雅典娜（*Athena*）从海上派来的两只毒蛇杀害。朱诺（*Juno*，即天后赫拉）也一直站在特洛伊人的对立面，主要是因为特洛伊王子帕里斯（*Paris*）没有将代表最美女神的金苹果判给她，也没有给雅典娜，而是给了维纳斯（*Venus*）。因为维纳斯向帕里斯许诺：促成他和世界上最美女人海伦（*Helen*）之间的婚姻，这也是特洛伊战争的起因。

《埃涅伊德》共 12 卷，我们摘录的是其中的第 4 卷。埃涅阿斯率众路过迦太基（*Carthage*）时，受到迦太基女王狄多（*Dido*）热情招待和大力支援，由于狄多女王爱上了埃涅阿斯，想让特洛伊人就在迦太基驻扎下去，但埃涅阿斯胸怀大志，肩负着族人生存的希望，一定要去神谕所指之地（*Hesperia*，即意大

363

利)。埃涅阿斯和狄多有过一夜情之后，竟暗自命令手下备船出发。当狄多发现时，特洛伊人已驶出港湾，命运多舛的狄多女王恼羞成怒，第一任丈夫被自己的哥哥皮格马利翁（Pygmalion）杀害，为了逃避凶残的哥哥，带着族人远离家乡塞浦路斯来到北非，原以为终于找到了自己的感情归属，哪成想又是梦一场。狄多安排好姐姐安娜接替自己的王位后，自杀殉情。

　　本书的"政治觉悟"很高，迦太基帝国于公元前146年被罗马共和国所灭，维吉尔在书中给出的理由是：历史上的迦太基女王被罗马人的祖先埃涅阿斯所抛弃，女王对迦太基后人立下遗嘱，世世代代与罗马人势不两立。而实际上地中海海上霸权和对通商贸易的主宰权是两国不共戴天的真正原因；书中称恺撒和屋大维的家族是埃涅阿斯的后代，似乎罗马向东部扩张吞并整个希腊地区也是理所当然，因为1000多年前希腊联军为了一个美女海伦，集10万之众，花了10年时间围攻特洛伊城，终于将其夷为平地，杀了特洛伊国王普里阿姆（Priam）和他的50位王子，埃涅阿斯作为特洛伊国王的亲戚，他的后人岂能不报这一箭之仇？

　　但故事终究是故事，历史归历史。据史料记载，迦太基城于公元前814年由推罗人（Tyrians）在北非海岸建立，此时埃涅阿斯至少死去300多年了，他是无法见到狄多女王的。学会理性分析作者所编故事背后的心理需求以及当时的社会心理环境，对于理解作品所表达的思想同样重要。

第六篇　《俄狄浦斯王》读书笔记

　　古希腊三大悲剧作家索福克勒斯（Sophocles，前496—前406年）与比他年龄小10岁的欧里庇得斯（Euripides，前485—前406年）死于同一年，另一位悲剧作家是埃斯库罗斯（Aeschylus，前525—前456年）。

　　《俄狄浦斯王》（Oedipus the King）是索福克勒斯悲剧的经典之作，也是希腊悲剧的最高成就。心理学家弗洛伊德将俄狄浦斯情结（Oedipus Complex）特指为青少年成长过程中的"恋母情结"。

　　俄狄浦斯年轻时曾到希腊中部的德尔菲（Delphi）的阿波罗神庙祈求过神谕，他当时的身份是科林斯（Corinth）的王子。神谕显示他命中注定杀父娶母，俄狄浦斯为了避免悲剧的发生，决定永远不再回科林斯，于是在荒野之外到处流浪。当他向忒拜城（Thebes，又译底比斯，埃及和罗马帝国均有此名之城）游荡时，在一个三岔路口，他与相向而行的一行人发生冲突，情急之下他杀了其中的4个人，只有一个仆人逃走了。不久之后，当他来到忒拜城附近时，遇到了斯芬克斯（Sphinx）之怪，斯芬克斯出难题祸害忒拜的人民，忒拜城的国王拉伊俄斯（Laius）刚死，王后犹卡斯塔（Jocasta）为了维护忒拜城的繁荣，昭告世人：谁能为民除害，铲除斯芬克斯（Sphinx），谁就是忒拜城的主人，王后犹卡斯塔（Jocasta）就嫁给他。俄狄浦斯（Oedipus）运用自己的智慧，解答了斯芬克斯之谜，为忒拜人民除了大害。成了忒拜城的新国王，娶了犹卡斯塔为妻。

俄狄浦斯成为忒拜城的新国王后，忒拜城依旧灾祸盛行，百姓请愿国王咨询占卜师，预测国运与未来，忒拜城的盲人预言家忒瑞西斯（Tiresias）道出了神谕。俄狄浦斯尽管不相信忒瑞西斯（Tiresias）的预言，但还是倍感困扰。当王后犹卡斯塔找到那个逃走的仆人时，俄狄浦斯确信是自己杀死了原来忒拜国王拉伊俄斯（Laius）。此时，科林斯的原牧羊人来到忒拜的王宫，告诉俄狄浦斯老国王已去世，要他立即回科林斯继承王位。俄狄浦斯告诉科林斯（Corinth）的牧羊人阿波罗的神谕，说自己不能回科林斯，牧羊人告诉俄狄浦斯，科林斯的老国王和王后不是他的亲生父母，他是被收养的，是一个忒拜城的牧羊人送给自己的，然后被科林斯的老国王和王后收养成为王子。

听到这个消息，王后犹卡斯塔脸色大变，俄狄浦斯要求王后犹卡斯塔将忒拜城的牧羊人找来对质，在事实面前，忒拜城的牧羊人终于承认：俄狄浦斯是拉伊俄斯和犹卡斯塔的亲生骨肉。真相大白。原来，犹卡斯塔生下俄狄浦斯之后，得知神谕俄狄浦斯将给王室带来灾祸，便命令忒拜城的牧羊人将孩子遗弃，没想到牧羊人不忍心，将他交给了科林斯的国王收养。听到这里，可怜的王后犹卡斯塔回到卧室上吊自杀身亡。

而俄狄浦斯痛苦之下刺瞎了自己的双眼，无奈于命运的捉弄，俄狄浦斯想通过对自己的惩罚来宽恕其后代的罪孽。他将犹卡斯塔的哥哥克瑞翁（Creon）召进王宫，让克瑞翁（Creon）辅佐儿子波吕涅克斯（Polyneices）统治忒拜，自己则开始了自我放逐的流浪生活。

第七篇 《理想国》读书笔记

柏拉图（Plato）的《理想国》（the Republic）记录了柏拉图的老师苏格拉底（Socrates）与几个雅典贵族之间探讨什么是理想人生的对话，是柏拉图对话录中最丰富的一本书。内容涉及神话、宗教、哲学、政治、伦理、社会学、心理学、优生学、教育学、文学艺术等方方面面，全书分为十卷，本书摘录了《理想国》的第二卷。苏格拉底没有留下任何文字作品，所有的思想和对话全部由其学生柏拉图整理，因而柏拉图也是西方哲学和社会科学思想的第一人。

雅典贵族克法洛斯（Cephalus）将苏格拉底（Socrates）和其他几个贵族请到自己家中……

克法洛斯（Cephalus）：我岁数大了，将不久于人世。没有年轻时那么多的欲望了，只愿意与智者谈谈人生。我自己这一辈子还是比较成功的，从父亲那里继承的家族财富有所增加，也算对自己的儿子们有个交代。但也许是人老力衰，也许将要去另一个世界，面对死亡时总会想到这辈子是否对别人做过一些错事。正如诗人品达（Pindar）写的那样："希望——温润着正义和崇高的灵魂，是人生的旅伴和衰老的守护神。"当一个富裕的人面对死亡时，他既不会无意地欺骗别人，也不会有意地欺诈别人；他既不欠别人的债务，也不欠给神的供奉，因此他会平静地走进地下。

苏格拉底（Socrates）：说得很好，但什么是正义呢？正义不仅仅是说真话和欠债还钱吧？

由此便开始了苏格拉底（Socrates）与四位雅典贵族关于正义问题的辩论。克法洛斯（Cephalus）年纪大了，将话题交给了自己的儿子玻勒马库斯（Polemarchus），便去休息了。

玻勒马库斯（Polemarchus）：正义就是支持你的朋友，反对你的敌人。

苏格拉底（Socrates）：你的朋友总是做正确的事，而你的敌人总是做错误的事吗？

玻勒马库斯（Polemarchus）：当我们的朋友做正确的事时，我们要支持他；当我们的敌人做错误的事时，我们要反对他。

特拉西马库斯（Thrasymarchus）：正义体现的是强者的利益，是强者的逻辑。

苏格拉底（Socrates）：强者可以发号施令，但号令需要别人去执行，执行的结果未必对强者有利，有时反而对他有害。

格劳孔（Glaucon）：正义只是一个概念，是一种名声或美德。在没有人监督的情况下，人是按照最有利于自己的原则行为，而不是正义原则行为。

在这里，格劳孔（Glaucon）讲了一个《盖吉斯的戒指》的故事（"the Ring of Gyges"见《理想国》第二卷），谁有了隐身戒指意味着他就有了做事不受别人监控的权力，他当然会按照有利于自己的方式行为。西方政治哲学中的权力制衡机制来源于此。

苏格拉底（Socrates）：正义就是善行和义举，来源于你自己的灵魂！不会受外在声望或奖惩所左右。正义是人的一种美德（virtue），如果我们还看不清楚什么是正义，可以将它放大到国家的层面来看看。一个国家的正义应该是不同阶层、不同职业的人各司其职，你最擅长做什么你就做什么，而不是什么最赚钱你就做什么。

由此苏格拉底（Socrates）提出了一个理想国家的建构，那就是理想的统治者应该是哲学王（Philosophic King），他们应该是国家的守护者（Guardians）。那么，如何培养国家的守护者群体呢？从优生学的角度，首先要保证未来守护者的遗传素质，让男性在25—50岁生子，让有美德身体强壮的人有更多生育后代的机会。其次是教育问题，让他们从小就接触音乐教育和体育（Gymnastics）锻炼，大一些要教他们数学、几何学、星象学知识，还要教他们战争方面的知识，让他们身临其境，到战场上去体会危险。

到了第八卷苏格拉底（Socrates）探讨了政府形式的问题，四种主要的政府形式会相互转化。僭主制（Tyranny）是僭越了君主权力的暴政；寡头制（Oligarchy）是以财富的多少来决定统治权；民主制（Democracy）是对自由的过度要求，因而经常演变成僭主制；贵族制（Aristocracy）是最好的人（有美德的人）来统治。显然，相对来说，苏格拉底（Socrates）更赞成贵族制。

阿德曼托斯（Adeimantus）：这样看来，在你的《理想国》里，不是人人都可以得到幸福。譬如国家的守卫者们就不能有自己的私有财产，甚至不能有私有的妻子和孩子。

苏格拉底（Socrates）：幸福原本就不是国家第一目标，只是它的副产品。

在第十卷中苏格拉底（Socrates）认为艺术活动是对模仿的模仿。他认为理念或真理是先于实际物质而存在的，现实的物质世界是对理念和真理的模仿，而艺术是对现实世界的模仿，因而离真理更远，这与他在教育上的"产婆术"是相一致的。教育只是将每个人灵魂深处的知识引发出来，而这些知识原本就是先于肉体而存在的理念或真理。最后，他探讨了灵魂的另外一种存在的可能，通过想象描述了死后灵魂的归属世界。

第八篇　《斐多篇》读书笔记

《斐多篇》（Phaedo）通过苏格拉底（Socrates）的学生斐多（Phaedo）之口，记录了苏格拉底（Socrates）在狱中死前最后一天与学生和朋友的对话。苏格拉底（Socrates）喜欢用"产婆术"与别人探讨问题，因为他坚信真理存在于每个人的灵魂之中，通过诘问可以让人们最终认识到真理。当然被诘问者也会发现自己思维中的很多谬误，有时会发现对自己以为了解的领域其实很无知。因为他经常在公开场合与别人讨论问题，很多被问得哑口无言的权势之士当然很尴尬和恼火，他最终以"不信神和腐化年轻人"的两项罪名，被判死罪。

在狱中最后一天的早上，苏格拉底（Socrates）支走了自己的妻子和儿子，为的是自己在太阳落山时喝毒芹行刑时，听不见他们的哭声，可以安静地开始他灵魂新的旅程。这一天主要是在与两个忒拜城（Thebes）的哲学家齐贝斯（Cebes）和西米亚斯（Simmias）探讨灵魂和死后的世界中度过的。

苏格拉底（Socrates）：灵魂（soul）是在出生之前就存在的，很多知识没有人教过我们，我们天生就有。譬如对物体大小的比较，对东西多少的判断，甚至对某些几何图形的直觉等，知识更像是对过去已知事物的回忆（Recollection）。

齐贝斯（Cebes）：好吧，也许灵魂在人出生之前就存在，但这并不说明人的灵魂不会随着肉体的死亡而消失。也许人死后，灵魂也就不复存在了。

苏格拉底（Socrates）：世界上的任何事物都有其对立的一面：有生就有死，有可朽就有不朽。人是可朽（mortal），神就是不朽（immortal）；肉体是可朽，那么与肉体相对立的灵魂呢？

西米亚斯（Simmias）：好吧，也许灵魂会在人死后仍然存在，它会在另一个地方、另一个生命开始时，进入这个生命里。但经过多次这样的生死，灵魂怎么能保证不被磨损而逐渐消亡呢？即便是灵魂在人死后仍然存在，也无法证明灵魂会不朽，或完好如初。

苏格拉底（Socrates）：朋友们，我并不是想向你们证明灵魂的不朽，我只是想说服我自己。今天傍晚，我的灵魂将开启它新的旅行，因为再也没有肉体对它进行束缚了。真正的哲学家，是不会害怕死亡的，因为死亡正是提供了了解灵魂和肉体之间关系的一个机会。

克里托（Crito）：（苏格拉底的弟子）老师，狱卒、关节都打通了，您是不是再考虑一下，我们可以去忒拜或是去其他的城市。这样的话，明年的这个时候我们还可以继续探讨哲学问题。

苏格拉底（Socrates）：克里托（Crito），我已经和你说过了，雅典人判我有罪，是他们的过错。如果我逃匿，那就是我的错误，我不会因为他们的过错，自己再去做错误的事情。另外，有件事情我要请你帮我办一下，我想向药神（Asclepius）供奉一只公鸡（因为毒芹药性的发挥是药神所起的作用），我死后，请你在向药神献祭时替我补上。

毒芹的药性逐渐从腿部向上越过心脏，两分钟后，他的眼睛不动了，克里托（Crito）用手替他抚闭了双眼和口。

第九篇 《政治学》读书笔记

亚里士多德（公元前384—前322年）是西方古代社会科学思想集大成者，柏拉图的弟子。后回马其顿自创学院，是亚历山大大帝的家庭教师。

亚里士多德思想所涉及的学科包括形而上学（Metaphysics）、逻辑学（Logic）、物理学（Physics）、心理学（Psychology）、伦理学（Ethics）、政治学（Politics）和诗学（Poetics）等。《政治学》分为八卷，本书节选了《政治学》的第三卷。

首先亚里士多德认为：人本质上是政治性动物，人无法离开社会而独立存在。从这个角度来说，国家（state 指城邦国家）优先于家庭和个体，因为整体优先于部分，因而研究国家的形成就显得非常重要。

从城邦国家的形成来看，各家庭形成了村落，村落最终形成了国家，因而国家的最终目的是满足其成员对好的生活的追求，也就是对幸福的追求。家庭中的人与人之间的关系有三种：主子与奴隶的关系、父亲与儿子的关系、丈夫与妻子关系。统治者与被统治者之间的关系更类似于丈夫与妻子的关系，因为只有这种关系是一种制度性的关系（institutional）。

《理想国》中柏拉图认为一致性（unity）越高的国家越好的观点是错误的，国家就是由不一致的群体组成的，如果一致性高是好的国家的标准，那么国家就不如一个村落，更不如一个家庭。柏拉图想通过共同的财产，甚至是共同的妻子、儿女这样一种方式，达到对国家的认同是行不通的，实际上越是公共的东西，越没有认同感。因而私产公用要比公产私用更能激起人们对国家和社会的认同。

亚里士多德显然对当时的城市国家和政府制度有了深入的分析和总结，对斯巴达、科林斯、迦太基、克里特等城市国家的立法机构的运作进行了比较。从第三卷开始对不同的政府形式的优劣进行了分析。从统治者的人数的多少来看可划分成三种：①君主制（Monarchy），它包括国王统治（Kingship）或皇权统治（Royalty）；②贵族制（Aristocracy）；③宪制（Constitutional Government）。偏离了这三种政府形式也相对应有三种不正常的或是异常的（Perversion）政府形式，僭主制（Tyranny）是对君主制的偏离；寡头制（Oligarchy）是对贵族制的偏离；民主制（Democracy）是对宪制的偏离。三种偏离的政府形式中，最好的是民主制，最坏的是僭主制。在亚里士多德看来，如果要说选择一个最好的政府制度的话，那就是中间阶级的宪制，这显然是与柏拉图所偏好的贵族制是完全不同的。

在这六种制度中，君主制是君主一人统治，君主有可能贤明，也有可能昏聩，有可能为百姓，也有可能为自己。但他的统治权是世袭的，具有合法性。但僭主制肯定是为统治者自己的，统治权不具有合法性。贵族制也是世袭的，统治者是一个集体，从贵族中选择那些有美德的人进入统治群体。但寡头制对统治者的选择标准是财富的多少，而不是个人的品德，没有钱的穷人是不可能进入统治群体的；中间阶级的宪制是以宪法制度为选择统治者的标准，这种宪法制度可以是选举制也可以是任命制，主要是根据官员的性质来决定。尽管民主制和宪制都是多数人轮流（in turn）进行统治，但民主制由于对自由的过分追求，容易将大多数人的共同意愿凌驾于制度之上，形成多数人的暴政，也容易被有领袖魅力的民众煽动者所利用，最终民众煽动者（Demagogue）篡夺统治权，成为僭主。

第四卷谈到了在宪制下，政府的三大权力（关于公共事务的商议权、行政权及司法权）、政府官员的选拔问题和执政时间等问题。第五卷探讨了国家内部产生革命的原因，及各种不同政府形式的转化。第六卷谈到了在现实国家中可能有几种政府形式同时并存的现象，好的政治体制依赖于不同的民情和历史，也依赖于对官员权力的合理分配。第七卷谈到了亚里士多德的理想国家是什么样子的，理想国家的终极目标是最大限度让公民追求其幸福和美好生活，政府应对战争时应该进行什么准备，政府应如何对待宗教和节日，政府对于国民健康应该做什么，政府对公民的结婚年龄、堕胎应有什么样的限制等。第八卷谈到了教育的问题，为了避免宪制政府的退化，培养城市国家的公民必须具备四种能力：读写能力、体育锻炼、音乐的教育、绘画的教育。

第十篇 《罗马十二帝王传》读书笔记

苏维托尼乌斯（69—122年），古罗马历史学家，最重要的现存作品是《罗马十二帝王传》（the Twelve Caesars），该书记录了尤利乌斯·恺撒（Julius Caesar）以及从奥古斯都（Augustus）到图密善（Domitian）这11位罗马皇帝的传记。苏维托尼乌斯是罗马从共和国转变成帝国时代的传记作家，他的作品不局限于官方资料,也来源于民间的传说。多方面的资料有利于我们对人物复杂性的理解,读者经过理性分析之后,会对人物本身有相对客观的认识。

我们收录了该书的第一章《尤利乌斯·恺撒》,因为恺撒在古罗马帝国中位置的重要性不言而喻,他是罗马从共和制走向帝制的关键性人物,以至于从奥古斯都开始的后续罗马统治者,均用恺撒(Caesars)作为皇帝的代名词。后来的俄罗斯帝国自认为是古罗马的继承人,也称自己的统治者为沙皇(Czar,俄语中的恺撒意思)。

从书中可以看出,恺撒在他走向罗马权力巅峰的过程中所表现出来复杂和矛盾的性格特点。他早年丧父,从年轻时就表现出来对权力的渴望,他撕毁了与骑士家庭背景的婚约,与科妮莉亚(Cornelia)结了婚(Cornelia的父亲曾四次担任罗马执政官)。为此罗马独裁者苏拉(Sulla,就是那位镇压斯巴达克奴隶起义的罗马贵族),要他与科妮莉亚(Cornelia)离婚,他不愿意,苏拉便派人追杀他。他东躲西藏,通过贵族亲戚向苏拉寻求和解。苏拉死后,他从小亚细亚急于回到罗马,策划阴谋,寻求更高的权力。后又与格奈乌斯·庞培(Gnaeus Pompey)和马库斯·克拉苏(Marcus Crassus)联手担任执政官,共同对抗元老院(Senate)中的反对力量,形成了所谓的"前三头同盟"。

为了维护与庞培之间的关系,恺撒将自己的女儿嫁给了庞培,以换取自己对高卢兵团的控制权。克拉苏死后,恺撒与庞培的关系逐渐恶化,最终两人兵戈相见,罗马内战爆发。庞培战败后逃往埃及,被埃及法老所杀,恺撒趁势占领了埃及,废黜了埃及法老托勒密十三世,法老的妹妹克里奥帕特拉(Cleopatra,即埃及艳后)被立为埃及统治者。

吞并埃及后,恺撒的势力如日中天,恺撒在罗马进行了一系列的改革,元老院的权力被进一步削弱。于是,以卡修斯(Cassius)和布鲁图(Brutus)为首的元老院贵族们秘密策划了对恺撒的刺杀,恺撒于公元前44年3月15日上午10时左右被众人刺杀于元老院,身上被匕首捅了23次。

后　记

本书最初的想法源于中央财经大学社会发展学院2004年探索的读书会培养方案，在探索的过程中，对人文及社会科学所关心和研究问题的渊源进行了思考。2016年开始在研究生中开设《西方人文社科经典原著选读》课程，选课人数达上千人次。最初设想的是读原著，但由于本人学识和能力所限制，无法阅读希伯来文、希腊文或拉丁文，只能选择比较容易得到的英文版译著，并得到了选课研究生的大力支持。

对于材料的选择和取舍是一件相当难的事情，一定会有读者要问，为什么选择这本书而不是另一本书？为什么选择这本书的这一章而不是别的章节？为什么是这个英文译本而不是别的英文译本？这里面的确有很多现实原因和个人的偏好，无法在此一一说明。但选择的基本原则是清楚的，那就是必须是经得起时间考验的经典文本。本书只是西方古代著作的一个小节选，基本上没有涉及中世纪、文艺复兴、启蒙运动时期及近现代西方名著，相对来说，学界对于西方古代经典文本看法的一致性也比较高。在人文社会科学诞生的早期萌芽状态，学科没有明显的分化，尤其是与人自身相关的学问。此时的文学、神话、宗教、哲学、政治、历史、地理、社会、心理、经济、教育、民俗等学科的思想萌芽遍布于原始文本之中，对这些经典的学习和分析有助于我们对东西方文明和文化的发展与分化有更进一步的了解和认识，有助于我们更加清醒认识和把握现代社会科学的研究问题和研究取向的脉络。

本书对于所选材料中西方出现的神名、人名、地名进行了前后一致性的注释，力求避免翻译上的混乱，本书试图成为具备一般英语阅读水平和能力的大学毕业生和普通读者的一座桥梁，通过这座桥梁自己可以去了解西方古代文明和文化的一鳞片爪，避免过多翻译所出现的词不达意或以讹传讹的现象。当然，本书节选的章节，只是一个引子，阅读所选书籍全文，方能全面体验文本所带给你的震撼和营养，但这必然需要付出更多的时间和努力。

有一位朋友听说我准备出这样一本书时，问了我一个非常好的问题：这本书的主线是什么呢？我想，本书的主线应该就是通过古代西方的文本，来探讨一下究竟什么是西方文化（Western Culture）或西方文明（Western Civilization）。或许这个主线太大，不是一两代人能说清楚的问题，更不是一两本书能解决的问题，但我们还是可以从西方古代的文字记录中，去了解古代西方社会所面对的各种冲突和思考的各种问题。理解西方文化或西方文明，可能首先要搞清楚文化或文明的概念问题。广义的文化是指在某一特定时期，一个地区或一个民族所共同创造的物质财富和精神财富的总和，狭义的文化是在某一特定时期，一个地区或一个民族所共同持有的思维方式、行为方式、生活方式、社会心理、风俗、价值观及信仰系统、意识形态和社会组织形式等方面。在这里我们主要探讨狭义文化定义下的东西方文化，有以下五点需要说明。

第一，文化是变化的、流动的。文化有传承功能，任何文化都是其传统和历史的传承，都是某一地区民族的先祖习俗的继续，但文化同时又是变化的、流动的。某一地区的文化在历史的长河中，受到外来文化的影响并同时影响外来的文化。若一个民族文化的核心部分没有改变，则这个民族的自我认同便不受影响。古代罗马人的风俗习惯和现代罗马人的风俗习惯会大不相同。我们现在的生活方式与我们的祖先也大不相同，尤其是大城市的居民，每天开车上下班，顺便到幼儿园或是中小学接送孩子，中午在单位食堂吃个饭，或是叫个外卖快餐已经成为城市上班族的生活常态。但我们从未认为自己更像西方人，而是更像自己的祖先；我们在买卖算账时用阿拉伯数字，上班时用着奥斯本电脑公司发明的笔记本电脑，享受着工作之后周日的休息，却没有体会到阿拉伯文化、美国文化和犹太文化对我们的冲击。所以，文化的某些方面会发生改变，另一些方面却保持着相对稳定，或不太容易发生改变。因此，文化是一个历史概念，时代发生了变化，内容也会发生改变，只不过有的部分改变较快、有的部分改变缓慢而已，没有自古以来就一直不变的文化，我们对某种文化的看法，可能是一种偏见或刻板印象。

第二，从地理位置上看，东西方是一个相对的概念。在古希腊的神话传说中，没有东西方文化概念，但的确有描述伊阿宋（Jason）去东方寻找金羊毛的故事。美丽的女巫美狄亚（Medea）之故乡——科尔基斯（Colchis），即现在黑海之滨的格鲁吉亚地区，应该是古希腊神话中的最遥远的东方之地了。特洛伊战争时期（约公元前12世纪）的特洛伊城在爱琴海的东岸，位于现在的土耳其最大港口城市伊斯坦布尔的东南方向的亚洲岸边，希腊人也并没有强调特洛伊人是东方人。在古希腊人的看法中，只有希腊人（Hellenes）与野蛮人（Barbarians）的区别，恰如中国商朝人称周边民族为东夷、西戎、南蛮、北狄

373

一样。即便是希腊人受到东方大国波斯帝国的入侵,他们也从未将自己定义为西方人。

第三,东西方概念逐渐从一个地理概念变化成一个文化概念。到了亚历山大东征时代,以及后来的古罗马时代,地中海文明圈开始区分自己和东方。亚历山大最远东征至印度河流域的旁遮普邦,北部到达乌姆河与锡尔河流域,即现在的乌兹别克斯坦、哈萨克斯坦一带。罗马帝国则明确将叙利亚行省看作东方行省,而波斯萨珊王朝被看成东方强大的竞争对手。在罗马帝国时代的后期,尤其是东西罗马帝国分裂之后,随着基督教在罗马帝国和欧洲北部地区的传播,东西方的概念区分越来越成为一个文化概念而不是地理概念。而公元7世纪阿拉伯地区伊斯兰教的兴起,更加重了这种东西方概念的文化内涵。从地理上看,东方已逐渐演变成欧洲之外的部分,西亚地区、阿拉伯半岛、埃及甚至非洲伊斯兰化的地区,都被看作东方。然而,公元5世纪匈人(Huns)阿提拉(Attila)对日尔曼部落的征服,公元13世纪蒙古人的西征,16世纪奥斯曼土耳其帝国的维也纳之围,使得东西方的文化和宗教隔阂与误解日益加深,欧洲甚至将被土耳其征服的希腊地区也称为东方。17世纪之后,随着美洲殖民地的建立和19世纪欧洲的工业革命生产能力的大幅提高,欧洲基督教国家日益强大,对世界资源的掠夺也日益加剧。欧洲学者也开始将东方分为近东(near-east)、中东(middle-east)和远东(far-east)分别进行研究,东西方概念的区分也开始有了意识形态和政治的味道。

第四,我们这里所指的西方文化,主要限定在思维方式、行为方式、生活方式、社会心理、风俗方面,而价值观、信仰系统、意识形态和社会组织形式则受到世界政治经济格局变化的较大影响,不做重点讨论。当进行这样的限定之后,我们再看看西方和东方的文化究竟有多大的差异呢?形成这种差异的原因究竟是什么呢?差异一定是有的,譬如西方神话中的天使有翅膀,而中国的神仙从来不需要翅膀;奥林匹斯主神宙斯也有七情六欲,和一位普通人没啥差别,而中国的神仙基本不会表现出情欲;西方的《理想国》里讨论的是社会公正问题,中国的《桃花源》关注的是与世无争的田园生活,或许关注点的不同恰恰反映了东西方思维方式的不同,以及人在实现自己社会价值时与外部世界互动方式的不同。但如果将特定的叙事文本,放在一个特定的时间(历史环境)和空间(地理环境)之中,就会发现差别其实没有我们想象的那么大了。恐惧来源于我们对事物的无知状态,对异族的摧毁和征服如果不是为了满足君王的权力欲望的话,那么很有可能来源于对异族的恐惧和无知。

第五,地理环境与历史环境在文化形成和融合中起到了重要的作用。地理环境和历史环境是我们理解阅读文本的基本心理环境，也就是我们要从心理上移情和置换文本的叙述者，从地理、气候、资源等自然环境和特定历史时期去试图理解文本所表述的内容和表述方式，我们才可以理解文本表述的内容和方式，也才能理解个体或群体行动的逻辑性与合理性。地理环境和历史环境先是影响一个民族的生活方式，而这种生活方式又会影响其思维方式和行为方式，进一步影响到社会心理、风俗习惯和价值观的形成，一旦形成了稳定的习俗和价值观，就会在更高的层次上形成民族的信仰体系、意识形态和社会组织形式，而在这个高层次上的差异，不同的民族就差别很大了。在一个相对稳定的历史时段中，如果没有外来文化的入侵，则本民族高层次的民族文化就相对稳定，并对低层次的民族文化起到指导作用。然而，当外来文化入侵时，高层次的民族文化最先都是抵抗的，随着在较低层次上的不断交流取舍，最终高层次的民族文化会与外来文化进行融合和整合，所以文化的融合是一个动态的交流过程。我们看到历史上许多民族在武力上征服了其他的民族，而在文化上却被被征服的民族所同化，也是这样一个过程。

从世界历史上看，一个民族一味地排斥外来文化，就是其逐渐衰落的原因，抑或排斥外来文化本身就是其衰落的一种表现。文化自信不仅反映在宏扬本民族的优秀文化，也反映了对不同于本民族的优秀文化的汲取与包容。正如柏拉图《理想国》所探讨的正义理论一样，如果每个人对正义的理解只与自己的切身利益相关，如果每个人对别人行为的判断只有朋友和敌人的区分，那么正义理念将不复存在，不同文化中人们相互理解的基础也将不复存在。人类早期留下的文字，是人类共有的精神文明和精神家园。对经典文本的学习，会加深对不同文化和文明的相互了解，而不是增加相互之间的敌意和误解，世界和平稳定和多种文化繁荣共存是人类共同的理想和目标，对不同文化背景下的经典文本的阅读和了解，能够帮助这一目标的实现。

附录1　希腊罗马神名对照表

希腊名	拉丁名
Cronus	Saturn
Zeus	Jupiter (Jove)
Hera	Juno (Saturnia)
Poseidon	Neptune
Hades	Pluto
Demeter	Ceres
Hestia	Vesta
Aphrodite (Cytherea)	Venus
Athena	Minerva (Pallas)
Apollo	Apollo (Phoebus)
Artemis	Diana
Ares	Mars
Hermes	Mercury (Cyllenian)
Hephaestus	Vulcan
Dionysus	Bacchus
Persephone	Proserpina
Eros	Cupid
Heracles	Hercules
Eos	Aurora

附录2　希腊常见诸神族谱关系图

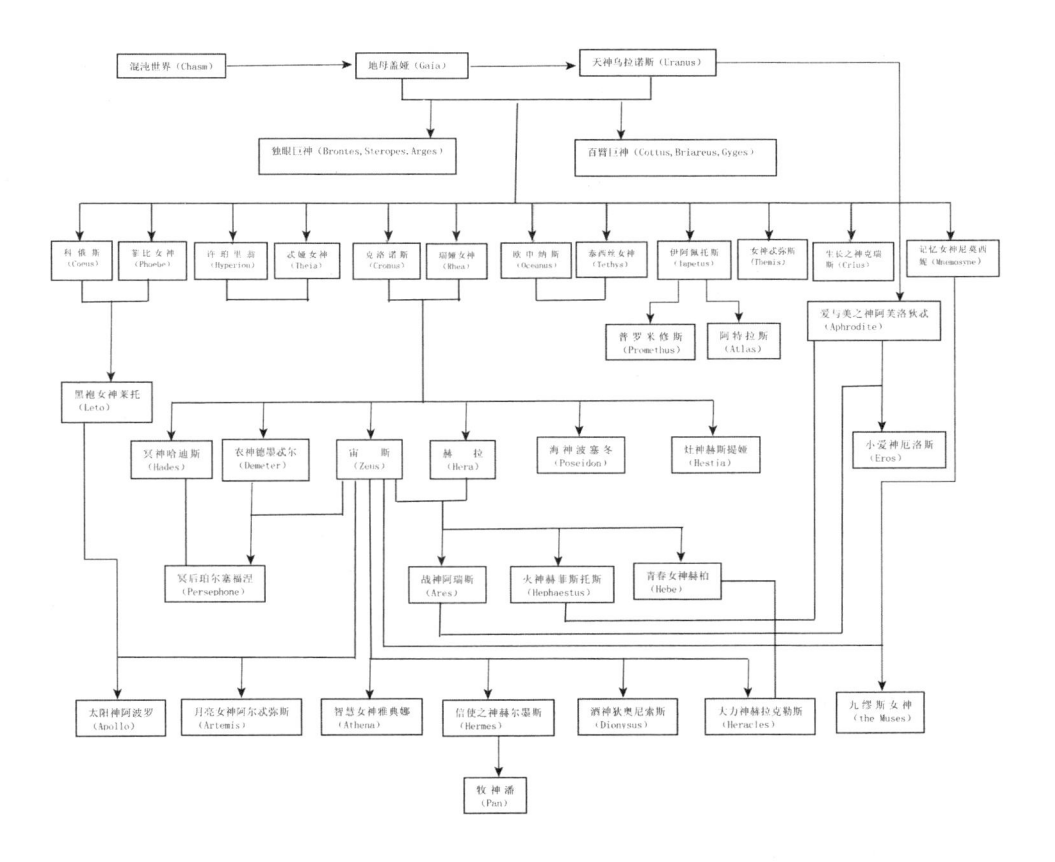

```
混沌世界(Chasm) → 地母盖娅(Gaia) ↔ 天神乌拉诺斯(Uranus)
                    ├── 独眼巨神(Brontes, Steropes, Arges)
                    └── 百臂巨神(Cottus, Briareus, Gyges)

十二泰坦：
  科俄斯(Coeus) — 菲比女神(Phoebe)
  许珀里翁(Hyperion) — 忒娅女神(Theia)
  克洛诺斯(Cronus) — 瑞娅女神(Rhea)
  欧申纳斯(Oceanus) — 泰西丝女神(Tethys)
  伊阿珀托斯(Iapetus) — 女神忒弥斯(Themis)
  生长之神克瑞斯(Crius) — 记忆女神谟涅摩叙涅(Mnemosyne)

伊阿珀托斯的子女：普罗米修斯(Prometheus)、阿特拉斯(Atlas)
爱与美之神阿芙洛狄忒(Aphrodite) → 小爱神厄洛斯(Eros)

菲比之女：黑袍女神莱托(Leto)

克洛诺斯与瑞娅之子女：
  冥神哈迪斯(Hades) — 冥后珀尔塞福涅(Persephone)
  农神德墨忒尔(Demeter)
  宙斯(Zeus) — 赫拉(Hera)
  海神波塞冬(Poseidon)
  灶神赫斯提娅(Hestia)

宙斯与赫拉之子女：
  战神阿瑞斯(Ares)
  火神赫菲斯托斯(Hephaestus)
  青春女神赫柏(Hebe)

宙斯的其他子女：
  太阳神阿波罗(Apollo)
  月亮女神阿尔忒弥斯(Artemis)
  智慧女神雅典娜(Athena)
  信使之神赫尔墨斯(Hermes)
  酒神狄俄尼索斯(Dionysus)
  大力神赫拉克勒斯(Heracles)
  九缪斯女神(the Muses)

赫尔墨斯之子：牧神潘(Pan)
```

说明：无箭头连线表示夫妻或情人关系，有箭头连线表示亲子关系。

377

附录3 犹太人十二支族谱关系图

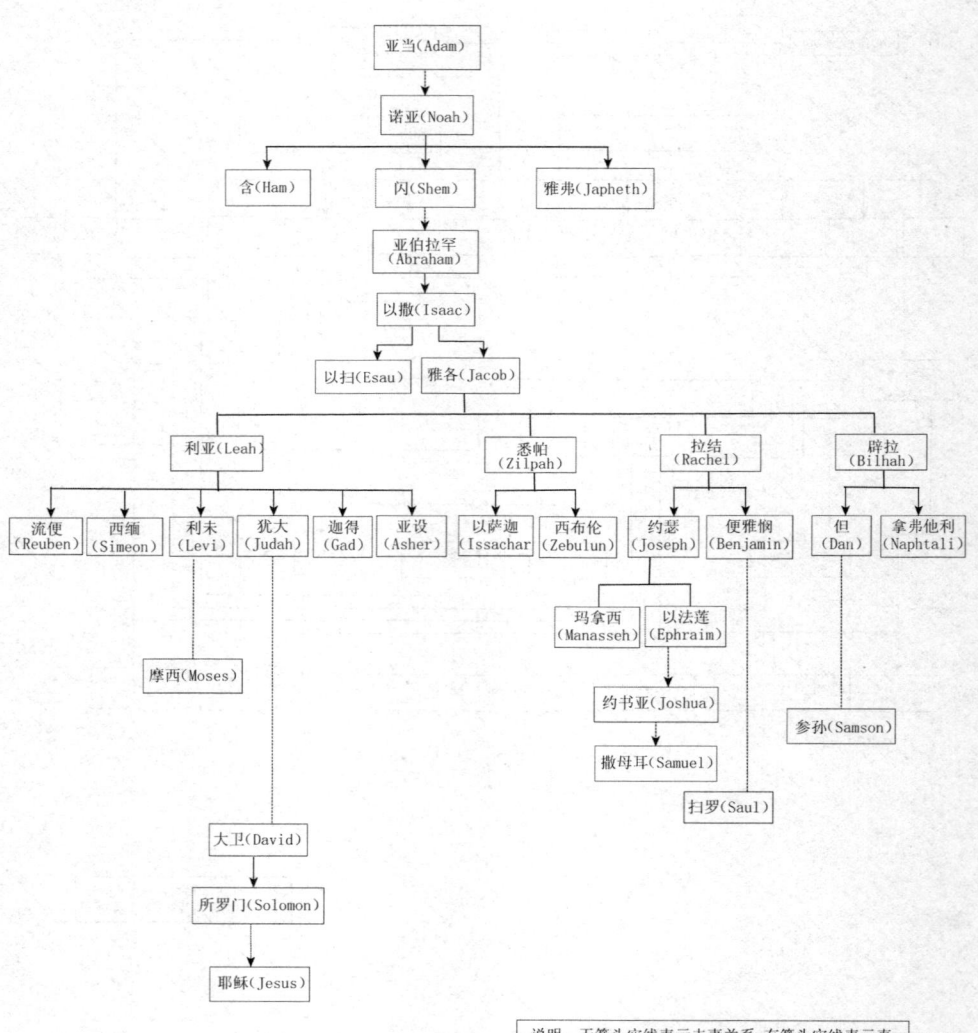

```
                        亚当(Adam)
                            │
                        诺亚(Noah)
                ┌───────────┼───────────┐
            含(Ham)      闪(Shem)    雅弗(Japheth)
                            │
                        亚伯拉罕
                        (Abraham)
                            │
                        以撒(Isaac)
                    ┌───────┴───────┐
                以扫(Esau)      雅各(Jacob)
    ┌───────────────┬───────────────┬───────────────┐
  利亚(Leah)     悉帕(Zilpah)    拉结(Rachel)    辟拉(Bilhah)
    │                │                │                │
┌─┬─┬─┬─┬─┐      ┌─┴─┐          ┌─┴─┐          ┌─┴─┐
流 西 利 犹 迦 亚    以萨迦 西布伦    约瑟 便雅悯    但  拿弗他利
便 缅 未 大 得 设   (Issachar)(Zebulun)(Joseph)(Benjamin)(Dan)(Naphtali)
(Reuben)(Simeon)(Levi)(Judah)(Gad)(Asher)
            │                      │              │
         摩西(Moses)          ┌────┴────┐      参孙(Samson)
            │                玛拿西    以法莲
            │              (Manasseh)(Ephraim)
            │                            │
            │                       约书亚(Joshua)
            │                            ⋮
            │                       撒母耳(Samuel)
            │                            ⋮
            │                        扫罗(Saul)
         大卫(David)
            │
         所罗门(Solomon)
            │
         耶稣(Jesus)
```

说明：无箭头实线表示夫妻关系，有箭头实线表示直系亲子关系，有箭头虚线表示隔代或旁系亲子关系。

主要参考资料

[1] 常耀信. 希腊罗马神话 [M]. 北京：外语教学与研究出版社，1981.

[2] 马可·福马罗利，弗朗索瓦·勒布莱特. 100名画古希腊罗马神话 [M]. 王珺，译. 桂林：广西师范大学出版社，2007.

[3] 阿兰·施纳普，弗朗索瓦·勒布莱特. 100名画古希腊罗马历史 [M]. 吉晶，高璐，译. 桂林：广西师范大学出版社，2007.

[4] 姚乃强. 西方经典文论选读 [M]. 上海：上海外语教育出版社，2003.

[5] 张中载，赵国新. 西方古典文论选读 [M]. 北京：外语教学与研究出版社，2006.

[6] 吴诗玉. 古希腊经典：阅读和讨论 [M]. 上海：上海交通大学出版社，2017.

[7] 奥古斯丁. 上帝之城 [M]. 玛库斯，译. 上海：世界图书出版公司，2011.

[8] 亚里士多德. 政治学 [M]. 本杰明，译. 上海：世界图书出版公司，2011.

[9] 马克·凯什岚斯基，帕特里克·吉尔里，帕特里夏·奥布赖恩. 西方文明史（第五版）[M]. 葛晓华审校/注释. 中国人民大学出版社，2008.

[10] 诺曼·戴维斯. 欧洲史 [M]. 郭方，刘北成，等译. 北京：世界知识出版社，2007.

[11] 西蒙·蒙蒂菲奥里. 耶路撒冷三千年 [M]. 张倩红，马丹静，译. 北京：民主与建设出版社，2015.

[12] 大卫·托马斯. 犹太人历史 [M]. 苏隆，编译. 北京：大众文艺出版社，2004.

[13] 亨利·林肯，迈克尔·贝金特，理查德·利. 圣血与圣杯 [M]. 李永成，等译. 北京：世界知识出版社，2008.

[14] Aristotle. The Philosophy of Aristotle [M]. Translated by J. L. Creed

and A. E. Wardman. New York: Penguin Group, 2011.

［15］Euripides. Ten Plays ［M］. Translated by Paul Roche. New York: Penguin Group, 1998.

［16］Hendrik Van Loon. The Story of Mankind ［M］. Beijing: Liaoning People's Publishing House, 2015.

［17］Hesiod. The Theogony ［M］. Translated by Glenn W. Most. London: Harvard University Press, 2006.

［18］Homer. The Iliad ［M］. Translated by Samuel Butler. Beijing: Liaoning People's Publishing House, 2018.

［19］Homer. The Odyssey ［M］. Translated by Samuel Butler. Beijing: Liaoning People's Publishing House, 2017.

［20］Ovid. The Metamorphoses ［M］. Translated by Horace Gregory. New York: Penguin Group, 2001.

［21］Plato. Phaedo ［M］. Translated by Benjamin Jowett. Beijing: Liaoning People's Publishing House, 2015.

［22］Plato. The Dialogues of Plato ［M］. Translated by Benjamin Jowett, etc. New York: Bantam Dell, 1986.

［23］Sophocles. The Complete Plays ［M］. Translated by Paul Roche. New York: Penguin Group, 2001.

［24］Virgil. The Aeneid ［M］. Translated by Patric Dickinson. New York: Penguin Group, 2002.